Interpreting Folklore

INTERPRETING FOLKLORE

Alan Dundes

INDIANA UNIVERSITY PRESS

Bloomington

Library of Congress Cataloging in Publication Data
Dundes, Alan.
Interpreting folklore.

Bibliography: p.
1.Folk-lore—Addresses, essays, lectures.
2.Folk-lore—Theory, methods, etc.—Addresses,
essays, lectures.   3.Folk-lore—United States—Addresses, essays, lectures.   I.Title.
GR66.D87   398'.042   79–2969
ISBN 0–253–14307–1   2 3 4 5 84 83 82 81

ISBN 0–253–20240–X pa

CONTENTS

Wet and Dry, the Evil Eye:
An Essay in Indo-European and Semitic Worldview

The Number Three in American Culture

The Crowing Hen and the Easter Bunny:
Male Chauvinism in American Folklore

A Psychoanalytic Study of the Bullroarer

Into the Endzone for a Touchdown:
A Psychoanalytic Consideration of American Football

"To Love My Father All":
*A Psychoanalytic Study of the
Folktale Source of* King Lear

The Hero Pattern and the Life of Jesus

REFERENCES

NOTES

Preface

———————————

The vast majority of published writings about folklore consist solely of descriptive data. One need only visit the nearest library and look under the catalog heading *Folklore* to discover that most books on the subject are merely collections of legends, jokes, proverbs, and the like. The emphasis has traditionally been placed on the recording and accurate presentation of authentic field-collected texts. There is nothing wrong with such collections. Quite the contrary. Every discipline depends for its very existence on the continual gathering of raw material. Without such material, there would be nothing for analysts to analyze or interpreters to interpret.

Yet there is relatively little interpretation of folklore. Much more energy has been devoted to questions of classification than analysis. Part of the impetus for the endless search for classificatory schema came from the practical need of storing and retrieving folklore in archival settings. Once an item of folklore has been filed in an archives, how can it be found again when requested by a researcher? If it were filed initially according to a logical classificatory format, then it can be a fairly simply matter to locate the item whenever it is sought. The large number of tale type indices based upon various national narrative repertoires attests to the long-standing interest in devising utilitarian classification systems. But collection and classification are not a substitute for analysis. Perhaps the arduous task of carrying out fieldwork, the tedious and time-consuming effort involved in transcribing tape-recorded interviews, and the abiding concern with archiving the huge amounts of data gathered have all combined to discourage folklorists from trying to understand the materials they collect and classify. But for whatever reason, folklorists typically stop their intellectual work with the presentation and identification of data. Thus a collection of folktales will be published, dutifully accompanied by appropriate tale type or motif index numbers. In European folklorists, the concern for the display of data is manifested in the cartographic method. This method, practiced in most European countries, consists essentially of placing different versions of the same custom or festival or idiom on a map. (The relevant data is typically gathered by questionnaire.) The resulting encyclopedic folklore atlases show page after page of the geographical distribution of one custom or another. The problem is that the fundamental question of meaning is never raised or discussed at all. Why should a particular custom or belief like the evil eye exist in the first place? Of course, folklore atlases, like tale type indices, are really only tools of the trade. They are not, or at least should not be considered, ends in themselves. But when scholars from other disciplines try to discover what folkloristics has to offer, all too often they are handed either a collection of myths or children's games or else an extensive series of maps showing the shapes of traditional breads or housetypes.

I believe that one reason for the reluctance of folklorists to attempt interpretations of their data is their tendency to treat "lore" as though it were totally separate from "folk." The tales, ballads, riddles, etc. are studied as entities independent of living human beings. A folktale may be tale typed, morphologically dissected, or mapped without regard to the fact that it is told by one human being to another. In contrast, I submit that the folk should be put back into folklore. I am interested in folklore because it represents a people's image of themselves. The image may be distorted but at least the distortion comes from the people, not from some outside observer armed with a range of a priori premises. Folklore as a mirror of culture provides unique raw material for those eager to better understand themselves and others. It should also be kept in mind that much of folklore is fantasy. Magic wands and dragons presumably don't exist (even though some people may claim they do!) but they exist in folklore and thus represent a challenge to folklorists concerned with interpretation. The apparent irrationality of much folklore poses problems for literal-minded, historically oriented folklorists. It is not easy to find a rationale for the irrational, to make sense of "nonsense," but that is what folklorists seriously interested in interpretation must try to do.

No doubt another reason why folklorists have been slow to interpret folklore is the speculative nature of much folklore interpretation. Folklore data or the "what" of folklore is empirical. One can collect a ballad and compare it with other versions of the same ballad or with other ballads. For example, one could identify it as a version of "Barbara Allen" and this identification can easily be verified by another folklorist. It is safe scholarship. On the other hand, when one turns to the question "why" (rather than "what"), one enters the ever treacherous area of interpretation. Interpretations often tend to be subjective rather than objective. It is a legitimate question whether one can effectively "prove" the validity of one interpretation over another. Nevertheless, I believe it is incumbent upon professional folklorists to offer interpretations of their data. They must make the best case they can for the particular interpretations they espouse. Ideally, the interpretations should be read out of the data rather than being read into the data! Some interpretations may be more plausible and convincing than others. What I am really arguing is that folklorists of the future must attempt to interpret folklore. They must try to answer the difficult question of why an item of folklore exists now or why it existed in the past.

My academic credo includes the conviction that each scholar should begin his research where previous scholars have ended theirs. This means in practical terms that one is obliged to read what others have written on the same subject. This is a rule honored, I'm afraid, more in the breach than in the observance. For one thing, previous scholarship on the evil eye or the bullroarer or the ritual number three may not necessarily or conveniently be in English (or the native language of the researcher). In my own folklore research, I have made a conscientious effort to locate previous relevant scholarship. I know that I may have failed to find some important sources—in this modern day of knowledge and publication explosion it becomes more and more difficult to find everything that has been published on a particular subject. This is especially true in folklore where a given topic may have been studied earlier by anthropologists, classicists, linguists, sociologists, and students of literature, among others. Having discovered as many sources as I could that treated a subject in which I had become interested, I tried to survey what was collectively known about that subject. Often I would find that what I had thought was my original idea had already been stated by other scholars who had considered the same issue. On other occasions, I would seek to add my own contribution to the stream of scholarship devoted to a given subject or problem. Generally speaking, the would-be contribution would take the form of a suggested interpretation or explanation of the subject.

Many different types of interpretation are possible and in theory I certainly subscribe to the desirability of multiple interpretations. In practice, my own interpretations tend to fall along quite specific intellectual lines. As the reader will soon learn, I favor relying upon folk metaphors. I assume that metaphors are meaningful, not accidental, and that there are consistent patterns of metaphor in every culture. These patterns may be cognitive (as in "Seeing Is Believing") or they may be symbolic (as in "Into the Endzone for a Touchdown"). In most cases individual informants are not aware of these cognitive and/or symbolic patterns. Yet I believe these patterns both reflect and affect behavior and thought in a given culture. Thus Americans may be three-determined in reporting the number of shots they allegedly heard fired in an assassination attempt or in designing multiple choice examinations (the third choice offered is more often the right answer to the test question), but these same Americans may not be consciously aware of the importance of the number three in American culture.

I believe the folklorist can, by analyzing folklore, discover general patterns of culture, and I would maintain further that a knowledge of such patterns can provide the means of raising levels of consciousness. So my analysis of male chauvinism in American folklore is not meant as a dry academic exercise but is rather an essay intended to show how folkloristic patterning acts as a critical cultural force in shaping opinion and prejudice. Similarly, my analysis of the possible symbolic content and function of American football is not simply a delineation of metaphorical patterning, but rather an implicit commentary on a facet of American society that typically discourages males from expressing physical affection towards one another. Folklore furnishes a socially sanctioned outlet for cultural pressure points and individual anxieties. By analyzing the folklore of a group (or of an individual), the folklorist may well succeed in the laudable goal of making the unconscious conscious.

Ultimately I suppose I am interested in the study of worldview. How do individuals perceive their world and their place in it?

Worldview is not an easy thing to study and the concept itself tends to resist rigorous definition. Even so, I would like to think that my analysis of the future orientation in American culture or of the wet-dry opposition in Indo-European and Semitic thought represents a small-scale attempt to isolate significant principles of worldview. Through an understanding of worldview principles, we should be better able to comprehend ourselves as well as others. Whether the result is a practical one such as realizing why a grant application has a better chance of success if there are three reasons (or even paragraphs) in support of it, or whether it is a more theoretical one such as trying to determine how and why the life of Jesus does or does not conform to the traditional Indo-European and Semitic hero pattern, is not the point. The point is rather that folklore cries out for interpretation. It is my sincere hope that this book of essays will stimulate others to join in the fascinating task of interpreting folklore.

Alan Dundes
Berkeley, California

Acknowledgments

"Who Are the Folk?" copyright © 1977 by the American Association for the Advancement of Science, first appeared in *Frontiers of Folklore*, edited by William Bascom, AAAS Selected Symposium No. 5, Westview Press, Boulder, Colorado, 1977. Reprinted by permission from the American Association for the Advancement of Science.

"Texture, Text, and Context" and "'To Love My Father All': A Psychoanalytic Study of the Folktale Source of *King Lear*" are reprinted by permission from *Southern Folklore Quarterly*, where they first appeared.

"Projection in Folklore: A Plea for Psychoanalytic Semiotics," copyright © 1976 by The Johns Hopkins University Press, first appeared in *MLN* 91 (1976):1500–33, and is reprinted with the permission of The Johns Hopkins University Press.

"The Curious Case of the Wide-mouth Frog," copyright © 1977 by Cambridge University Press, first appeared in *Language in Society* 6 (1977):141–47, and is reprinted by permission of Cambridge University Press.

"Thinking Ahead: A Folkloristic Reflection of the Future Orientation in American Worldview," copyright © 1969 by The Catholic University of America Press, first appeared in *Anthropological Quarterly* 42 (1969):53–71, and is reprinted by permission of The Catholic University of America Press.

"Seeing Is Believing" is reprinted with permission from *Natural History* Magazine, May, 1972. Copyright American Museum of Natural History, 1972.

"Wet and Dry, the Evil Eye: An Essay in Indo-European and

Semitic Worldview" is reprinted by permission of the Folklore Society (England).

"The Number Three in American Culture" first appeared in Alan Dundes, *Every Man His Way: Readings in Cultural Anthropology,* © 1968, pp. 401–23. Reprinted by permission of Prentice-Hall, Inc., Englewood Cliffs, New Jersey.

"The Crowing Hen and the Easter Bunny: Male Chauvinism in American Folklore" first appeared in *Folklore Today: A Festschrift for Richard M. Dorson,* Bloomington, Indiana: Indiana University Research Center for Language and Semiotic Studies, 1976, pp. 123–38; and is reprinted by permission of Richard M. Dorson.

"A Psychoanalytic Study of the Bullroarer," copyright © 1976 by the Royal Anthropological Society, first appeared in *Man* (n.s.) 11 (1976):220–38; and is reprinted with permission from the Royal Anthropological Society.

"Into the Endzone for a Touchdown: A Psychoanalytic Consideration of American Football," copyright © 1978 by the California Folklore Society, first appeared in *Western Folklore* 37 (1978):75–88, and is reprinted by permission of the California Folklore Society.

"The Hero Pattern and the Life of Jesus," first published in the *Protocol of the Twenty-fifth Colloquy of the Center for Hermeneutical Studies in Hellenistic and Modern Culture,* 12 December 1976 (Berkeley, 1977), is reprinted by permission.

Interpreting Folklore

Who Are The Folk?

To discuss folk or folklore in the context of the advancement of science seems somewhat paradoxical. For the long-standing pejorative association of error with folklore as with such other terms as myth, superstition, old wives' tale, etc., would make it appear that folklore is precisely what science has advanced *from*!!! Folk medicine continues to be contrasted with scientific medicine—the implication clearly being that in an ideal world the former should be completely replaced by the latter. I hope to show that this definition of folk and folklore is false and, furthermore, that one essential part of the science of folklore includes the study of the folklore of science (and scientists).

The discipline of folkloristics began in the nineteenth century. To be sure, one can find precursors. In the late eighteenth century Herder had used such terms as *Volkslied* ("folksong"), *Volksseele* ("folk soul") and *Volksglaube* ("folk belief"). His famous anthology of folksongs, *Stimmen der Völker in Liedern*, was first published in 1778–79, but folkloristics proper, in the sense of the scholarly study of folklore, did not emerge until later. The Grimm brothers published the first volume of their celebrated *Kinder und Hausmärchen* in 1812, but the English word *folklore* was not coined until Thoms first proposed it in 1846. Closely tied to currents of romanticism and nationalism, the serious study of folklore found an enthusiastic audience among individuals who felt nostalgia for the past and/or the necessity of documenting the existence of national consciousness or identity. By the last decade of the nineteenth century, national folklore societies had been formed in Europe and the United States: among them, the Finnish Literature

Society, 1831; the English Folk-Lore Society, 1878; and the American Folklore Society, 1888.

The critical difficulty in the various nineteenth-century usages of the term *folk* lay in the fact that it was inevitably defined as a *dependent* rather than an *independent* entity. In other words, *folk* was defined in contrast with or in opposition to some other population group. The folk were understood to be a group of people who constituted the lower stratum, the so-called *vulgus in populo*—in contrast with the upper stratum or elite of that society. The folk were contrasted on the one hand with "civilization"—they were the uncivilized element in a civilized society—but on the other hand, they were also contrasted with the so-called savage or primitive society, which was considered even lower on the evolutionary ladder.

Folk as an old-fashioned segment living on the margins of civilization was, and for that matter still *is*, equated with the concept of peasant. The way in which folk occupied a kind of middle ground between the civilized elite and the uncivilized "savage" can be perceived in the emphasis placed upon a single culture trait, the ability to read and write. The folk were understood to be "the illiterate in a literate society," as opposed to the primitive peoples, who were ethnocentrically labelled "preliterate" (implying that they would achieve literacy as cultural evolution progressed). More recently the term was changed to "nonliterate." (The ethnocentric bias in labelling other peoples continues with such terms as "developing," "underdeveloped," or "non-Western.") The key to this definition of folk is "in a literate society." It was not simply that an individual could not read or write, but that he lived in or near a society that included a literate elite. The association of folk with rural is similarly defined. Rural is implicitly compared with urban. The folk were rural because they could be contrasted with city dwellers. Primitive people since they supposedly lacked cities could not be termed rural.

In terms of the assumed unilinear cultural evolutionary sequence of savagery, barbarism, and civilization through which all peoples were believed to pass, the folk were more or less considered as barbarians. More civilized than savages, the folk had not yet attained civilization. However, the folk were believed to have retained survivals of savagery. Since the elite (which included anthropologists and folklorists) was vitally interested in its own origins, it sought to collect the traditions of its adjacent folk. These traditions could then be compared with the supposedly fuller versions to be found among savage societies. Through this form of the comparative method, historical reconstruction of the origins of the elite, literate, civilized European cultures was to be undertaken.

Let me illustrate the nineteenth-century view of folk and folklore by citing several passages from one of its most eloquent and articulate spokesmen, Andrew Lang. I feel that Lang's essay "The Method of Folklore," which appeared in his *Custom and Myth* published in 1884, is a representative statement.

> There is a science, Archaeology, which collects and compares the material relics of old races, the axes and arrow-heads. There is a form of study, Folklore, which collects and compares the similar but immaterial relics of old races, the surviving superstitions and stories, the ideas which are in our time but not of it. Properly speaking, folklore is only concerned with the legends, customs, beliefs, of the Folk, of the people, of the classes which have least been altered by education, which have shared least in progress. But the student of folklore soon finds that these unprogressive classes retain many of the beliefs and ways of savages . . . The student of folklore is thus led to examine the usages, myths, and ideas of savages, which are still retained, in rude enough shape, by the European peasantry." (1884:11).

Here we find the folk defined as peasants, lower-class and lacking the benefits of education and "progress."

Lang's answer to the question What is the method of folklore? shows very well his conception of folk.

> The method is, when an apparently irrational and anomalous custom is found in any country, to look for a country where a similar practice is found, and where the practice is no longer irrational and anomalous, but in harmony with the manners and ideas of the people among whom it prevails . . . Our method, then, is to compare the seemingly meaningless customs or manners of civilised races with the similar customs and manners which exist among the uncivilised and still retain their meaning. It is not necessary for comparison of this sort that the uncivilised and the civilised race should be of the same stock, nor need we prove that they were ever in contact with each other. Similar conditions of mind produce similar practices, apart from identity of race, or borrowing of ideas and manners. . . . Our method throughout will be to place the usage, or myth, which is unintelligible when found among a civilised race, beside the similar myth which is intelligible enough when it is found among savages. A mean term will be

found in the folklore preserved by the non-progressive classes in a progressive people. This folklore represents, in the midst of a civilised race, the savage ideas out of which civilisation has been evolved. (1884:21−22, 25).

The notion of "non-progressive classes in a progressive people" is obviously analogous to the "illiterate in a literate society." The folk possessed what Lang called a "mean term," the intellectual link between civilized and primitive.

If we were to list the principal characteristics of folk as defined by nineteenth-century scholars, we might include the following traits:

SAVAGE or PRIMITIVE	FOLK or PEASANT	CIVILIZED or ELITE
Pre- or non-literate	Illiterate	Literate
	Rural	Urban
	Lower stratum	Upper stratum

Because folk was defined primarily with respect to its supposed relationship to the civilized or elite, folklore was presumed to exist only where a civilized or elite group existed. Thus large parts of the world, deemed uncivilized by ethnocentric European intellectuals, had no folk and hence no folklore. North and South American Indians, Australian aborigines, native peoples of Africa, etc., were not civilized and therefore did not constitute folk in the strict sense of the term. In large measure then, the term *folk* in its initial meaning referred to European peasants and to them alone. To this day, some European folklorists consider peasant life to be the subject of their inquiries. Such folklorists study the totality of the life of peasants, not just selected genres such as folktales or ballads. This study is sometimes called folklife rather than folklore and it corresponds to what American anthropologists call ethnography (except that American anthropologists consider that ethnographic description can be carried out with respect to any people anywhere in the world).

One might expect this narrow nineteenth-century definition of *folk* as "European peasant" to have disappeared, but it has not. One rarely hears the music of the American Indian referred to under the rubric of folk music or the art of the Australian aborigine listed as folk art. Folk music and folk art still tend to be restricted to European or European-derived cultures. Only a few genres of folk literature, for example, folktale, are considered to be cross-cultural. Yet how is it that American Indians can have *folk*tales but not folk music and folk art? Of course, they have music and art, but it is typically referred to as "primitive" or "non-Western" or some other such value-charged ethnocentric term. In Latin America, for example, folklorists insist upon the nineteenth-century folk-as-peasant definition. In 1948, American folklorist Ralph Steele Boggs entered into a spirited debate with Argentinian folklorist Bruno C. Jacovella on this very question of the exclusion of so-called primitive peoples from consideration by folklorists. Boggs pointed out that while the concept of folk as initially conceived did refer exclusively to European peasants, it was later expanded to include primitive societies. Boggs cited the title of G.M. Theal's *Kaffir Folk-Lore* (London, 1886) as an example of the expanded usage. It is true that British folklorists were willing in theory to consider a broader use of the term. In the 1914 edition of *The Handbook of Folklore*, we find the following discussion of the beginnings of folklore study. The study "began with the observation that among the less cultured inhabitants of all the countries of modern Europe there exists a vast body of curious beliefs, customs, and stories, orally handed down from generation to generation, and essentially the property of the unlearned and backward portion of the community." Then it was noted "that similar, and even identical beliefs, customs, and stories, are current among savage and barbaric nations." Accordingly, this definition of folklore was offered: "the generic term under which the traditional Beliefs, Customs, Stories, Songs and Sayings current among backward peoples, or retained by the uncultured classes of more advanced peoples, are comprehended and included" (Burne 1914:1–2). Jacovella's response was that the study of American Indian peoples belonged to the discipline of ethnography or anthropology and therefore they should not be included as folk to be studied by folklorists.

The continued use of the narrow definition of folk as peasant excluded not only primitive peoples but urban ones as well. And American anthropologists are partly to blame for this. Redfield proposed an ideal typology, in which folk and urban were at opposite ends of a continuum. In this scheme, it would be absurd to speak of urban folklore. Peasants as they moved from a rural area to a city might bring some of their folklore with them, but the idea that urban dwellers could constitute a folk or actually many different folk groups, each with its own folklore, was hardly tenable to anyone subscribing to Redfield's dichotomy. In his 1953 essay, "What is Folk Culture?" Foster tried to refine the Redfield distinctions. He suggested that a folk society was not a whole society, not an isolate in itself. It was rather "a 'half-society,' a part of a larger social unit (usually a nation)." The folk component of the larger unit bore a "symbiotic spatial-temporal relationship to the more complex component, which is formed by the upper classes of the pre-industrial urban center." Here the folk are defined, once again, in terms of opposition to the upper class and to an urban center. By this definition, Foster says, "true primitive cultures are excluded from the folk category. They are, in theory at least, isolates, which are complete in themselves" (1953:163). Foster's distinctions are remarkably close to the nineteenth-century restricted definition of folk. (Foster's elitist bias is also manifested in his acceptance of *gesunkenes Kulturgut* theory, which argues that folk culture retains "sunken" scientific and artistic materials from the upper classes of earlier centuries.) Foster concludes that "folk cultures will disappear in those places where a high degree of industrialization develops"; and "true folk cultures can hardly be said to exist in countries like the United States, Canada, England, and Germany, though in peripheral areas there are perhaps marginal manifestations. It also seems improbable, in view of the trends of the modern world toward industrialization in all major areas, that new folk cultures will rise" (1953:171).

If modern folklorists accepted the nineteenth-century definition of the folk as illiterate, rural, backward peasants, then the study of the lore of such folk might well be strictly a salvage operation and the discipline of folklorists might in time follow the folk itself into oblivion. Certainly it is conceivable that eventually all the peasants of the world will become urbanized or, at least, so much influenced by the urban centers as to lose their peasant qualities. The impact of the mass media—transistor radios, motion pictures, and the like—has tended to encourage standardization of food, dress, language, etc. But if we look at the question Who are the folk? in a new light, we shall see that the folk are *not* dying out; that there are folk cultures alive and well in the United States, Canada, and Europe; and that new folk cultures are bound to arise.

I have defined folk in the following way. "The term 'folk' can refer to *any group of people whatsoever* who share at least one common factor. It does not matter what the linking factor is—it could be a common occupation, language or religion—but what is important is that a group formed for whatever reason will have some traditions which it calls its own. In theory a group must consist of at least two persons, but generally most groups consist of many individuals. A member of the group may not know all other members, but he will probably know the common core of traditions belonging to the group, traditions which help the group have a sense of group identity" (Dundes 1965:2). With this flexible definition of folk, a group could be as large as a nation or as small as a family. One can speak of American folklore or Mexican folklore or Japanese folklore in the sense that there are items of folklore shared by all or nearly all members of the group in question. Presumably most Americans, for example, know who Uncle Sam is (and what he looks like), can sing "Jingle Bells" or "Happy Birthday to You," and are familiar with such idioms as o.k. Each family has its own folklore, often involving a mixture of traditions from each parent's side of the family. Family folklore might include accounts of how the family came to settle where it did or how the family name evolved. It might include a family whistle (a tune or sequence of notes) used in public places, for example, in a department store, to assemble members to depart for home. It might include a reference, normally derogatory, to a member of the family with an unfortunate personal characteristic, such as being stingy or having a boarding-house reach. The allusion in the family circle might take the form of "Don't pull an Aunt Josephine on me!"

But there are many other forms of folk in addition to nation and family. Geographical-cultural divisions such as region, state, city, or village may constitute folk groups. In the United States, one can speak of the folklore of New England or the Ozarks, the folklore of California, the folklore of, and about, San Franciso. Even more obvious as folk groups are those of an ethnic, racial, religious, or occupational character. Each ethnic group has its own folklore, as does each occupational group. Baseball players, coal miners, cowboys, fishermen, lumberjacks, and railroadmen all have their own lingo, legends, and in-group jokes. It should be noted that this is not idle speculation on my part. Decades of fieldwork have demonstrated conclusively that these groups do have their own folklore. Moreover, as new groups emerge, new folklore is created. Thus we have the folklore of surfers, motorcyclists, and computer programmers. From this perspective, it would be absurd to argue that there is no folklore in the United States and that industrialization stamps out folk groups and folklore. There may be a diminution in the number of peasants, but peasants constitute only one type of folk. Industrialization has in fact created new folklore, for example, the folklore of computers.

Marxist folklorists have made a useful contribution with respect to the folklore produced or inspired by industrialization. They saw that the concept of folk had to include both peasant and proletariat, that is, folk in the country and folk in the city. However, Marxist theory erred in limiting folk to the lower classes, to the oppressed. According to strict Marxist theory, folklore is the weapon of class protest. It cannot be denied that some folklore does express protest. Numerous folksongs, for example, articulate discontent with social ills, racism, and other issues. But there is also right-wing folklore expressing the ideology of groups of a conservative political philosophy. If one carries Marxist theory to its logical extreme, then on that day when the perfect society is achieved, there will be no oppressed group, hence no folk and no folklore. But the fact is that while there is factory folklore and the folklore of labor unions, there is also folklore of big business and big businessmen. The traveling salesman joke cycle, for example, is clearly a reflection of capitalistic free enterprise as well as a vehicle for a city slicker trickster's attempt to seduce a country farmer's daughter.

With this modern conception of folk, we see that we can no longer think of the folk in monolithic terms as a relatively homogeneous group of peasants living in a symbiotic relationship with an urban center. Folk is not a dependent variable but an independent variable. We must see members of modern societies as members of many different folk groups. A summer camp can constitute a folk group (with its own folksongs, initiation rituals, and customs). Many of these folk groups may be considered as part-time folk. One participates in a summer camp, for example, for a month or two. The experience may be repeated for several summers, but being a member of a summer camp "folk" is not the same as being a full-time member of a homogeneous peasant community. Yet there are plenty of summer camp folklore traditions. Moreover, the same individual who can claim membership in a summer camp group may also belong to a number of other folk groups, formed by religious, ethnic, or occupational ties. These groups may overlap. For instance, a Catholic Afro-American who attended a Boy Scout summer camp would al-

most certainly know Catholic folklore, Afro-American folklore, and
Boy Scout folklore.

One important consequence of the notion of part-time folk is the
possibility for the study of code-switching. As an individual moves
from one of the folk groups to which he belongs to another, he must
shift mental gears, so to speak. A man normally wouldn't tell jokes
exchanged in a military setting at a Church-sponsored meeting. It
could be argued that the amount or importance of the folklore of
part-time folk groups, such as summer camps, is much less than the
folklore of peasants, but I believe that to be a subjective value judgment. All folk groups have folklore, and the folklore of such groups
provides a socially sanctioned framework for the expression of critical
anxiety-producing problems as well as a cherished artistic vehicle for
communicating ethos and worldview.

I should like to demonstrate the rich variety of folk groups by using
selected examples of a single genre, the joke. A given folk group may
utilize any number of folklore genres, for example; superstition, reci-
pe, folk dance. For this reason it would take a book-length discussion
to document the folklore of any one folk group. One might have a
chapter on legends, another on proverbs, a third on folksongs, and so
forth. My purpose is not to document the existence of any folk group
in particular but rather to suggest that there are many folk groups
besides "peasants." In this way, I hope to provide a partial answer to
the question Who are the folk?

Jokes about groups do provide an index of the existence of such
groups. Sometimes the jokes about groups are told only by group
members; sometimes only by nonmembers; sometimes by both. Context is often critical. Catholics may tell anticlerical jokes and Jews may
tell anti-Semitic jokes, but usually not in the presence of non-group
members. Military groups have rich folklore. I recall from the late
1950s a Navy sea story (the generic term for stories told to while away
the hours of a long sea voyage). A famous sea captain had an incredi-
bly good record. Every time there was a crisis, the captain would rush
down to his cabin to consult something and then he would return on
deck to make a correct decision, such as "come right to course 270," or
"commence firing." The officers and crew wondered what it was that
gave him the inspiration or confidence, but no one knew. Finally, one
day the old captain died at sea—of natural causes. Curious about the
captain's secret source of knowledge, the executive officer went to the

captain's stateroom and opened up his safe. Inside was a single piece of paper on which was written: Port, left; starboard, right.

This anecdote is easily localized to adapt to other folk groups. For example, consider the following bit of bank folklore, which circulated in the 1930s. "There was this old bank employee, a cashier, who started every day by going to his desk, opening the top drawer, looking at a piece of paper, and putting it back. Finally, after forty years of flawless service to the bank, he retired. After he left, curiosity was just overwhelming and the other employees just had to look in his desk for the piece of paper. In the top drawer, they found and read it, "The red figures must equal the black ones."[1] Here is a musical variation: "There was a famous conductor who was greatly respected in all of the music circles throughout the world. Before every concert, right before he raised his hands for the orchestra to begin playing, he would take a small piece of paper out of his pocket, read it, and put it back into his pocket. He never failed to perform this little ritual which the musicians had long since taken for granted and which they ignored. One night, however, the maestro dropped the little piece of paper. The concertmaster picked it up and accidentally and innocently read it. The message was brief. All it said was: 'Violins on the right, violas on the left.'"[2]

From this kind of data, one can see that there are an infinitude of folk groups. The Navy constitutes a kind of folk; bankers are another; musicians yet another. Moreover, each of these groups may in turn be shown to consist of smaller constituent folk groups. For example, within the general folklore of musicians, we may point to the special folklore (especially folk speech) of jazz musicians (as opposed to other kinds of musicians). The idea that a particular folk group may in fact consist of a lumping of smaller folk groups is not idle theory. (The notion is implicit in defining folk from a nation to a family.) The critical test is inevitably whether or not there is folklore of, and about, such smaller groups. Let me illustrate this important point by referring to the widespread joke cycle involving "the priest and the rabbi," surely one of the best known cycles in American folklore. Dozens of examples of this cycle continue to be in active circulation. Typical is the following text collected from a Protestant informant in 1964:

A Catholic priest and a rabbi were driving down the highway one day, the priest behind the rabbi in the same lane. They came to a stoplight and the rabbi applied his brakes and came smoothly to a stop. The priest, however, was lost in meditation and failed to notice the rabbi's stoplights and slammed into his car doing 40 mph, completely demolishing both autos.

A squad car pulled up and a large Irish cop came over with ticket book in hand. After surveying the situation and learning that the first was a rabbi's car and the second a Catholic priest's, he came over to the priest and said (in a heavy accent):

"Sure and I'm sorry to bother youse, father, but how fast was the rabbi going when he backed into you?"[3]

Of course, no one needs extensive proof to accept the fact that there is folklore of, and about, Jews and Catholics in the United States. In this sense, Jews constitute a folk and so do Catholics. What may or may not be quite so obvious is that each of these folk groups consist of a variety of smaller groups. For example, within the broad framework of Catholicism, one finds numerous Orders, each with its own identity and its own attributed characterological traits. Typically, there are a Dominican, a Franciscan, and a Jesuit (although the particular groups and their sequence may vary in accordance with the identity of the joketeller and the makeup of his audience). In one such story, the three are in the middle of a meeting when the lights go out. "Undeterred by the darkness, the Dominican stands up and says, 'Let us consider the nature of light and of darkness, and their meaning.' The Franciscan begins to sing a hymn in honor of our little sister darkness. The Jesuit goes out and replaces the fuse."[4] The practicality of the Jesuit in contrast with the more mystical nature of the Franciscan seems praiseworthy, but the Jesuit is not always seen in such a favorable light.

> There was a Jesuit and a Dominican on shipboard. There was a little bit of contention—you know the old rivalries between the orders. Well, somehow or other, the Jesuit fell overboard and was immediately surrounded by sharks. It looked bad for a while, but they just swam around in a circle and finally swam away. Oh, there was a secular there, too, and he says, "The saints be praised, it's a miracle!" But the Dominican said, "No, just professional courtesy."[5]

Among non-Catholics, there may be relatively little knowledge of ongoing inter-Order rivalries and stereotypes. But within Catholicism one can identify specific folk groups—and one can do so on the basis of the in-group folklore itself. The point is that *it is in folklore that folk groups are defined*. In much the same fashion, one can discover within Judaism such distinctions as Orthodox, Conservative, and Reform Judaism.

> A Jewish couple residing in a gentile area were struggling with the annual Chanukah-Christmas problem of whether they should deprive their children of a Christmas tree or desecrate their home with a Christian object. The father thought of a solution. He called the orthodox rabbi, explained the problem, and asked if there were a "Broche" [blessing] which he could say to decontaminate the Christmas tree. The rabbi replied, "A Klog aff dir" [A curse on you], and slammed the receiver on the hook.
> The man was taken aback, but then on consideration decided to try the conservative rabbi. He replied that he understood and appreciated the problem, but that there was no conceivably appropriate "Broche" so there was nothing he could do.
> As a last resort, the father turned to the reform rabbi. This rabbi replied, "A Christmas tree I know, but what's a 'Broche'?"[6]

The same three groups are involved in a joking comparison of the recitation of the Shema, the most common prayer in Judaism: *Shema Yisrael, Adonai Elohaynu, Adonai Echad* ("Hear O Israel, the Lord Our God, the Lord is One"), (Deut. 6:4).

> When an Orthodox Jew recites the Shema, he says, "Shema Yisrael, Adonai Elohaynu, Adonai Echad."
> When a Conservative Jew recites the Shema, he says, "Shema Yisrael, IdonKnow Elohaynu, IdonKnow Echad." [Hear O Israel, I don't know God, I don't know one.]
> When a Reform Jew recites the Shema, he says, "Shema Yisrael, Ideny Elohaynu, Ideny Echad," [Hear O Israel, I deny God, I deny one.][7]

In a descending scale of religious faith, we have the pious Orthodox Jew followed by a near-agnostic Conservative and then an atheistic Reform Jew.

Moving from religion to science, we find folklore defining similar subgroups. Consider the following typical specimen of the folklore of academe:

A chemist, a physicist, and an economist are marooned on a desert island without food. Suddenly a cache of canned goods is discovered, but there is no opener. The chemist begins looking about for chemicals in their natural state so he can make up a solution that will dissolve the tops of the cans. The physicist picks up a rock and begins calculating what angle, what force, what velocity he will need to strike the can with the rock in order to force it open. The economist merely picks up a can and says, "Let us assume this can is open." [In a variant, "Let us assume we have a can opener."]

In many academic disciplines, including both the natural and the social sciences, one can find a sharp division between those individuals interested in theory and those interested in solving practical problems. Economists are frequently singled out for comment, however, because of their penchant for "as if" model-building in lieu of working with empirical data. Within the natural sciences, similar stereotypes exist. Here is a typical text, told in 1969 by a statistician:

A physicist, a statistician, and a mathematician were in an airplane flying over Montana. They looked out and saw below a herd of sheep all of which were white, except one which was black. The physicist began calculating the number of black sheep in the universe, based on the sample. The statistician began calculating the probability of a black sheep occurring in any given herd. The mathematician, on the other hand, knew that there exists at least one sheep that is black, ON TOP![8]

In view of the fact that any group can theoretically be subdivided into smaller subgroups (there are, for instance, various specializations within physics), the question might arise: Just how small can a folk group be? I have argued that for purposes of definition, a folk group could consist of as few as two individuals. It is possible for two individuals to develop a special set of traditions including gestures, slang expressions, and so forth. This would certainly be a very restricted and limited "folk." I suppose one might be tempted to test the limits of the definition by asking if one person could constitute a "folk." If an individual created a set of idiosyncratic gestures, terms, etc., would he be a "folk" unto himself and would his gestures, terms, etc., be folklore? I would say no on the grounds that the notion of folk does imply some form of collective plurality. Individuals do have idiosyncrasies, but at least two individuals would have to share them before I would be comfortable in calling such behavior traditional or folk. I must stress that the idea of a two-person folk group is essentially a matter of theory. I don't know any two-person folk groups. The family is surely the smallest folk group presently studied by folklorists. I should also point out that most of the folk groups actually studied, that is, religious, occupational, or ethnic groups, consist of thousands of individuals.

It is worth recalling that not all members of a folk group necessarily know one another. If we speak of the folklore of Mormons or the folklore of lumberjacks, what we mean is that body of folktales, legends, folksongs, superstitions, folk speech, etc., that is shared collectively by Mormons or lumberjacks. No one lumberjack is likely to know every single item of lumberjack folklore. If we were to represent the folkloristic repertoire of each individual lumberjack as a circle, then the totality of lumberjack folklore existing at any one point in time would be the sum of all the areas obtained by combining all the circles. In most cases, there would be overlap between one circle and another, that is, between the repertoires of any two lumberjacks, but the degree of overlap might vary with the ages of the two individuals, where they lived (Maine or Oregon), and their life experiences. Probably no two circles would be perfectly congruent—no two individuals know precisely the same folklore. By the same token, it is at least theoretically possible (though not very likely) for two circles to share no common ground. Thus lumberjack A and lumberjack B might conceivably share no traditions in common but lumberjack C and others would presumably share lumberjack folklore with both A and B.

Folklorists have rarely sought to ascertain just how many individuals in a folk group actually know and use a particular item of folklore. (Nor have folklorists sought to investigate exhaustively the *entire* folklore repertoire of a single informant. There have been extensive collections of folktales from a single raconteur but that same informant's knowledge of folksong or folk speech or games may not have been tapped at all.) Questionnaires are more common in European folkloristics, but even there it would be difficult to provide hard data attesting to the fact that a given item of Irish folklore was known to every single Irishman.

Let me illustrate the difficulty of determining the size of a folk group. In the United States, there is folklore concerning the *Reader's Digest*. It would not be easy to ascertain just how many Americans have heard one or more of the following three items of *Reader's Digest* folklore. The *Reader's Digest* sells more than 18 million copies monthly and most copies are read by more than one reader. Of those Americans who do not read the *Reader's Digest* regularly, many have read it at one time or another, perhaps in a doctor's or dentist's waiting room. I venture to say that not all of the total number of Americans who have read or who are to some extent familiar with the *Reader's Digest* will have heard each of the three jokes about to be cited. But the jokes exist and can be collected from informants. And so we have indisputable de facto evidence that a folk who creates, transmits, and enjoys these jokes also exists. I frankly do not know how many Americans make up that folk, except that it is a number greater than two!

> Q. How do you keep a WASP uninformed?
> A. Take away his *Reader's Digest*.
> Q. How do you keep a WASP misinformed?
> A. Give it back to him.[9]

The joke itself suggests that the folk in question may include WASPS, WASP being an item of folk speech, a traditional acronym for White Anglo-Saxon Protestant. (I would think WASP is an item of folklore known by a goodly portion of the entire American population.) The jokes comment upon the average American's propensity to depend upon digests or summaries of news and information, not to mention the alleged inaccuracies in such synopses.

Do you know the *Reader's Digest* version of the Star Spangled Banner?

This joke confirms the *Reader's Digest* tendency to abridge materials, even whole books, as well as its penchant for patriotic subject matter. The third example plays upon the formula quality of the writing, the favoring of success stories written in the first person, and the general themes of political conservatism and religion.

A man was on a geophysical survey and he was assigned to the
Arctic Pole for about six months in this little shack. And every day
he'd go out and he'd measure the rainfall. And the only thing he had
to read in this shack were stacks and stacks of *Reader's Digests* from
about 1945. So he started to read them and pretty soon he thought,
"Well, I think I could write a story for *Reader's Digest* 'cause I think I
have the format down." So he wrote a story and sent it off to *Reader's
Digest*. And a while later he got back a nice letter which said, "Dear
Sir, We enjoyed your article, "I fucked a Polar Bear" very much. Except, we are a family magazine and it's not exactly our type of article,
but we like your style—keep trying." So the man thought he'd gone
wrong somewhere so he read about 300 more *Reader's Digests* and he
said, "Ah, I think I've got it now." So he wrote another story and sent
it off. And pretty soon he got back an even nicer letter—"Dear Sir,
We are very interested in you and we're quite pleased with your story,
"I fucked a Polar Bear for the FBI," But still, we *are* a family magazine
and we don't think this is what Mr. and Mrs. America are looking for,
but please, please keep writing and keep submitting your material to
us as we like your style." So he read some more and finally he wrote
another story and sent it off and a week later he got a check and a
letter that said, "Congratulations, sir, here is a check for your story.
We're very happy to have accepted it and we're pleased to announce
that your story "I fucked a Polar Bear for the FBI and found God"
will appear in our next issue."[10] [In another version the anti-
Communist theme is parodied, the final article title being "I fucked a
Russian bear for the FBI and found God." One informant indicated
that this joke was in circulation in 1949 in the New York area.]

If these items constitute folklore—and I cannot imagine on what
grounds they could possibly be excluded—then to the question "Who
are the folk?" we would have to answer: anyone who has told or heard
any of these items. Members of the folk in question are not limited to
a family or a region or a religious, occupational, or ethnic group. Now
we can see the inadequacy of the nineteenth-century definition of the
folk as the illiterate in a literate society. The folk in this case (and in
the case of the "port-starboard" messages *written* on slips of paper) are
literate. They are regular or, at least, occasional *readers* of a nationally
(actually internationally) distributed magazine. Nor are the folk in this
instance rural or lower-class. Many would surely be urban and
middle-class, if one were interested in making such distinctions or
using such labels. For the modern folklorist, there is no paradox whatsoever in speaking of an urban folk. There are urban folk just as there
are rural folk.

One final issue remains, which I should like to discuss briefly. This is the matter of the relationship between science and technology on the one hand, and folklore on the other. Partly because folklore was wrongly tied to illiteracy, it was wrongly assumed that as literacy increased, folklore would decrease. Technology, especially as it impinged upon communication techniques, was thought to be a factor contributing to the demise of folklore. Not true! The technology of the telephone, radio, television, Xerox machine, etc., has increased the speed of the transmission of folklore. What used to take days, weeks, or months to cross the country can now move around the world in a matter of seconds. Moreover, the technology itself has become the subject of folklore. Experimental scientists (and engineers) constitute a folk group with their own folklore. For example, Murphy's Law and its corollaries are an excellent illustration of the folklore of this group. Many versions of Murphy's Law exist, but the most common is "If anything can go wrong, it will." In this traditional parody of the scientific penchant for reducing the universe to principles and laws, we find that even experimental errors can be codified into a "law" that guarantees predictability and regularity, two important desiderata of the scientific community.

So technology isn't stamping out folklore; rather it is becoming a vital factor in the transmission of folklore and it is providing an exciting source of inspiration for the generation of new folklore. The rise of the computer symbolizes the impact of technology upon the modern world. My point is that there is a folklore of, and about, the computer. Among computer programmers, one can find elaborate, quite technical in-group jokes, some involving pseudo-programs and others involving the specialized terminology of various computer languages. As early as 1958 one joke concerned the difficulty for the computer in handling metaphor. Thus "The spirit is willing but the flesh is weak" was translated by the computer into "The liquor is good but the meat is terrible."

Even the wider American public has come to accept the computer as a feature, if not a character, in contemporary folklore. Old traditional issues such as the nature of God and the nature of man appear in new guises in the folklore of computers. Man's fear of being replaced by the machine is a prominent theme in this folklore. (The concern of workers that they may be replaced by increasing automation in factories is a very real one.) Many computer jokes begin with the premise that it is possible to feed all of the world's knowledge into a computer. Let me close my discussion by citing three examples of this modern folklore.

1) All the greatest scientists of the world gather together and decide they are going to find out the answer to the ultimate question—Is there a God? So they build this gigantic computer, the most complex and fantastic computer the world has ever seen. They program all the knowledge of the world into it, and finally they are ready to feed in The Question. So they feed it in, and the machine blinks and whirs and buzzes for some time, and finally the answer comes out . . . "There is now!"[11]

2) A skeptic was being shown around the biggest computer facility in the world. He was told that all human knowledge had been programmed into the computer and that he was welcome to ask the computer any question he wished. The computer would answer it. "Any question?" "Yes, any question." So the man said he'd like to ask the question "Where is my father now?" "Fine," said the computer operator and he punched in the question. After several seconds of flashing lights and a series of clicks, a printout appears saying, "Your father is on a fishing trip off the coast of Baja California." "Is that right?" asked the computer operator. "No," said the man, "That's wrong. My father is at a meeting of the American Association for the Advancement of Science in Denver." "Are you sure?" asked the operator. "Yes, I just spoke to him last night." "Well, let's try it again." The question was punched in, "Where is my father now?" Again after lights and clicks, the printout appeared, "Your father is on a fishing trip off the coast of Baja California." At this point, the computer facility man is really concerned. The installation has cost millions of dollars. "Let's try it once more." This time, besides the question "Where is my father now?" the additional instruction is given to search all memory banks. After the lights and the clicks, the printout appears, "Your father is on a fishing trip off the coast of Baja California; the man who is married to your mother is at a meeting of the American Association for the Advancement of Science in Denver."[12]

There is widespread genuine anxiety that the use of the computer to gather personal data may bring us to the point where dossiers contain more information about a person than the person himself knows. More and more often, people are demanding (and receiving) the right to have access to their personnel files. The final example suggests that it is folklore itself—including the joketelling process—that ultimately separates man from machine, or does it?

3) A super computer is built and all the world's knowledge is programmed into it. A gathering of top scientists punch in the question: "Will the computer ever replace man?" Clickity, click, whir, whir, and the computer lights flash on and off. Finally a small printout emerges saying, "That reminds me of a story."

Who are the folk? Among others, *we* are!

Texture, Text, and Context

Folklore, as a discipline, will never be adequately defined unless or until all the various genres or forms of folklore are rigorously described. Attempts to define folklore by means of criteria *external* to the materials of folklore are doomed to failure. Superstitions, for example, cannot be properly defined on the basis of whether or not an informant believes a particular superstition to be true or valid. If superstition or any other form of folklore is defined in such a way, the problem arises as to what to call "Breaking a mirror is seven years' bad luck" when the informant does not himself believe that breaking a mirror has anything to do with bad luck.[1]

Perhaps the most common external criterion used to define folklore is the way in which folklore is transmitted. Folklorists are wont to say that folklore is, or is in, "oral tradition."[2] Yet many forms of folklore are not transmitted orally at all. A boy may learn to play marbles or skip stones by watching other boys play. Nonverbal folklore such as gestures, games, and folkdance cannot be said to be truly in *oral* tradition. Even the "oral" as opposed to "written" dichotomic criterion, in the final analysis, can be shown empirically to be untenable. There are numerous written forms of folklore. Examples of folklore which are primarily written include: autograph book verse, automobile names, flyleaf rhymes (e.g., book-keepers), latrinalia, and traditional letters (e.g., chain letters). A more serious handicap to the definition of folklore by means of its mode of transmission is that a good many aspects of culture are transmitted in exactly the same way that "folklore" is.[3] For example, a farm boy may learn to drive a tractor either by watching his father drive or by receiving verbal (i.e., *oral*) instruction or both. Yet it is doubtful whether any folklorist would include tractor driving per se as an example of folklore. In the same way, individuals learn to put toothpaste on their toothbrushes and to deposit coins in parking meters. It should be clear that the mode of folklore's transmission is in no way limited to folkloristic materials and that, consequently, it is of limited aid in defining folklore as distinct from other cultural materials. From this, one could with reason say that definitions of folklore which depend completely upon such terms as "oral," "tradition," and "transmission" are of questionable utility in explaining to someone who has no idea what folklore is what folklore is! Yet Utley's recent attempt to grapple with the problem of definition concludes with his so-called operational definition which consists essentially of the "orally transmitted" criterion.[4] In another recent study devoted in part to the same bête noire, Maranda maintains that "the process of transmission is the key for defining what folklore is."[5] However, both of these folklorists are aware that form, in fact, is and in theory should be the decisive criterion for defining folklore. It must be *internal*, not external, criteria which are used to define folklore. There is no harm, of course, in noting that folklore is transmitted like other aspects of culture, but it should be understood that this in no way materially contributes towards a definition of folklore which might differentiate it from other aspects of culture transmitted in the same fashion.

The problem then of defining folklore boils down to the task of defining exhaustively all of the forms of folklore. Once this has been accomplished, it will be possible to give an enumerative definition of folklore. However, thus far in the illustrious history of the discipline, not so much as one genre has been completely defined.[6] At the present time, if a beginning student asks his folklore instructor what a proverb is or what a superstition is, he is more often than not told to read a book of proverbs or superstitions and that he will, upon completing this assignment, know what a proverb or superstition is. A standard work on the proverb *begins* with the statement that "The definition of a proverb is too difficult to repay the undertaking." The student is told that "An incommunicable quality tells us this sentence is proverbial and that one is not." Since the quality is incommunicable, it follows that "no definition will enable us to identify positively a sentence as proverbial."[7] Stith Thompson not only confesses that he cannot really answer the question of what exactly a motif is, but he

argues that "it makes no difference exactly what they are like."
Thompson's attitude towards the problem of definition is equally evident in his discussion of his specialty, the folktale. After remarking
that "no attempt has ever been made to define it exactly," Thompson
goes on to say *in the course of writing a definition of folktale for a folklore
dictionary* that this lack of basic definition is a "great convenience . . .
since it avoids the necessity of making decisions and often of entering
into long debates as to the exact narrative *genre* to which a particular
story may belong."[8]

The same deplorable situation is found in discussions of other
genres. With all the wealth of scholarship devoted to the ballad, it still
remains extremely difficult to tell someone who has never heard one
sung just exactly what a ballad is. Why is it, an African student wants
to know, that an African narrative song which focuses on a single
incident is *not* a ballad. Whereas in the natural sciences items may be
defined before there are even instruments powerful enough to see
them, in folklore the materials may be easily seen and heard, but still
they have not been defined.

In an effort to encourage the definition of the various forms of
folklore and thus eventually the definition of the field of folklore itself,
I would like to propose three levels of analysis, each of which can aid
in the task of definition.[9] With respect to any given item of folklore,
one may analyze its texture, its text, and its context. It is unlikely that
a genre of folklore could be defined on the basis of just one of these.
Ideally, a genre should be defined in terms of all three.

In most of the genres (and all those of a verbal nature), the texture is
the language, the specific phonemes and morphemes employed. Thus
in verbal forms of folklore, textural features are linguistic features.
The textural features of proverbs, for example, include rhyme and
alliteration.[10] Other common textural features include: stress, pitch,
juncture, tone, and onomatopoeia. The more important the textural
features are in a given genre of folklore, the more difficult it is to
translate an example of that genre into another language. Hence the
texture of fixed-phrase genres (genres in which the wording as well as
the content is fairly constant) may virtually preclude the possibility of
translation. For instance, tongue twisters are so dependent upon textural features that only rarely do they diffuse from one linguistic
community to another, particularly if the languages concerned are not
genetically related. On the other hand, folktales, which are free-

phrase rather than fixed-phrase like tongue twisters, can traverse linguistic boundaries much more easily. It is likely that the textural distinction between fixed-phrase and free-phrase forms of folklore may be just as important for folklore diffusion theory as von Sydow's distinction between active and passive bearers of tradition.[11]

Since the study of texture in folklore is basically the study of language (although there are textural analogs in folkdance and folk art), textural studies have been made by linguists rather than by folklorists. Moreover, because of the many theoretical and methodological advances in linguistics, there has been a tendency among some linguists to try to define folklore genres upon the basis of textural characteristics alone.[12] To attempt this is to commit what I would term "the linguistic fallacy," that is, to reduce the analysis of folklore to the analysis of language. One of the most obvious theoretical weaknesses of such an approach is the fact that textural features are rarely, if ever, limited to just one form of folklore. Rhyme is a textural feature of some proverbs, but the fact that rhyme is also found in some riddles means that it is of limited value in distinguishing a proverb from a riddle. However, it may well be that certain textural features may be of great use in defining folklore genres when used in conjunction with features obtained from the analysis of text and context.

The text of an item of folklore is essentially a version or a single telling of a tale, a recitation of a proverb, a singing of a folksong. For purposes of analysis, the text may be considered independent of its texture. Whereas texture is, on the whole, untranslatable, text may be translated. The proverb text "Coffee boiled is coffee spoiled" may in theory be translated into any language, but the chances that the textural features of rhyme will survive translation are virtually nil. A text may be subjected to structural analysis just as its texture may be subjected to structural analysis. However, the results of such analysis will be the delineation of folkloristic structure in contrast to the delineation of linguistic structure obtained through the analysis of texture.[13] Most of the work of folklorists has been with text. Texture has been left to interested linguists, while context, the third level of analysis, has been almost completely ignored.

The context of an item of folklore is the specific social situation in which that particular item is actually employed. It is necessary to distinguish context and function. Function is essentially an abstraction made on the basis of a number of contexts. Usually, function is an analyst's statement of what (he thinks) the use or purpose of a given genre of folklore is. Thus one of the functions of myth is to provide a sacred precedent for present action; one of the functions of proverbs is to provide a secular precedent for present action. (Note that the citation of proverbs in African judiciary proceedings is analogous to the citation of cases as legal precedents in our own culture.) This is not the same as the actual social situation in which a particular myth or proverb is used. To say that a clan origin myth bolsters the ego of a clan is not to say exactly how, when, where, to whom, and by whom the myth is uttered on a given specific occasion. The important difference between general discussions of function and specific detailed accounts of context may be seen by taking the riddle genre as an example.

Whereas folklorists have long been unwisely content to publish just riddle texts, anthropologists have prided themselves upon their inclusion of some mention of the functions of riddles. Accordingly, in the latter's preface to their riddle collections, they may list some of the various functions of riddles, e.g., their use in courtship ritual. However, they rarely, if ever, give any indication of just which riddles in their corpus are used for which functions.[14] In one sense context is given but it is given without reference to individual texts. Thus it is not truly *con* text. Perhaps there is some question as to why it is so important to record context along with text (and texture). (Note that the failure to collect folklore in the original native language means that texture is not collected.) One reason for collecting context is that only if such data is provided can any serious attempt be made to explain WHY a particular text is used in a particular situation. Let me illustrate this point with a hypothesis about riddles.

In a recent structural study of riddles, a type of riddle termed oppositional was distinguished.[15] In oppositional riddles, two descriptive elements appear to conflict in such a way that the two elements seem not to belong together, e.g., "What has eyes and cannot see?" The first descriptive element, "has eyes," and the second, "cannot see," do not appear to belong together, i.e., do not appear to form an integral whole or unit. Only upon formal enunciation of the answer, "potato," can the two separate elements be properly and logically joined. Recalling the curious but widespread use of riddles in courtship ritual, one might be led to hypothesize that the reason for this function is that oppositional riddles provide miniature structural models for marriage in that marriage relates two unrelated principals. In fact, in exogamous societies it is culturally mandatory that the bride and groom—like the riddle's descriptive elements—not be closely related. Here, then, the structure of the context (social situation) in which two separate individuals or rather family units are joined together is paralleled by the structure of the text used in that context. Unfortunately, there is little evidence to affirm or negate this hypothesis. In those cultures in which riddles are used in courtship ritual, there is no indication as to whether oppositional riddles are used more than nonoppositional riddles. Statements that "riddles were used during the courtship of young people" or that "the bridegroom received the right to sit beside the bride only in the event that he, with his groomsmen, solved the riddles which were propounded him" provide no help.[16] The only evidence is that of literary instances, e.g., in folktales where the prospective groom is tested by being asked to solve a riddle (cf. motif H551). In addition, there are ballads (Child numbers 1, 46, and 47) in which the solving of riddles is a condition of marriage. In these folkloristic materials, there is some evidence that oppositional riddles are employed. Thus in "Captain Wedderburn's Courtship," there are a chicken without a bone and a cherry without a stone, among others. In folktales, the marriage tests frequently consist of "impossible tasks" (motif H1010) or "paradoxical tasks" (motif H1050). Paradoxical tasks are commonly structured as oppositional riddles: coming neither naked nor clad, coming neither with nor without a present, or coming neither riding nor walking. The solution to the task resolves the contradiction just as the answer to an oppositional riddle resolves the apparently contradictory descriptive elements.

The probable psychological significance of courtship riddles would seem to support the hypothesis here proposed. Concern with "questions and answers" or the feared examination in dreams has long been interpreted as a traditional expression of a dread of sexual ineptness. Thus the riddle imposed upon the folktale hero is an impotence threat. In the case of oppositional riddles, he is asked to put two unlike things together so that they stay together. The two things (descriptive elements) are placed next to each other by the poser of the riddle, but only if the protagonist gives the correct answer can these things be properly joined. The sexual symbolism is obvious enough. In this connection, it is worth noting that it is not sufficient to know whether oppositional riddles rather than nonoppositional riddles are used in courtship ritual, but it might be important to know exactly what type of oppositional riddle was used. If, for example, privational contradictive oppositional riddles are employed, the present hypothesis would be considerably strengthened. In this type of oppositional riddle, the second of a pair of descriptive elements constitutes a denial of a logical or natural attribute of the first. In English riddles, most of the privational contradictive oppositions involve comparison with the human body. Wolfenstein, in her brief but brilliant discussion of this type of riddle, has called attention to the clear theme of castration.[17] In most of the examples, a physical part of the body fails to function: eyes can't see, ears can't hear, legs can't walk, and so forth. If this type of riddle were employed in courtship ritual, then the groom would in all probability be expected to remove the innuendo or threat of castrative impotence. By giving the correct traditional answer, the prospective groom removes the threat of physical dysfunction.

The above hypothesis is admittedly highly speculative. However, regardless of the validity of the hypothetical explanation of one of the most common riddle functions, surely one can see the advantage, or rather the absolute necessity, of recording context. It is not enough to know that in such and such a culture riddles are used in courtship ritual. It is essential to know just which riddles are so used. Are oppositional riddles used more often than nonoppositional riddles? If oppositional riddles are used, what type of oppositional riddle is most common? Is the most common type the privational contradictive? It should be realized that even in the case of folklore genres for which structural delineations of the basic subtypes have not been made, the context of individual texts can still easily be recorded. In other words, even if the collector does not know the difference between one type of a riddle and another, he can still, as a matter of elementary fieldwork methodology, record context.

The importance of collecting context is especially obvious in the study of jokes. Variants of jokes, recorded without context, may be of value to historic-geographers plotting paths of diffusion, determining degrees of cognation, and postulating developmental sequences of subtypes, but contextless jokes are of limited value to the social scientist. Two of the most vital constituents of contextual structure are the person telling the joke and the audience listening to it. It is a commonplace that context can influence text (and also texture in the sense that a taboo lexical item will be used in one situation, but not in another), but actual concrete published examples of such influence are not common. This is partly because of the folklorists' overwhelming penchant for unadorned, often even unannotated, texts. The influence of audience or addressee is illustrated in the following joke collected in 1961 from the Dean of Men at a small college in southern Indiana.

The inmates of a mental institution were told that they would be released if they could do three things. They had to take their left hand and tap their right wrist, right elbow, and right shoulder, saying as they did so, "This is my wrist," "This is my elbow," and "This is my shoulder." The first of the three volunteers approached the examining psychiatrist and he tapped his wrist, saying, "This is my wrist." However, in the second part of the test, he mistakenly tapped his wrist again while saying "This is my elbow." "Sorry," said the psychiatrist, "you'll have to remain here." The second man succeeded in tapping his wrist and elbow, but when he said, "This is my shoulder," he tapped his elbow instead of his shoulder. The third man hit all three targets and identified them properly. "Congratulations," said the psychiatrist, "that's wonderful. We'll see that you're released immediately. But tell me, how is it that you do this so well?" "Oh," said the man tapping his head, "I just used my ass."

The joke was related at a Naval Reserve meeting by an adult male to a group of four other males. It was a typical situation in which American men attempt to demonstrate their masculinity to other men by telling jokes with some sexual content. In response to a question from me, the raconteur said that he used an alternative punch line if his audience included women, namely, "Oh, I just used my head." In this case, the narrator slaps his buttocks instead of his head. My informant recalled that upon one occasion in addressing a mixed audience, he began to tell this particular joke. He noticed by the middle of the joke that one woman in the audience was frowning and squirming uncomfortably. It was clear that she knew the "males only" punch line and that she was embarrassed at the prospect of the utterance of the taboo word "ass." The raconteur interrupted his anecdote to assure the woman the joke would be all right. (This, in itself, demonstrates how audience behavior, e.g., facial expression, can influence the telling of a story.)

Here is evidence that a knowledge of context can explain variations in text and texture. If, on the other hand, context data were not available, the folklorist would possess alternate punchlines of text without much possibility of determining the specific reason for alternation. Context cannot always be guessed.

The identity of the narrator is just as crucial as the identity of the audience. Specifically, just as the sexual makeup of the audience can influence text and texture, so can the sexual identity of the raconteur be a critical factor. This may be seen by comparing two versions of a henpecked husband tale collected recently.[18]

Three henpecked husbands determine to get back at their wives. Being henpecked, they can't really rebel, so they decide to obey their wives and to do exactly what they're told to do.

A month or so later, the men are together in a bar. The first says, "Well, we were eating supper and I accidentally spilled a little tiny bit of gravy on the tablecloth. So my wife says, 'Go ahead, spill gravy all over the table!' So I did—I turned that gravy bowl over; I smeared the stuff all over the table. I sure got even with my wife!"

The second says, "Well, I was comin' in the door and wind caught it, and it slammed shut. My wife, she hollers in at me, 'Go ahead, tear it off the hinges.' So I did. I ripped that damn door right off the hinges. I sure got even with my wife!"

The third one said, "We were in bed and I was trying to get my wife to make love and I was fooling around a little and my wife, she says, 'Cut it out!'—Ever see one of these things up close?"[19]

This joke was told by a thirty-year-old male schoolteacher to a twenty-two-year-old married female folklore collector. The informant's wife was present during the joke and when it was over, she offered an alternate ending:

". . . and I was fooling around a little and my wife, she says, 'Knock if off!' (with the gesture of raising a hand and swinging it as if one were swinging a pendulum), "How do you put one of these things back on?"

The psychological significance of the correlation of text variation with context should be apparent. The man's version eliminates the female's genitals while the wife's version castrates the marauding male. The alternate punch lines support several psychoanalytic hypotheses concerning male and female sexuality in Western culture. The point here, however, is that without the minimal context data, that is, the sex and relationship of the informants, the texts would be much less meaningful.

It was noted earlier that while textural features cannot in and of themselves define a genre of folklore, they may be of some supplementary value in defining folklore forms. The same may be said for contextual features. Context alone cannot always define a genre, inasmuch as a given social situational slot may be filled by any one of a number of different genres. For example, in a oneupsmanship context between children, a child might employ a riddle, a taunt, a joke, a catch tale, or a game. On the other hand, there are cases where contextual data is critical in distinguishing one genre from another. One such case involves a riddle or proverb. Both riddles and proverbs are based upon topic-comment constructions which are often metaphorical. However, in riddles, the referent is to be guessed, that is, the answer is presumably known by the poser of the riddle, but not by the addressee. In proverbs, the referent is already known to both utterer and audience. Sokolov has suggested that the transformation of proverb to riddle is a matter of an intonation change. He says, "Sometimes, only by means of a single change of intonation, a proverb is transformed into a riddle: 'Nothing hurts it, but it groans all the time.' In the proverb they are speaking of a hypocrite and a beggar, but in the riddle, by those very same words, a swine is meant."[20] But it should be clear that proverb context is not the same as riddle context. That there are textural (in this case intonational) distinctions cannot be gainsaid, but the primary difference is contextual. It is the different contexts which are responsible for the differences in intonation. Either individual A is asking B to guess the referent, swine, of a *riddle*, or A is commenting to B upon the actions of someone, action already known to B, by means of a *proverb*. The context is crucial. Consider the following Burmese text:

> Ma thi thu   kyaw thwar:
> Thi thu   phaw sar:
> The one who does not know about it may walk over it;
> The one who knows about it will dig it up and eat it.

As a riddle, the referent (answer) is a potato (or anything which grows underground); as a proverb, the statement is applied in many different situations where someone is ignorant of something valuable which is not readily apparent. In such instances, the statement is, *by context*, a proverb. My informant noted that the text functioned as a proverb

more than as a riddle. One can easily see how misleading it would be
if just the text alone were given (particularly if intonation features
were not recorded). It is doubtful whether a non-Burmese could have
guessed from the text alone that it could be a proverb.

   The collection of context is essential for all genres of folklore, but it
is absolutely indispensable for proverbs and gestures. Yet the majority
of proverb collections provide just texts. This is contextless folklore
collection. Proverbs, as examples of a fixed-phrase genre of folklore,
must be recorded in the original native language so that texture will
also be preserved. But what about context? Context is just as important as texture and yet it is almost never recorded. As a final illustration of the necessity for the collection of context, another Burmese
proverb will be considered.

        Sait ma so: bu:
        Kywè mi: to dè

which might be rendered, "I am not angry, but the buffalo's tail is
shorter." Having recorded both text and texture, can we say what the
proverb means? Do we know when, how, and why the proverb might
be used? It might be useful to think of the text of a proverb as somewhat analogous to that portion of an iceberg which is above the water
and readily visible to the naked eye. That upon which a proverb is
based may be invisible or beneath the surface, but the experienced
folklorist knows how to plumb the depths. To put the matter another
way, a proverb may be likened to T. S. Eliot's "objective correlative"
in that it is often an expression of a specific situation or chain of events
which serves to evoke a particular emotion or attitude.[21] Consequently, a discussion of a proverb without mention of what the proverb
evokes is as fruitless as studying literary allusions without knowing to
what the allusions allude. If there is oral literature, there is also oral or
native literary criticism. Folklorists have erred in simply recording
bare texts and assuming that they would undertake all the analysis (or
literary criticism) that was needed. The informant's opinions about his
materials are rarely solicited and yet they should be. Informants
should be asked what they think the significance of their materials is.
The collection of native literary criticism in no way precludes the
standard types of analysis conducted by folklorists. But besides Melville Jacobs' brilliant analyses of Clackamas Chinook oral literature,

there should be analyses of the same materials made by the Clackamas Chinooks themselves.

With regard to the Burmese proverb mentioned above, one can see quite easily that what is unsaid is much more important than what is said. In fact, the text alone is almost meaningless to members of another culture. First of all, as with many proverbs in Asian and African cultures, the proverb is the last sentence in a tale.

A farmer goes to the field to plow it. He works from morning to noon. He is hungry and waiting for his wife to bring his lunch. After a few hours, he cannot wait any longer. He cuts the tail off the buffalo which has been pulling the plow. He bakes it and eats it. The wife finally comes with his lunch and asks him whether he is angry with her. He replies, "I am not angry, but the buffalo's tail is shorter."

We now have some idea of the meaning of the proverb, but what about its use? The proverb is used when one is mildly angry with someone. In other words, one is angry, but one forgives. The proverb is most often used by a husband to his wife or a wife to her husband. Ideally, the collector should himself observe the context of the texts he records. However, in practice, there is usually an artificial context in which an informant is talking to a collector and/or his tape recorder. Thus it is incumbent upon the professional folklorist to seek to elicit the context in those instances where it cannot be directly empirically observed by him. A useful technique is to ask the informant to make up a situation in which the proverb might appropriately be cited. Unfortunately, on the whole, folklorists are inclined to limit supplementary data to "where, when, and by whom a saying is used." In other words, for publication in most of the folklore journals one needs only the bare text of the proverb with an indication that it was collected, say, in Bloomington, Indiana, on 31 July, 1962 from Maung Than Sein, a native of Magwe, Burma. But does this tell us what the proverb means or how it is used? There is nothing wrong with recording an informant's name and address and the place and date of collection, but one should not delude oneself into thinking that one has thereby recorded context. Such minimal informant data is a beginning, not an end.

Texture, text, and context must all be recorded. It should be noted that texture, text, and context can each be subjected to structural analysis. Emic and etic units can be distinguished at each level. There are emic slots in contexts which can be filled by etic examples of particular genres. In a given contextual slot, e.g., one involving social protest, a number of different genres may be employed, such as jokes, proverbs, gestures, and folksongs. On the other hand, a given genre, e.g., the riddle, may fill a number of different contextual slots. This is exactly parallel to the structural analysis of text. In the case of folktale structure, for example, emic slots in texts can be filled by different etic units, that is, different motifs (allomotifs) may be used in a given motifeme. Moreover, the same motif (etic unit) may be used in different motifemes (emic unit).[22] Texture may be analyzed in similar fashion.

The interrelationships between the three levels remain to be seen. A change in context can apparently effect a change in texture (e.g., a female narrator or audience may cause the substitution of a euphemism for a taboo word). In a previous study of proverbs, it was noted how textural structure underlined textual structure (e.g., the two parts of an equational proverb rhymed: coffee boiled is coffee spoiled).[23] In the present study, it was suggested that the structure of riddle texts might underlie the structure of riddle context (i.e., oppositional riddles used in courtship ritual).

With regard to the perplexing problem raised initially, that of the definition of folklore, it would seem that the first task of folklorists ought to be the analysis of text. Text is less variable than texture and context. In the case of free-phrase genres, textural features may be of little value with respect to defining these genres. In the case of fixed-phrase genres, textural features may be fairly stable, but they are rarely limited in their distribution to a single genre. Contextual criteria are similarly of limited value for purposes of definition. However, probably the best definitions of the various forms of folklore will be based upon criteria from all three levels of analysis. For this reason, it is probably a mistake for the folklorist to leave the analysis of texture to linguists and the analysis of context to cultural anthropologists. The well-rounded folklorist should hopefully attempt to analyze all three levels. Once all the genres have been rigorously described in these terms, it will no longer be necessary to rely upon such vague definitions as those depending upon such external criteria as the means of transmission. Furthermore, the vital relationship between folk and folklore, now virtually ignored by text-oriented folklorists, may finally be given the attention it so richly deserves.

Projection in Folklore
A Plea for Psychoanalytic Semiotics

———————⟫⬦ ⬦⟨———————

Folklore *means* something—to the tale teller, to the song singer, to the riddler, and to the audience or addressees. A given item of folklore may mean different things to different tale tellers or to different audiences. It may mean different things to different members of the same audience; it may mean different things to a single tale teller at different times in his life. This seems obvious enough. But despite the assiduous collection of scores and scores of folklore texts, there has been precious little attention paid to what these texts mean.

In the nineteenth century and before, folklore was thought to be a *dead* survival from ages past rather than a *live*, functioning part of the present-day world of man. Even as late as 1931, Ruth Benedict, writing the entry on folklore for the prestigious *Encyclopaedia of the Social Sciences*, observed that "folklore has not survived as a living trait in modern civilization" and "thus in a strict sense folklore is a dead trait in the modern world."[1] To be sure, one can find easily enough bona fide evidence of survivals. Consider, for example, the name of the month September, which is our ninth month. It is derived from the Latin word for seven (as October is from eight, November from nine, and December from ten). Reconstructing history from etymology, we can see that if September were the seventh month, then the first month of the year must have been March rather than January, and in fact the onset of spring makes much better sense metaphorically as the appropriate time to signal the birth of a new year. In Europe, the designation of January first as the beginning of the new year is a relatively recent innovation. But the point is that folklore can hardly be limited to survivals. The folklore of social protest and the folklore of

33

computers demonstrate convincingly that folklore *is* a living trait in the modern world.

One difficulty impeding the study of meaning of folklore stems from the fact that a goodly portion of folklore is fantasy, collective or collectivized fantasy. I do not refer here to any Jungian sense of a collective unconscious. The evidence available from the *Motif-Index of Folk-Literature* shows quite plainly that few if any narrative elements have universal distribution.[2] Quite the contrary, most narrative traditions have strictly circumscribed areas of distribution. The localization of fantasy is empirically demonstrable. Trolls are found in Scandinavia; leprechauns only in Ireland, *menehune* only in Polynesia.[3] The cultural relativity of fantasy is also suggested by the fact that it is only Christians who report seeing visions of the Virgin Mary. Those who argue that a given example of fantasy is universal rarely cite data from aboriginal Australia, Africa, or the Indian peoples of South America. It is true that all peoples have folklore and in that sense folklore could conceivably qualify as a universal. However, the particular folklore possessed by a particular folk varies from culture to culture even though historically related peoples share some folklore in common. When I speak of folklore being collective, I mean that a myth or a folksong is known by more than a single individual. An item of folklore is known by several individuals, usually many individuals, and it is transmitted from person to person, often over the course of generations. Collective folklore differs from individual dreams. Dreams appear to be similar to narratives in part because they are related in words. But a dream may or may not be sufficiently intelligible or interesting to be related by a second party to a third party. Folktales, in contrast, like all folklore, have passed the test of time, and are transmitted again and again. Unlike individual dreams, folktales must appeal to the psyches of many, many individuals if they are to survive.

The fantastic dimensions of folklore have been consistently disregarded by folklorists and members of other disciplines studying folkloristic data. These scholars prefer instead to concentrate upon collection, classification, storage (in archives), comparison, and endless searching for the oldest cognate versions of a particular piece of folklore. The history of folklore scholarship is by and large a series of attempts to dehumanize folklore. I mean dehumanize quite literally. Considering "folklore" without reference to "folk" is commonplace in folkloristics. Whether one assigns motif or tale type numbers, or attempts to structurally dissect a given folklore text, one can effectively forget about the fact that folklore is used as a means of traditional communication between humans.

The influence of semiotics upon folkloristics has not been altogether salutary. The scholarship of semiotics seems bloated with pompous terminology and littered with competing unintelligible abstract formulations, formulations which seem far removed from any close contact with empirical data. For semiotics, although ostensibly concerned with meaning, tends to emphasize the *logical* rather than the *psychological* facets of the data being examined. Semiotic analyses generally treat the composition or structural patterning of a text to the exclusion of any concern for possible psychological meanings of that text. Structuralism perceived as one branch of semiotics should be considered as being essentially a rigorous means of descriptive ethnography. Structural analyses attempt to tell us *what an object is*, not what the object is for or what it means. To be sure, there is nothing wrong with descriptive ethnography. On the contrary, one needs to know the nature of the object one is studying. It is only that pure structuralism has a tendency to stop after describing in agonizing detail an object's actual or imagined constituent elements and the patterns of interrelationships between those elements. In short, however useful semiotics may be for honing the tools of description and classification in folkloristics, it has yet to prove itself in the study of the meaning of folklore. Thus, for example, Propp's important *Morphology of the Folktale* gives us an unrivaled view of the nature of Indo-European *Märchen*, but Propp's delineation of thirty-one functions (or what I have rechristened motifemes, following Kenneth Pike) does not explain why the fairy tale pattern should exist in the first place or what, if anything, it means.[4]

I believe that one reason why structuralism is sweeping through folkloristics (which habitually maintains a respectful pace of a decade or so behind advances in linguistics theory) is that the shift from diachronic to synchronic methodology posed no serious threat to the folkless study of folklore. At first, practitioners of the historical and comparative methods were adamantly opposed to structuralism, which they felt gave short shrift to historical and comparative dimensions. But in time, it was realized that the same nonpsychological bias could prevail. Instead of plotting the distribution of motifs or quaint customs on maps—as is done in European atlas work in folkloristics, one could stick the very same "butterflies" on another kind of board and proceed to dissect them. Butterfly collection of antiquarian days had finally advanced to the point of demonstrating that a butterfly was a mediating model consisting primarily of two wings in opposition—if I may somewhat facetiously and unfairly describe the binary penchant of Lévi-Straussians.

Interestingly enough, structuralism has opened up anew the question of the existence of the unconscious, but it has done so in a curiously unproductive way from my point of view. It is true that matters of grammar and syntax are not conscious—in the sense that individuals perfectly well able to speak a language cannot articulate the underlying grammatical or syntactical principles governing their speech acts. But this is hardly the unconscious of the Freudian variety in which materials, often of a taboo nature, are repressed and disguised.

It is my contention that much of the meaning of folkloristic fantasy is unconscious. Indeed, it would have to be unconscious—in the Freudian sense—for folklore to function as it does. Among its functions, folklore provides a socially sanctioned outlet for the expression of what cannot be articulated in the more usual, direct way. It is precisely in jokes, folktales, folksongs, proverbs, children's games, gestures, etc. that anxieties can be vented. If a person knew exactly what he was doing when he told a joke to his boss or to his spouse (or if the boss or spouse knew what he was doing), the joke would probably cease to be an escape mechanism. Man needs such mechanisms. That is why there will always be folklore, and also incidentally why there is always new folklore being created to take care of new anxieties—I refer, for example, to the folklore of bureaucracy transmitted so effectively by the office-copier machine.[5]

The unconscious nature of so much of folklore makes the study of meaning difficult though not impossible. It is difficult because it is not easy to elicit native testimony about such meanings. Unconscious symbolism is just as hard for informants to articulate as is the grammar of the languages they speak. Moreover, just as there are competing modes of grammatical analysis, so also are there competing schools of symbolism. So if the informant cannot enlighten the folklorist with respect to meaning—either by telling him about it initially or by corroborating an educated guess of the folklorist, how can the meaning of folklore be investigated?

Fortunately, there is patterning and system in folklore, and it is this remarkable consistency which can assist the folklorist interested in meaning. Jakobson and Bogatyrev in 1929 pointed out that the Saussurean distinction between *langue* and *parole* could be applied to folklore.[6] Accordingly, an individual folkloristic performance or communication act bore the same kind of relationship to the general folkloristic code that an individualistic speech act did to the language as a whole. I believe symbolism works in a similar fashion, so that the symbol employed in any one given folkloristic (con)text may be related to a general system of symbols. This does not mean that I think any one symbol is necessarily universal. In fact, I know of no symbol which is reported from all peoples, just as I know of no myth which has universal distribution. What I am saying is that within a culturally relative system of symbols, the use of a particular symbol may be remarkably consistent. I hasten to add that symbols—as opposed to signs—may carry multiple meanings. (I realize that some semioticians consider symbol a subcategory of sign, but I prefer to treat them separately.)

I intend to illustrate the above by referring to several specific examples of folklore; but before I do so, I should like to mention briefly the crucial device of projection. In psychology, projection refers to the tendency to attribute to another person or to the environment what is actually within oneself. What is attributed is usually some internal impulse or feeling which is painful, unacceptable, or taboo. The ascription of feelings and qualities of one's own to a source in the external world is accomplished without the individual's being consciously aware of the fact. The individual perceives the external object as possessing the taboo tendencies without recognizing their source in himself.[7] I might mention that Charles S. Peirce was aware of the existence of projection. He wrote, "I think it is probably true that every element of experience is in the first instance applied to an external object. A man who gets up out of the wrong side of the bed, for example, attributes wrongness to almost every object he perceives. This is the way in which he experiences his bad temper."[8] Despite the triviality of the example, the aptness of the insight remains valid. Of course, Freud said it too and with specific reference to folklore: "As a matter of fact, I believe that a large portion of the mythological conception of the world which reaches far into the most modern religions, is *nothing but psychology projected to the outer world*."[9]

I should also point out *en passant* that the discipline most concerned with projection is psychology and yet psychologists rarely think of folklore in connection with projection. Lindzey's *Projective Techniques and Cross-Cultural Research* published in 1961, for example, contains not even a mention of folklore.[10] For psychologists, projective techniques involve the utilization of tests or devices such as Rorschach or T.A.T. (Thematic Apperception Test). As a folklorist, I would argue that such devices are a priori artificial techniques usually imposed upon hapless subjects from outside the cultures of many of the subjects. How many peoples around the world are accustomed to interpreting inkblots? It is a question whether the results of such tests reflect the personalities of the test-takers or the test-makers! Folklore is quite different. The projective materials, if folklore is indeed projective, come from within the culture. It has been created, passed on, and enjoyed for considerable time long before the analyst arrives upon the scene. Folklore as autobiographical ethnography, as a mirror of culture, is a natural projective test—as opposed to the artifical schemata designed by psychologists.

If one admits there is no such thing as a culture-free test, projective or otherwise, one ought in theory to be delighted to have native or folk projective tests, that is, projective materials devised by a people themselves. Consider the New Year's practice found in Finland and elsewhere which calls for boiling lead and pouring bits of it into water. Someone then "reads" the shapes formed by the lead to predict the fortunes of individuals in the coming year. Reading lead shapes is somewhat similar to reading inkblots. By the same token, there are folkloristic analogues to sentence completion, word association, or storytelling psychological tests. For example, there is a popular American party game in which "It" is sent out of the room while supposedly those remaining are engaged in making up a story. "It" is told that he will be summoned shortly and asked to guess the story plot. After "It" leaves, the group members are told that there is no story, but that "It" will make up his own story upon his return. The trick is that to each of "It's" questions, the group will answer only yes or no, according to whether the last orthographic letter in "It's" question is a vowel (plus "y") or a consonant. Thus if "It" asks, "Is it a story about me?" a member of the group would answer yes. The question, "Does it take place on earth?" would require a no response. (In a variant, the rule is 'yes' if the last letter of the last word falls within the first half of the alphabet, no for the last half.) What usually happens in this game is that the story "reconstructed" by "It" often reveals interesting facets of "It's" own personality. A psychologist would probably say that "It" projects his own anxieties, thoughts, wishes, etc. upon the minimal structuring provided by the mechanical replies of the group.

The above party game and most of the examples of folklore I shall discuss will be familiar ones. This is intentional. Typically, anthropologists offer elaborate exegeses of some esoteric symbolic system which their audience cannot really confirm or reject inasmuch as they are completely dependent upon the data provided by the anthropologist for any knowledge of the culture under examination. It is for this reason that I have chosen examples from American folklore. I assume that most Americans will have personal acquaintance with the data. Let us begin with a jump rope rhyme.[11]

> Fudge, fudge, tell the judge
> Mama's got a newborn baby.
> It ain't no girl, it ain't no boy
> Just a newborn [or 'common', or 'plain ol'', or 'ordinary'] baby.
> Wrap it up in tissue paper
> Throw (send) it down the elevator.
> First floor, miss
> Second floor, miss, etc. [until the jumper misses]

What does this rhyme mean? Were we to ask little girls jumping rope to it to give us a full *explication de texte*, what would we elicit? What does "fudge" mean? Here we have a typical piece of concrete data and what would conventional semiotics do with it? Why is there a judge? Is it merely a matter of 'judge' rhyming with 'fudge', or 'fudge' rhyming with 'judge'? Folklore is admirably concise and I am persuaded that whatever is contained in a folkloristic text is meaningful—even if we do not always have full insight into what the meanings may be. What I am unalterably opposed to is the all too commonly vouchsafed platitude that folklore is bound to contain irrational nonsense which has no meaning. Why would individuals bother to remember something and repeat it with such gusto if it had no meaning? It seems clear that if an item remains in tradition, it must have meaning for the carriers of the tradition.

We can see that the jump rope rhyme reflects sibling rivalry. A newborn baby is a threat to the older children who may resent all the attention paid to it by their parents. We know that there is often a wish on the part of older children to dispose of the new baby. Wishful thinking and wish fulfillment are, of course, widely found in folklore.[12] There is more than a hint that Mama has committed a crime in producing a sibling rival. The crime is signalled in the first line insofar as a judge is to be informed (and possibly the punishment for the 'crime' of throwing the baby away is projected to the judge). But why fudge? If one thinks of the color and texture of fudge, *and* is also familiar with infantile sexual theory, one can arrive at a possible explanation. In the days before sex education was taught in elementary school, young children in our culture did not always understand the true nature of childbirth. After having been told by a parent that a baby brother or sister was present in mother's obviously expanding abdomen and that it would soon come out to join the family, the often bewildered child frequently assumed that this new baby would come out of the stomach area the same way the child understood that all materials exited from its own stomach, namely, via the anus. The equation of feces with babies is reported extensively in the psychoanalytic literature, but I doubt that any little girl jumping rope would offer such an interpretation of the possible meaning of 'fudge.' Yet there is additional evidence, for cultural symbols rarely occur in unique single texts. Another children's rhyme, though not one used for jumping rope, goes as follows:

> Milk, milk, lemonade
> Around the corner, fudge is made.

Gestures accompanying this rhyme point in turn to several areas of female anatomy (breasts, vulva, and anus). However distasteful or crude one may find the rhyme, one cannot very well deny the explicit equation of fudge and feces. Returning to our original jump rope rhyme, we can now better understand the action taken. Wrap it up in tissue (toilet) paper, throw it down the elevator. The new baby is 'giftwrapped to go,' namely, to be flushed down the toilet-elevator. Notice also that the more skillful the jumper, the greater the number of floors or distance the baby is sent away, thereby providing a most effective means of "passing" judgment on or "wasting" a sibling rival.

It should not be necessary to say that sibling rivalry is a normal feature of family life. However, since parents often interfere with or restrict overt acts of violence directed by one child towards another, it is clear that some outlet is necessary for the expression of the hostility which is bound to occur. Rhymes against babies are just as healthy as are rhymes against parents, e.g., Step on a crack (line); break your mother's (father's) back (spine). In terms of projection, it would be interesting to know whether individual children intentionally stepped on sidewalk cracks or intentionally avoided doing so, and then correlating such behavior with the overall personalities of such children and their stated attitudes towards each parent.

Children's projections of parents occur more commonly in narrative form than in rhymes. Fairy tales, for instance, are essentially stories about children and their relationships to siblings and parents. The "step" relationship is a convenient device to allow full-fledged hatred. A girl can, with clear conscience, hate wicked stepsisters, or a wicked stepmother. Fairy tales with girl protagonists may include wicked sibling rivals as well as a wicked mother in the form of a stepmother or witch. Fairy tales with boy heroes may include the same kind of wicked brothers plus a male antagonist in the form of a monster (e.g., dragon) or a giant. Let me select one fairy tale found primarily in England and the United States to illustrate the nature of symbolic projection. Once upon a time, a boy named Jack lived *alone with his mother!* That very opening should give pause to anyone with a psychological bias. In boy-centered fairy tales, the father is often portrayed as missing or dead—which allows the boy to be "alone with his mother." (In girl-centered fairy tales, the mother is similarly missing or deceased, which allows the girl to be alone with her father.) As most will remember, Jack trades his milk-giving cow to an old man who gives him some beans in exchange. Jack's mother insists, at the sight of the beans, that he throw them out of the window. (I shall refrain from commenting upon each and every symbol.) The next day, a huge beanstalk is discovered. Jack's mother begs him not to ascend, but he disobeys. Up in the beanstalk world, there is a cannibalistic giant who often in some vague way is linked with Jack's father—e.g., the giant allegedly stole Jack's father's treasures. Fortunately, someone up there helps Jack. It is Mrs. Giant. Did it ever strike you as somewhat peculiar that Mrs. Giant would help a total stranger, a young boy, taking sides against her own husband? (In this Oedipal projection, the upper world is an extension of the lower one.) In this connection, it may be worth recalling where Mrs. Giant hides Jack—it is in her oven. (The symbolism of ovens in European folklore generally is quite consistent.[13]) Consider, for example, the initial morpheme of the verb *fornicate* and in this context, note the poetic justice in the best known version of tale type 327A,[14] Hansel and Gretel, according to which Gretel tricks the witch into being burned to death in her own oven. In any event, the stupid old giant fails to see Jack hiding in his wife's oven. Finally, Jack rushes down the stalk with the giant in close pursuit. As it happens, down at the bottom of the stalk waiting with a hatchet in her hand is Jack's mother. Taking the hatchet, Jack cuts down the stalk, an act which causes the death of the giant. The story ends with Jack living happily ever after *with his mother.*[15]

Surely the maternal aid in both the upper and lower worlds can be understood as a projection of the young boy's point of view in terms of an Oedipal struggle against the villainous giant. From Jack and the Beanstalk, I should like to turn to another example of projection. This example is not folklore, but it is dependent upon folklore and folkloristic associations. One reason for using the example is to show that projection is such an important device that it may utilize even historical events rather than relying solely upon the traditional forms found in folklore proper.

The example of projection I have in mind is the first lunar landing. I must insist that nothing of what I am about to present should be understood as in any way demeaning the very real and splendid achievement of landing on the moon. My sole purpose is to try to demonstrate how large a part folkloristic projection plays in all our lives—whether we are aware of it or not.

First of all, there is the name of the lunar mission: Apollo. I should stress here that it is precisely in the selection of names and symbols that those of us interested in psychoanalytic semiotics are afforded prime data. It might well be erroneous to interpret a detail which was an integral part of the scientific apparatus, but the choice of the name Apollo is not such a detail. In theory, the mission might have had any one of a hundred names. The name Apollo is a conscious or perhaps unconscious invocation of traditional mythology. And in mythology round the world, we find the most pressing problems of earthly bodies projected onto heavenly bodies. In this light, constellations and their names in different cultures may appropriately be studied as native projective Rorschach gestalts. As for planet names in our own culture, it is interesting that earth falls between Venus and Mars, love and

war, perhaps even life and death. Has earth separated god and goddess lovers just as in the widely diffused Oedipal sky-father/earth-
mother myth (motif A625, World parents; sky-father and earth-
mother)[16] in which a culture hero forcibly pushes the sky back out of
the connubial embrace with the earth in order to provide living space
for man?

To return to the lunar mission, who is Apollo and what, if any, is
his relationship to the moon? Apollo the sun is the brother of Diana
the moon. Thus mythologically speaking we have a brother trying to
reach or land on his sister. And what are the semantic associations of
Diana? One of the most obvious is virginity. Diana is traditionally
associated with chastity.

Once the projective metaphor has been pointed out, it is easy
enough to see its consistency. Among the principal problems to be
overcome in the Apollo missions was gaining enough power to escape
the gravitational pull of the earth. The standard term for this power
was "thrust." Keeping in mind that the mythological associations of
earth include 'mother,' we have the astronauts trying to get up enough
thrust to escape the gravitational pull of mother earth. (I shall not
dwell on the symbolism of rockets other than to recall that "to have a
rocket in my pocket" can be a euphemistic phrase for masturbation
(cf. "pocket pool").)

I have spoken of the name of the mission, but what were the names
of the three astronauts and who was the first man on the moon? Neil
Armstrong. Why was Armstrong the first? Was it mere alphabetical
order? No, it was not because in that event, *Al*drin would have been
first, not *Ar*mstrong, or Collins. Could it have been the association of
Jack Armstrong, the all-American boy, hero of radio adventure serials
of several decades past? And could it have been the very name
Armstrong was deemed appropriate because it literally refers to a
strong body extremity? A well placed television camera allowed all
other earthlings to voyeuristically watch as Armstrong's leg emerged
from the capsule and stepped upon the surface of the moon. Certainly
it made symbolic sense for the name of the *first* man to stand on the
moon to begin with the *first* letter of our alphabet. Who can remember
the names of any of the men who made the *second* lunar landing? The
point is that the moon could only be violated once. No one cares who
the other violators were. It is, after all, only on a maiden voyage that a
bottle of champagne is broken over a ship's hull. Once on the moon,

the astronauts put up an American flag, a common symbolic ritual act for claiming virgin land for one's mother country (or fatherland). We may have here the same projection which led earlier generations of American explorers into what Henry Nash Smith has so aptly termed the "Virgin Land."[17] What did the astronauts bring back as souvenirs of their conquest? Pieces of rock. In this context, the whole mission involved going out to get a piece of virgin moon to show off to one's peers back home—a super masculinity dream come true! Americans surely wanted to get to the moon before the Russians did. The fantasy I have just delineated is not a universal one—in some cultures the moon is considered masculine rather than feminine. But in American culture, the moon is definitely feminine. It even has maternal associations of a cow jumping over it or being made of green cheese. The image of a 'man in the moon' may even suggest an idealized intrauterine one. The maternal associations of the moon hint at an Oedipal projection and in English, the choice of the name Apollo at least permits the possibility of a homonymic pun on sun/son. So the sun/son who leaves mother earth to be the first to violate the virgin moon (sister, mother) may well be related to American fantasy—regardless of the purely scientific features of the mission.

The lunar mission brings to mind the interweaving of folklore and history. The point is that historical events and personages may serve as anchors for flights of projective fantasy. I believe many historians seriously err in dismissing or ignoring elements which they label as spurious or apocryphal. Folklore, as an item of folk speech—think of the phrase "that's (just) folklore"—means error, that is, something to be carefully weeded out of otherwise accurate historical source material. As a folklorist, I have learned to respect what the folk say and think about history regardless of the historicity of their words and thoughts. What happened is important, but no less important is what people think happened or what people wish had happened. Folk history may tell us more about folk than about history, but surely that is worth knowing. The folk history of George Washington, for example, includes his famous confrontation with his father over the chopping down, not of a beanstalk, but of a cherry tree. Actually, George, a son in that anecdote, is more celebrated for his paternal role. Why is it, for instance, that George is reputed to have slept in so many beds on the east coast of the United States. Signs proclaim that George Washington *slept* here, not ate, drank, or visited here. Of course, if he is considered to be the *father* of our country then the verb choice is apt—just like the particular style of monuments *erected* to honor him.[18]

But can there be any validity to the projections discussed thus far? I can anticipate the most obvious objection. The reader may have watched the lunar landing himself and he did not think of any associations of Apollo-Diana, brother-sister incest, etc. He did not think of the lunar landing as a violation of the moon. Any tension he may have felt was strictly due to his genuine concern for the safety of the astronauts. But sometimes the tension was excessive. Some individuals refused to believe that the lunar landing actually occurred. Rather, they assumed that the whole event was simply a fictionalized television program. Several individuals suffered breakdowns evidently precipitated by the successful lunar landing.[19] Here I must reiterate the important point that folkloristic projection is often, though not always, unconscious. Rarely is the nature of the projection consciously recognized. I am always amused by would-be critics of the Oedipal reading of the Oedipus story when they claim that the Freudian interpretation is invalid because Oepidus didn't *know* that he was killing his father and marrying his mother. Of course, he didn't know consciously. That is precisely the point. It is the bringing of the unconscious into the purview of the conscious which is difficult and painful for the psyche. Projection is one of a number of psychological defense mechanisms which provides an unconscious screen or arena for the display of the causes of anxiety and it is for this reason that folkloristic projections are so indispensable as tools in the human arsenal for mental health.

The unconscious nature of symbols and projections does present a serious challenge to those folklorists who are seeking meaning in folklore. But materials which have entered the unconscious can also be brought out of the unconscious. One characteristic which is helpful in the study of folkloristic projections is the play upon 'literal versus metaphorical.' Sometimes seeing projections as literalizations of metaphors or, if one prefers, as metaphorical transformations of literal statements can greatly aid in deciphering the unconscious content of folklore. Let me illustrate this by briefly considering an important detail of the American wedding ritual. One of the high points of the ritual involves the bride's casting her floral bouquet to the females in attendance. What is the meaning of this act? I wish to reiterate my firm conviction that semiotics must ultimately be concerned with meaning. One can analyze the structure of American weddings and note the binary oppositions between bride and groom, married and unmarried, etc., but unless semiotics can take account of the symbolic, projective aspects of ritual, it can never be more than a purely descriptive technique as opposed to an explanatory one. The throwing of the bridal bouquet involves homeopathic magic and therefore metaphors or, if one prefers, as metaphorical transformations of literal just as contagious magic is analogous to simile. Most poetic tropes have structural analogues in types of magic. Synecdoche, for example, corresponds to the principle of *pars pro toto* in magic practice. In terms of the literalization of metaphor, the bride is through the ritual act of throwing away her floral bouquet signifying her willingness to be, or intention of being, *deflowered*. Interestingly enough, the flowers, once separated from the bride, furnish an example of contagious magic inasmuch as the lucky girl who catches the bouquet is said to be the next to marry.

I might mention several other examples of the literalization of metaphor in American folklore. There is an American superstition which states that if one wants to ensure that one's newborn baby will rise in the world, one should carry it up a flight of stairs shortly after birth. The metaphorical notion of rising in the world is thus literally carried out. Literalization of metaphor can also occur in folktales. I think, for instance of tale type 311, Rescue by the Sister, in which there is a forbidden chamber. The heroine, as one may remember, opens the interdicted door whereupon an egg or key becomes bloody. The symbolism of telltale blood marking an egg or key after opening a forbidden door seems to be a projection of defloration. What is also of interest is the sight that the heroine sees in the forbidden chamber. Commonly she finds the decapitated bodies of her older sisters. The literalization of metaphor is, if I am correct, exemplified by the vivid depiction of girls who have quite literally lost their maiden heads!

An even better example of the literalization of metaphor in folkloristic projections may be found in yet another genre, namely nursery rhymes. "There was an old woman who lived in a shoe; she had so many children she didn't know what to do." Now what possible connection could there be between a woman living in a shoe and having a superabundance of children? Upon reflection, we may recall that there is a traditional connection between shoes and marriage. Not only does Cinderella find her prince charming through the perfect fit between her foot and a glass slipper, but in American culture, we continue to tie old shoes on the bumpers of cars carrying newlyweds off on their honeymoon. With respect to the Cinderella story (tale type 510A), it might be observed that very few versions have the shoe made of glass. Cox in her 1892 study of 345 versions of Cinderella found only six instances of glass slippers. However, the occurrence of the glass slipper in the celebrated Perrault version of Cinderella may explain the widespread popularity of this element. I shall refrain from commenting on the theory that the slipper in question was not really made of glass but was rather a mistranslation of the French word "vair" which was a kind of fur,[20] a theory which strongly suggests that interpretations of folklore can involve almost as much symbolic projection as the folklore itself. The mystery of the association of shoes with marriage and children is partly solved by another version of the Mother Goose rhyme reported from the Ozarks of the 1890s. "There was another old woman who lived in a shoe. She didn't have any children; she knew what to do." The consistency of the symbolism should be apparent. In nursery rhymes, in fairy tales, in post-wedding customs, the same symbolic equation is found. This supports the idea that symbol patterns are culturewide. One could easily cite additional illustrations, e.g., Cock a doodle doo; My dame has lost her shoe [a real challenge for transplant surgeons]; Her master's lost his fiddling stick. They don't know what to do."[21] So it may be that participants in a wedding cannot articulate any rationale for the custom of tying shoes to the car bumper, but that does not mean that the custom is a "meaningless" survival. The marriage car carries off the shoe trophies just as the groom will later carry his bride across the threshold of their dwelling, the latter custom being perhaps a metaphor for the successful initiation of male-dominated sexual intercourse.

Now I fear I may perhaps have done a serious disservice to my thesis by having utilized so many examples of sexual symbolism. Some may think that I have badly misconstrued the term *semiotics* as being the scientific study of the "seamy." I must stress that projection in folklore is *not* limited to sexuality. Any anxiety-producing topic can find expression in projective form. For example, there is projection in the modern urban legend in which a family is obliged to take its old grandmother along on a vacation trip. In a remote area, grandmother dies and the family is forced to curtail its vacation. Strapping the body to the roof of the Volkswagen, the family starts for home. En route they stop for lunch during which time the car plus grandmother's corpse is stolen. Sometimes the absence of the body causes delay in probating grandmother's will. I have argued that this legend reflects American attitudes towards the older generation and towards death. In terms of wishful thinking, there is the wish that grandmother should die and that someone else should dispose of the body. In terms of the literalization of metaphor, grandmother is "taken for a ride," if I may be permitted to use the appropriate gangster idiom. The normally unutterable mercenary interest in grandmother's demise also finds expression in the concern about the delay in probate.

Similarly there is projection in the standard legend of the medical school prank in which a group of medical students crossing a toll bridge leave a cadaver's arm holding the coin in the surprised and shocked grasp of the tollbooth attendant. Medical students have anxiety—at least initially—about handling cadavers and probably also about paying their way through life at the expense of the health of their patients. After all, the families of patients are charged for operations whether the operations are successful or not. Doctors have to learn to be dispassionate objective practitioners who are able to leave their patients' medical problems, e.g., anatomical parts such as an arm, behind them even as these problems literally hold the lucrative financial rewards of medical practice. Notice that in this projection, the fear and shock of taking money from a dead man's hand is displaced from the medical students to the outside world, the tollbooth attendant.[22]

Racism is another anxiety-producing problem which is expressed in folkloristic form. Let us briefly consider the folksong "John Henry." A popular folksong, this ballad tells the sad story of a black steel-driver who wages a valiant struggle against the steam drill. He wins the battle, but the victory is Pyrrhic for in the end John Henry dies. I have had white, middle-class school teachers tell me they use this folksong in the classroom as an example of Afro-American folklore. They like the ballad's depiction of the increasingly important issue of man versus machine. This is all well and good, but as a projection, John Henry is little more than the white stereotype of what black men should be. John Henry is strong, doggedly loyal to the white boss, and he dies doing the white man's work. He is, in short, a projection of the ideal "good nigger." He even dies with his hammer in his hand—no threat there to the white womanhood of the south. The ballad of John Henry is thus more part of white folklore about blacks than Afro-American folklore, and its continued use in schools promoted the image of the strong, docile, Uncle Tom figure of the black male so ardently desired by whites.

The unconscious projective aspects of folklore make its use all the more insidious and perhaps dangerous inasmuch as few individuals are aware of the semiotic implications of the projection. Racism is nonetheless virulent for its being unconscious. Many whites may not see the racism in an advertisement for "flesh-colored bandaids" but it is there all the same. A terse bit of Afro-American folklore conveys a unique indictment of the use of white folklore in classrooms containing black students. There's the young black girl who asks a question of the mirror on the wall. "Mirror, mirror on the wall, who's the fairest one of all?" and the mirror answers, "Snow White, you black bitch, and don't you forget it!" In an educational system and society where the values come from white folklore, there is not much potential for a positive self-image for black students. Americans inherited from Europe an entire semiotic of color in which black was evil and white was good. Even a lie, if it's white, is all right. "Black is beautiful" is a conscious attempt by the black community to fight the semantic set of countless words (blackmail, blackguard, blackball, black list, etc.) which assert the contrary.[23]

Racist projections are also found in literature and I do not want to give the impression that projections are limited to folkloristic form. Let me cite just one illustration from children's literature. *Charlie and the Chocolate Factory* is a popular children's book, which was made into a motion picture. The cover blurb calls it "an uproarious morality tale by the world-renowned storyteller, Roald Dahl." And it is a highly moral story, poking fun as it does at a gluttonous eater, a spoiled little rich girl, a fanatic gum chewer, and a television addict. But as some readers may recall, there is a chocolate factory run by Willy Wonka. Who is it that does all the work at the factory? The work is done by the Oompa-Loompas. Who are the Oompa-Loompas? They are pygmies "imported direct from Africa." "Their skin is almost black" and Willy Wonka "shipped them all over here, every man, woman and child in the Oompa-Loompa tribe. It was easy." He "smuggled them over in large packing cases with holes in them, and they all got here safely." "They love dancing and music."[24] According to Willy Wonka, the Oompa-Loompas came willingly because they were told they could have all they wanted to eat (at the company store)! It is hard to know whether this white projection of contented 'lumps' of black slave labor is conscious or unconscious on the author's part, but its potential impact upon a generation of children (and parents) in terms of continuing a stereotype is devastating. Curiously, the title of the book (and the name of the little boy hero) revolves around the name Charlie, the standard slang term in Afro-American folklore for the 'white man.'

Projections are to be found in all types of literature including comics, television, and motion pictures. My plea for psychoanalytic semiotics is based primarily upon folklore only because I am most familiar with folkloristic data. It is equally imperative that popular culture be understood as projective materials. One thinks of the generic "Western" with its rugged individual hero who often has to take the law into his own hands, vigilante-style, in order to prevail over the "bad guys" and to establish law and order, thereby protecting property rights. Similarly, we might look at Star Trek, which relates the adventures of an eternally floating bastion of American values in the context of a popular science fiction television program series. Typically the space ship makes an *uninvited* visit to some alien culture which somehow threatens the existence or safety of the ship (or the ship is itself invaded by the alien culture). Often the progress of the space ship is imperiled or stopped. Its leader heroes, of obvious Anglo-Saxon ancestry (Kirk, Spock, Scotty, McCoy), assisted by various assorted ethnic underlings who obey rather than give orders, take whatever action they deem necessary to *free* the ship. Since the ship's name is Enterprise, we have an all too thinly disguised projection of what Americans will do in the name of free enterprise. And what does the crew of the Enterprise do? The usual solution consists of converting or destroying the alien cultures. Only after such justifiable homicide can the United Starship (=U.S.) Enterprise return to its set course—in accordance with its 'manifest destiny.'[25] It is not hard to see how the Western-vigilante and Star Trek projections could lead to the American officer in Viet Nam who explained in all seriousness that "It was necessary to destroy the village in order to save it."

Projection can involve placement in the far distant past or the far distant future. This is why one can study projection in myth, the far distant past, or projection in science fiction, the far distant future.

The plots and the dramatis personae are strikingly similar in both myth and science fiction. In sum, it is the projection which is crucial, not so much the time and place or local coloring. It is the removal from reality to fantasy which allows the human spirit free rein to portray its spiritual struggles and play out its moments of anguish. Yet sometimes, even fantasy does not afford sufficient disguise for such activities, not without recourse to what I would call projective inversion.

Most of the projections discussed thus far have been more or less direct translations of reality into fantasy. The code of symbols permits a healthful rewriting of a problem on earth into a disguised arena where it may be happily resolved. So the lunar landing might be interpreted as an extended metaphor for the American male's quest to break the silver (umbilical) cord or maternal apron strings in order to seek a virgin bride. But there are some human problems which evidently require more elaborate disguise.

One of the finest examples of projective inversion in folklore is the one first analyzed by Otto Rank in his brilliant monograph, *The Myth of the Birth of the Hero*, first published in 1909. In this classic study, Rank attempts to explain why the Indo-European hero should so often be born of a virgin mother and why he should be abandoned to die immediately upon being born. According to Rank, it is an Oedipal plot from the son's point of view. A virgin mother represents a complete repudiation of the father and especially his normal necessary role in procreation.[26] In Oedipal theory, it is supposedly the son who would like to get rid of his father (which would thereby reserve his mother for his exclusive use) but a narrative in which a son deposed or disposed of his father would produce considerable guilt. Thus, according to Rank, the child's wish to get rid of the father is neatly transposed in the myth to the father's getting rid of the child. Rank called this projection, but I would call it projective inversion. The son's wishful thinking is projected in inverted form so that the father does everything he can to kill the son. One obvious advantage of such projective inversion is the avoidance of guilt. The son need not feel guilt for wanting to get rid of his father inasmuch as the traditional fantasy projects the 'crime' and the presumed responsibility for the crime upon the victim. Projective inversion permits one to blame the victim. Rather than feeling guilt, the son-hero can justifiably take Oedipal revenge and kill the villainous father figure.

In the psychological literature, it seems that both kinds of projection, that is, direct translation from inner thoughts to outward manifestation, as well as what I am calling projective inversion, fall under the same general rubric of projection. Freud, for example, in his 1911 paper, "Psycho-Analytic Notes upon an Autobiographical Account of a Case of Paranoia," remarks how the "proposition 'I hate him' becomes transformed by *projection* into another one: 'He *hates* (persecutes) me, which will justify me in hating him'."[27] I would call the transposition of 'I hate him' into 'He hates me' an example of projective inversion. Moreover, in terms of a possible generative grammar of folktales, one could imagine predictable rewrite rules governing when a taboo-laden wish would be transformed—active to passive, subject to object. Instead of the hero or heroine doing something to a parent surrogate or sibling, the rival does that very thing to the hero or heroine. Boys wishing to eliminate father figures can be rewritten as kings-fathers attempting to eliminate sons. Girls wishing to eliminate mother figures can be rewritten as queens-stepmothers attempting to eliminate daughters.

Insightful as Rank was with respect to the Oedipal features of the standard Indo-European hero pattern, he seems to have missed the analogous projective inversion in heroine (Electra) narratives. Rank says, for example, "The father who refuses to give his daughter to any of her suitors, or who attaches to the winning of the daughter certain conditions difficult of fulfillment, does this because he really begrudges her to all others, for when all is told he wishes to possess her himself. He locks her up in some inaccessible spot, so as to safeguard her virginity."[28] It is not at all clear why Rank is willing to accept the literalness of a father's concupiscence for his daughter but not his presumed hatred of his newborn son.

If we examine a typical Electral folktale, e.g., tale type 706, The Maiden Without Hands, we find projective inversion. The typical girl's wish to eliminate her mother and marry her father is expressed in projective form. The mother dies (not through any fault of the girl) and the father wants to marry someone just like the dead mother. After some search, he decides to marry his own daughter. In the folktale, the heroine cuts her hands off because she will not marry her father. Why should the heroine take this drastic action? Those who would claim that the father's incestuous wish to marry his daughter is a literal reflection of reality ought to offer some explanation for the daughter's act of cutting her hands off. In part, it might be a macabre literalization of a metaphor insofar as the father has asked for his daughter's *hand* in marriage. But one difficulty with this literal approach is: why should the daughter be punished for the father's crime? On the other hand, if we assume this might be an instance of projective inversion, then the father's wish for the daughter is in fact an expression of the daughter's unconscious wish for the father. This would explain why it is the daughter, not the father, who is punished. Hands are commonly used in initiating masturbatory fantasy and therefore they might provide appropriate 'sinning' objects to be punished.

The rationale for the punishment of the girl is also relevant to the fate of Cordelia in Shakespeare's *King Lear*. Critics have been troubled by Cordelia's death. In the majority of the literary versions of the plot, Cordelia takes her own life. *King Lear* is derived ultimately from "Love Like Salt" (tale type 923) which in turn is an abridged version of a major form of the Cinderella cycle, namely tale type, 510B, The Dress of Gold, of Silver, and of Stars (Cap o' Rushes). As in tale type 706, The Maiden Without Hands, an apparently lecherous father wants to marry his daughter. But if this father-daughter incest is a projective inversion of a daughter's sexual desire for her father, then the 'original' sin is Cordelia's and Lear truly is "a man more sinn'd against than sinning." From this perspective, Cordelia's triumph over her dead mother and her two sibling rivals for the final exclusive attention of her father is a punishable offense. Incidentally, the adaptation of this projective inversion (tale type 510B) by Shakespeare means that *King Lear* is a girl's fairy tale told from the father's point of view.

In some versions of tale type 706, the maiden's hands are miraculously restored, sometimes through the intervention of the Virgin Mary herself. In the present context, it is worth remarking that the Virgin Mary could be construed as a religious projection of a young girl who is impregnated by a heavenly father. Christian mythology, of course, has an Oedipal projection to go along with the Electra projection. A hero who is born of a virgin mother may represent the Oedipal ideal. As Rank observed, a virgin mother means that one's father did not succeed in gaining sexual access to one's mother. Moreover, the doctrine of consubstantiation claims the son and the father are one, the begotten is the begetter. Through this projection, one is doubly protected: one's mother is virgin, and one is in some sense interchangeable with one's father. According to this argument, Christian mythology is an ideal projection for European family structure, containing as it does both Oedipal and Electral components. For those who are skeptical about viewing mythological beings as projections of human beings, I might mention that it is not only in Christianity that one finds explicit references to god the father, among other kinship terminological parallels. The ruling god of the Roman pantheon was Ju*piter* whose name includes "piter," surely cognate with one of the most widespread Indo-European roots, namely the one for father, including Sanskrit "pitar-" and Latin "pater."[29]

Let me give an additional example of projective inversion from modern American legend. The gist of the legend is a report that Negro youths have castrated a young white boy in a public bathroom. Like all legends, it is told as true, and in fact several years ago (1969) it was reported repeatedly by telephone to various police stations in San Francisco. The legend's sudden popularity was almost certainly related to the discussion of the bussing of school children in San Francisco to achieve desegregation. Now historically one may ask which race has castrated which race? It is surely whites who castrated blacks as punishment for actual or imagined crimes. But in this exemplar of urban folklore, through projective inversion, the whites have metamorphosed their own fears of the stereotyped superphallic Negro male into a form where their victim becomes the aggressor. The wish to castrate black males is projected to those males who are depicted as castrating a white boy. This makes it possible to blame the black victim for the crime the white would like to commit. Just as in the myth of the birth of the hero, the wisher can through projective inversion punish in fantasy not himself but the victim of his aggression. It is the evil parent (king, giant) who is guilty, not the child. It is the black who is guilty, not the white.

It was no mere coincidence that the increased circulation of the legend in the San Francisco Bay Area occurred at the same time bussing was being discussed. This raises, once again, the question of the interrelationship of historical event to folkloristic projective fantasy. Some scholars tend to feel that historical and psychological approaches are mutually exclusive, but I believe this to be a serious error. Frequently a historical event may rekindle an old projection or inspire a new one. It has been suggested, for example, that the elephant joke cycle of the early 1960s might be related to the rise of the Civil Rights movement of the same period. Elephants, like blacks, are associated by whites with African origins. In the joke cycle, elephants were typically described in terms of color "Do you know why elephants are gray? So you can tell them from bluebirds" and in terms of making phallic leaps down from trees upon unsuspecting victims "Why do elephants climb trees? To rape squirrels." The Civil Rights movement aroused longstanding fears among whites that the superphallic militant Negro male might assert himself with respect to former white oppressors. As mentioned in the analysis of the previous legend, castration, symbolic or literal, is one solution. How do you keep an elephant from charging? Take away his credit card. How do you keep an elephant from stampeding? Cut his 'tam peter off.[30]

In the same way, I believe it is possible to show historical roots for other recent American folkloristic phenomena. For example, the spate of "dead baby" jokes in the early 1970s provides a challenging instance. What's red and hangs from the ceiling? A baby on a meathook. What's red and sits in the corner? A baby chewing on a razor blade. It is never easy to make sense of nonsense, but that does not mean that nonsense is meaningless. These jokes told by post-pubertal adolescents may reflect simple sibling rivalry, but that would not explain why this particular cycle became so popular in the early 1970s. Sibling rivalry, after all, has presumably always existed. I would hazard a guess that new techniques of contraception (including the pill) and especially the liberalized laws governing abortion have generated more discussion (and guilt) concerning the "murder" of babies. Contraception and abortion measures may have encouraged a higher incidence of sexual activity among teenagers and this might also account for the expression of literally murderous wishes that babies be eliminated.

Perhaps a more graphic example of the connection between historical events and folkloristic fantasy is "streaking." Streaking consists of one or more persons running naked through a public place. Is it only coincidence that it became a national phenomenon during the Watergate political scandal of the 1970s? I would argue that streaking is a projective protest against the Watergate *coverup*. Whatever individualistic exhibitionistic impulses streaking may have fulfilled, it also served to emphasize the demand that Watergate details be uncovered or disclosed publicly. Accordingly, it might be possible to say that streaking is in part a ritual literalization of a metaphor. It is certainly interesting that once the Watergate coverup was stripped away, streaking stopped.

Whether or not a particular joke cycle, legend, or public ritual derives from a historical impetus is not crucial for the present argument. The issue is whether or not there is a projective aspect to the collectivized forms of fantasy we call folklore. If there is such an aspect, then I believe there are important implications for semiotics which, as I have noted previously, tends to concentrate upon rules, formulas, binary paradigms, and the like. If one examines the gamut of semiotic studies which have been made thus far, one can see that the projective aspect has been almost totally ignored. For example, one of the finest examples, in my opinion, of semiotic analysis is Paul Bouissac's insightful descriptions of various circus acts. In his essay "Poetics in the Lion's Den: The Circus Act as a Text," Bouissac analyzes the constituent elements of a lion act performance. He even describes some of the many standard tricks as metaphorical, e.g., the lion walks in the center of the ring to be ridden by the man, or the lion straddles two stools allowing the man to bend under him and carry the lion on his shoulders. Bouissac's analysis is fine as far as it goes.[31] My point again is that semiotics seems to stop with description, classification, and typology whereas description, classification, and typology ought to be beginnings not ends. Circus acts, like zoological gardens, involve man's attitude towards animals and towards animality—including human animality. Part of the thrill and pleasure in circus and zoo is the implicit struggle of man versus animal. The animals are caged and kept in check, just as man's own animal nature is supposed to be. Yet there is always the possibility, the danger, or the risk, one could call it, that the animal will escape the bonds of man or, to put it metaphorically, that emotion and passion will escape the bonds of reason.[32] One of the techniques used to keep the animal or animality in check consists of requiring the animal, in this case, a lion, to perform human acts. In terms of projective inversion, one is tempted to suggest that although men would like to yield to "animal" desires and to perform animal acts, this is not a guilt-free wish. Hence, through inversion, it is pretended that animals would like to be like humans. The more human the behavior performed by the animal, the more complete the projective inversion. The inversion is hinted at by such tricks in which the animal is first ridden by the man and then later is carried by the man. The latter trick would appear to reverse the normal roles of man and beast. Whether or not my particular analysis of a lion's act in terms of projection is valid, the issue, it seems to me, is the necessity of adding a consideration of projection to conventional semiotic analysis.

In my view, psychoanalytic semiotics could be applied to a wide variety of phenomena, folkloristic and otherwise. One could, for example, imagine such a study of the bullfight. But besides studying the structure of the bullring or the social hierarchy of the various participants, one could also perceive the matador versus the bull as a projection. It is not just man versus animal, culture versus nature, but a projection of traditional male rivalry in Spanish (and other Mediterranean) cultures. In a homosexual battle of masculinity, it is critical just who penetrates whom. If the matador penetrates the bull properly, then the bull becomes feminized (as symbolized by having one or more of his extremities (tail, hoofs) cut off as trophies.)[33] As a projective drama, the bullfight is a ritualized cognate of ordinary verbal dueling as found among adolescent youths. In fact, we have similar ritual behavior in American culture.

One of the most common gestures, obscene or nonobscene, in the United States consists of giving a rival or enemy the "digitus impudicus" better known in folk parlance as "the finger." There are endless variations in style and technique to "flipping the bird," as it is termed in California, but the overall impact of the insult is the same. Yet I suspect that relatively few Americans have ever thought about precisely what the gesture signifies. It is enough to know that to be the addressee of such a gesture constitutes sufficient grounds to reply in kind or to engage in a physical fight. A whole host of lesser public phallic gestures share a similar import—I refer to sticking out one's tongue or thumbing one's nose, often termed the Shanghai gesture.[34] The words which, as often as not, accompany the gesture make the meaning fairly clear, e.g., fuck you, screw you, up yours, etc. Strangely enough, even professional students of obscenity appear to have missed the underlying semiotic significance of this gesture cum locution. Since the famous four-letter word refers to a pleasurable act, Sagarin in *The Anatomy of Dirty Words,* argues that to tell someone "go fuck yourself" as an insulting order is absurd. He quotes Albert Ellis to the effect that it would be more appropriate to give the command "go unfuck yourself."[35] What Sagarin and Ellis seem not to understand is that the basic gesture signifies that the addressee is a passive homosexual. To be the recipient of the phallic finger is to assume the 'female' position or role. The idiom "to put someone down" reflects the winner's stance while "to get the shaft" reflects the loser's. When an opponent is urged to carry out the act all by himself, passive homosexuality is coupled with implied imaginary masturbatory behavior. I might also mention that the present analysis of this extremely common gesture would explain why the word "ass" can refer both to a woman's genitals (as in "a piece of ass") and to the buttocks area—of a male (as in "I'm going to kick your ass").

For those who think that such types of symbolic phallic fighting are unusual, I would call their attention to the existence of comparable ritual phenomena in many other cultures. In the cockfight, a Balinese version of which was so admirably analyzed by Geertz, handlers attached spurs consisting of "razor sharp, pointed steel swords, four or five inches long" to the legs of their cocks with the hope of annihilating the cocks of their opponents.[36] From the point of view of symbolic projection, the cockfight is isomorphic with kite-fighting in which men attach broken glass to their kite strings and then once the kites are aloft, the men maneuver so as to sever the kites of their rivals.

The possibility of identifying projective isomorphisms in folkloristic fantasies opens up a new dimension in the study of folklore. Folkloristic phenomena which may be historically unrelated may nevertheless share a common projective structure and function. For example, I earlier alluded to George Washington as our founding father. Why do we Americans have founding fathers and no founding mothers? In the various recountings of the "birth" of our nation, we invariably find references to forefathers and founding fathers. This reflection of male chauvinism goes back to Old World folkloristic projections, which not only consistently deny women's role in procreation, but in fact insist upon depicting men as fulfilling the role singlehandedly.

In a "man's world," women themselves are defined in terms of men. Before marriage, a girl is in theory a "virgin," a term evidently derived from the Latin word for man (*vir*).[37] If to be married, a woman gives up her maiden name which is, of course, her *father's* name, and exchanges it for her husband's name. At her wedding, she is pronounced "wife" in the phrase "man and wife." Wife is a term like woman which is defined in relationship to man, e.g., with man. (It is theoretically possible for the pronouncement to have been "man and woman" or even "woman and husband.") The linguistic derivation of "woman" from "man" is also literally expressed in mythic projective form as in the creation of Eve from Adam's rib. But the irony is that even though woman may derive from man, man in fantasy tries to become a womb-man, that is, a man with a womb. In an Old Testament setting where the most famous bosom belongs to Abraham, it is no surprise to learn of Noah's construction of a womb-like ark which floats in a flood for approximately nine months. Similar examples abound in classical mythology. One might mention the sowing of dragon's teeth to produce all-male offspring, or the marvelous creation of Athene from the brow of Zeus, making her truly a literal brainchild of the male. The bolstering of male egos via folkloristic projections continues in modern America. A rotund Santa Claus delivers gifts down our chimneys, the very same chimneys through which male storks deliver the babies they *carry!* Perhaps an even more striking male usurper of female procreativity is the Easter Bunny, who delivers eggs! These various and sundry folkloristic projections are clearly not historically related—there is no connection between the stork as the bringer of babies and the Easter Bunny. But from the perspective afforded by psychoanalytic semiotics, they may be seen as sharing common projective content.

There is yet one additional point I should like to make about projection in folklore. I fear I may have implied that viewing folklore as projective material is a mechanical, reductionistic technique. Quite the contrary, for there is great variety in the projective dimensions of even a single item of folklore. One may recall that I began this whole discussion with the statement that folklore means something and that it may mean different things to different performers and to different audiences. To the extent that all artistic creativity is autobiographical, all artistic creativity is projective. Moreover, the way in which individuals interpret artistic creativity is also autobiographically projective. Each age and each individual in an age is free to interpret art, music, and literature anew. And so it is with folklore. It is not simply, then, that folklore as fantasy contains projective material. Each individual who tells a tale or who hears a tale cannot help but project his own personality into that tale. This is why the study of projection in folklore cannot be limited to the text alone. The process of projection also occurs in the very act of communicating an item of folklore.

Let me illustrate the multiplicity of meanings, or the projective potential, of a single text with a final example. This text was related to me in 1964 by a black male informant from Alabama. "Governor Wallace of Alabama died and went to heaven. After entering the pearly gates, he walked up to the door of a splendid mansion and knocked. A voice inside exclaimed, "Who dat?" Wallace shook his head sadly and

said, "Never mind, I'll go the other way." First of all, the item is older
than 1964 inasmuch as a similar joke was told during World War II
with Adolf Hitler as the protagonist confronted by a voice in heaven
with a pronounced Jewish accent. In the present version, the projective aspects include the wishful thinking (for Wallace's death) and Wallace's being sent to hell by his own prejudice. The historical fact of
Governor Wallace's having stood dramatically at the door of the University of Alabama to deny admission to black students is also relevant
(as is no doubt the context of a black informant telling the joke to a
white folklorist). But the joke may function as a projective text for
whites as well as blacks. What is understood by individual whites
when they hear the stereotyped dialect "Who dat?" Clearly the implication is that a Negro is inside the mansion. But individuals differ
markedly as to the identity of the Negro voice. Some think it is God;
others think it might be Saint Peter. A few assume it is a doorman or
gatekeeper or other menial. The joke itself does not say. I would argue
that it is projection on the part of the interpreter in making a judgment as to the identity of the speaker. Similarly, some whites claim
they understood from "Who dat?" that heaven is now integrated,
while others assumed that heaven has been completely "taken over"
by Negroes. None of this is articulated in the joke proper, but it is
part of the joke as semiotic text. Folklore is not only projective material, but it allows, if not encourages, projection on the part of participants in the act of communicating folklore. In fact, I would go so far
as to argue that if folklore did not provide a socially sanctioned outlet
for projection, it would almost certainly cease to exist. The problem
in folkloristics is that while we have literally thousands upon
thousands of folklore texts recorded—think of all the folktales,
folksongs, and legends in print, the projective part of the semiotic text
has not been recorded and so it is that we continue to have lore without reference to folk.

If the interpretation or understanding of a folkloristic item also involves projection, then it is perfectly obvious that scholarship in general has a projective aspect. Maybe there are even national characterological tendencies in scholarship just as there are unquestionably
individual idiosyncratic biases at work no matter how purportedly objective any scholar claims to be. This means that there could be a
personal projective aspect to my present argument that folklore fantasy may be based upon projection. Yet if there is truth in dreams,

then there may be truth in dreams within dreams as well. So whatever my personal need may be to interpret folklore in terms of projection as opposed to listing identifying motif numbers or segmenting folkloristic discourse into elegant syntagmatic or paradigmatic schemata, I would hope that there is notwithstanding some objective validity to the notion of treating folklore as projective material.

From this all too cursory consideration of selected examples of jump rope and nursery rhymes, fairy tales, legends, and rituals, I have tried to show that projection is an inherent feature of folklore. Whether the issue is sibling rivalry, Oedipal or Electral impulses, male envy of female procreativity, or racism, projection offers a guilt-free means of exploring the problem. If semiotics is to become a seminal science of signs and symbols, it must be willing and able to analyze fantasy as fantasy, that is, in terms of projection. For humans, projection provides protection. Folklore, although *collectivized* fantasy, does meet the psychological needs of individuals. Indeed it is literally and figuratively custom-made for the purpose. If projection provides a means of translating inner thoughts into outer expression, then psychoanalytic semiotics ought to try to show from close analysis of such expressions what these inner thoughts are. By this means, psychoanalytic semiotics could become a kind of magic lantern which might afford new illumination for us in our unceasing quest to study and enjoy some of the marvels of the mind of man.

The Curious Case
of the Wide-mouth Frog

In the early 1970s, a strange piece of whimsy circulated orally in the United States. The modern joke in question concerned a "wide-mouth" frog who evidently lacked the knowledge of what to feed its newborn babies. In the course of his or her attempts to question other animals about their normal regimes of infant diet, the wide-mouth frog is eventually put in the position of having to radically alter its customary speech pattern. This piece of folklore thus contains an explicitly metalinguistic aspect. Let me present representative texts of the story before discussing its possible significance.

> There once was a mommy wide-mouth frog and a daddy wide-mouth frog. They had a baby wide-mouth frog. They didn't know what to feed their baby wide-mouth frog so the daddy wide-mouth frog went to the zoo to ask mommies what they fed their babies. When he got there, he asked the mommy giraffe, "Mama Giraffe, whaddaya feed your BABIES?" [spoken with a wide open mouth]. The giraffe (in a very dignified voice) "I feed them leaves from the highest trees." "OH, IS THAT SO?" [again spoken with a wide mouth]. Then he asked the mommy rhinoceros, "Mama Rhinoceros, whaddaya feed your BABIES?" The rhinoceros (in a deep voice) "I feed them mud from the swamp bottoms." Again the wide-mouth frog says, "OH, IS THAT SO?" Then he asked the mama hippopotamus, "Mama Hippopotamus, whaddaya feed your BABIES!" "I feed them little wide-mouth frogs." "oh, is that so?" [with a small tight mouth, in a soft voice].[1]

It should be obvious that most of the power of the joke lies in the performance and specifically in the shifts of "dialect" from wide-mouth speech, to normal speech, and finally to "narrow-mouth" speech. To fully appreciate the story, one needs to do more than *read* the text of the joke. Rather, one should *hear* and *see* it performed. The critical paralinguistic and kinesic features essential to the joke's performance cannot really be successfully translated into the format required by the orthographic exigencies of the printed page. Let me nevertheless present a second version before attempting to analyze the joke.

> A wide-mouth frog goes to the zoo and he hops into the lion's cage. And he says, "Hello, Mrs Lion! I'm a wide-mouth frog. What do you feed your babies?" [spoken with mouth widely extended]. Mrs Lion says, "Go on, get out of here. I don't have time for you." And so he hops out into the tiger's cage and says, 'Hello, Mrs Tiger. I'm a wide-mouth frog. What do you feed your babies?' And Mrs Tiger says, 'Go on, go 'way.' So he hops into the alligator cage and says, 'Hello, Mrs Alligator! I'm a wide-mouth frog. What do you feed your babies?' 'Wide-mouth frogs.' 'Oh, really?' [spoken with lips pursed and brow furrowed in sudden sincerity].[2]

The informant indicated having heard alternative punch lines: "Is that so?" or "You don't say." Still other informants reported such alternatives as an abrupt implosive almost hiccoughed "OH!" or an equally fascinating final sequence in which the wide-mouth frog (narrator) forms a large "OH" with the mouth shaped as if making a huge yawn but just in the nick of time before uttering a sound, the frog purses or puckers its lips as tightly as possible in order to produce the /iu/ diphthong (McDavid 1953:107) or diphthongal vowel (Kurath & McDavid 1961:113) instead.

Informants who told or were told the story of the wide-mouth frog could say relatively little about what it might mean. This is not unusual. A joke, like beauty, tends to be its own excuse for being and can often be enjoyed without either the joketeller or his audience being able to provide a fully articulated exegesis. However, a joke does not exist *in vacuo* but rather it exists in a society where it embodies or reflects concerns of that society. The question is thus what concerns, if any, of American society are to be found in the short saga of the wide-mouth frog? How could a sudden change in speech pattern, under threat of death, be relevant to America in the 1970s? To suggest an answer to these questions, let us examine some of the details of the story.

One theme of the joke appears to be the contrast between an open and a closed society. The frog is free in contrast to the various animals in the zoo who reside in cages. One might go so far as to argue that there is symbolic or iconic phonological isomorphism in so far as the frog in the open society speaks in a wide-mouth or open fashion. At the end of the joke, the frog in order to survive has to curb its natural way of speaking. It must speak literally and figuratively in a closemouthed way in order to stay alive. The frog must keep its mouth shut to remain free. Perhaps one possible moral is that free speech is dangerous in a closed society (the zoo). However, in some versions, the animals questioned by the wide-mouth frog are not described as being in a zoo. Another possible interpretation not at all incompatible with the foregoing turns on the notion that big-mouth individuals of whatever political or ideological persuasion inevitably come to grips with the pressures arising from the practice of continually talking 'big'. The harsh realities of life often demand that a habitually outspoken individual learns to take advice and perhaps to change his customary style of presentation of self.

While one can understand and admire the adaptiveness of the frog who abruptly and drastically changes his mode of speaking, there is something pathetic as well as absurd in a frog's being forced to deny his wide-mouth nature. (Note that in one of the versions presented above, the frog bothers to proclaim to each animal visited that he is a wide-mouth frog, suggesting that he is proud of his identity.) The irony is that the danger of being eaten comes from a creature who does possess a truly wide mouth, typically it is a hippopotamus or alligator. But since these creatures speak normally (at least as judged by the dominant society), their wide mouths are not socially significant. It is only the frog who is singled out on the basis of a single physical characteristic: its wide mouth and its wide-mouth manner of speaking.

Another version of the joke, a somewhat unusual version admittedly, provides an important clue as to the possible meaning of the joke. Here is that version:

> There is a wide-mouth frog standing in her kitchen. She hears a commotion outside and looking out of her window, she notices a crowd standing around a tree. She goes outside and asks, "WHAT'S HAPPENING?" [speaking with a big mouth]. A person answers,

"They're hanging a wide-mouth frog!" [talking "regular" as the informant put it]. "oh, I didn't know!!!" [spoken with a very small, tight mouth].[3]

The reference to a lynching as well as the use of the phrase "What's happening?" strongly suggests that the joke is really about a facet of race relations in the United States. "What's happening?" is a standard greeting formula in Afro-American speech. This hints that the wide-mouth frog might be in some sense a black—even if only a white stereotype of one. The lynching, of course, refers to a long disgraceful period in American history when white vigilante groups did hang blacks without even so much as a pretense of holding a formal trial.

If the joke is really about white attitudes towards black speaking patterns, we can more reaily understand the joke's popularity in the 1970s. With increased integration through court-ordered school bussing, for example, more and more whites became familiar with black speech patterns. Many whites were both fascinated and repelled by black speech. On the one hand, they delighted in imitating it (mostly in private) and this might explain part of the pleasure for both the joketeller speaking in a wide-mouth dialect and the audience listening to it. On the other hand, most educators, classroom teachers, and the white community in general publicly attack black dialect, demanding that black students learn to talk (and write) "white." In the joke, the wide-mouth frog is forced to do just that in order to continue living (not be eaten, not be hanged). The implication is clearly that if the wide-mouth frog wants to be successful in the larger animal community, he must stop talking like a wide-mouth frog. Black announcers on white radio stations (as opposed to black stations) or black newscasters on major network television stations certainly talk "white"—often eliciting exclamations of praise from white listeners who mistakenly marvel at the sight of a black individual speaking without a trace of black dialect. A wide-mouth frog can "pass," so to speak, by denying his normal speech pattern even though this means denying any relation to the poor wide-mouth frog being hanged. If a wide-mouth frog wants to remain secure in the kitchen of her home—the kitchen like the concern with feeding babies emphasizes the fundamental nature of an orality theme, she must conform to the dominant majority's speech pattern and renounce any connection with wide-mouth brothers and sisters who cannot or will not change. It should also be noted that a wide-mouth frog who doesn't speak like a wide-mouth frog is still in fact a wide-mouth frog. Perhaps this suggests a white view that even if a black makes a concerted effort to talk "white," he cannot ultimately be "white." He remains black.[4]

Some additional support for the present interpretation of the joke comes from the visual evidence from the phonetic articulation of the joke and from a longstanding detail of the white stereotype of the Afro-American. In the earliest European stereotypes of Africans, we find references to the thick or protruding lips of the Negro (George 1958). This stereotypic detail carried over to the New World. In American folk speech, there is a slighting reference to someone's rolling or lighting a cigarette with too much lip motion consisting of an admonishment such as 'Don't nigger-lip it'. McDavid (1951:32, n. 4) even noted a 1949 newspaper account which claimed that the Negro cannot pronounce postvocalic /-r/ in *beard, bird, bard* because his lips are too thick. The dialogue in the wide-mouth frog joke makes extensive use of words with initial labial consonants or other consonants which entail pronounced lip movement. "What do you feed *your* babies?" involves an initial /w/ in "What" followed typically by an extended or exaggerated /y/ in "your." Often the performance includes an accentuation of the two bilabial /b/s in 'babies'. Even more convincing is the iconic nature of the initial consonants in each of the three words of the key phrase "wide-mouth frog." In the one version in which the frog proudly proclaims his identity "I'm a wide-mouth frog" this phonological patterning is especially striking. /w/ is a labial, followed by a diphthong that can easily be extended with lips wide. /m/ is a labial which is also followed by a diphthong that can easily be extended with lips wide. /f/ is a labial followed by an American /r/, which tends to involve the lips, to share something of the traits of a /w/.[5] Even though the majority of versions have the key phrase uttered by the alligator rather than the frog, the phonological contrast between the labial patterning of the next-to-the-last line and the final punch line remains. The dynamic labial movement in these words is contrasted with the relatively static labial features in the articulation of the punch line. Also the common use of the diphthong /iu/ in the punch line also draws special attention to the position of the lips. They protrude but they do so in an extremely tightly controlled manner. The particular diphthong itself may be relevant. McDavid

(1953:107, 109, 114) states that although it occurs in such words as *puke, beautiful, music, tube, due, new, suit, sumach, grew, blew* in New England as well as along the Chesapeake Bay and the Carolina and Georgia coast, it has an old-fashioned connotation. He further observes that although it may have social prestige in England, it strikes most Americans as being unnatural and affected. Reed discusses it under the rubric of "fancied elegance" (1967:32). The /iu/ diphthong thus smacks of phonetic hypercorrection. The implication might be that the wide-mouth frog in trying to conceal her identity over-corrects her speech.

There is yet another piece of evidence supporting the present interpretation of the wide-mouth frog. In American minstrelsy of the nineteenth century, part of the stereotype of the Afro-American was his large mouth. Whites took pleasure in acting out their stereotypes of blacks. In a recent thorough study of minstrelsy, we learn that "emphasis on the black man's supposedly large lips and mouth was not new. From the beginning of minstrelsy, white minstrels had made themselves up to appear to have huge mouths, an important part of the physical stereotype that set blacks off from whites" (Toll 1974:254). If a huge mouth was part of the minstrel stereotype of the Afro-American, the wide-mouth frog may be seen as a continuation of that tradition. As whites enjoyed talking like blacks (or watching white minstrels in blackface talking like blacks), so the wide-mouth frog joke provides a modern socially sanctioned outlet for whites to talk black. The paradox is that what the whites who talk black say is that blacks ought to be forced to talk white!

One might legitimately ask why there should be need for a façade of fantasy to express stereotypic traits. Why not delineate the stereotype in undisguised fashion? Part of the answer might be that it is always easier to treat unpleasant material in fantasy rather than in reality. Fantasy has always served as a screen for the projection of racism and this includes literary as well as folk fantasies. But part of the answer might be that the civil rights movement of the 1960s made it more socially unacceptable to express blatant racism directly. An interesting example from children's literature is Roald Dahl's popular *Charlie and The Chocolate Factory*, first published in 1964 and later made into a film. In this moralistic fable (in which children who are greedy or who chew too much gum or who watch too much television are appropriately punished), all the work at Willy Wonka's chocolate factory is carried out by "Oompa-Loompas" whose "skin is almost black," who were "imported direct from Africa" by being "smuggled over in large packing cases with holes in them." We are also told "They are wonderful workers . . . They love dancing and music. They are always making up songs." Perhaps Dahl (1964:72–6) was not fully conscious of the racist implications of his portrait of the Oompa-Loompas, but racism need not be conscious to be destructive. Animals are commonly used in such racist fictional fantasies. For example, it is quite likely that there is a racist rationale underlying the appeal of King Kong, a huge gorilla—gorillas come from Africa!—who in a classic 1933 film carries off a screaming white woman (to whom he is greatly attracted) to the top of a tall building. The fact that the film was being remade in 1976 suggests that the racial tensions involved remain a vital factor in American society. In any event, there can be no doubt that fantasy, sometimes utilizing animal characters, can be used to express and communicate racist projections. If I am correct, then the curious case of the wide-mouth frog is at least clear, although unfortunately it is not solved.[6] The idea that a minority group must change its speech pattern under pain of death may overstate the parameters of the problem (although the attempted imposition of Afrikaans upon South African blacks led to riots and death in 1976) but the problem is a very real one in the interrelationship of language and society. It may be that social judgments based upon distinguishable linguistic differences are likely to last as long as ethnocentrism and prejudice do. Then again perhaps calling attention to the double standard and hypocrisy of a "wide-mouth" alligator preying on a frog because of its "wide-mouth" may ultimately lead to greater tolerance for linguistic diversity.

Thinking Ahead

A Folkloristic Reflection of the
Future Orientation in American Worldview

———————————⟫⊶ ⊷⟨———————————

The study of worldview has intrigued anthropologists for some time. Malinowski's statement (1922:517) is typical: "What interests me really in the study of the native is his outlook on things, his *Weltanschauung* . . . Every human culture gives its members a definite vision of the world . . ." Robert Redfield, perhaps the one anthropologist most interested in the subject, defined worldview as "the way a people characteristically look outward upon the universe" (1953:83). More recently, Geertz has stated that a people's worldview is "their picture of the way things, in sheer actuality are, their concept of nature, of self, and of society" (in Dundes 1968:303). Generally, it is assumed that worldview, in the sense of a cognitive set by means of which people perceive, consciously or unconsciously, relationships between self, others, cosmos, and the day-to-day living of life, is patterned (Kluckhohn 1949:358; Redfield 1953:86).

Part of the problem in analyzing worldview structure stems from the fact that worldview is often implicit rather than explicit. It is unlikely that informants are any more consciously aware of their worldview (cf. Foster 1966:387) than they are of the grammatical principles which underlie the language they speak. Nevertheless, worldview, like grammar, can through rigorous ethnographic description become subject to conscious thought. But how then can the would-be student get at the task of describing worldview?

If one holds a holistic concept of culture and if one accepts the notion of the all-pervasiveness of worldview within a given culture, then in theory one could begin anywhere, with any bit of cultural material, in the search for worldview. One could find clues to worldview in kinship data, grammar, child-rearing details, agricultural techniques, or any one of a thousand bits and pieces of culture. Each anthropologist could thus logically begin a study of worldview from the data with which he is most familiar. However, there are some very good reasons for electing to utilize folklore as source material for the study of worldview.

To the extent that folklore constitutes an autobiographical ethnography of people, it provides an outsider, e.g., the visiting ethnographer, with a view of the culture from the inside-out rather than from the outside-in. Not only is folklore a people's own description of themselves and hence possibly less subject to the influence of the ethnographic reporter's unavoidable ethnocentric bias than other kinds of data, but it is frequently the case that in folklore implicit worldview principles and themes are made explicit (cf. Kluckhohn 1949:359). Unfortunately, the great potential of folkloristic data for studies of worldview is more often recognized than realized by anthropologists. Melville Jacobs in his important study of Clackamas Chinook myths and tales, *The Content and Style of an Oral Literature*, devotes a whole chapter to worldview but, alas, the chapter consists of only five pages. Occasionally genres other than myth, for example, proverbs (cf. Raymond 1954; Shimkin and Sanjuan 1953), have been utilized for the extrapolation of worldview. Probably one of the most interesting studies thus far is that made by a Hungarian folklorist, which revealed that one individual tale-teller's personal worldview was remarkably similar to the worldview expressed in the folktales collected from that individual (Erdész 1961). But despite these and other studies (e.g., Forde 1954), it would appear that folklore as source material for the serious study of worldview has yet to be tapped.

As a test case for the feasibility of using folklore for worldview analysis, I have selected one aspect of American worldview, or at least one distinctive feature said to be an attribute of American worldview, namely, the futuristic orientation, to see whether or not there is any folkloristic data manifesting this alleged attribute. If folklore does in fact provide a concrete form in which implicit worldview is often made explicit, and if American worldview includes a future orientation, then one would expect to find that orientation expressed in American folklore.

There is one apparent problem in using American folklore as source material and that is the fact that so much of that folklore is patently derived from European tradition. Certainly one could find without difficulty cognate forms of many American proverbs in England and other Old World cultures. Yet what is really most important in the present context is a proverb's occurrence and specifically its frequency of occurrence in the United States. In a way the critical issue is whether or not it is possible to distinguish "American worldview" from "Anglo-American" or "English" or even "Western European worldview." It is the inevitable vexing question of where or how the would-be analyst should make his arbitrary "cuts." The task of distinguishing multi-cultural relativism, cultural relativism, sub-cultural relativism, and perhaps ultimately individual relativism is a terribly challenging and frustrating one. Are there elements of American worldview distinct from Western European worldview? Are there elements of American Negro worldview distinct from general American worldview? I suggest that though there are common elements, i.e., similarities, in the worldviews of related peoples, there are also important differences. Sometimes the differences may entail degree rather than kind. Thus, for example, one might find future orientation in Europe but not always in as intensified a form as in the United States. Similarly, one might find past orientation in the United States, but not to the extent that one can find it in tradition-bound areas of Europe. In a number of rather striking instances, it is precisely the slight but definite changes introduced in American versions of European folkloristic items which seem to signal crucial differences in general American and European worldviews.

That Americans are future-oriented has been noted by a number of observers (e.g., Williams 1952:405; Florence Kluckhohn 1953:349), but rarely is any detailed evidence cited. A representative statement is made by Florence Kluckhohn when she writes: "Americans, more than most people of the world, place emphasis upon the future—a future which we anticipate to be 'bigger and better'" (1953:349). One of the relatively few attempts to document this future-orientation was made by Evon Z. Vogt in his study of a Texas community. A chapter entitled "Living in the Future" begins: "To look forward to the future, to forget or even reject the past, and to regard the present only as a step along the road to the future, is a cherished value in American culture and a conspicuous feature of life on the frontier. This future-time orientation and associated value emphases on "progress," "optimisim," and "success" have had a profound influence on the settlement and development of Homestead" (1955:93). Nevertheless, his data (most of which are in the form of verbatim statements taken from the appropriate sections of high school student autobiographies, the sections dealing with career expectations—hardly a random sample!) are from just one community. While it is tempting to generalize about *American* worldview on the basis of informants from a single community, it is obviously sounder, methodologically speaking, to utilize data from a wider sampling of the American people. Of course, Vogt may be assuming (and quite rightly in my opinion) that general American values and worldview are manifested in the statements elicited from his Texas informants. The point is that documentation for the assertion that Americans in general are future-oriented is not offered.

In American folklore there is plenty of relevant evidence and this evidence is for the most part not regional. Rather the proverbs, folk metaphors, and other traditional linguistic clichés and formulas are found throughout the United States. It should also be noted that a future-orientation in American folk speech does not exist in a cultural vacuum. The penchant for valuing the future highly may well be correlated with a tendency to denigrate or ignore the past. Furthermore, the different attitudes towards past and future in American worldview are in turn part of a larger, more comprehensive paradigm. If one were to delineate a portion of this worldview paradigm, one might well include the following associated dichotomies:

Past	— Future
Before	— After
Backward	— Forward
Behind	— Ahead
Beginning	— End
Old	— New
Traditional	— Original

However, the principal aim of the present essay is to examine the tendency of Americans to look, think, and plan ahead as it is expressed in folklore (especially folk speech).

Americans look into the future in part because they are end-oriented. "The ends justify the means." "All's fair in love and war." Beginnings and origins are not so important in a future-oriented society. It is the end which counts. "Tall oaks from little acorns grow." Whether the end is catching worms or saving stitches, one's actions are directed towards such future ends. "The early bird catches the worm." "A stitch in time saves nine." The positive attitude towards ends is revealed by such phrases as to be the "end" or the "living end" or to be "endsville" or to refer to something as the "be and end all," though there may well be anxiety about "making ends meet." Obviously, the great concern with the "happy ending" in popular films and novels is another example.

Americans invariably want "something to look forward to." They have been so conditioned since earliest childhood. One of the most recurrent questions directed to young children from parents, teachers, and other adults is: "What do you want to be when you grow up?" Children thus learn to be curious about "what's in store" for them. When they join such organizations as "Future Farmers of America" or "Future Homemakers of America," they are attempting to keep "the end in sight," which they are encouraged to believe is a good thing. They soon discover that the question "where am I now?" is not nearly as pressing as "where will I be 'x' years from now?" (even though in 'x' years the identical question will be repeated). They invariably "hope for the best" and dream that some day their "ship will come in" or that some day their "prince will come" as it is stated in one form of the ideal of romantic love, in this case in a song from the movie *Snow White*. Actually, many folksongs aid in the enculturation process, e.g., the various verses of "She'll be comin' around the mountain when she comes." The same is true of popular songs: "There's gonna be a great day." Children in secondary schools evaluate their peers, not so much in terms of present status as in terms of future promise. Consider the category "most likely to succeed," among others. In this future-oriented context, it is certainly no accident and it is certainly appropriate that pregnant American women refer to themselves as "expecting"!

A striking example of future-oriented worldview is found in American greeting and leave-taking rituals. While to be sure there are present-oriented formal greetings: "How do you do?" and "How are you?", these are purely rhetorical questions. Informal greetings, in contrast, may involve genuine requests for information. (It is noteworthy in any case that most American greetings are phrased in *question* form perhaps suggesting the possibility of change in state or status.)

While there are past-oriented informal greetings, e.g., "How have you been?" the most common are future-oriented: "How are things going?" "What's up?" "What's new?" "What's happening?" "What's the latest?" "What's with you?" When one is asked "How are things going?" one is being requested for a prediction as to the direction of change. Are things going well, better than yesterday, and are they going to be even better tomorrow? The common greeting "What's new (with you)?" emphasizes the tremendous concern with novelty. Americans thirst for the new and for "news." Yet the news must be new. "There is nothing deader than yesterday's news(paper)." Novelty must always be just around the corner, in the future. Once it is introduced, it is no longer new or news. It is the *anticipation* of the new, the constant taking and retaking of political polls to try to predict the direction of news which appeals to most Americans. Novelty itself "wears off fast." The future becomes present and is shunted immediately and ignominiously into the category of past. Even in the greeting context, one often hears "So what else is new?" as a means of signalling that one has already heard a piece of news. A possible historical factor which may have encouraged the positive attitude towards what is new is, quite obviously, the emigration pattern from Europe and elsewhere to the United States. People cut past ties with the Old World to come live in the New World. (Interesting is Tillich's insight [1966:66] that whereas Europe is endangered by the curse of the past, America is endangered by going ahead without looking back.)

In leave-taking formulas, there is similarly an overt reference to a future action. "See you later," "See you around," "Be seeing you," "See you," "You all come back and see us," "We really must get together one of these days," etc. One can, of course, simply say "good-bye," but the fact is that one normally does make a reference to future activity: "Good-bye, enjoy your lunch," or "Good-bye, have a good time at the party," etc., or there is a request for future action, "Say hello to ____ for me [when you see him]." (It is true, of course, that similar "I'll be seeing you" formulas occur in European languages, e.g., German, French, and Spanish. However, one is tempted to distinguish semantically between "until we meet again" which, after all, could be never and a positive assertion promising a definite future meeting, "I'll see you later.")

Before continuing with future-reflecting folklore per se, it might be well to consider briefly the related folkloristic repudiation of the past. If "thinking ahead" is good, then "looking back" is bad! The various folkloristic responses to present and past mistakes will illustrate the point: "Don't worry about it"; "Everybody makes mistakes"; "Nobody's perfect"; "Let bygones be bygones"; "Never mind about that"; "No use crying over spilled milk"; "That's water over the dam"; "It doesn't make a particle of difference"; "Let it go"; "I don't give a damn"; "To hell with it"; "Don't bother with it"; "Don't mention it"; "No regrets"; "I'll overlook it this once"; "Don't let it happen again"; "Oh that's all right"; "Forgive and forget"; "Forget it"; etc. One finds a similar philosophy displayed in some superstitions. There is danger in turning towards the past. For example, it is supposed to be bad luck for a person to retrace his steps once he has set out to do something. The implication is clearly that one must go forward, never backward. One thinks also of the idea that "lightning never strikes twice." Literally interpreted, this is a superstition about the supposed characteristics of lighting. However, metaphorically interpreted, the phrase suggests the nonrepetitive nature of history. It affirms novelty and emphatically denies that the future will conform to the pattern of past events. Even if one has been successful in the past, one is expected to point towards the future. One risks the displeasure of his peers if he "rests on his laurels." It is not necessarily that "History is bunk," but rather the idea that one cannot change the past. Thus there is no point in being a "Monday morning quarterback" (and commenting critically on events which took place on the football field the preceding Saturday or Sunday). For Americans, only the future is subject to change. Americans thus accept the past fatalistically (as opposed to past-oriented societies who accept the future fatalistically!). "That's the way the ball bounces (cookie crumbles)" etc.

The favoring of future over past also has correlates in the penchant for new rather than old, and for child rather than parent. It is the new generation which counts. Politicians depend upon slogans like "New Deal" or "New Frontier." American manufacturers invariably replace their products (laundry soaps, toothpastes, cigarettes, television sets, etc.) with *new*, improved versions, which are presumably intended to make consumers dissatisfied with last year's "obsolete" model. It is the newcomer, the newlyweds, the tenderfoot, the freshman, and, in acting, the "new faces," who attract the greatest interest. There are awards for the "rookie of the year." There are few for the second-year man. He is already "old hat," an accepted part of the present and past. (Cf. "Sophomore slumps" among college students.) Nobody wants to be an "old fogy," "old-fashioned," or "behind the times" (cf. also the somewhat unflattering associations attached to such stereotype characters as the LOL [Little old lady] and the "dirty old man"). Instead, one wants to be *avant garde*, "ahead of his time," part of the "wave of the future." The idea is if one looks (thinks, plans) ahead, he can get ahead. "Where there's a will, there's a way."

It is not only the past which is sacrificed to the future; it is also the present. Sometimes it is an unpleasant present which is denied in favor of a reference to a brighter future. "Better luck next time" and "Tomorrow's another day" are examples. In addition, there is the proverbial cry of baseball fans backing a loser: "Wait till next year." Yet the "wait and see" philosophy may offer hope in the more immediate future for "The ballgame's never over until the last man is out." "Where there's life, there's hope." But it is not just the unpleasant present which is denied. Americans are so future-oriented that they are discontent even with pleasant presents. For the present reality, no matter how good it is, can never be as good as the future might be. Other peoples on the face of the earth might be discontent with the present but for a different reason. For them the present may represent a departure (deemed unfortunate) from the more perfect past. With Americans and their belief in efficiency, evolution, progress, perfectibility, etc., "the best is yet to come." Whatever one has, one hears, "You ain't seen nothin' yet" or "If you think this is _____, wait until you see _____." The same kind of sentiment is expressed in the American military slogan: "We have not yet begun to fight." (Other future-oriented military phrases include: "Don't fire until you see the whites of their eyes" and "I shall return.") Nevertheless, in American culture, one never does catch up with the carrot on a stick in front of the donkey; one never does reach the "pot of gold at the end of the rainbow." (Now *there* is a compact folkloristic expression of American worldview!)

The present is but "preparation" for the future, a future which never comes: "Tomorrow never comes." (cf. the Boy Scout motto "Be Prepared" and the notion of "prep" schools). Consider the educational *cursus honorum*. Middle-class Americans try to do well in high school, not because they really enjoy high school but because they want to be admitted into college. They then try to do well in college, not because of college per se, but because they want to get into medical school, law school, graduate school, etc. There is always the next diploma, a still better meal ticket, until the final reward (cf. "went to his reward" as a folk circumlocution for dying), a place in heaven, when presumably the deferred reward is deferred no longer.

It should be noted that it is not just pleasure alone which fills the future. Futurism is not necessarily associated with optimistm. An example of futurism plus pessimism would be reflected in the idea of "putting something aside for a rainy day." Thus it is not just pleasure which may be postponed; pain may also be put off into some future realm. Pain in American includes paying cash or being unable to purchase a desired item because of an insufficiency of cash on hand. This pain is postponed by means of the installment plan: buy now; pay later. Indeed, the whole "credit" way of life is based upon future payment for present actions. But whether one buys now and pays later *or* pays now to receive later—as in medical insurance, life insurance, and retirement plans, the same future orientation pervades the philosophy. In *life* insurance, for example, according to most plans, one receives (or one's heirs or beneficiaries receive) only after life has ceased. This is why some Americans often "look forward" to the prospective demise of a "loved one"(!) as an effective means of obtaining wealth, thus fulfilling an American ideal of "getting rich quick." Even when some Americans buy antiques, which are ostensibly objects belonging to the past, the underlying motivation is frequently the hope that the items purchased will increase in value. "Just think how much this will be worth x years from now" and "how much it will bring on the open market."

Certainly, the future orientation permeates American business theory and method. It is glaringly apparent in advertising. "There's a Ford in your future" would be one obvious example. It is not enough merely to "keep up with the Joneses," although that at least would eliminate the possibility of falling behind or being passed by. Rather, one is urged to "be the first on your block" to purchase a particular item. Whether it is a matter of "How to win friends and influence people" or "30 days to a more powerful vocabulary" or the standard pictorial drama of "before" (=past or perhaps present) and "after" (=future), the pattern of perfectibility or improvement in the immediate or even distant future is a recurrent one. Perhaps the most blatant example of futurism in American business concerns the an-

nouncement of only so many more "shopping days left until Christmas." When Christmas finally does come, it is frequently an anti-
climax. It would appear that it is buildup and the anticipation of the
future which pleases the American aesthetic palate. The present picture is never as glamorous or as thrilling as the "previews of coming
attractions" led us to believe the feature "coming soon at your neighborhood theater" would be. At concerts and at prizefights, the audience is inevitably informed about what is coming and, more often
than not, the promise of the "next" presentation succeeds in making
the present evening pale by comparison.

Nowhere is the future-orientation and the emphasis upon buildup
more clearly displayed than in the punch line joke. Here is an admirable example of how folklore encapsulates worldview and, more specifically, how the structure of folklore delineates in microcosm the
structure of worldview. In most American jokes, the whole joke is
told for the sake of the final line. So much of our art (and sex) aesthetic depends upon achieving a climax (cf. Lee in Dundes 1968:341).
The final response to the joke provides an index to the success or
failure of the joketeller. The structure of the joke reflects the whole
cultural propensity to build towards a bigger and better end, in this
case a punch line which provokes or evokes loud laughter. (Even the
sequence of jokes in a joke-telling session may illustrate this tendency
as one joke is followed by another, which is told by someone other
than the first joketeller with the conscious or unconscious competitive
hope that the second joke's punchline will be more climactic than the
punch line of the first.) Americans also prefer that the joke be new or
at least one that they have not heard before.

All this is in sharp contrast to the oral literature of past- rather than
future-oriented peoples. Among most past-oriented peoples, it is the
past, the known, which is valued. It is more likely that beginnings
(e.g., creation myths) rather than ends (e.g., punch lines) matter.
American Indian audiences already know the plot of the tale and they
enjoy the entire episode, not just the final punch line. One might
speculate that one possible reason for the paucity of punch line jokes
among American Indians—at least the less acculturated ones—is that
punch line jokes would not appeal to a people without a future-climax
building worldview.

There are also specific types or genres within American jokelore
which seem to reflect the future orientation. One thinks of the cross-

breed riddle: "What do you get when you cross a ____ with a ____?" (e.g., a hoot owl with a nanny goat: a hootenanny). Here it is clear that the end desired dictated the particular means used (cf. Abrahams and Hickerson 1964). Perhaps the ultimate in end-directed American folklore is a group of riddles in which the riddler offers his audience the answer and asks them for the question, e.g., the answer is 9W, what is the question? ("Is it true, Herr Maestro Wagner, that you spell your name with a 'V'?") In this light, the extremely popular joke cycle which consists of what are called "shaggy dog stories" may be seen as a metacultural parody of future-oriented worldview. The shaggy dog story consists of a long, often a *very* long buildup to what is usually regarded as a disappointing punch line—it frequently depends upon a pun or a perverted proverb (cf. Brunvand 1963). The audience's reaction is usually that the poor punchline was not worth the long build-up. One is reminded of the phrases "to win the fur-lined bathtub" or the "solid gold chamber pot" which are used ironically on the occasion of a remarkable action by someone else. In both cases, the reward is less than was expected or deserved. If the shaggy dog story builds expectations and then denies them, it may be said to be playing upon the future-oriented, goal-directed worldview of most Americans. On the other hand, the specific fact that the great effort expended upon the buildup of the joke did not result in an appropriate pay-off punch line may well be a realistic appraisal of the fallacy of living for the future, inasmuch as the "future-becoming-present" is, as we have noted, almost always something less than the long anticipatory period had prepared us for. When one finally gets to the punch line, the "end" of the joke, it just wasn't worth it. In shaggy dog stories, the "end" does *not* justify the means! Of course, the frustration of expectations in jokes is comic; in life it may be tragic!

Having found some indications of future-oriented worldview in American folklore, one is tempted to undertake studies comparing the worldviews of two or more cultures. There have been few enough attempts to describe single worldview systems; consequently, the literature on comparative worldview is, to put it mildly, very sparse. The opportunity for investigating comparative worldview in the present essay arises because most of the cultures of the world have, or at least had, a past-oriented rather than future-oriented worldview (Cf. Heilbroner 1959:18–21). Americans have reworked many Old World cultural elements and, predictably enough, the American versions of customs with European cognates reveal the unmistakable influence of future orientation. For example, in the celebration of All Souls Day in Europe, respect is paid to the dead, that is, to the ancestors, to the *past*. (The same is true of All Saints Day inasmuch as saints are part of the past.) In the United States, the Halloween festival has been converted to a celebration for *children*, not parents. Though remains of departed spirits survive in the form of ghosts and other creatures, memorial visits to the graves of ancestors have been replaced by parents giving treats to children who threaten to play pranks on them. In accordance with a futuristic optimistic view, the child—who represents the future—is bribed to be good. The emphasis is upon the child, the future, rather than upon the deceased ancestors, the past.

A similar past-future comparison is afforded by birthday rituals. In Norwegian tradition (and presumably in the traditions of other past-oriented cultures), a child who reaches the age of seven celebrates the seventh year just passed. In other words, the child and his family take pride in what *has been* accomplished. But in American tradition, a child who is seven years old celebrates his arrival into a new status, the next year. Frequently, there are *eight* candles or *eight* spanks—the spanks possibly marking one more than the number of years since the original spank administered by the obstetrician. The eighth candle or spank is explicitly "one for good measure" or "one to grow on," a clear push towards the future. (An alternative custom involves a pinch instead of a spank with the accompanying verbal formula: "A pinch to grow an inch.") Note also that American children when questioned about their age will often say not, "I'm seven," but "I'm seven and a half" or "I'm seven going on eight" or even "I'll be eight in January," which is a clearcut refusal to accept the past and present coupled with a definite penchant for looking ahead.

There is a partial contradiction in children wanting to be older. They want to be older because they anxiously await the future and the future for them as individuals involves their becoming older. On the other hand, there is a point at which an individual is no longer "young" and "full of promise." The "new" or "younger" generation suddenly becomes the "older generation." The moment a man becomes a father, he becomes his child's "old man." Naturally, a member of the older generation is a part of the present or status quo, at best, or a part of the past at worst. Such a generation is destined to be forgotten, to be replaced by a new generation, new breed, etc. The critical point in American culture is not clear and obviously it could vary somewhat in individual cases. Possibly it is around age 30 ("Don't trust anyone over thirty"), a multiple of the American ritual number three (Dundes 1968:401–24). Up to thirty, one is a comer, a good prospect, someone on the make. After thirty, one has joined the Establishment. The vagueness of critical age criterion lies in the vagueness of "middle age." When in American culture does a young man become middle-aged? *In any event, it is certain that the older one becomes, the less future he has!* Since American culture is future-oriented and since individuals are frequently measured in terms of potential and possible future productivity, there is much more interest in young people than in middle-aged or old people. It is difficult to grow old in a youth-oriented culture and individuals may dye their hair or refuse to admit their age in an attempt to "pass" for a more youthful version of themselves. With less to look forward to before entering their "second childhood," there may develop a tendency to look back to the "good old days": "When you and I were young, Maggie." In a future-oriented, child-oriented society, one can understand why parents live for, or perhaps more aptly, live through, their children. Thus, as an individual's own future begins to diminish and his prospects dim, he shifts his aspirations to the future of his children or grandchildren.

In contrast, one finds that in past-oriented societies individuals are measured in terms of age and how much *past* experience they have. The older they are, the wiser they are thought to be and the more respect they deserve. Children take pride in their parents' achievements and boast of their ancestors. (In American culture, in contrast, it is the parents who boast of their children's accomplishments, while children may actually consider it a disadvantage to be the son of a famous father.) It is easy to see, futhermore, that residence patterns are related to worldview. In a past-oriented worldview, young people must move in with one set of parents. One continues to live in with one's past. A new element, that is, a bride (or groom) is absorbed into the previous (=past) pattern. In contrast, in future-oriented worldview one finds *neo*local residence. Newlyweds want to make their own future away from the "dead hand of the past." In fact there is even resistance to the idea of the past—in the form of parents or in-laws eventually moving into the young people's household.

In addition to Halloween and birthday ritual, one may profitably examine divination theory for an instructive differentiation between past and future oriented worldview. In a past-oriented culture (e.g., most of the cultures of Africa), divination is defined largely as determining *past* causes of present states. Thus a diviner may be asked to discover why a given person has become ill or why there is a drought. In contrast, in American culture, divination techniques normally concern the *future*, e.g., predicting the sex of an unborn child or the identity of one's future mate. Thus diviners in African (and other past-oriented) societies seek past origins, that which has caused the present. In future-oriented American society, diviners are used primarily to predict what the future will be or bring, that is, what the present will become, *not* what has caused the present. This does not mean that there are no references to the future in a past-oriented society. The point is rather that in such a society the future is determined by events in the past. Accordingly, the folklore prophecies of a child's future greatness or a hero's future death are all set in the past. Often the predictions are made even before the child is born. The future is totally controlled by the past. In one sense—from the perspective of a future-oriented society—such individuals really had no future at all. Similarly, in modern American culture, the minority who depend upon astrology and daily horoscopes are undoubtedly more past- than future-oriented. They may desire to know their future (a goal consistent with the dominant American worldview), but they assume that its course has already been determined by past events, e.g., by the sign of the zodiac under which they were born. True future orientation, allied as it is in American culture to individualism, rugged individualism, and achieved rather than ascribed status, is more typically associated with the notion of making one's own future rather than passively playing out the part prescribed by a predetermined procrustean pattern esablished in the past.

An individual is expected to have a hand in creating his own future. One admires a "man who knows where he's going" especially if he seems to be someone who will be "going far" or "getting somewhere," while one may disdain a man with "no future," a "man who doesn't know where his next meal is coming from." Consider the common insult technique in American folklore of directing the future action of an enemy. I am going to tell him "where to get off"; "to jump in the lake"; "what he can do with his —." More important, Americans judge one another, not on the basis of what an individual *is*, but on the basis of what he *will do or become*. Past-oriented societies differ greatly from future-oriented societies in their ways of evaluation and decision

making. In a past-oriented society, one acts and judges others in accordance with the presumed wishes of one's ancestors, that is, according to a paradigm of the past. In a future-oriented society, one acts in
accordance with how one thinks one's parents or, more probably,
one's peers (or one's children) will judge or react to the planned action.
A principal worry is "What will the neighbors say?" Proposals are
often couched in such language as "what would you say to the idea of
—" or "what do you say we go to —." Typical negative judgments
express the same futurity: "I don't think he'll ever get the hang of it";
". . . ever set the world on fire"; ". . . ever get off the ground"; . . .
ever amount to much." Healthy skepticism is signalled by: "That remains to be seen"; "That'll be the day"; "That I'd like to see"; "I'll
believe it when I see it." Even outright warnings intended to dissuade
someone from a particular action are cast in terms of future consequences: "You'll be singing a different tune"; "You're going to get
yours"; "You'll never get away with it"; "Some day you're going to get
it" (it being "comeuppance"). Americans wonder and worry about
how people and events will "turn out." They hope that bad things will
"come out in the wash," leaving a bright future!

The significance of the future orientation in American worldview as
it is revealed in American folklore is relevant, I feel, to both teaching
and research. In educational philosophy, the past versus future orientations are critical. In past-oriented educational systems, students are
expected to know (typically via verbatim memorization) the "classics"
of the past. So it is that if the future must conform to the patterns of
the past, then students must record in their notebooks and minds
exactly what their professors tell them (cf. Adams in Dundes
1968:507). Many past-oriented professors still insist on the memorization of facts and rote learning right up until the final examination,
which demands a full regurgitation presented for inspection. The
technique was designed to make the young old, to bring the past into
the present, and to guarantee its continuation in the future. In
future-oriented educational philosophy, students are taught to critically question the past in order to build a new and different future.
From this perspective, students are no longer sponges to soak up the
allegedly infallible wisdom of the professor. The emphasis is upon
change, not the changeless; upon the new, not the old; upon original-
ity, not conformity to tradition; upon relativity, not upon absolutes;
upon the future, not the past!

The implications of a future-oriented worldview for research are no less important than those for teaching. It is once again the contrasts of future- and past-oriented cultures. A culture past-oriented, say, in terms of acculturation theory, is likely to conceive its future in terms of its past. Thus the Ghost Dance and other nativistic movements like the cargo cults invariably consist of future projections involving glorified reinstatements of the past. Similarly in research, scholars in a past-oriented society would be intent upon demonstrating how well present and future events "prove" the validity of one or more authorities of the past. But scholars in a future-oriented culture would be likely to evaluate the past in terms of the future. Thus they might anxiously peruse the works of the past looking for hints of precursors indicating future trends. The point is that methodologically they would probably start with the particular trend and then go back to the past to find prefigurations of it. This is why scholars in a future-oriented society write the *conclusions* of their papers *first!* They are end-, not beginning-, oriented. With the "end in sight," they begin the search through past studies to find the means to their end, that is, the data to support their conclusions. Even the ritual formula of the scientific method which demands that a hypothesis be tested reflects the futuristic bias. *In theory*, one proposes a "new" hypothesis which one tests (or which one asks colleagues to test) in *future* experiments. But in *practice* isn't the hypothesis really a tentative conclusion in disguise? It is analogous to writing the introduction to a paper only *after* the conclusion is written, an introduction in which one pretends to test various assumptions. This is perfectly understandable in the light of end- or future-oriented worldview. Where one is going is more important than where one has been!

The basic philosophy of induction or "reading back" from empirical data like folklore to "prior" organizing principles like worldview is end-oriented. One begins with the known and the known is the *end* or consequence. One searches for causes to explain effects. The association of inductive reasoning with future-orientation is also indicated by the nuances of the word *induce*, meaning "to bring forward or bring about," as in "inducing a hynotic state." In contrast, the logic of deduction entails working from given (past) premises to projected conclusions. As in inductive reasoning, one begins with the known, but in this case the known is the beginning, not the end. Deductive reasoning is therefore beginning-oriented rather than end-oriented. It is true that deduction is nominally concerned with delineating future events, but the future in a deductive system is totally controlled by the past premises, usually assumed without question. It is analogous to the closed future dictated by past-oriented astrological data previously mentioned. The past orientation of deduction is also signalled by its additional meanings of tracing derivations or descents. In any case, whether induction or deduction is employed, the passionate concern with "prediction" in science overrides all. One does not have science, it is sometimes said, unless one can predict, that is, unless one can foretell the future accurately! It is surely no accident that a future-oriented society worships prediction.

One of the most fascinating offshoots of scientific prediction is science fiction. Here again is an opportunity to compare past- and future-oriented societies. In past-oriented societies, the principal projections of interpersonal relations such as parent-child or sibling struggles are placed in the past, the far distant past. The normal expression of fantasy is found in the form or genre of myths. In contrast, in future-oriented societies such as ours, there seems to be a tendency for the myths of the *past* to diminish in force but this is accompanied by a tendency to project the nuclear and conjugal family traumas into the far distant future by means of a science fiction setting. Thus the modern monsters are creatures found in space or produced by mad scientists of other worlds. They differ only slightly from the traditional chimerical monsters of the past. One of the critical differences is the matter of the time setting: future as opposed to past.

The fact that I began this essay with my conclusion—American folklore *will* reflect the future orientation in American worldview— *will*, I hope, not offend anyone. I trust by such a beginning I did not raise expectations which were not fulfilled! As I have noted above, the technique of beginning with the end in sight and then writing or rewriting an introduction to match the conclusion is well known in academic circles even though it may not always be readily admitted. I can only say in conclusion that I hope that *future* research will confirm the present analysis. Time will tell!

Seeing Is Believing

———————————————>◦ ◦<———————————————

Whether from early memories of playing "peek-a-boo," "showing and telling" in school, or learning the opening phrase of the national anthem—"Oh, say can you see"—the primacy of vision in American culture is affirmed again and again as infants grow to adulthood. Americans are conditioned from childhood to believe that "what you see is what you get."

There is more to such a phenomenon than at first meets the eye. That Americans rely more on vision than on other senses doesn't mean that they are aware of it. Nor does it mean that it is a peculiarly American trait. People everywhere rely on their senses to perceive their world and order their experiences, but since my data are derived from American folk speech, I cannot speak about others. In any case, because I have been taught to mistrust hearsay, I have decided to take a look at the evidence for a visual bias and to see for myself.

In Western thought, a distinction has commonly been made between sensory perception and reasoning. The power of reason is presumably the superior of the two. According to Aristotle, there are five senses—sight, hearing, smell, taste, and touch—which provide data generally deemed less trustworthy or, at least, frequently illusory, compared to the information that is provided by the faculties of rational thought. Subjective versus objective and body versus mind are other expressions of this distinction between the sensory and the rational. If we assume, however, that reasoning cannot take place without some reference to metaphor, then it is certainly possible that much American logic and reasoning is closely tied to metaphor in general and to visual metaphor in particular.

86

The allegedly inferior sensory experiences seem to be ranked according to how effective or reliable a given sense is assumed to be. In American culture, the sense of sight is normally the first of the five senses to be listed. However, whether sight is actually more useful or crucial for perception than the other senses is a moot question and, in fact, does not require an answer to show that a cultural bias for the sense of sight really exists. In the present context, it is not the literal meaning of sight that is important, but the metaphorical. I believe that, metaphorically speaking, Americans tend to *see* the world around them, rather than hear, feel, smell, or taste it. It may be no accident that Americans *observe* laws and holidays.

American speech provides persuasive evidence to support the notion that "vision" is used as a metaphor for "understanding." Consider, for example,the classic punning proverb, "'I see,' said the blind man, as he picked up his hammer and saw." The oppositional structure in this text is produced by the juxtaposition of sight and blindness. Here is a clear distinction between literal and metaphorical seeing. Literally a blind man cannot see, but figuratively he certainly can.

Americans consistently speak of "seeing" the point of an argument when, in fact, an argument is not really seen but comprehended. Intellectual positions, or "perspectives," are frequently referred to as points of *view*. When articulated, they may be introduced by such formulas as, "As I see it" or "It all depends on how you look at it."

American culture is pronouncedly concerned with empiricism, and this empiricism is explicitly visual. "Seeing is believing" and "I'm from Missouri" (which means "you've got to show me") are indications of the emphasis on seeing something for oneself and the tendency to distrust anyone else's report of a given event. "I saw it with my own (two) eyes" is a common authenticating formula, as is the invitation to "see for yourself."

Without sight, there may be disbelief or lack of faith: "I'll believe it when I see it," "That I've got to see," or "I can't picture that." Even though the reliability of vision may be questioned—"There's more to this than meets the eye"—in general, people tend to believe what they see. Thus, when something is really out of the ordinary, we say, "I couldn't believe my eyes." Something that is incredible or unbelievable is termed "out of sight," a phrase dating from before the end of the nineteenth century.

Imagination is sometimes called "the mind's eye," but why should the mind have an eye? Probably for the same reason that patients want doctors "to see them." Telephone conversations or other purely oral-aural channels are not considered entirely satisfactory. Actually, the patient is probably relieved by *his* seeing the doctor. Seeing the doctor, in turn, is part of the widespread cultural insistence upon interviews. Literally, the word *interview* refers to A seeing B and B seeing A.

Consider the nature of American tourist philosophy—sightseeing. To "see the sights" is a common goal of tourists, a goal also reflected in the mania for snapping pictures as permanent records of what was seen. Typical travel boasting consists of inflicting an evening of slide viewing on unwary friends so that they may see what their hosts saw.

This is surely a strange way of defining tourism. Visiting a foreign locale certainly involves all of the sensory apparatus. There are exotic smells and tastes, and the opportunity to savor new foods and experience the "feel" of a foreign setting is as important in understanding a country and its people as seeing them. One reason Americans frequently fail to enjoy touring as much as they might may be their almost compulsive tendency to see as many sights as possible. The seeing of many sights is, of course, consistent with a tendency to quantify living, and, specifically, with the desire to get one's money's worth.

When shopping, whether in foreign countries or at home, Americans are reluctant to buy anything "sight unseen." They prefer "to look something over," "to walk into something with their eyes open." A thorough inspection theoretically allows one to "see through" a pretense or fake. And obviously, a product can only "catch a person's eye" if he sees it.

Public "images," too, are part of the visual pattern. But why, after all, should a person have to be depicted in a term such as image? Even though looks may be deceiving ("Never judge a book by its cover"), it seems clear that packaging that appeals to visual aesthetics is equally effective whether one is hawking cigarettes or automobiles or selling political candidates.

The reduction of persons or events to purely visual terms is also evident in the use of the popular slang phrase for a detective: "private eye." By the same token, sleep is commonly referred to as "shut-eye," which obviously singles out only one aspect of the dormant state. Furthermore, it also implies that the waking state is marked chiefly by having one's eyes open.

As I collected examples of folk speech, I soon found that comparison of vision with the other senses reaffirmed the superiority of sight. That a "seer" can make predictions by gazing into a crystal ball, for example, suggests that vision is more effective than the other senses in fore*seeing* future events.

The same bias in favour of the visual is found in American greeting and leave-taking formulas. Examples include: "See you around," "I'll be seeing you," or "I haven't seen so-and-so in ages." Greetings may also be couched in visual terms. "It's good to see you," Americans say, rather than, "It's good to hear, smell, or feel you."

There seem to be relatively few complimentary references to hearers, smellers, talkers, and touchers. "Look, but don't touch" hints at a delight in gawking (girl-watching), and possibly at a cultural distaste for body contact. Someone who is "touchy" is not pleasant to have around. A "soft touch," which sounds as if it should have a positive connotation, is a slang term for a dupe or easy mark.

One of the most interesting pieces of evidence supporting the notion of visual superiority over the other senses is that the original version of "Seeing's believing" was presumably "Seeing's believing, but feeling's the truth." That most Americans have dropped the second portion of the proverb does not seem to be an accident. Rather, it reflects a definite penchant for the visual as opposed to the tactile. Originally, the proverb denigrated "seeing" in favor of "feeling."

Comparisons between the visual and the aural are the most common, however, with hearing considered second best. Consider "Believe nothing of what you hear and only half of what you see." Although caution is urged against believing everything one sees, seeing is surely depicted as being more reliable and trustworthy than hearing. Compare the following two statements: "I hear that X has just moved to Miami," and "I see that X has just moved to Miami." The first statement is possibly true, possibly not true: there is an element of doubt. The second, in contrast, seems to be a statement of fact.

Other instances are found in legal parlance. Although judges hear cases, there is no doubt that *hearsay*, that is, aural-oral, evidence is not in the same league as that offered by an eyewitness. Actually, the word *witness* indicates that the person was physically present during an event and saw with his own eyes the activities in question. If so, then the term *eyewitness* is redundant. Strangely enough, at *hearings* there is an insistence that *hearsay* evidence be rejected and that only *eyewitness* testimony be accepted. On the other hand, it is interesting to recall that Justice is depicted as being blind. Justice cannot see and presumably blindness guarantees fairness. But of course, sometimes even an innocent man may be guilty "in the eyes of the law."

The eye is also more powerful than the ear insofar as it is regarded as an active rather than a passive agent. The eye looks, peers, or gazes. There is seductive power in the eye, as in "giving a girl the eye," and the malevolent power of the eye is manifested in "the evil eye." The ear, by contrast, is a passive receptacle. There is little evidence of evil ears. Remember also that "big brother is watching you," not listening to you, although bugging rooms with microphones makes listening more likely than watching. Note also that voyeurs, or Peeping Toms, are considered to be worse than eavesdroppers. The active versus passive with respect to seeing and hearing may also be implied by the connotative differences between "spectators" and "audience."

Marshall McLuhan and his followers have suggested that the oral-aural channels of preliterate or, rather, nonliterate man may be enjoying a renaissance. According to this view, as man becomes literate, written language—which must be seen to be read—takes priority over the oral. Recently, however, radio and television have created postliterate man, whose world is once more primarily oral-aural. Many Americans learn the news of the day by hearing it on the radio rather than by reading it in newspapers. Even on television, the argument says, the news is mainly told, not shown. Then, too, telephone conversations are replacing letter writing more and more.

One can contend, however, that television has replaced radio, and thus the visual still supersedes the purely aural. Americans still prefer to get agreements in writing rather than to trust a gentleman's handshake (a tactile sign) or take someone's word or say-so (oral sign) for a contract. Once an agreement is down in black and white, Americans watch out for, and read, the small print, with an "eye" toward avoiding an unfavorable set of conditions.

If Americans do have a deep-seated penchant for the visual sense, as I have tried to suggest by examining American folk speech, the question of what it means remains to be answered. It is not just a matter of being able to see more clearly why Americans tend to look for men of vision to lead them. Much more important is the influence of folk metaphors on scientific thought. American science is not culture-free, no matter how devoutly American scientists wish that it were or think that it is.

As an anthropologist, I am struck by the fact that American anthropologists insist upon being participant observers (not voyeurs!) when they go into the field so as to gain insight into the worldviews of other cultures. Why "insight"? Do all examples of problem solving by insight actually involve visual perception? And why worldview?

Anthropologists do not always agree whether man is active or passive with regard to worldview. Bronislaw Malinowski, for example, tended to consider man passive: he depicted man as being molded by the impress of a culturally patterned, cookie cutter kind of worldview, which imposed its structure upon human minds. "What interests me really in the study of the native," Malinowski said, "is his outlook on things, his *Weltanschauung.*" "Every human culture gives its members a definite vision of the world." In contrast, Robert Redfield, by defining worldview as "the way a people characteristically look outward upon the universe," suggested that man was a more active participant. In any case, whether man passively accepts a culturally determined worldview or actively creates a worldview system, the visual bias in the very search by anthropologists for worldview is evident.

It has been observed that for Americans the universe is essentially something they can draw a picture or diagram of. But surely a person's world is felt, smelled, tasted, and heard as well. This propensity for visual metaphorical categories may produce distortion in attempts to describe facets of American culture. It is unlikely that such distortion would even be noticed, since the distortion, like beauty, is strictly in the subjective eye of the beholder. But what happens when Americans or American scientists seek to describe features of other cultures or the features of the natural world?

It is at least possible that by looking for the worldview of other peoples, we run the risk of imposing our own rank-ordering of the senses upon data that may not be perceived in the same way by the people whose cultures are being described. If we are truly interested in understanding how other peoples perceive reality, we must recognize their cognitive categories and try to escape the confines of our own.

This history of man is full of instances of one group's conscious or unconscious attempts to impose its particular set of cognitive categories upon another group. The imposing group typically claims that its categories represent the true nature of reality (as opposed to the categories of the victimized group, which are deemed odd at best and false at worst). Whether it is nineteenth-century American linguists searching in vain for Latin cases (for example, the dative or accusative) in American Indian languages, or a modern Western physician, unaware of his own cultural bias in favor of the number three, trying to persuade an American Indian, who believes in the sacredness of the number four, that only three doses or inoculations are sufficient (as in a series of three polio shots), the issue is the same.

This is why it is essential for Americans (and for other peoples as well) to become aware of their dependence upon cognitive categories such as the visual metaphorical mode I have been talking about. Armed with this awareness, it is possible to appreciate more fully the aptness of the visual metaphor. Ruth Benedict used to explain why so many social theorists failed to notice custom or culture: "We do not see the lens through which we look." A conscious recognition of our visual bias may help make the lens visible. We must never forget the possible relativity of our own sensory perception categories.

Inventories of the same or similar sense categories found in other cultures may help. Clifford Geertz reports, for example, that the Javanese have five senses (seeing, hearing, *talking*, smelling, and feeling), which do not coincide exactly with our five. The delineation of such differences may teach us just how culture-bound or culture-specific our own observations of nature may be. We tend to delude ourselves into thinking we are studying the nature of nature, foolishly forgetting that we cannot observe raw or pure nature. We can perceive nature only through the mediation of culture, with its panoply of culturally relative cognitive categories.

Much of the study of "natural history" often turns out to be "cultural history" in disguise. Theories and ideas about the natural world are invariably couched in terms of a specific human language and are based upon data obtained from human observation. With human observation expressed in human language, one simply cannot avoid cultural bias. Searching for culture-free descriptions of nature may be a worthwhile goal, and perhaps man will one day succeed in achieving it. In the meantime, we must be wary of mistaking relatives for absolutes, of mistaking culture for nature. Cross-cultural comparisons of sense categories may not only reveal critical differences in the specific senses, but also whether or not the apparent priority of vision over the other senses is a human universal. For the moment, we can do little more than wait and *see*.

Wet and Dry, the Evil Eye

An Essay in Indo-European and Semitic Worldview

——————⟫⟩·❦·⟨⟪——————

I should like to dedicate this essay to the memory of Ernest Jones whose brilliant application of psychoanalytic theory to the materials of folklore has served as a continual inspiration to me over the years. I must also thank Stanley Brandes, Robert Coote, Osama Doumani, George Foster, Steve Gudeman, Barbara Kirshenblatt-Gimblett, Wendy O'Flaherty, Felix Oinas, Saad Sowayan, and Tim White for valuable references and suggestions.

The evil eye is a fairly consistent and uniform folk belief complex based upon the idea that an individual, male or female, has the power, voluntarily or involuntarily, to cause harm to another individual or his property merely by looking at or praising that person or property. The harm may consist of illness, or even death or destruction. Typically, the victim's good fortune, good health, or good looks—or unguarded comments about them—invite or provoke an attack by someone with the evil eye. If the object attacked is animate, it may fall ill. Inanimate objects such as buildings or rocks may crack or burst. Symptoms of illness caused by the evil eye include loss of appetite, excessive yawning, hiccoughs, vomiting, and fever. If the object attacked is a cow, its milk may dry up; if a plant or a fruit tree, it may suddenly wither and die.

Preventive measures include wearing apotropaic amulets, making specific hand gestures or spitting, and uttering protective verbal formulas before or after praising or complimenting a person, especially an infant. Another technique is concealing, disguising, or even denying good fortune. One may symbolically disfigure good looks, for instance, by purposely staining the white linen of a new dress or placing a black smudge of soot behind a child's ear (Rodd 1968:160–61, cf.

93

Crooke 1968:2:6), so as not to risk attracting the attention of the evil eye. This may be the rationale behind behavior as disparate as the veiling common in Arab cultures, the refusal in Jewish culture to say "good" when asked how one's health or business is—the safe reply is "not bad" or "no complaints"—the common tendency among millionaires in Europe and America to insist upon dressing in rags, and the baseball custom in the United States of not mentioning that a pitcher has given up no hits. (The mere mention of a possible "no-hitter" would supposedly jinx the pitcher and result in a batter's getting a base hit of some kind.)

In the event of a successful attack by the evil eye, there are prescribed diagnostic and curative procedures available. One may first need to ascertain whether or not it is a true case of the evil eye and second, if it is, who is responsible for it. Sometimes, the agent, who was perhaps an unwitting one, is involved in the ritual removal of the evil eye and its ill effects from the victim. He may, for instance, be asked to spit on the victim's face (cf. Dodwell 1819:235–36).

Although widespread throughout the Indo-European and Semitic world, the evil eye belief complex is not universal. In the most recent cross-cultural survey Roberts found that only 36 percent of the 186 cultures in his world sample possessed the evil eye belief (1976:229); and he suggested that the belief "probably developed in the old world, particularly in India, the Near East, and Europe" (1976:234). From this and other surveys (e.g., Andree, Seligmann), it is clear that the evil eye appears to be largely absent in aboriginal Australia, Oceania, native North and South America, and sub-Saharan Africa. The few rare reports of its occurrence in Africa, apart from the Maghreb where it flourishes, suggest Islamic influence. In Latin America, the evil eye was surely part of the general Spanish and Portuguese cultural legacy. Yet within the Indo-European and Semitic world, it is difficult to think of a more pervasive and powerful folk belief than the evil eye.

The scholarship devoted to the evil eye goes back to classical antiquity. Many of the ancients referred to it and Plutarch (46–120 A.D.) featured it in one of the dialogues in his Table Talk (V, Question 7) "On those who are said to cast an evil eye." The dialogue begins as follows: "Once at dinner a discussion arose about people who are said to cast a spell and to have an evil eye. While everybody else pronounced the matter completely silly and scoffed at it, Mestrius Florus, our host, declared that actual facts lend astonishing support to the common belief." Sometimes the passing references indicated belief in the evil eye, sometimes disbelief. In his insightful homily "Concerning Envy," written in the fourth century, Saint Basil remarked ". . . some think that envious persons bring bad luck merely by a glance, so that healthy persons in the full flower and vigor of their prime are made to pine away under their spell, suddenly losing all their plumpness, which dwindles and wastes away under the gaze of the envious, as if washed away by a destructive flood. For my part, I reject these tales as popular fancies and old wives' gossip" (Saint Basil 1950:469–70).

One of the issues often discussed was whether the evil eye was a conscious or unconscious power. The famed Arab historian Ibn Khaldûn (1332–1406) tended to consider the power of the evil eye as deriving from an involuntary act and, for this reason, to be distinguished from intentionally malicious sorcery. In section 27 of chapter 6 of the *Muqaddimah* (1967:170–71), Ibn Khaldûn commented on the evil eye, calling it a natural gift, something that is innate and not acquired, not depending upon the free choice of its possessor. He ended his discussion as follows: "Therefore it has been said: 'A person who kills by means of sorcery or a miraculous act must be killed, but the person who kills with the eyes must not be killed.' The only reason for the distinction is that the person who kills with the eyes did not want or intend to do so, nor could he have avoided doing so. The application of the eye was involuntary on his part." Ibn Khaldûn's distinction, somewhat analogous to the modern differences between first and second degree manslaughter, is not held by all writers on the evil eye. Some (e.g., Mackenzie 1895; Cutileiro 1971:274) suggest that some cases of the evil eye reflect an evil disposition on the part of the person possessing the power while others believed to have the power are "innocent of any ill design."

During the Renaissance a number of treatises were devoted to the evil eye. Representative are Enrique de Villena's "Tradado del Aojamiento" of 1422, Leonardus Vairus's "De Fascino" of 1589, Martinus Antonius Del Rio's "Disquisitionum magicarum" of 1599–1600, Joannes Lazarus Gutierrez's "Opusculum de Fascino" of 1653, and Joannes Christianus Frommann's "Tractatus de Fascinatione" of 1675. These and subsequent surveys often contain valuable data. For example, Nicola Valletta in his *Cicalata sul fascino volgarmente detto jettatura* of 1787 ended his discussion with a series of thirteen queries, designed very much like the modern questionnaire, about the evil eye and the *jettatura*, the casters of the evil eye. Valletta's queries were: 1) Is the evil eye stronger from a man or from a woman? 2) Is it stronger from someone wearing a wig? 3) Stronger from someone who wears glasses? 4) Stronger from a pregnant woman? 5) Stronger from monks and, if so, from which order? 6) If the evil eye does approach, after the attack, what effects must be suffered? 7) What is the range or limit of the distance at which the jettatura can be effective? 8) Can the power come from inanimate objects? 9) Is the evil eye stronger from the side, from the front, or from behind? 10) Are there gestures, voice quality, eyes, and facial characteristics by which jettatura can be recognized? 11) What prayers ought to be recited to protect us against the jettatura of monks? 12) What words in general ought to be said to thwart or escape the jettatura? 13) What power then have the horns and other things? (Valletta 1787:152). Valletta then asked anyone who had had experience with the evil eye to get in touch with him and added that he would be happy to pay for any information furnished.

The steady flow of treatises continued in the nineteenth century. Italian scholars in particular were intrigued with a phenomenon that flourished unabated in their country. Typical are Giovanni Leonardo Marugj's *Capricci sulla jettatura* in 1815, and Michele Arditi's *Il fascino, e l'amuleto contro del fascino presso gli antichi* of 1825, and Andrea de Jorio's *La Mimica degli Antichi* of 1832, which was especially concerned with the traditional gestures used to avert the evil eye.

Modern scholarship on the evil eye may be truly said to have begun with Otto Jahn's pioneering essay, "Über den Aberglauben des bösen Blicks bei den Altern," which appeared in 1855. It, like so many of the early treatises, concentrated upon ancient Greek and Roman examples of the evil eye, but it differed in its honest and erudite consideration of all facets of the evil eye complex, including the obviously phallic character of so many of the apotropaic amulets. By the end of the nineteenth century, numerous essays had been written on the evil eye, though most of them were limited to descriptive reports from one particular area. Among the more general surveys of the subject was Jules Tuchmann's remarkably detailed series of articles on "La Fascination," which began to appear in the French folklore journal *Mélusine* in 1884 and continued intermittently until 1901. Tuchmann's massive and impressive collection of citations on the evil eye drawn from a huge variety of sources in many languages (Gaidoz 1912) may well have been the inspiration for folklorist Arnold van Gennep's delightful parody of the doctoral dissertation writer who tried but failed to write the definitive work on the evil eye (van Gennep 1967:32–36). A better-known nineteenth-century survey work is Frederick Thomas Elworthy's *The Evil Eye*, first published in 1895.

The next major effort, perhaps the most ambitious of all, was the encyclopedic two-volume work by oculist S. Seligmann, *Der Böse Blick und Verwandtes*, published in 1910. This, or the 1922 version *Die Zauberkraft des Auges und des Berufen*, remains probably the best single source of information on the subject, at least in terms of sheer quantity of ethnographic data. Other landmark studies of the evil eye in the twentieth century include Westermarck's extensive consideration of the evil eye in Morocco (1926:414–78) and Karl Meisen's two comprehensive essays (1950, 1952) in the *Rheinisches Jahrbuch für Volkskunde*, the first covering the evil eye in the ancient and early Christian eras and the second treating the medieval and modern periods. Also worthy of mention are oculist Edward S. Gifford's *The Evil Eye: Studies in the Folklore of Vision* (1958), classicist Waldemar Deonna's marvelously learned and brilliant *Le Symbolisme de l'Oeil*, posthumously published in 1965, psychiatrist Joost A. M. Meerloo's *Intuition and the Evil Eye: The Natural History of Superstition* (1971), and a collection of anthropological essays on the evil eye, *The Evil Eye*, edited by Clarence Maloney (1976). This latter group of fifteen essays consists primarily of ethnographic description and makes little reference to the voluminous literature devoted to the evil eye in classics, folklore, and psychiatry. It does, however, include a long, important paper by John M. Roberts, "Belief in the Evil Eye in World Perspective," which carefully canvasses 186 diverse cultures to see if the evil eye occurs and, if so, with what other cultural variables it might meaningfully be statistically correlated.

The works mentioned thus far are essentially overviews of the evil eye belief complex, but it should be noted that there are a number of valuable books and monographs on the evil eye in a given culture. Among the best of these are investigations in Scotland, R. C. Maclagan's *Evil Eye in the Western Highlands* (1902); in Spain, Raphael Salillas's *La Fascinación en España* (1905); in Finland, Toivo Vuorela's *Der Böse Blick im Lichte der Finnischen Überlieferung* (1967); and in Sardinia, Clara Gallini's *Dono e Malocchio* (1973). When one adds to these the literally dozens upon dozens of notes and articles that discuss the evil eye either en passant or in some depth, it is clear that one has an unmanageable number of sources available to consult for relevant information.

Despite the enormous bibliographic bulk of the evil eye scholarship, it is not unfair to say that there have been few attempts to explain the evil eye belief complex in terms of a holistic integrated theory. By far the majority of the discussions of the evil eye consist solely of anecdotal reportings of various incidents. Anthropologist Hocart summed up the situation aptly when he said (1938:156): "There is a considerable literature about the evil eye, but it does little more than add instances to instances." Unfortunately, the situation has not changed; and as Spooner puts it (1976:281): "Permutations of practice do not appear to lead to a satisfactory formulation of theory."

Formulations of theories of the evil eye do exist. Recent speculations about the possible origin and significance of the evil eye have included the suggestion that it is related to gaze behavior perhaps involving gaze aversion, common in many animal species (Coss 1974). With regard to gaze behavior, Erikson proposes (1977:50, 58) that an infant experiences the unresponsive eye of an adult as a rejecting, hostile environment or "Other" (as opposed to self). Thus, according to Erikson, "the unresponsive eye becomes an evil one." It has also been claimed that the evil eye is an ancient type of hypnotic phenomenon (MacHovec 1976). But probably the most widely accepted theory of the evil eye contends that it is based upon envy. In his celebrated *Folkways*, first published in 1906, Sumner argued that the evil eye depended upon primitive demonism and envy. According to Sumner (1960:434), "It is assumed that demons envy human success and prosperity and so inflict loss and harm on the successful."

There is no question that envy is somehow closely related to the evil eye. This is clear in the earliest Near Eastern texts we have. The word *envy* is etymologically derived from the Latin *invidia*, which in turn comes from *in videre*, thus ultimately from "to see" or "seeing" as Cicero first observed (Elworthy 1958:7; cf. Odelstierna 1949:72, n.1). To see something is to want it, perhaps. A common reaction to seeing a desirable object is to verbally admire it. An expression of admiration or praise is understood to imply at least a tinge of envy. Envy can accordingly be expressed either by eye or by mouth (or by both). Schoeck considers the evil eye to be a universal expression of malevolent envy (1955), but Spooner has criticized the envy theory, noting (1976:283) that "although it is perfectly valid and necessary at one stage of analysis, the anthropologist should attempt to build models at a higher stage of abstraction." Spooner might also have realized that no theory can be persuasive unless or until it enables one to explain the particulars of a given custom or segment of human behavior. How does the notion of envy explain, for example, the specific details of fruit trees withering, the common symptom of yawning, or the various gestures, such as spitting, employed to ward off the evil eye. Spooner does ask why, since envy in some form is probably universal, it should give rise to the evil eye in some societies but not in others (1976:283). One can only conclude that whereas envy is surely a component of the overall evil eye complex, it is not sufficient in and of itself to explain the complex in all its concrete detail.

The same difficulties inhere in suggestions that the evil eye complex provides an outlet for the expression of aggression, or that it acts as an agent of social control. The question that must be addressed is: why does the evil eye manifest itself precisely in the forms that it does? Why are very young children and infants especially susceptible to the effects of the evil eye? Or, why is the butterfat content of milk in a churn magically removed?

Psychoanalytic interpretations of the evil eye have also been partial. Because many of the apotropaic amulets and gestures have unmistakable phallic elements (Valletta 1787:18–25; Jahn 1855; Michaelis 1885; Wolters 1909; Elworthy 1958:149–54; Seligmann 1910:II:188–200; Deonna 1965:180–81), it has long been obvious that the male genitals are involved in some way with the evil eye complex. Since phallic gestures like the *fica* (Leite de Vasconcellos 1925:92) were used to ward off the evil eye, and since males often touched their genitals upon seeing a priest or other individual thought to have the evil eye (Valla 1894:422n; Servadio 1936:403; n. 8) then it is not unreasonable to assume that the evil eye threatened to make men impotent (Seligmann 1910:I:199; Servadio 1936). But if the evil eye constituted a danger to masculinity, why was it believed that a weaned infant who has returned to the breast would grow up to have the evil eye, and why was the evil eye especially damaging to *female* animals, such as cows? Roberts attempted a factor analysis of various features associated with the evil eye in his cross-cultural survey; he found the highest correlation with milking and dairy production though he was unable to explain this linkage (1976:241, 258). Of course, psychoanalysts have also argued that the eye could be a female symbol (Reitler 1913:160) with "the pupil representing the vagina, the lids the labia, and the lashes the pubic hair" (Tourney and Plazak 1954:489). Is the eye a phallus, or is it a vagina, or is it both (or neither)? And how would this possibly relate to injury to cows and their milk supply?

Géza Róheim suggests (1952:356) that the key to the whole evil eye belief is oral jealousy and oral aggression. This would illuminate the apparent connection with nursing children as well as the appropriateness of the use of spitting or oral incantations to avoid the evil eye. But in this case, it would not be so obvious why phallic means should be equally effective. Róheim does not succeed, in my opinion, in reconciling the oral and phallic elements in the evil eye complex.

Freud himself, writing about the evil eye in his 1919 essay on the 'uncanny,' considered its origin to be fear of envy, coupled with the device of projection. "Whoever possesses something at once valuable and fragile is afraid of the envy of others, in that he projects onto them the envy he would have felt in their place" (1959:393). Tourney and Plazak follow this psychiatric tack by emphasizing the eye as an organ of aggression. They suggest (1954:491) that "with the utilization of the projective mechanism, fear of the evil eye may represent the manifestation of one's own aggressive impulses attributed as being apart from the ego and acting in turn against it. A need for punishment because of guilt over hostility and aggression can be realized in the suffering of a recipient from the influence of the evil eye." Through projection, the original would-be aggressor is spared feelings of guilt because "I hate you" or "I envy you" has been transformed into "You hate me" or "You envy me." By means of this projective transformation, the active becomes the passive, the aggressor becomes the victim. This may explain why the rich and powerful are so often thought to have the evil eye—popes and nobility have frequently been said to have it. The poor envy the rich and powerful, but this envy is transformed into the rich casting an evil eye at the poor. But this psychiatric notion does not really explicate all the particulars of the evil eye belief complex either.

A plausible theory of the evil eye must be able to account for most, if not all, of the elements in the complex, including the manifestly male and female components. Consider the following modern Greek cure for the evil eye, which involves the formula (Dionisopoulos-Mass 1976:46): "If it is a woman who has cast the eye, then destroy her breasts. If it is a man who has cast the eye, then crush his genitals." In a variant (Hardie 1923:170), "If a man did it, may his eyes fall out. If a woman did it may her eyes fall out and her breasts burst." In India, we find the same alternation of male and female attributes. According to Thurston (1907:254):

> When a new house is being constructed, or a vegetable garden or rice field are in flourishing condition, the following precautions are taken to ward off the evil eye:
> a. In buildings—
>   1. A pot with black and white marks on it is suspended mouth downwards.
>   2. A wooden figure of a monkey, with pendulous testes, is suspended.
>   3. The figure of a Malayali woman, with protuberant breasts, is suspended.
> b. In fields and gardens—
>   1. A straw figure covered with a black cloth daubed with black and white dots is placed on a long pole. If the figure represents a male, it has pendent testes, and, if a woman, well-developed breasts. Sometimes male and female figures are placed together in an embracing posture.
>   2. Pots, as described above, are placed on bamboo poles."

Since the evil eye is as dangerous to female breasts (including cow's udders) as to male genitals, it is necessary for the magical counter-measures to defend against both threats. The question is: what theoretical underlying principle or principles, if any, can explain the whole range of phenomena believed to be caused by the evil eye, from the withering of fruit trees, to the loss of milk from cows to impotence among males. The striking similarity of evil eye reports from different cultures strongly suggests that whatever the rationale behind it may be, it is likely to be cross-culturally valid.

I suggest that the evil eye belief complex depends upon a number of interrelated folk ideas in Indo-European and Semitic worldview. I should like to enumerate them briefly before discussing them in some detail.

    1. Life depends upon liquid. From the concept of the "water of life" to semen, milk, blood, bile, saliva, and the like, the consistent principle is that liquid means life while loss of liquid means death. "Wet and Dry" as an oppositional pair means life and death. Liquids are living; drying is dying!

2. There is a finite, limited amount of good—health, wealth, etc.—and because that is so, any gain by one individual can only come at the expense of another (cf. Foster 1965). If one individual possesses a precious body fluid, semen, for instance, this automatically means that some other individual lacks that same fluid.

3. Life entails an equilibrium model. If one has too little wealth or health, one is poor or ill. Such individuals constitute threats to persons with sufficient or abundant wealth and health. This notion may be in part a projection on the part of well-to-do individuals. They think they should be envied and so they project such wishes to the have-nots. On the other hand, the have-nots are often envious for perfectly good reasons of their own.

4. In symbolic terms, a pair of eyes may be equivalent to breasts or testicles. A single eye may be the phallus (especially the glans), the vulva, or occasionally the anus. The fullness of life as exemplified by such fluids as mother's milk or semen can thus be symbolized by an eye and accordingly threats to one's supply of such precious fluids can appropriately be manifested by the eye or eyes of others.

I am not claiming that any of the above folk ideas or principles are necessarily consciously understood by members of Indo-European and Semitic cultures. They may or may not be. What I am proposing is that they are structural principles of thought among the peoples of these cultures. I hope to show that they explain not only the evil eye but a vast range of traditional behavior ranging from tipping to some specifics of burial customs.

Documentation for the folk idea that life is liquid is amply provided by Richard Broxton Onians in his brilliant tour de force, *The Origins of European Thought about the Body, the Mind, the Soul, the World, Time, and Fate*, published in 1951. Onians is able to explain one of the rationales behind cremation. Burning the dead expedites the "drying" process, the final removal of the liquid of life (1951:256). He remarks on the Greek conception of life as the gradual diminishing of liquid inside a man (1951:215). I would add that the metaphor probably made sense in light of what was empirically observable in the case of fruits, among other items. Juicy grapes could become dry raisins; plums could become prunes, etc. With increasing age, the human face becomes wrinkled and these inevitable wrinkles could be logically construed as signs of the same sort of drying process that produced the wrinkles in raisins and prunes. It should also be pointed out that this Greek conception is also a manifestation of the notion of limited good (Foster 1965, Gouldner 1965:49–51). Man is born with only so much life force and he is therefore ever anxious to replenish it. Milk and wine are obvious sources of liquid (1951:227), noted Onians, and he correctly observes the content of toasts in this connection. One drinks "healths." What Onians failed to understand is that healths are supposedly drunk to *others*, that is, accompanied by such verbal formulas as "Here's to you," "Here's to your health," or "Here's long life to you." What this means in terms of limited good, I submit, is: "I drink, but not at your expense. I am replenishing my liquid supply, but I wish no diminution in yours." The very fact that a drinker mentions another person's *health* before drinking implies that if he did not do so, that person's health might suffer. In other words, drinking without a formulaic prophylactic preamble might be deleterious to the other person's health. In an unusual volume published in 1716 entitled *A Discourse of Drinking Healths*, we find this thought articulated: "And what strange Inchantment can there be in saying or meaning, As I drink this Glass of Wine, So let another Man perish" (Browne 1716:19).

Lévi-Strauss, in a rare instance of ethnographic fieldwork, reports on a custom observed in lower-priced restaurants in the south of France (1969:58–60). Each table setting includes a small bottle of wine but etiquette demands that one does not pour the contents of the bottle into one's own glass. Rather the wine is poured into the glass of an individual at a neighboring table. This individual will normally reciprocate by pouring the contents of his bottle into the initial pourer's glass. Lévi-Strauss explains this custom in terms of a structural principle, namely the principle of reciprocity: "Wine offered calls for wine returned, cordiality required cordiality." This is not an implausible explanation, but this custom which reflects an attitude towards wine remarkably different from that towards food, as Lévi-Strauss himself notes, may also exemplify the special rules governing the incorporation of liquids among Indo-European and Semitic peoples. The notion of limited good—as applied to the essential liquids of life—requires one to offer beverages to others. If one drinks without regard to one's neighbors, one risks being envied and becoming the object or victim of an evil eye. The reciprocity of courtesy is demonstrated in a Gaelic incantation against the evil eye reported from the island of Skye in the Hebrides. When washing in the morning (Mackenzie 1895:39), a person may recite:

> Let God bless my eye,
> And my eye will bless all I see;
> I will bless my neighbor
> And my neighbor will bless me.

Numerous reports attest that eating in public is thought to be especially dangerous with respect to the evil eye. Westermarck (1904:211; cf. Gifford 1958:48–50), for example, notes that "the danger is greatest when you eat. To take food in the presence of some hungry looker-on is the same as to take poison; the evil—*i-bas*, as the Moors call it—then enters into your body. When you commence eating, everybody must either partake of the meal or go away." In Egypt, Lane 1895:262) reports that his cook would not purchase the fine sheep displayed in a butcher's shop because "every beggar who passes by envies them; one might, therefore as well eat poison as such meat." A report that appeared in the Russian paper *Ilustriravansk Mir* in 1881 (according to Gordon 1937:306) reflects a similar belief: "The Russian government turned over a convict sentenced to die to the Academy of Science for the purpose of testing the powers of [the] evil eye. The prisoner was starved for three days during which a loaf of bread was placed in front of him of which he was unable to partake. At the end of the third day, the bread was examined and found to contain a poisonous substance." Gordon (1937:307) observes that while the story proves nothing—the bread could easily have been spoiled by being kept in a damp cell for three days—the very fact that a newspaper could print the report shows the readiness of the public to believe in the power of the evil eye.

One technique used in restaurants to avert the dangers of the evil eye is to offer onlookers some of one's food. In Spanish restaurants, for example, any person waiting to be seated at a table is frequently invited by patrons already eating to join them or share their food. This formulaic offer is inevitably refused but the point is that the invitation is made. Foster (1972:181) has described this very well:

In Spain and Spanish America—to this day in small country inns—a diner greets each conceptual equal who enters the room with "*Gusta [Usted comer]?*" ("Would you care to share my meal?"), thereby symbolically inviting the stranger (or friend) to partake of the good fortune of the diner. The new arrival ritually replies "Buen provecho" ("Good appetite," i.e., may your food agree with you), thereby reassuring the diner that he has no reason to fear envy, and that he may eat in peace. The entrant normally would not think of accepting the invitation, and the courtesy appears to have the double function of acknowledging the possible presence of envy and, at the same time, eliminating its cause.

After commenting upon the probably similar functioning of such ritual predining formulas as the French "bon appetit," Foster proceeds to discuss the necessity for offering something to a waiter in a restaurant. Since a waiter may also envy a diner, he needs to be given something to ensure his good will, namely, a tip. In a fascinating brief survey of analogues to the word *tip* in a number of European languages, e.g., French *pourboire*, German *Trinkgeld*, Spanish *propine*, Portuguese *gorgeta*, Polish *napiwek*, Swedish *drincs*, Finnish *juomarahaa*, Icelandic *drykkjupeningur*, Russian *Chaevye* [*den'gi*], and Croatian *Napojnica*, Foster concludes that the English word *tip* must come from *tipple*, which means "to drink." (This is obviously much more likely than the folk etymology often encountered that *tip* is an acronymic formation from "to insure promptness" or *tips* from "to insure prompt service.") While Foster is surely correct in stating (1972:181) that "a tip, clearly, is money given to a waiter to buy off his possible envy, to equalize the relationship between server and served"; he fails to comment on the possible significance of the fact that the waiter is invited to *drink* (as opposed to eat). In the light of the present argument, it is precisely liquids which must be offered to avert the evil eye.

The use of a liquid bribe, so to speak, is also found in other evil eye contexts. For example, in Scotland,

A well-informed woman, an innkeeper, said that in cases where a person possessed of the Evil Eye admired anything belonging to another, no injury could follow if some little present were given to the suspected person on leaving . . . In the case of churning the small present naturally takes the form of a drink of milk to be given to anyone suspected of the Evil Eye, and so a reciter said that one should always, for safety's sake, give a visitor a drink of milk, and stated further that the beneficial effect was added to if the one who gives it

first takes a little of it herself before handing it to the stranger" (Maclagan 1902:122–123).

The suggestion that the efficacy of the "tip" is increased if one first
takes a little of the milk before offering it to the stranger is reminiscent
of one of the folk theories of the evil eye, which claims a connection
exists between breast-feeding practices and the evil eye. One notion is
that an infant allowed to drink freely from both breasts (rather than
from just one) will grow up to have the evil eye. Another notion is
that an infant once weaned who is allowed to return to the breast will
likewise grow up to have the evil eye. Representative ethnographic
data includes the following. In India (Crooke 1968:1:2), "One, and
perhaps the most common theory of the Evil Eye is that 'when a child
is born, an invisible spirit is born with it; and unless the mother keeps
one breast tied up for forty days, while she feeds the child with the
other (in which case the spirit dies of hunger), the child grows up with
the endowment of the Evil Eye, and whenever any person so endowed
looks at anything constantly, something will happen to it.'" In Greece
(Hardie 1923:161), "It is known, however, that if a new-made mother
suckles her infant from both breasts without an interval between, her
glance will be baleful to the first thing on which it rests afterwards.
Again, should a mother weakly yield to the tears of her newly weaned
son and resume feeding him, he will, in later life, have the evil eye."
(This belief could function as a socially sanctioned charter or justification for mothers weary of breast-feeding and anxious to finalize weaning.) Similarly, in Greece, one of the things that can cause the evil eye
is "if the baby resumes breast feeding after having been interrupted
for a few days or weeks" (Blum and Blum 1965:186, 1970:146).
Analogous informant testimonies concerning the presumed causal relationship between reversing the weaning act and the evil eye have
been reported in the Slovak-American tradition (Stein 1974) and in
Romania (Murgoci 1923:357). (The folk theory that weaning reversal
can cause the evil eye would seem to offer support to psychoanalyst
Melanie Klein's claim that the primary prototype of envy in general is
the infant's envy of the "feeding breast" as an object which possesses
everything (milk, love) the infant desires [Klein 1957:10,29].) In all
these cases, the infant is displaying what is construed as greedy behavior. Either he wants both breasts (when one is deemed sufficient)
or he wishes to return to the breast after having been weaned (perhaps

thus depriving a younger sibling of some of the latter's rightful supply of the limited good of mother's milk). An infant who gets more milk in this way is likely to become an adult who also attempts to get other forms of material good in this same way, that is, at someone else's expense. Thus he will be an adult with the evil eye, a greedy individual who, craving more than he deserves, or needs, may seek to take from the bounty of others. (In this context, it might be more apt to say that *tip* derives not just from *tipple*, but ultimately from *nipple*.) One wonders if the yawning symptom of victims of the evil eye might not be reminiscent of weaning insofar as the mouth in the act of yawning is constantly opening without obvious material benefit.

Confirmation of the importance of weaning and sibling rivalry in the evil eye belief complex comes from a curious detail in a remarkable legend which itself serves as a charm against the evil eye. The text typically involves the personification of the evil eye, usually as a female demon, perhaps a Lilith, child-stealing figure. A saint or archangel encounters the she-demon and forces her to reveal all of her names (through the recitation of which she may henceforth be controlled) and to return any infants she has already carried off or devoured (cf. Gollancz 1912; Hazard 1890–91; Naff 1965:50–1; Montgomery 1913:259–62; Gaster 1900; Fries 1891; and Perdrizet 1922:5–31). Gaster cites a Slavonic version of the legend (1900:139–42) in which it is the devil who steals and swallows a sixth infant after having similarly disposed of five previous ones. The mother Meletia dispatches her brother Saint Sisoe to recover her infants. When he confronts the devil and demands the return of the infants, the devil replies, "Vomit thou first the milk which thou hast sucked from thy mother's breast." The Saint prays to God and does so. The devil, seeing this, regurgitates the six infants, who are safe and sound. In two seventeenth-century Greek versions cited by Gaster, the same motif recurs. Two saints, Sisynnios and Sisynodoros, demand that the villain Gylo return the children of their sister Melitena. The She-demon Gylo replies, "If you can return in the hollow of your hand the milk which you have sucked from your mother's breast I will return the children of Melitena." The saints pray and "they vomited at once into the hollow of their hand something like their mother's milk." Gylo then brings up the abducted children and reveals her other names (Gaster 1900:143–45; cf. 147–48). If the brothers' regurgitation of mother's milk equals the restoration of infants, then one might logically assume that swallowing mother's milk is symbolically equivalent to destroying infants. Since the protagonists are brother and sister, we appear to have a case of sibling rivalry revolving around the allocation of mother's milk. Incidentally, the name of the personification of the evil eye, Gylo, may, according to Perdrizet (1922:25) who has studied the legend in some detail, be related to the Arab *ghoul*, which may in turn be related to the Babylonian *gallou*, which means "demon." The root may possibly be related to a variety of Indo-European words associated with greediness in drinking. Consider French *goulu*, meaning "gluttonous," or *gueule*, meaning "the mouth of an animal," with *gueulee*, meaning "a large mouthful." In English, it may be related to such words as *gullet, glut, gulp, gully*, and possibly *gurgle, gobble, gorge*, and *gurgitation*. *Gulch* once meant "drunkard" or "to swallow or devour greedily" while *gulf* once referred to a voracious appitite (and may derive from the Greek for bosom). To engulf means to swallow.

Water *is*, of course, necessary for the sustenance of life, and life itself is empirically observed to begin in some sense with an emergence from a flood—of amniotic fluid, perhaps providing a human model or prototype for creation myths involving supposed primeval waters or floods (cf. Casalis 1976). But it is the metaphorical and symbolic quests for water that are most relevant to our consideration of the evil eye. Onians explains that the idea that life is liquid and the dead are dry accounts for the widespread conception of a "water of life" (1951:289). The search for the water of life in fairy tales (cf. motif E80, Water of life), which is found throughout the Indo-European and Semitic world, as well as the common quest for the fountain of youth (cf. motif D1338.1.1, Fountain of youth), certainly support the notion that liquid is life. Hopkins (1905:55) distinguishes the two motifs, arguing that the "fountain of youth" comes from India while the "water of life" stems from Semitic tradition. In any case, the magic liquid can cure wounds and even bring the dead back to life. It can also rejuvenate, making the old young again. If the passage of life consists of the gradual diminution of finite fluids, then the only logical way to reverse the process would be to increase one's fluid supply. Whether fluids were taken internally (by drinking) or externally (by bathing, baptism, or being anointed), the life-giving or -renewing principle is basically the same.

If increases in liquid mean health, then decreases might signify the opposite (Onians 1951:212–14). I think it is quite possible that the English word *sick* comes ultimately from the Latin *siccus*, which means "dry." The total loss of liquid, that is, loss of life, would mean death. And this is why in the Indo-European and Semitic world, the dead are specifically perceived as being thirsty. The following custom is typical (Canaan 1929:59): "Water is not only essential for the living but also for the dead. As in ancient days so also now the Palestinian is accustomed to place for the dead a jar containing water; the only difference is that we often find on the tombs a shallow or deep cup-like cavity. Some believe that the soul of the dead visits the tomb and expects to find water to quench its thirst; therefore they that visit the tombs of the dead fill these cups with water." Onians in writing of the thirst of the dead notes (1951:285) that in Babylonia the provision of water to the dead fell to the deceased's nearest kinsman. This kinsman was known as a man's "pourer of water." One Babylonian curse was: "May God deprive him of an heir and a pourer of water." The widespread distribution of the conception of the thirsty dead has been amply described (cf. Bellucci 1909 and especially Deonna 1939:53–77).

Certainly the presumed thirst of the dead is a major metaphor in ancient Egyptian funerary ritual. According to Budge (1909:34), one of the oldest of the ceremonies performed for the dead was called the "Opening of the Mouth." The deceased was told, "Thy mouth is the mouth of the sucking calf on the day of its birth (Budge 1909:60, 156, 209). Various offerings of food and libation were presented to the deceased, most of them specifically said to come from the Eye of Horus. "Accept the Eye of Horus, which welleth up with water, and Horus hath given unto thee" (Budge 1909:147; cf. 117, 129, 185). The Eye of Horus as a breast or other body part containing liquid is understood to refresh the deceased by offering him the necessary additional "fluid of life" to replace the fluids lost before death or during the process of mummification (Budge 1909:46, 52).

In the light of the centrality of liquid as a metaphor for life, it makes sense for envy to be expressed in liquid terms. The have-nots envy the haves and desire their various liquids. Whether it is the dead who envy the living (as in vampires who require the blood of the living and who are commonly referred to as "bloodthirsty"), the old who envy the young, or the barren who envy those with children, it is the blood, the sap or vitality of youth, the maternal milk, or masculine semen that is coveted. The notion of limited good means that there is not really enough to go around. Thus an admiring look or statement (of praise) is understood as a wish for precious fluid. If the looker or declarer receives liquid, then it must be at the expense of the object or person admired. So the victim's fruit tree withers from a loss of sap or his cow's milk dries up. The point is that the most common effect of the evil eye is a *drying up* process.

There have long been clues revealing the desiccating nature of the evil eye. A thirteenth-century Dominican, Thomas of Cantipré, claimed that if a wolf and a man meet and the wolf sees the man first, the man cannot speak because the rays from the wolf's eye dry up the *spiritus* of human vision, which in turn dries up the human *spiritus* generally (Tourney and Plazak 1954:481). At the beginning of the twentieth century, twenty-three informants in Spain mentioned *secarse*, "drying out," as one of the characteristic symptoms of the evil eye (Salillas 1905:44). An interesting clinical parallel is provided in a case of schizophrenia where a nurse believed a private eye (not a detective but an actual eye) was watching her and that it had the power to draw vital body fluids from her (Tourney and Plazak 1954:488).

One of the oldest texts extant that treats the evil eye is a Sumerian one; it too confirms the association with water. It begins, "The eye *ad-gir*, the eye a man has . . . The eye afflicting man with evil, the *ad-gir*. Unto heaven it approached and the storms sent no rain." The evil eye even takes away water from the heavens. The Sumerian text suggests the cure involves "Seven vases of meal-water behind the grinding stones. With oil mix. Upon (his) face apply" (Langdon 1913:11–12, cf. Ebeling). One may compare this with a Neapolitan charm from Amalfi (Williams, 1961:156), which is nearly four thousand years later: "Eye of death, Evil Eye, I am following you with water, oil and Jesus Christ." The protective power of fluids including water is apparent in many ancient texts referring to the evil eye. For example, in the *Berakoth*, a book of the Babylonian Talmud, we read, "Just as the fishes in the sea are covered by water and the evil eye has no power over them, so the evil eye has no power over the seed of Joseph" (Simon 1948:120(20a), 340(55b)). On a portal plaque from Arslan Tash in Upper Syria, a Phoenician incantation text inscribed in an Aramaic script of the early seventh century B.C. (Caquot and Mesnil du Buisson 1971) urges the caster of the evil eye to flee. It begins, according to Gaster (1973 but cf. Cross 1974:486–90) with these words: "Charm against the demon who drains his victims." This suggests the antiquity of the idea that the evil eye constitutes a threat to the body fluids. In modern Saudi Arabia, a person who is accused of having the evil eye may be labelled by the adjective *ash-hab* which means "grey and desiccated." A person with the evil eye is thus one who is dried out, in need of liquid refreshment.

Once it is understood that the evil eye belief complex depends upon the balance of liquid equilibrium, it becomes possible to gain insight into various apotropaic techniques. For example, on the back of a large number of ancient amulets used to keep the evil eye away appears a Greek inscription meaning "I drink." Bonner (1950:213) and other scholars puzzled by this inscription felt that this meaning was inappropriate and suggested alternative translations such as "I am hungry" or "I devour." But if these meanings were intended, one might ask, why should "I drink" appear so often. Bonner even went so far as to suggest the "perhaps the 'error' occurred on the first specimen manufactured in some important workshop and was slavishly copied." The point is surely that the folk know (in some sense) what they are doing—even if scholars do not. In the light of the present hypothesis, "I drink" makes perfect sense as the inscription of an anti–evil eye amulet.

Or consider the following detail of a contemporary Algerian Jewish custom. Whoever removes the effects of the evil eye from someone afflicted evidently runs some risk of having the effects transferred to him. "Pour éviter que le 'mauvais oeil' enlevé au malade ne pénètre en lui, l'opérateur après avoir terminé absorbe un verre d'un liquide quelconque (eau, anisette, vin, etc.) que lui offrent les parents du malade" (Bel 1903:364). Clearly, the incorporation of liquid—whether it is water or wine is immaterial—is thought to guard against the dangerous effects of the evil eye.

Structurally speaking, the various apotropaic methods employed to avoid or cure the evil eye ought to be isomorphic. But how is showing a phallus or the fica isomorphic with spitting? I would argue that all these amulets or gestures signify the production of some form of liquid. Whether the liquid is semen or saliva, it provides proof that the victim's supply of life force is undiminished. Spitting is also an act of insult and it is quite likely that spitting as a counteractant to the evil eye represents a devaluation of the victim. In other words, a beautiful baby whether praised or admired or not represents a potential object for attack by an evil eye. If one spits on the baby (or asks the possessor of the evil eye to spit on the baby), one is mitigating the praise or admiration expressed. It is as if to say this is not a beautiful, admirable object (and that is should not be subject to an evil eye attack). On the other hand, spitting involves the projection of liquid for all to see. Crombie (1892:252) was quite right in remarking that saliva seemed to contain the element of life, but he did not realize that saliva can also be symbolically equivalent to semen (cf. Onians 1951:233, n.5). The initial consonant cluster *sp* occurs in both *sputum* and *sperm*, suggesting the emission of liquid, but even more persuasive is the unambiguous metaphorical evidence provided by the idiom "spitten image" (or "spit and image" or "spitting image"), used to refer to a child who greatly resembles his father (cf. Jones 1951a:63, 273). The symbolic equivalance is also attested in jokes. Legman (1968:584) reported the following abbreviated text collected in Scranton, Pennsylvania, in 1930; "Two twins are conversing in the womb. 'Who's that bald-headed guy that comes in here every night and spits in my eye?'"

The important role of saliva in the evil eye belief complex is confirmed by an interesting practice reported in Greece and Saudi Arabia. In the Oasim district in north central Saudi Arabia, in cases where someone is afflicted by the evil eye and it is not known who caused the misfortune, someone representing the victim, usually a small male child, stands in a public area, for example, outside a mosque with a small bowl half filled with water and asks each male passerby to spit into it. This is done so as not to embarrass anyone in particular by accusing that person of having the evil eye. After everyone or, at least, a good many individuals have expectorated into the container (or made a pseudo-spitting gesture), the container is taken to the victim who drinks half the contents and anoints his body with the other half. In eastern Greece in the beginning of this century, a village girl fell ill. Her mother, fearing that the cause was the evil eye, hired a curer (female) to go to the church to collect forty spits in a glass from people going into the church. The curer kept track of the number of spits by counting kernels of corn. When she counted forty kernels, she brought the glass to the victim who drank it. The victim recovered within a few days. However aesthetically unpleasing or hygienically unsound such a practice may be adjudged by nonmembers of the cultures concerned, the cure certainly does exemplify the principle of liquid intake as a counteractant to the evil eye.

As for the Malabar custom described earlier, the male figures with pendulous testes or female figures with protuberant breasts used to ward off the evil eye can also be understood as liquid-bearing symbols. The large testes and breasts presumably represent an abundance of semen or milk. (The overturned pot may suggest that the abundance is so great that hoarding is not necessary.) The symbolic equivalence of breasts and eyes is suggested by a variety of data. In ancient European iconography circles with short lines radiating from the circumference were used to symbolize both eyes and breasts (Crawford 1957:41, 48, 96, 98; cf. Deonna 1965:64; Meerloo 1971:36). In contemporary German folk speech, dozens of idioms support the fact that "Eine der merkwurdigsten Gleichsetzungen im Vokabular der Sexualsprache ist Auge = Brust" (Borneman 1971). The interchangeability of eyes and breasts is also obvious from an examination of different versions of the folktale or legend "Present to the Lover" (Aarne-Thompson tale type 706B). Its summary reads "Maiden sends to her lecherous lover (brother) her eyes (hands, breasts) which he has admired" (cf. Williamson 1932, González Palencia 1932). Further data come from contemporary tattooing. "Open eyes are tattooed on American sailors' lids or around their nipples because the sailors believe that such tattoos will keep watch for them when they are tired or asleep" (Parry 1933:136), a belief probably identical to the one that accounts for the widespread Indo-European custom of painting an eye on either side of the bows of ships and boats (Hornell 1923, 1938). But the important point here is that the eyes are sometimes drawn around the nipples, which would exemplify the breast-eye equation.

Similar folkloristic data suggests that testicles and eyes may be symbolically equivalent on occasion. In Irish mythology, we find motif J229.12, Prisoners given choice between emasculation and blinding, an alternative reminiscent of Oedipus' self-imposed punishment of blinding for a sexual crime. (For a discussion of blindness and castration as allomotifs, see Dundes 1962:102.) One may note the same allomotifs in another European narrative setting. The plot summary of Aarne-Thompson tale type 1331, The Covetous and the Envious, is as follows: Of two envious men one is given the power of fulfilling any wish on the condition that the other shall receive double. He wishes that he may lose an eye. Legman (1975:611) reports a version from New York City in 1936: "A Jew in heaven is told that whatever he asks for, Hitler will get double. He asks that one of his testicles be removed." This kind of incontrovertible data strongly supports the idea that testicles and eyes are in some sense interchangeable. We can now better understand the modern Greek formula cited earlier, in which it is wished that the possessor of the evil eye suffer crushed genitals or burst breasts, in other words, that his or her vital fluids be wasted. (The wish for breasts to burst may also imply a wish for the death of a female evil eye caster's infant—an event which might tend to cause the mother's unused breasts to swell to the bursting point.)

One detail we have not yet explained is the singularity of the evil eye, and I mean singularity in the literal sense. Why the evil *eye* instead of evil *eyes*? In most languages the idiom for *evil eye* expresses this notion of a single eye. To my knowledge, none of the previous scholarship devoted to the evil eye has even raised this elementary but intriguing question. Any plausible theory of the evil eye should be able to account for it.

To better understand this facet of the evil eye belief complex, we may profitably examine ancient Egyptian beliefs. According to Moret (1902:40–47), all living things were created by eye and voice. Life was an emission of fecund light from the Master of rays. Above all, it was the sun Ra who was the primary creator, using his eye, the sun, "Eye of Horus." (For the sun as a heavenly eye generally, see Weinreich 1909). The solar virtues of the gods were transmitted to the pharaoh through a magical fluid called *sa*. That *sa* which flowed in the veins of the pharaoh, son of Ra, was the "liquid of Ra," the gold of the sun's rays. *Sa* was emitted by a process termed *sotpou*, a verb used to describe the shooting forth of water, flames, and arrows and the ejaculation of semen (Moret 1902:47,n.2; cf. Róheim 1972:162). Another source of life, incidentally, besides the liquid of Ra, was the milk of Isis (Moret 1902:48, n.1), which suggests that the symbolic equivalence of semen and milk is of considerable antiquity (cf. Jones 1951b:233; Legman 1975:139, 367).

The curious verb *sotpou* with all its nuances reminds us of the term *ejaculation* for the action of the evil eye. Francis Bacon in 1625 spoke of the act of envy producing an "ejaculation" of the eye; and many reports of the evil eye among Greeks and Greek-Americans use the term *ejaculate* in speaking of preventatives, e.g., ejaculating the phrase "garlic in your eyes" (Lawson 1910:14; Georges 1962:70). The eye shoots forth its rays just as the Egyptian sun, the eye of Horus, emitted its life-force liquid, *sa*. The sun's rays, according to Ernest Jones

(1951b:303) are often regarded as "a symbol of the phallus as well as of semen." The phallic interpretation of the sun with its rising perceived as a metaphorical form of erection was first suggested more than a hundred years ago (Schwartz 1874; cf. Jones 1951b:278, 285) and it certainly puts solar mythology in a new light! What is important in the present context is that the sun is both phallus and eye. Noteworthy also is that *jettatore*, the common term in southern Italy for the possessor of an evil eye, and *ejaculation* come from the same Latin root.

In 1910 Ernest Jones commented, in the course of discussing the power of the eye in hypnotism, on various beliefs in magical fluids including so-called magnetic fluid. (In this connection it is of interest that a report of the evil eye mechanism in Corsica [Rousseau 1976:6] suggests that the force involved may be a kind of fluid, a fluid that is released after an unguarded compliment or expression of admiration.) Jones noted (1910:239) that the magnetic fluid was principally emitted from the hypnotist's eye; and he suggested that such a belief in the influence of the human eye, for good or ill, had its origin in the notion that the eye and its glance were symbolically regarded as the expression of the male organ and its function. Freud too spoke of "the substitutive relation between the eye and the male member which is seen to exist in dreams and myths and phantasies" (1959:383–84). In the case of the phallus, one is tempted to observe, the glance might come from the glans. If one looks at the glans of a penis, it is not impossible to imagine it as an eye, the urinary meatus serving as a surrogate pupil.

What is startling about this notion is that iconographic representations of the phallus with an eye do occur. A number of scholars have noted the existence of the *phallus oculatus* (Seligmann 1910:2:28; Servadio 1936:405; Perdrizet 1922:31; Deonna 1965:70), but none have theorized about its significance. The idea of a phallus with an eye is no stranger than contemporary risqué puns on *cockeye* (Legman 1968:241). Even more germane is some striking evidence from Arabic folk speech. In the fifteenth-century Arabic classic *The Perfumed Garden* (Nefzawi 1963:166, 176), epithets for a man's sexual parts include *el aâouar*, "the one-eyed," and *abou aîne* "he with one eye." The Arabic word for eye is similar to the Hebrew word *ayin*, which means both "eye" and "well" (Gifford 1958:81). One of the biblical verses used in phylacteries to ward off the evil eye was Genesis 49:22: "Joseph is a fruitful bough, even a fruitful bough by a well," because of the understood play on words. Joseph and his descendants were fruitful even though next to a well (= eye). The strength of the liquid metaphor even in the twentieth century is perhaps signalled by the fact that "*Maiyeh*, water, in colloquial Arabic is also used as the name of male semen, the life medium" (Canaan 1929:58).

The folk notion of the penis as the one-eyed also occurs in Walloon folklore. According to an anonymous report in *Kryptadia* (1902:24), a traditional epithet for the phallus is *li bwègne*, a dialect form of *le borgne*, which means "one-eyed." We are told that this remarkable appellation can be understood by the "ressemblance vague que la gland et ses lèvres présentent avec un oeil et ses paupières." However, the resemblance cannot be all that v̆ague if we find the same one-eye idiom in other cultures! The traditionality of the Walloon metaphor is confirmed by the reporting of an additional illustration: "sainnî-s-bwègne," which is explicated as "saigner son borgne, c'est-à-dire pisser." If bleeding or, more figuratively, draining the one-eye refers to urination, then this would certainly support the idea that an eye containing liquid might represent a phallus!

We need not go so far afield as Arabic and Walloon folklore for the idea that a *third eye*, like a *third leg*, can be a circumlocution for the phallus. The fact that the phallus is the *third* eye or leg would be in accord with the phallicism of the number three in Indo-European tradition, with the phallus cum testiculis perceived as a triform cluster (Dundes 1968:420, n.1). The phallus as the one-eyed has been reported in American folklore. One of the "unprintable" folk beliefs from the Ozarks collected by Vance Randolf in 1946 has been published by G. Legman. It concerns the custom of the so-called dumb supper by means of which young women learn the identity of their future husbands. In most versions of the custom, the girls prepare a supper in total silence and then await the arrival of the first male visitor, who is supposedly a spouse-to-be. In Randolf's account of a prank played around the turn of the century, a "local ruffian" overhears the plans of two young girls near Green Forest, Arkansas. Here is part of the story: "Exactly at midnight the two girls sat down and bowed their heads. The door opened very slowly, and in came a big man walking backwards, clad only in a short undershirt. Approaching the table he bent forward, took his enormous tool in hand, and thrust it backwards between his legs, so that it stuck right out over the food on the table. One of the girls screamed and fled into the 'other house' crying 'Maw, maw, he's thar! He's come a long way, an' he's only got one eye!" (Legman 1975:823). Whether or not the prank actually occurred is immaterial in the present context. What is important is that a narrative collected in 1946 refers to a phallus as a one-eyed man.

Even more striking is the widespread joke reported from both America and Europe in which fleas conceal themselves in various parts of the female anatomy, agreeing to meet the next day to compare notes. The flea who spent the night in the vagina reports that a bald-headed, and in some versions a one-eyed, man entered and spat on him (Legman 1968:585–586). This is not only another instance of the phallus described as one-eyed, it also exemplifies the equivalence of spitting and ejaculation.

If a healthy eye, that is, a phallus, can spit or ejaculate, then an unhealthy one cannot. Given this logic, it is not impossible to imagine that a larger, more powerful eye may rob a given eye of its ability to produce liquid, or of the precious liquid itself. The idea that an evil eye absorbs or sucks up liquid as opposed to a good eye, which emits liquid, is paralleled by an analogous folk belief attached to snakes and serpents. La Barre in his insightful discussion of the phallic symbolism of serpents observes that snakes are commonly endowed with such body image features as feathers or hair, despite the fact that "no snake in the world has either hair or feathers" (1962:61). Snakes are also believed to be able to suckle human breasts and to drink milk (La Barre 1962:94; cf. Aarne-Thompson tale type 285, The Child and the Snake, in which a snake drinks from the child's milk bottle). The point is that phalluses in the form of snakes or evil eyes are thought to have the power of stealing precious liquids.

If the phallus is the "one-eyed," then it is at least reasonable to speculate that one-eyed objects or persons in folklore might have phallic connotations. The tale of Polyphemus (cf. Aarne-Thompson tale type 1137, The Ogre Blinded) might be examined in these terms. Odysseus makes his escape by thrusting a burning mass into the giant's single eye. It may be of interest that one reported technique for removing the threat of an evil eye is to "blind the eye" (Westermarck 1926:1:434–35; Stillman 1970:90), while another entails a "symbolic burning of the eye" (Stillman 1970:85), which would be an extreme form of desiccating it. Analogous perhaps to the rationale of cremation discussed earlier, this technique would remove all liquid from the hostile eye.

With respect to Polyphemus, Comhaire (1958:26) remarks that

while Homer consistently speaks of the one eye of the Cyclops, he does mention eyebrows in the plural. This suggests that the eye may be a nonliteral or symbolic one. As early as 1913, Reiter suggested that the eye of Polyphemus represented the father's phallus and that Odysseus's blinding of Cyclops represented a son's castration of his father (cf. Glenn 1978:151–52). Reitler's Freudian discussion began with a consideration of a curious Austrian folk toy. It is a little wooden man. When his head is pushed down, a potent phallus emerges from under his clothing. Not only does this toy equate the head with the phallus, but the head of the toy has three eyes. Besides the usual two, a third one appears above them right in the middle of the forehead. Reitler assumes the third eye represents the phallus (1913:161).

In folk tradition, the eye of the one-eyed giant is centered (cf. motif F531.1.1.1, Giant with one eye in middle of forehead). Onians presents much evidence to show that the head is the male genital organ displaced upward (1951:109–10, 234, n.6). If the head can represent the male genital organ, and if the phallus is perceived as a single eye, then it would be perfectly appropriate for the eye to be centrally located. One must remember, after all, that single eyes situated in the middle of foreheads do not occur in nature. We are dealing with fantasy. The importance of the middle of the forehead is also signalled by the idea in Lebanese-American custom that a counteractant blue bead (against the evil eye) "to be truly effective should suspend from the forehead to lie between the child's eyes" (Naff 1965:49). The location of the third eye in the middle of the forehead is also paralleled by the efficacy of the middle finger, the so-called digitus infamis or digitus impudicus (Seligmann 1910:2:183–84), in warding off or curing the ill effects of the evil eye. Typically, spittle is placed on the middle finger and applied to the infant's forehead (Napier 1879:35). The phallus is often considered to be a third leg placed obviously in the middle between the two regular legs.

The equivalence of eye and phallus may be suggested in ancient Egyptian mythology when Horus battles Set. Set tears out one of Horus's eyes and Horus counters by tearing off one of Set's testicles. In this connection, it is interesting that the Eye of Horus presented to the deceased in Egyptian funeral ritual is said to be the one devoured by Set, who later vomited it up (Budge 1909:134–135, 255); and even more significantly, the deceased is told, "The Eye of Horus has been

presented unto thee and it shall not be cut off from him by thee"
(Budge 1909:128, 245). In a variant text, "The Eye of Horus hath
been presented unto thee, and it shall not be cut off from thee" (Budge
1909:184).

In Irish mythology, we find Balor, a famous robber, who had an
eye in the middle of his forehead (Krappe 1927:1–43). Interestingly
enough, Balor's was an evil eye and he used it to steal a wonder cow.
The use of an evil eye to steal cattle is, of course, very much a part of
the evil eye complex in the Celtic world and elsewhere. The evil Balor
is eventually slain by his grandson Lug who, as prophesied, "thrust a
red-hot bar into Balor's evil eye and through his skull so that it came
out on the other side" (Krappe 1927:4). The antiquity of this notion of
a male third eye is suggested by its possible occurrence in Sumer,
where Enki (Ea) allegedly bore the epithet "Nun-igi-ku, the god with
the gleaming eye." Reportedly this was described as "the god with the
holy eye in his forehead" (Van Buren 1955:164, 169). In Indic
mythology, Siva has a third eye. In light of the hypothetical phallic
association of the eye in the forehead, it is of more than passing interest that Siva's cult consisted largely of the worship of his phallus
(O'Flaherty 1975:137). The third eye of Siva has been interpreted in
an erotic sense (O'Flaherty 1969).

I should like to suggest a logical, albeit magical, paradigm that also
supports the idea that there is a phallic component of the evil eye. The
paradigm is based upon the principle of homeopathic magic, in which
a form of a dangerous object is itself used as a prophylactic countera-
gent. In Turkey and surrounding areas, for example, blue eyes are
considered to be dangerous, perhaps evil eyes (Westermarck
1926:1:440). Lawson (1910:9), who had blue eyes, reported how
difficult this made the conduct of fieldwork in Greece. He was often
taken aback at having his ordinary salutation, "Health to you," answered only by the sign of the cross. Yet the color blue in the Near
East is also regarded as protective against the evil eye (Westermarck
1926:1:440; Lawson 1910:12–13). The "like against like" principle also
applies to eyes themselves. Eye amulets are commonly used (Westermarck 1926:1:459; Elworthy 1958:133). Bonner has noted that "the
commonest of all amulets to ward off the evil eye consists of an apotropaic design which has been found on numerous monuments, and
which, though subject to slight variations, remains the same through
several centuries. It represents the eye, wide open, subjected to var-

ious injuries and assailed by a variety of animals, birds and reptiles" (Bonner 1950:97, cf. 211). The technical name of this design, Bonner discovers, is reported in a passage in the *Testament of Solomon*, an important source for the study of demonology dating perhaps from early in the third century (McCown 1922:108). In this passage, each of the thirty-six decans, or segments, of the zodiac is required to tell the king his name, his power, and the means of guarding against him. The thirty-fifth says, "My name is Rhyx Phtheneoth. I cast the glance of evil at every man. My power is annulled by the graven image of the much suffering eye." Conybeare's translation of the relevant passage (1899:38) is "The thirty-fifth said: 'I am called Phthenoth. I cast the evil eye on every man. Therefore, the eye much-suffering, if it be drawn, frustrates me.'"

The paradigm then can be sketched as follows. The color blue causes the evil eye but the color blue is used on amulets to ward off the evil eye. An eye causes the evil eye but an image of an eye is used to ward off the evil eye. Now something, that is, something analogous to an algebraic unknown, causes the evil eye, but an amulet or gesture representing a phallus or vulva wards off the evil eye. If our paradigm is valid and our reasoning is correct, then one of the "causes" of the evil eye must be the phallus or vulva.

The horseshoe and crescent moon—charms of both shapes are used to ward off the evil eye—could represent the female genitals. The symbolic equation of eye and female genitals is substantiated by a well-known pretended obscene riddle. A version recounted by Bessie Jones of Georgia to enliven a discussion workshop at a folk festival in Berkeley, California, in 1963, is representative: "What's round and hair all around it and nothin' but water comes out?" The answer is "Your eye." (Cf. riddles 1425, 1426, and 1443–44, "Hair Above, Hair Below" in Taylor 1951.) The vulva as maleficent object would also explain Frachtenberg's observation that "the glance of the eye of a woman during her menstruation period was extremely dreaded by the Zoroastrians" (1918:421). Clearly, a woman who was losing blood, a life fluid, would represent a threat to the life fluids possessed by others (potential victims of the evil eye). According to a limited-good worldview, the loss of menstrual blood would require making up the liquid deficit—at someone else's expense.

The association between the eye and the genital areas may also explain the curious belief that too much coital activity (Meerloo 1971:54) or excessive masturbation will lead to blindness. Masturbatory ejaculation causes a loss of liquid and the eye would reflect this by dimming with each successive loss. Gifford (1958:166) reminds us of Francis Bacon's note that the ancient authorities believed "much use of Venus doth dim the sight." Bacon was puzzled that eunuchs were also dim-sighted but if their organs could not produce semen, then this lack of liquid life force might be responsible for poor vision—at least according to the folk theory. The logic is remarkably consistent. If the loss of liquid causes blindness, then the addition of liquid can cure blindness. Urine, for example (cf. the trade name of a solution to refresh eyes: *Murine*!) was commonly used to cure the effects of the evil eye as well as for eye diseases generally (Gifford 1958:66). Mother's milk is as effective a form of eye medicine as liquid from a male source. Numerous reports relate that "a few drops of mother's milk directly from the breast is also a favorite remedy for inflamed eyes" (Gordon 1937:313). "If a few drops of his mother's milk are poured into his eyes, the child will have good eyesight" reads a typical Hungarian superstition (Róheim 1952:353). Urine and mother's milk are evidently effective male and female curative fluids.

The phallus or the vulva as a liquid-seeking evil eye would explain why the evil eye is singular. But it may not be entirely clear why a phallus or a vulva should be perceived as liquid-seeking. To understand this, it is necessary to consider an important folk theory of sexuality, namely, that coitus is dangerous and debilitating insofar as it may result in a loss of liquid. Legman refers to the fantasy that "sexual intercourse is 'weakening' to the man, but not to the woman, because he 'loses' a fluid, the semen, which she receives" (1975:653). Legman relates this fantasy to the notion of the succubus. Earlier Ernest Jones (1951b:120) had suggested that "the simple idea of the vital fluid being withdrawn through an exhausting love embrace" was related to the vampire belief. Jones also (1951b:179) cited the fascinating folk belief that the devil has no semen and that "he can impregnate a woman only by having first obtained some semen by acting as a Succubus to a man." The crucial point with respect to the evil eye complex is that it is not farfetched to claim that the eye as phallus or vulva poses a threat to the victim's vital fluids. The widespread idea that hunters should refrain from sexual intercourse just before a hunt (or warriors before a battle or athletes before a game) is very likely related to the notion that a man has a finite amount of energy and this energy might be siphoned off or drained by the female genitals. The empirically observable fact that a man can manage only a limited or finite number of erections, hence sexual acts, within a given period of time while a woman, at least in theory (and fantasy—cf. Legman 1968:356–60 for the "unsatisfiable female"), can indulge in an infinite number of sexual acts might account for the idea that males have "limited good" with respect to semen.

In like manner, the Arab practice of *Imsák*, the special art of delaying the male orgasm (Nefzawi 1963:30), is probably selfishly intended to decrease the loss of precious semen rather than altruistically increasing the sexual pleasure of females. The idea that "women emit a special fluid at orgasm similar to the semen in men," which Legman calls a superstition "once almost universally believed at the folk level" (1968:403), would encourage such a practice. If the male succeeded in drawing fluid from the female genitals while at the same time retaining his own fluid, he would presumably suffer no diminution in the finite amount of his life force. The fact that most males are unable to prevent ejaculation no doubt accounts for the widespread fear of female demons who threaten to suck a male victim dry in one way or another (cf. Legman 1975:134).

This battle of the sexes for precious liquid of life is quite explicit in Chinese sexual theory. In this theory, the Yang-Yin distinction includes a male-female component. According to one authority, the Chinese believed that "while man's semen is strictly limited in quantity, woman is an inexhaustible receptacle of Yin essence." (Weakland 1956:241). Men were supposed to retain their semen insofar as possible and to use the sexual act as a means of "absorbing the woman's Yin essence." According to the folk theory, "this art of sexual intercourse with a woman consists of retraining oneself so as not to ejaculate, thus making one's semen return and strengthen one's brain" (Weakland 1956:240). Since men wanted children (especially sons), they were "supposed to ejaculate only on those days when the woman was most likely to conceive . . . On all other days the man was to strive to let the woman reach orgasm without himself emitting semen. In this way the man would benefit by every coitus because the Yin essence of the woman, at its apex during the orgasm, strengthens his vital power . . ." The goal is absolutely clear. Man was to retain his vital essence while drawing the essence from his female sexual partner. In Chinese folklore, one finds dangerous, beautiful women who delight in draining their male sexual victims dry (Weakland 1956:241–42). While the evil eye was reported "to be no less common amongst the native population of northern China than it was and still is in Europe" (Dennys 1876:49), it seems to be largely absent from China (cf. Seligmann 1910:1:43). But even though the evil eye complex is not a major element in the Chinese folk belief system, the Chinese perception of coitus in terms of gaining or losing sexual fluids seems to be paralleled by similar folk theories among Indo-European and Semitic peoples.

In Uttar Pradesh in northern India, it is believed (Minturn and Hitchcock 1966:74) that excessive sexual activity may cause minor illness and that "sexual intercourse is thought to make men in particular weak and susceptible to disease because the loss of one drop of semen is considered the equivalent of the loss of 40 drops of blood." Moreover, "the longevity of several men is attributed to complete abstinence in their later years." Clearly the loss of vital fluids through ejaculation is believed to diminish a finite supply of life energy. An Andalusian expression (collected in Andalusia by my colleague Stanley Brandes in 1976) confirms that the same reasoning is traditional in Spain: "Si quieres llegar a viejo, guarda la leche en el pellejo." "If you want to reach old age, keep your semen within your skin."

Essentially the same folk idea is described in Kinsey's *Sexual Behavior in the Human Male*.

> "For many centuries, men have wanted to know whether early involvement in sexual activity, or high frequency of early activity, would reduce one's capacities in later life. It has been suggested that the duration of one's sexual life is definitely limited, and that ultimate high capacity and long-lived performance depend upon the conservation of one's sexual powers in earlier years. The individual's ability to function sexually has been conceived as a finite quantity which is fairly limited and ultimately exhaustible. One can use up those capacities by frequent activity in his youth, or preserve his wealth for the fulfillment of the later obligations and privileges of marriage" (Kinsey, Pomeroy, and Martin 1948:297).

Kinsey goes on to remark that medical practitioners have sometimes claimed that infertility and erectal impotence were the results of the wastage of sperm through excessive sexual activity in youth and that Boy Scout manuals for decades informed countless youths "that in order 'to be prepared' one must conserve one's virility by avoiding any wastage of vital fluids in boyhood," which presumably was an attempt to appeal to self-interest to curb self-abuse, the common euphemism for masturbation. That a woman's genital area is perceived as a dangerous mouth posing a threat to the male genitals is confirmed not only by the vagina dentata motif (F547.1.1) but perhaps also by the use of the Latin *labia* for the outer and inner folds of skin and mucous membrane of the vulva. *Labia*, of course, means "lips" (cf. La Barre 1962:89n) and lips drink up liquid.

In the context of the evil eye belief complex, I suggest that showing the phallus or making the fica gesture (which symbolically shows a phallus in a vagina) affirms the prospective victim's ability to produce semen. The ability to produce liquid is explicit in a curious detail in Lebanese-American custom. An exorcist who specialized in combatting the effects of the evil eye maintained that a child was not cured until he had urinated. She insisted that "no one should kiss a child while he is being read over and not until he has urinated after the eye has been expelled." Asked why this was necessary, she replied, "It's just natural. That's the way it is supposed to be" (Naff 1965:50). From the present perspective, the child's cure from the ill effects of the evil eye is demonstrated by his ability to make water, to produce liquid normally. (This would also be consonant with the fact that urine is sometimes reported to be an effective agent in curing the effects caused by the evil eye (cf. Pitrè 1889:245; Kirshenblatt-Gimblett and Lenowitz 1973:73).) It is, in sum, entirely consonant with the wet-dry hypothesis.

There is yet another way of blinding the evil eye and that is by defecating upon it. An unusual marble bas-relief reported by Millingen in his paper delivered in 1818 shows a man lifting his clothing to allow his bare buttocks to sit upon a large eye, which is also being attacked by a host of animals (cf. Elworthy 1958:138–41; Deonna 1955:93–94; 1965:180). This belongs to the same tradition as the painting unearthed as Pompeii next to a latrine, in which a man squats in a defecating position between two upright serpents next to a woman whose feet are pierced by a sword. Above the squatting man is inscribed *Cacator cave malum* (Magaldi 1932:97; cf. Deonna 1955:94). Seligmann (1910:1:302–3) notes that excrement is sometimes used to counteract the effects of the evil eye, e.g., in the case of a cow whose milk has gone dry, but he does not attempt to explain why excrement should be so used. Róheim (1955:28–31) suggests that "the magical value of excrement is based on the infantile anal birth theory" in which very young children equate the act of defecation with the act of giving birth. Thus, according to Róheim, "The defecating child is the mother; the excrement, the child." Róheim remarks that in Scotland, a calf can be protected against the evil eye if some of its mother's dung is put into its mouth (1955:25); and he interprets this as meaning the witch cannot "eat" the child with her evil eye because the child is eating the witch (bad mother, excrement). Says Róheim, "To possess the evil eye means to have oral aggression or a desire to eat the child" (1955:7). If the production of feces is equivalent to giving birth to a child, then defecation could be construed as an alternate means of proving one's fertility. But like spitting, the act of defecation can also have an insulting aspect. Defecating on the evil eye could also be a means of repudiating and defiling it. If the eye were that of an all-powerful and ever-watchful parent or all-seeing god, then a child (or an adult considering himself a child vis-à-vis his parents or a deity) might take pleasure in depositing feces in or on that eye (cf. Jones 1951b:176).

Deonna (1965:183) reminds us of a formula employed in Asia Minor by a mother attempting to keep the evil eye away from her child. The mother addresses the possible possessor of the evil eye as follows: "Que ton oeil soit derrière de mon enfant." Deonna wonders if wishing that the eye be positioned at the child's rear might be related to the curious custom of painting an eye at the bottom of chamber pots sold at fairs. Such chamber pots are reported in England, Scotland, and France, among other places, where they are commonly used in wedding customs (Monger 1975). In Stockport, Cheshire, a premarriage ceremony includes the groom's friends presenting him with a chamber pot. It is decorated with the names of the bride and groom and a large eye is painted on the bottom of it with the words "I can see you" (Monger 1975:52). Later the man and his friends take the pot to a tavern and everyone drinks from it. In Scotland, a chamber pot filled with salt was given as a wedding present to the groom. Miniature chamber pots were sold at the Aberdeen market in the mid 1930s "usually inscribed with the words 'For me and my girl' or with an eye at the bottom" (Monger 1975:56–57).

Van Gennep (1932:I:161–162) reported French versions of the custom, including one called *Saucée* (which one is tempted to translate as

"soused" or "wet through"), from Revel-Tourdan in the Dauphiné district, in which melted chocolate was poured into a chamber pot with
an eye design at the bottom in such a way as to leave the eye clear.
After the chocolate hardened, other ingredients were added, such as
white wine or champagne, grated chocolate, balls of chocolate,
creams, etc. The concoction was taken later to the nuptial chamber
after the bride and groom were considered to be asleep. The bride had
to drink first, then the groom. Monger (1975:58) suggests a possible
though admittedly highly speculative, connection to a supposed ancient eye-goddess cult in the Middle East (Crawford). However, it is
more likely that it and the Scottish custom mentioned above are vestigial fertility rituals. Salt, as Ernest Jones convincingly demonstrated,
is a symbolic substitute for semen (1951a:22–109), and thus a
chamber pot filled with salt is a container full of semen given to the
groom. Newlyweds are especially concerned with performing the sexual act satisfactorily. Tourney and Plazak observe that "the nuptial
pair may fear impotence, frigidity or sterility" and that apotropaic
charms are used to demonstrate that the threatened genitalia are safe
(1954:491–92). If the eye at the bottom of the chamberpot represents
the parental or peer group's attempt to observe the first connubial act
of intercourse (cf. the words "I can see you") then the act of pouring
in chocolate (a sweet, sublimated substitute for feces) might be
analogous to defecating upon the evil eye.

If the evil eye represents the threat of impotence and/or the lack or
loss of the necessary sexual fluids, then it would make sense to drink
from an evil eye container. The chamber pot, an obvious receptacle for
the passing of liquid, is converted through ritual reversal into a drinking goblet allowing for the incorporation of a potent liquid. (The ritual
may also signal that a part of the body hitherto associated primarily
with excretion will be employed in a new and different way.)

In the context of defecating upon the evil eye, it might be worth
conjecturing that the common drinking toast "Here's mud in your
eye" may stem from the same psychological source. The person who
drinks is incorporating the liquid of life. The liquid is taken at someone else's expense. This other person, rather than taking in vital fluid,
receives the end product of digestive incorporation in his eye. Certainly the above-mentioned wish "May your eye be at the posterior of
my child" is not all that different from "Here's mud in your eye."

In terms of the possible symbolism of body parts, it is conceivable that the anus could constitute a metaphorical eye. This is suggested by a number of standard joke texts. One traced by Legman back to the late eighteenth century tells of a man who puts his artificial glass eye in a glass of water before retiring and swallows it by mistake. He visits a proctologist who after examining him exclaims, "I've been looking up these things for thirty years, but this is the first time anyone ever looked *back* at me!" (Legman 1975:515). Another involves a drunk who attempts to convince a bartender that he is sober: "Drunk? Hell, I'm not drunk. I can see. Look at that cat coming in the door there. It's got only one eye, hasn't it?" The bartender replies that the cat has two eyes and, besides, it is not coming in but going out (Legman 1975:822). In both Italian and Spanish, there are metaphorical references to the anus as an eye. From Liguria in Italy, we have the following example. A young girl refused to drink her coffee because she noticed coffee grounds in it. Her mother asked, "Ti ae puia che o te o l'euggio de cu?" which might be rendered "Are you afraid that it will stop up the eye of your ass?" i.e., cause constipation. Similarly, *ojo* means *culo* in Andalusia. In this connection one recalls Chaucer's reference at the end of his celebrated Miller's Tale to duped Absolon kissing Alison's "naked ers" with the words "And Absolon hath kissed hir nether ye." The nether eye was thus known in the fourteenth century.

To the extent that the evil eye has an anal cast, it would be perfectly reasonable to confront a threatening anus with anal power. In this light, an unusual Spanish ritual and charm against the evil eye might be cited (Diego Cuscoy 1969:502). According to this account, since individuals who give the evil eye are generally known as such, one turns a child's back or an animal's butt towards them when they are seen approaching. Then one thinks mentally or recites in a low voice the following text:

Tres garbanzitos	Three little chick peas
tiene en el culo:	He has in the ass;
quitale dos,	Away with two
déjale uno.	Leave one.
Virate p'al monte	Turn towards the mountain
virate p'al mar,	Turn towards the sea
virate el culo	Turn your ass
y déjalo andar.	And let it go.

This would seem to be consistent with the *Cacator cave malum* pattern noted earlier.

Most folklorists eschew symbolic analysis, and they may therefore be skeptical of the analysis of the evil eye proposed in this essay. But even leaving aside the symbolic considerations, one cannot avoid the obvious psychological aspects of the evil eye. Sometimes the possessor of an evil eye used the power for both psychological and mercenary advantage. In Scotland, fear of the evil eye led people to bribe or buy off the potential evil eye inflictor (Maclagan 1902:30–31, 47). One informant reported that Mrs. MacE. "was believed to have the Evil Eye very strongly, and people would do almost anything rather than offend her, so general was the impression that she could injure any person if she wished to do so" (Maclagan 1902:69). There are similar accounts from Italy. "I know also a most disagreeable woman whose daily task of running errands is made profitable by propitiatory tips, lest she blight her patrons, their children, or their cattle" (Mather 1910:42). In America (Gordon 1937:219), "one case in Philadelphia came up before a magistrate recently in which a dark-haired little old Italian woman was terrorizing the neighborhood. For many years she had extracted large sums of money from those who came under the influence of the evil eye. She also sold charms made out of bones of the dead, articles of ivory, stones, and herbs, wrapped in rag bags." These are surely examples of transforming what might be a liability into a kind of asset.

Occasionally, there have been attempts to put the power of the evil eye to good use. One of the most unusual of these attempts took place in Sassari in Sardinia near the end of the last century. According to the report (Edwardes 1889:326–27), the evil eye was enlisted to battle a plague of locusts: "Not long ago, Sassari elected a mayor who openly scoffed at the priests. This gentleman was not, however, a thorough type of the modern Sassarese. For though he condemned religion, he was sufficiently in the thrall of superstition to give his earnest sanction to the employment of a youth gifted with the evil eye. The country happened to be plagued with locusts. There was no remedy except the evil eye. And so the lad was perambulated about the district, and bidden to look his fiercest at the insufferable ravagers of vineyards, gardens, and the rich orchards of the north. Even when the locusts remained unmoved by this infliction, the mayor's faith in the remedy was unchanged. They had requisitioned an 'evil eye' of comparative impotency, that was all. It behoved them, therefore to find a person better gifted than the lad they had used."

Evidently, humans are more likely to be intimidated by the evil eye than locusts are. In 1957, a committee of the U.S. Senate charged with investigating possible connections between organized crime and labor interviewed an Italian racketeer from New York City. The committee was told that the evil eye had been used to keep unhappy employees on the job. According to Gifford's account (1958:103), the racketeer was hired by one employer simply to come in once or twice every week or so to glare at the employees. The employer found that it was enough to have this individual come in and look at the workers to keep them at their work.

Most of the time, however, the possessor of the evil eye is shunned and ignored. In Morocco, "A person who is reputed to have an evil eye . . . is not allowed to take part in feasts or gatherings . . . he must not pitch his tent near the tents of others" (Westermarck 1926:426). Like accusations of witchcraft, accusations of possessing the evil eye give social sanction to ostracizing an individual, often transforming him into a pariah. Pitrè (1889:247) is one of the relatively few scholars to express sympathy for the poor soul who may be unfortunate enough to be victimized by an accusation of possessing the evil eye: "The *jettatore* has no name, no friends, nor the possibility of a social life . . ."

The evil eye, like so many forms of human custom and superstition, is condemned automatically by so-called educated members of Western elite societies. But it should be realized that the evil eye, like most customs, serves an invaluable projective function. When an infant becomes ill or dies, there is potentially a great deal of guilt and shame felt by parents. The evil eye belief complex provides a nearly foolproof mechanism that allows the anxious parents to shift the responsibility and blame for the misfortune upon someone else, perhaps even a total stranger whose eyes are a different color from the parents'. Similarly, if a cow's milk dries up or a favorite fruit tree withers, it is not the fault of the owner of the cow or the tree: The evil eye caused these calamities.

Even the diagnostic and protective techniques involved in the evil eye belief complex may provide important psychological supports. A small child who feels ill is assured of a great deal of parental attention. In Italian and Italian-American tradition, a bowl or shallow dish filled with water and a drop of olive oil may be placed on his head to determine whether or not his discomfort has been caused by the evil eye. Whether the child or parents believe in the efficacy of the procedure or not, most children surely enjoy being the cynosure of all eyes. Thus whatever evil results from the evil eye, there is also a beneficial aspect of the belief complex.

The concern in this essay has been not so much with the evil eye per se, but with the attempt to understand the folk ideas or worldview principles underlying it. The delineation of the wet-dry opposition and the idea of limited good is, however, not just an idle intellectual exercise. There are applications to be made that may lead to a better understanding of cultural differences. For example, in the United States, the idea of limited good is not as common as in the Old World. Instead, it has been argued that an idea of unlimited good prevails (Dundes 1971). In theory (as opposed to practice), there is enough "good" for everyone to have his fair share. One could also argue that the collective guilt felt by citizens of the United States for their relatively high standard of living accounts for their attempts to "tip" less fortunate countries by offering them substantial foreign aid. Just as many wealthy individuals turn to philanthropy as a means of salving their consciences (for enjoying the possession of more goods than they need for simple survival) so the have-nations feel impelled to help the have-nots by offering grain surpluses and other aid.

But there are some substantive differences. In American culture, praise is not only permitted but expected. One can praise the beauty of an infant or a friend's new house or dress without giving offense or causing anxiety. But Americans need to remember when they travel in other parts of the Indo-European and Semitic world that praise can be considered threatening. When a new acquaintance literally gives a visiting American the shirt off his back (which the American may have admired), it is not necessarily because of friendship so much as because of fear of the evil eye. By the same token, Americans, who from infancy are accustomed to hearing and receiving lavish praise for even the slightest deed, should not be offended when praise is not forthcoming from colleagues from cultures in which belief in the evil eye remains a vital force. One American woman married to an eastern European told me she had never understood why her in-laws so rarely praised her or her children. She took it personally, not realizing that their unwillingness to indulge in the public praising so common among Americans might have been due to the cultural imperatives demanded by the evil eye complex. To praise is to invite disaster in evil eye cultures.

The contrast between American conventions of socialization and those of evil eye cultures is quite pronounced. American children are typically asked to perform and show off in front of family and friends (and sometimes even strangers). Not so in evil eye cultures. The case of the Syrian and Lebanese Americans is instructive. "Experience taught that to show off a 'smart' child in front of people, especially strangers, is to invite the eye to strike him" (Naff 1965:49). The same is reported for northern India: "Because of the belief in the evil eye, a visitor who followed the American custom of admiring the baby, praising its unusual healthiness, good looks, or well-kept appearance would cause panic rather than pride, and a village mother would no more show off her baby to the admiration of a visitor than an American mother would deliberately expose an infant to a contagious disease" (Minturn and Hitchcock 1966:111–12).

For most of the Indo-European and Semitic world, the philosophy articulated by Herodotus and Horace prevails with respect to fame and fortune and the praise thereof. Herodotus in Book VII, chapter 10, of the *Persian Wars* speaks of lightning striking the tallest trees. "See how god with his lightning always smites the bigger animals, and will not suffer them to wax insolent, while those of a lesser bulk chafe him not. How likewise his bolts fall ever on the highest houses and the tallest trees. So plainly does he love to bring down everything that exalts itself." Horace says, "It is the mountaintop that the lightning strikes" (*Odes* 2.10). A low profile is essential to avoid the envy of one's peers or the gods. Certainly one element of the evil eye complex is the "fear of success" (Haimowitz and Haimowitz 1966). This is analogous to the underdog theme in American culture—politicians and athletic teams prefer to be the underdog because they ardently believe that front runners and the favored are likely to be overtaken and defeated. In the same ode Horace says, "Whoever cultivates the golden mean avoids both the poverty of a hovel and the envy of a palace." This is an ideal—to be neither envied nor envier.

One needs enough liquid to live but that means not too little and not too much. But eventually the finite amount is depleted. "For dust thou art, and unto dust shalt thou return." If drying is dying, then death is dust. The American slang idiom "to bite the dust" reflects not only the convulsive act of a dying man whose mouth may touch the earth, but also the same wet-dry continuum that I have suggested underlies the whole evil eye belief complex.

In the Judeo-Christian tradition, ideas of the afterlife include a solution to the problem of the imagined thirst of the dead. For heaven or paradise or the promised land is one which flows with milk and honey (Genesis 3:6, Exodus 33:3, Jeremiah 11:5, etc.). The phrase "and the hills shall flow with milk" (Joel 3:18) strongly suggests that there may be an infantile prototype for this metaphor, namely, the initial postnatal breast-feeding constellation. In the idealized afterlife, one is finally safe from the evil eye. Here there is plenty of milk and honey—enough for an eternity of replenishment. With unlimited liquid, one is free to enjoy life eternal. On the other hand, in hell, we have excessive heat—fire and water are presumably in opposition. And one thinks of the plight of the unfortunate Tantalus, perpetually consumed by thirst he is unable to slake because the waters cruelly recede whenever he bends down to drink.

In conclusion, it seems reasonable to argue that the wet-dry opposition is just as important as the hot-cold opposition, which has been frequently studied by anthropologists and students of the history of medicine. Perhaps it is even more important. Classical humoral pathology in fact included all four distinctions: heat, dryness, moistness, and cold (cf. Story 1860:697, Lloyd 1964). In this connection, it is noteworthy that a reported native classification of foods in northern India included hot, cold, dry, and wet (Minturn and Hitchcock 1966:73). If the wet-dry distinction does underlie the evil eye belief, then the distribution and age of the complex would tend to suggest that the wet-dry opposition is much older than its articulation among the ancient Greeks concerned with humoral pathology. Rather, it would appear that the formulations of humoral pathology simply formalized a folk theory already in existence. One must keep in mind that all of the so-called humors were fluids, and for that matter, the term *humor* itself comes from the Latin *umor*, meaning "fluid" or "moisture." It is even possible that the idea of an exceptionally dry sense of humor might imply that the normal state of humor was wet!

Foster (1978) has assumed that the wet-dry distinction has disappeared in Latin America. He asks, "But why have the moist/dry qualities disappeared—apparently everywhere—in contemporary systems?" Foster answers his own question by suggesting that the

moist-dry component so basic to classical humor pathology is less critical than the hot-cold distinction. "Heat and cold, and not moistness
or dryness, are the primary causes of illness," argues Foster, who is, of
course, speaking only of conscious articulation of theories of illness
causation. If the wet-dry opposition is related to the evil eye belief
complex (not to mention beliefs about the dead), one might take issue
with the idea that the wet-dry distinction has disappeared and also
with the idea that it is less critical than the hot-cold dichotomy with
respect to folk theories of disease. On the contrary, I believe there is
ample evidence to support the notion that the opposition between wet
and dry is a fundamental folk idea, albeit an unconscious one, in
Indo-European and Semitic worldview, a folk idea which is,
metaphorically at any rate, a matter of life and death. With respect to
the ideal of moderation, I can only hope in closing that my argument
holds water but that my ideas are not all wet. God forbid that anyone
who disagrees with me should give me a withering look, or tell me to
go dry up and blow away.

The Number Three in American Culture

———————⟫•⟪———————

Nothing is as difficult to see as the obvious.
—BRONISLAW MALINOWSKI,
A Scientific Theory of Culture

Ever since the publication of H. Usener's monograph in 1903, no one has questioned the importance of the number three in Greek and Roman culture. Subsequent investigations of classical literature, law, and medicine (Göbel, Goudy, Tavenner) have served only to confirm the pattern. More recent scholarship (Deonna, Dumézil) has demonstrated the existence of the pattern in most of Western civilization and has suggested it may be a characteristic of Indo-European culture. Some of the more convincing pieces of evidence are provided by mythology and, more specifically, by the widespread occurrence of triads of deities. Typical examples would be the Babylonian Ea, Anu, and Enlil, and the Hindu Brahma, Vishnu, and Shiva. Also pertinent is the widespread distribution of single gods with three heads (Kirfel). However, relatively few of the numerous studies of the number three have concerned themselves with the "three-determinism" of contemporary thought.

In a valuable study which appeared the same year as Usener's, Raimund Müller suggests that modern European culture is just as three-oriented as classical culture was. Unfortunately, because Müller's essay was published in a somewhat obscure graduate exercise program, it has had little influence. As for American culture in particular, only one of the studies made by classicists and Indo-Europeanists (Lease) and some of the latest of a long line of overtly

Christian treatises seeking to reveal the presence of the Trinity in nature (e.g., Strand) have documented in any detail that the number three is of ritual importance in the United States.

One should realize that three is not a universal pattern number. There are several pattern numbers, each with its own distribution. The majority of American Indian cultures have four as their ritual or sacred number. Sometimes a member of Euro-American culture is surprised or amused at the American Indian's obvious cultural insistence upon fourfold repetition. Parsons (1916:596) remarked on the "obsessive character" of the Zuni use of four. Earlier, Buckland (1895:96) had mistakenly thought that all American Indians had four as their ritual number, but he was unaware of the ritual five among numerous tribes in western North America (Jacobs 1959:224–28: Lowie 1925:578). The occurrence of five in South America and in China (Geil) suggests that the ritual use of five may be of considerable antiquity. Of course, American Indians are not particularly bothered by what appears to us as an exaggerated use of four or five repetitions, just as we are not irritated by our own equally persistent use of threefold repetitions.

It should also be noted that three is not the only pattern number in American culture. In fact, there is clearly a plurality of pattern numbers—two, seven, and twelve are three obvious examples. Certainly, philosophical dualism is very much a part of American culture and individuals do dichotomize. Common polarities include: life/death, body/soul, and male/female. Indeed, although Lease (1919:72, n. 2) suggests that the primary divisions of the human arm and leg, not to mention the finger, tend to support trichotomic thinking, the anatomical datum would appear to reinforce "two" rather than "three." There are two sexes, two ears, eyes, nostrils, arms, legs, and so forth. These universally recognized pairs would help to explain why dualism is probably worldwide. Whether one uses such criteria as dual social organization (e.g., in moiety systems) or some variation of a "self-other" or "us-them" dichotomy (e.g., as in exogamy), there seems little doubt that "two" is more widely distributed in the world than "three." In American culture one finds quite frequently that there are alternative classification schemes: one binary and one trinary. The present thesis is not that the number three is the only numerical native category in American culture, but rather that it is the predominant one.

The following general statements about the nature of trichotomy may be of interest: (1) Often three appears to be an absolute limit; there are three terms or three categories and no more. In folk speech one can give three cheers for someone, but not two or four. (And each cheer may consist of "Hip, Hip, Hooray.") The starter for a race will say "One, two, three, go." He will not count to two or four. (Cf. the three commands "On your mark, get set, go.") The alphabet is referred to as the ABCs and in the common folk simile, something is as easy as ABC; one does not speak of learning his ABs or his ABCDs. (2) If there are more than three terms, the additional ones will not infrequently be defined primarily in terms of one of the three basic terms, usually one of the extremes. For example, in shirt sizes, one finds small, medium, and large. The size "extra-large" is certainly linguistically and very probably conceptually derived from "large," rather than possessing separate individual status. (3) One source of trichotomies consists of positions located in reference to some initial point. The golfer tries to shoot par for the course. He may, however, shoot "under" par or "over" par. In music, the point of reference may be "middle C," which serves, for example, as a midpoint between the base and treble clefs in addition to functioning as a point of reference from which to describe voice ranges (e.g., "two octaves above middle C"). (4) On the other hand, a third term may be the result of splitting a polarity. If A and B represent two extremes, then a trichotomy may be achieved by establishing their average, median, or mean as a midpoint. Or if "early" and "late" represented extremes in describing arrivals and departures, then "on time" would presumably be the midpoint. Obviously, in some instances, it is difficult to say whether the midpoint or the extremes came first. (5) Another common means of trichotomy formation is the merging or combining of two terms so that one has A, B, and AB. In *Robert's Rules of Order* it is stated that "an amendment may be in any of the following forms: (a) to insert or add, (b) to strike out, or (c) to strike out and insert." In theory, any polarity can be converted to a trichotomy by this or the immediately preceding principle. Moreover, it is decidedly easier to move from two to three (cf. Usener 1903:323) than from three to two. The majority of the most common trichotomic schemes in American culture could not easily be put into a dichotomic mold. (6) The strength of the trichotomic tendency is indicated in part by its "repetition compulsion." In a considerable number of tripartite schemes, each of the three units in question may itself be divided into three parts. Each of these parts may in turn be broken down into three subdivisions and so on almost ad infinitum. (7) A final generalization concerns the special case of the triune or the three-in-one. In some trichotomies the three subdivisions are not separate and independent; instead they are part of a whole. The doctrine of the Trinity as opposed to a doctrine of tritheism illustrates this form of trichotomy.

We may now turn to specific examples of trichotomy in American culture. One of the very best sources for the study of native categories is folklore. Folklore, consisting as it does of native documents or autobiographical ethnography, is prime data for investigations of cognitive patterning. A number of scholarly studies have described the frequent occurrence of "three" in European folklore (e.g., Lehmann, Müller) and indeed the overwhelming consistency of trifold repetition in both classical and modern European folklore led the distinguished Danish folklorist Axel Olrik to claim that the "law of three" was one of the fundamental epic laws governing the composition of folk narrative. There has also been a Christian-anthropological treatise (Seifert) that has sought to demonstrate threeness as a manifestation of the Trinity in the myths of primitive peoples. This is questionable, but certainly in Euro-American folktales there are three brothers, three wishes, three magic objects, and often a three-day interval of waiting or fighting. In jokes, which are the modern equivalents of *märchen* (fairy tales), there are commonly three principals: an Englishman, an Irishman, and a Scotchman; a minister, a priest, and a rabbi; or a blonde, a brunette, and a redhead. Structurally, there are usually three action sequences in such jokes. Three is equally popular in other genres of American folklore.

In American folksongs there are numerous examples of trebling and it is doubtful whether many singers are fully conscious of it. For example, in many songs the verse consists of a line which is repeated three times before being followed by a final line. Typical illustrations include: "John Brown's body lies a moulderin' in the grave . . . but his soul goes marching on"; "John Brown had a little Indian . . . one little Indian boy"; "Polly put the kettle on . . . we'll all have tea"; "Go tell Aunt Rhody (Nancy) . . . her old grey goose is dead"; "Lost my partner, what'll I do? . . . skip to my Lou, my darlin'"; etc. In other instances, a word or phrase is thrice repeated: "Row, row, row your boat," "Mary had a little lamb, little lamb, little lamb," "Do you know the muffin man, the muffin man, the muffin man?" "Did you ever see a lassie, a lassie, a lassie?" and such other favorites as "Buffalo gals, won't you come out tonight?" "Joshua fit the battle of Jericho," "Here we go round the mulberry bush," and "London Bridge is falling down," to list just a few.

The number three also figures prominently in American superstitions. Sometimes, it signifies luck: "Third time's a charm." Sometimes it is the opposite: "Three times a bridesmaid, never a bride," "Three on a match is bad luck," and "Going down for the third time" (i.e., drowning). Riddles as well as superstitions may reflect triadic form. The celebrated riddle of the Sphinx, which is very old and very widely distributed, is a particularly noteworthy example, especially if one considers that, in a way, the riddle constitutes a folk definition of man: "It first walks on four legs, then on two, then on three legs." In many versions the "morning, noon, and night" time trichotomy is used as a metaphor for the "three" ages of man—"Four legs in the morning, two legs at noon, three legs at night"—making the tripartite categorization even more explicit.

The pattern is also found in traditional games. In the popular parlor game of tic-tac-toe, whose title itself is trinary, the object of the game is to get three x's or ciphers in a row. In card games, three of a kind or sequential runs of at least three cards may be important. In games such as "Hearts," where each individual passes cards to his neighbor, the number passed is three. The playing cards themselves are of interest. While there are four suits (possibly a reflection of a Chinese origin), there are but three face cards in American decks of cards. When it is realized that some European sets have four face cards, and further that the particular face cards in American culture are a King, Queen, and Jack, a secular trio of father, mother, and son, the three penchant becomes more apparent.

Threeness also occurs in team games or sports. In the "national pastime" threes abound. In baseball there are nine players; nine innings; three outs; three strikes; first, second, and third base; left, center, and right field; and often three umpires. Moreover, both batting and fielding averages are calculated to three places, pitching "earned run averages" (ERAs) consist of three digits, and box scores commonly list "runs, hits, and errors"—all follow a ternary pattern. While the patterning is not perfect (a walk is earned by four balls), three does seem to be the prevailing number. Batters are measured in part by the number of RBIs (runs batted in) and whether or not they hit over .300. (Is it just a coincidence that this particular percentage is singled out?)

Other sports in the United States reveal similar patterning. In football, the "line" consists of seven men (another magic number), but is divided into a left side, center, and right side in common parlance. The left and right sides consist of three slots: guard, tackle, and end. The backfield has four men, but only three linguistic slots: quarterback, halfback, and fullback. (This is analogous to the front, side, and back yards of a house, in that four areas are labeled with just three basic designatory terms, and perhaps analogous also to the three instruments found in the normal form of the string quartet: violins, viola, and cello.) Obviously, there are other number patterns present in football. Ten yards is the immediate objective and there are four attempts (downs) permitted to attain this goal. However, a field goal is three points and a touchdown is six points.

In professional boxing, bouts take place in a "ring," which is surrounded by three strands of rope. Rounds consist of three minutes of fighting. A comparison of American and European practices once again reveals the American bias. Whereas fights in Great Britain and most of continental Europe are judged by the referee alone, in the United States the winner is determined by a referee and two judges, i.e., by three votes.

One could find many additional examples from other American sports, but perhaps most striking are the following points. In many instances, only the first three participants to finish a race receive official recognition. Similarly, in horse racing the three possibilities are win, place, and show. Noteworthy also is the fact that in many American games there is more than the binary possibility of winning or losing. The third alternative, that is, drawing or tying, allows the choices "win, lose, or draw," which is consistent with trichotomic patterning. Even the partisan cheers at athletic events often consist of three words, e.g., fight, team, fight, hold that line, get that ball.

Another form of spectacle, the circus, though not strictly speaking a game, provides a rather striking example of trichotomy. Besides the obvious difference between a one-ring show and a three-ring circus, the latter being an excellent example of the "three-in-one" type of trichotomy, among American circus performers there has historically been a burning desire to do things in triplicate. Specifically, there were attempts to "turn a triple somersault from a trapeze bar to a catcher's hands as a grand finale of the flying return act" and to "do a triple from a springboard" (May, 1932:249). The goal, though culturally appealing, was extremely difficult physically and a host of would-be triplers actually broke their necks in attempting this feat (May 1932:255). The existence of trebling in circus acts and of the "three-in-one" tent show may serve to illustrate how a particular widespread pattern of culture can be manifested in a single aspect of culture, an aspect which might easily be overlooked.

Another revealing aspect of folk culture concerns naming conventions. Perhaps the trichotomy here is attributable in part to the theory and methodology of logical definition itself. In formal definitions, the trinary criteria are term, genus, and differentia. In any event, scientific names for plants and animals are often in trinomial form, giving genus, species, and variety. In American culture most individuals have three names, any of which may be converted into initials: John Fitzgerald Kennedy to JFK. Most formal documents have space for three names and individuals with only two names may be obliged to indicate "none" or n.m.i. (no middle initial) in the middle name slot. Significantly, it is the last or third name which is the principal identifier. The clumsiness of this sytem has led to the practice on many forms of requesting that the last name be given first. Organizations as well as individuals have three-word names. Typical titles of American organizations include: American Anthropological Association (AAA), American Medical Association (AMA), and Ku Klux Klan (KKK). In some instances, the organization's title has more than three words, but there are still only three initials: Daughters of the American Revolution (DAR), Parents and Teachers Association (PTA), and Congress of Industrial Organizations (CIO). In addition to individuals and organizations, there are the names of projects—Tennessee Valley Authority (TVA)—of chemical products—trinitrotoluene (TNT)—and of tests—Thematic Apperception Test (TAT). The names of the *three* major television networks are: ABC, CBS, and NBC. In fact, often the set of three initials has virtually replaced the words for which they stand: COD, DNA, DOA, FBI, FOB, GOP, LSD, MGM, RIP, RPM, TKO, USO, and VIP. The item may be a local family expression such as FHB (family hold back), a command directing family members to refrain from taking too much food so that guests will have enough; however, most of the items are national in scope, as in the case of the common abbreviation for the whole country: USA. The preeminence of the three-letter gestalt is also suggested by SOS, in which the Morse Code signals consist of three dots, three dashes, and three dots.

A final bit of folkloristic evidence for the existence of a trichotomic pattern in American culture is provided by folk speech. The model for America's rhetorical heritage includes such triple constructions as *veni, vidi, vici* (and it was surely no accident that all Gaul was divided into three parts) or *liberté, égalité, fraternité*. Small wonder that American political style favors: life, liberty, and the pursuit of happiness; a government of the people, by the people, and for the people. Political slogans likewise may consist of three words: I Like Ike; We Shall Overcome. But nonpolitical folk expressions are equally three-structured: beg, borrow, or steal; bell, book, and candle; blood, sweat, and tears; cool, calm, and collected; fat, dumb, and happy; hither, thither, and yon; hook, line, and sinker; hop, skip, and jump; lock, stock, and barrel; me, myself, and I; men, women, and children; ready, willing, and able; signed, sealed, and delivered; tall, dark, and handsome; Tom, Dick, and Harry; and wine, women, and song. Railroad crossing signs warn motorists to "stop, look, and listen." Advertising clichés manifest the same structure. A skin cream advertisement maintains: "she's lovely, she's engaged, she uses Pond's." The breakfast cereal Rice Krispies is represented by "Snap, Crackle, and Pop." Commercial products such as SOS scouring pads and 3-in-1 Oil use three in their names, while others claim to have an essential three-initial ingredient (Shell gasoline has TCP) or to operate on three levels (such as fighting headaches three ways). Superman, a mass media folk hero for American children, is introduced in threes: "Faster than a speeding bullet, more powerful than a locomotive, able to leap tall buildings at a single bound. It's a bird! It's a plane! It's Superman!" Superman's own formula is "Up, up, and away."

Many American verbal rituals are in the same tradition. The various countdowns before the starting point of events may be in threes: ready, set, go; or ready, aim, fire. The auctioneering phrases "Going once, going twice, sold" and "Going, going, gone" are examples. There is also the barker's cry: "Hurry, hurry, hurry," often followed by "Step right up." American judicial rituals also provide illustrations. The cry of "hear ye" or "oyez" repeated three times is one, while the oath sworn by a witness is another. A witness is sworn by asking him to repeat "truth" three times, as he must do when he swears to "tell the truth, the whole truth, and nothing but the truth." Similarly, in wedding ritual, there is the promise to "love, honor, and obey."

There are many more examples from American folk speech. Some are in rhyme: "First is worst, second the same, but third is best of all the game." Some are not: "A minute in your mouth, an hour in your stomach, a lifetime on your hips"; or the Army credo, one version of which directs, "If it moves, salute it! If it doesn't move, pick it up! If you can't pick it up, paint it!" Even more interesting is the American tendency to build triple constructions from original single ones. Thus starting from "Those who can, do," one moves to add, "Those who can't teach". In final form, one has "Those who can, do; those who can't, teach; and those who can't teach, teach teachers!" The same pattern is reflected in a popular American leave-taking formula: "Be good." The second stage: "If you can't be good, be careful" is followed by the third: "If you can't be careful, have fun" (or "name it after me").

It is not just in American folklore that the trichotomic and trebling tendency is found. Almost every aspect of American culture is similarly three-patterned. One may examine food, clothing, education, social organizations, religion, time, or any other aspect of American culture and one will find abundant examples of trichotomy. Yet, most Americans are unaware of the pervasiveness of this pattern. It might therefore be worthwhile to observe a small portion of this patterning.

Americans customarily eat three meals a day (at morning, noon, and night). One must remember that three meals a day is by no means a universal custom. Moreover, while the actual number of artifacts employed to move the food from a container to the mouth may vary with the kind of meal and its formality, there are only three basic implements: knife, fork, and spoon. With respect to silverware, it is of interest that Emily Post, an authority on American etiquette, states that one of the important differences between place settings in formal and informal dining concerns the number of forks. On formal occasions, there should be no more than three forks (and three knives), whereas in informal dining, the three-fork limit is absent. In many American homes the sets of china include three plate sizes: bread and butter, luncheon, and dinner. While the number of courses served at a meal is, like the number of eating implements, determined in part by the occasion and place, one might conceivably consider that dinners served in average restaurants consist of three parts: soup or appetizer;

entree with vegetable or salad; and dessert with coffee. (One might define the segments of the continuum of a meal served in a restaurant on the basis of the number of times the waiter or waitress removes dishes or brings a new set of food items to the table.) In any event, while the number of courses is admittedly open to question, it is true that entrees are commonly divided on menus into meat, poultry, and fish. And it is equally true that patrons order their steak to be cooked rare, medium, or well-done. The beverage choice may be "coffee, tea, or milk." If an alcoholic beverage were desired, the choice might be beer, wine, or whiskey. Noteworthy is one dessert commonly served in restaurants, Neapolitan ice-cream with its three flavor layers: chocolate, strawberry, and vanilla.

Of theoretical interest is the fact that the smallest detail may reveal the same patterning present in larger aspects of culture. Such a detail is the cutting of sandwiches. While it is true that the cutting of sandwiches is almost always binary, the way in which sandwiches are cut in half may be significant. In restaurants sandwiches are usually halved with a diagonal cut so that the patron is presented with two triangular halves. At home, however, sandwiches are often cut to form two rectangles. The point is that when the sandwiches are cut into rectangles, there is no opposition to the basic binary division, but rather a reinforcement of this pattern. The rectangle has four sides which consist of *two* pairs of parallel lines, i.e., its length and its width. In contrast, when the sandwiches are cut into two triangular sections, the resultant three-sided figures represent trinary, not pure binary division. Note also that on the rarer occasions when sandwiches are divided into four rather than two sections, the same kind of 'restaurant-home' patterning prevails. In a restaurant the sandwich is normally divided by means of two diagonal cuts into four *triangular* sections:

At home, the mother making smaller sandwich sections for her younger children is more likely to divide the sandwich into four square sections:

From this, one might be led to hypothesize a possible association of "two" with informal occasions as opposed to the association of "three" with more formal occasions. In any case, sandwiches, surely a very popular item on the American menu, consist of two bread covers and a "middle". Sometimes the "middle" consists of three components, such as bacon, lettuce, and tomato (the BLT sandwich). The popularity of the club sandwich or triple decker, in which three slices of bread are used, is also worth noting.

Clothing is as rewarding a subject as food for the study of cultural patterns. As noted earlier, many articles of clothing come in three sizes: small, medium, and large. Moreover, generally speaking, American clothing is worn in three layers. Beneath the layer visible to one's fellows lie *under*garments (e.g., underwear). For outside wear and for warmth, one may don such outergarments as an *over*coat. Thus with respect to any one part of the body, for example, the feet, one might find socks, shoes, and overshoes. That this is a manifestation of culture patterning is suggested by the fact that not all cultures prescribe three layers of clothing. Socks and underwear are not universal. One is tempted to suggest that the body is divided into three basic parts for clothing purposes. In terms of standard indoor apparel, one ordinarily covers the feet, the lower torso up to the waist, and the upper torso above the waist. In men's clothing, for example, these three parts are dressed separately. Shoes and socks are put on after shorts and trousers. Undershirt and shirt clothe the third unit of the body. Although stylistic features do vary, men's sport jackets more often than not have three buttons down the front and often, though not always, there are three buttons sewn on the cuffs of the jacket. The usual number of outside pockets on such jackets is three and in the upper one of these pockets, one may place a handkerchief. The handkerchief may be folded into a triangle so that one point protrudes or, in a fancy dress variant, the handkerchief may be folded so that three points protrude.

The subject of folding is a most fascinating microcultural detail. For example, a binary versus trinary distinction occurs with respect to folding letters. Personal or social letter paper should be folded once, thus forming two parts. In contrast, business letter paper is ordinarily folded twice, thus "dividing" one letter into three parts (Post 1960:503). Note that the two-part letter is informal and the three-part letter is formal, a distinction paralleling one made previously in connection with alternative ways of cutting sandwiches. (The association of tripartite division with formality is also manifested in the ritual folding of the American flag into triangles on ceremonial occasions.) The outside of the envelope provides further data. On the front of the envelope, one writes the address of the person to whom the letter is to be sent and this address is frequently divided into three parts. On the first of the three lines, one puts the addressee's name, usually preceded by one of three titles: Mr., Mrs., or Miss, e.g., Mr. Alan Dundes. The second line typically has a number, a street name, and the word *street* or its equivalent, e.g., 985 Regal Road. The third line consists of city, state, and ZIP code (or zone number), e.g., Berkeley, California 94708. The two versus three distinction occurs on the first line. The use of two names may indicate a close and personal relationship between the sender and addressee, while the use of three names or two names plus the middle initial very probably indicates that there is some social distance and a certain amount of formality in the relationship. (The most intimate relationship, that signalled by a reciprocal "first name" arrangement, is of course not feasible in written as opposed to spoken tradition.) The formalizing effect of the presence of a third party upon a previous two-party group is also relevant (Simmel). (Cf. the folk judgment: two's company, three's a crowd!)

Some examples of American material culture have already been discussed, but there are many more. Traffic lights are usually divided into three parts: red/stop, yellow/caution, and green/go. Superhighways commonly have three lanes (the middle one of which contributes to a metaphor for American political positions: left, right, and middle of the road). Freeway signs often list the next three exits. Standard gear shifts in automobiles have traditionally been divided into forward, neutral, and reverse. While this might appear to be necessary, the further division of forward into first, second, and third gears is not. Even the modern automatic shift systems have a low gear and two drive positions. Some makes of cars come in three degrees of quality, although obviously the idea of first-rate, second-rate, and third-rate is disguised.

Moving away from automobiles, we may note some other examples of American technological culture. Until recently most record players and tape recorders had three speeds; there are three major types of motion picture film (8, 16, and 35 millimeter); stoves and window fans may have settings of low, medium, and high; toasters frequently have settings for light, medium, and dark; modern light bulbs have three settings for three degrees of brightness; and typewriters have single, double, and triple spacing. Cold drink vending machines usually offer three choices and one may make a choice by depositing a nickel, dime, or quarter. In slot machine gambling, the winning combination may be three of a kind, e.g., three lemons.

The pattern is also found in the telephone. On modern telephones, one finds that on the dials there are groups of three letters which correspond to one finger slot. Moreover, the United States and Canada have recently been divided into more than one hundred telephone areas, each identified by a three-digit area code. By means of this system, DDD (Direct Distance Dialing) has been established. Other three-centered features include the three-digit numbers for information (411) or repair (611), not to mention the standard basic time unit of telephone calls: three minutes. While the telephone is not as obvious an example as the three-color American flag, it is influenced by the same general culture pattern.

The American educational system reflects the pattern too, with its breakdown into primary, secondary, and higher education. It is in primary or elementary school that the three R's (Reading, 'Riting, and 'Rithmetic) are taught. Higher education consists of three degrees: bachelor's, master's, and doctoral. In colleges where a credit system is employed, the usual number of credits needed to be promoted is thirty, a multiple of three. Most college courses are worth three credits and they ordinarily meet three times or three hours a week. The college school year is divided into two semesters, Fall and Spring, plus a summer session. (A trimester scheme, in which the three school year units are equal, is in effect at a few colleges.) Frequently, a "social organizational" distinction is made between freshmen and upperclassmen, with the latter consisting of three classes: sophomore, junior, and senior. (The alternate distinction of lower division versus upper division is in the binary cultural category and provides an illustration of the dichotomy-trichotomy choice.) Interestingly enough, this scheme parallels the professorial rankings in which at least linguistically there is a distinction between "instructor" and the upper three ranks: assistant professor, associate professor, and (full) professor. While at college, a student may specialize in the humanities, the social sciences, or the natural sciences. If he distinguishes himself, he may receive his bachelor's degree *cum laude*, *magna cum laude*, or *summa cum laude*. In graduate schools, doctoral candidates may be examined in three major fields of specialization and their thesis committees consist of at least three members. Even educational philosophy and methodology is three-bound. One teaching technique consists of "Preview, Teach, and Review," which keeps its tripartite form in an analogous folk pedagogical principle: "Tell 'em what you're going to tell 'em, tell 'em, and tell 'em what you told 'em."

American social organization, like American education, is under the influence of the pattern. The continuum of the American population is divided into upper, middle, and lower classes. These distinctions have even been further refined so that the upper class yields upper-upper, middle-upper, and lower-upper. In the same way, American intellectual levels are highbrow, middlebrow, and lowbrow. American government is divided into three branches: executive, legislative, and judiciary. While the legislative branch is bicameral, it is of interest that senators are elected for six-year terms with a stagger system so that only one third can be changed at one time. In terms of sociopolitical geographical units, most Americans feel loyalty to their community, their state, and their country.

Perhaps the best example of trinary social organization is found in the American military system, which consists of the Army, Navy, and Air Force. With a supreme Secretary of Defense, one has a prime illustration of the division of a unity into three parts, a secular parallel to the sacred Trinity. Each of the services has a system of rank based in part upon three. In the Navy, for example, the three initial grades are: Seaman Recruit (one stripe), Seaman Apprentice (two stripes), and Seaman (three stripes). The sequence of unrated men, that is, SR, SA, and SN, does not continue; instead a new sequence begins: Third Class Petty Officer (one chevron), Second Class Petty Officer (two chevrons), and First Class Petty Officer (three chevrons). Although there is a Chief Petty Officer grade, his uniform and status are quite different from PO3, PO2, and PO1, different enough so that the apparent binary split between "officers" and "men" is in fact trinary: officers, chiefs, and men. This trichotomy is even more obvious when the criteria of separate messing and berthing and the extension of privileges (e.g., the time of the expiration of liberty or shore leave) are taken into account. A threefold division of officers is less obvious (and there is, of course, a system of four stripes rather than three) but junior officers include: Ensigns, Lieutenants Junior Grade, and Lieutenants. Senior officers include Lieutenant Commanders, Commanders, and Captains. Flag officers include Rear, Vice, and Full Admirals.

Army social organization is similar, although triangular infantry organization was replaced in 1957 by a pentomic plan. However, historically, Army units have been based on a three-in-one breakdown (Lease, 1919:67). A battalion consisted of three rifle companies, a rifle company of three rifle platoons, and a rifle platoon of three squads. A strong survival of triangular organization is found in the Boy Scouts, the American analog of primitive puberty initiation societies. The ranks include tenderfoot, second class, and first class scouts. Thereafter, the accumulation of merit badges and the satisfaction of various requirements permit a scout to attain the ranks of Star, Life, and Eagle Scout. An Eagle Scout may, upon the earning of additional merit badges, be awarded Eagle Palms: a Bronze Palm (5 badges), a Gold Palm (10 badges), or a Silver Palm (15 badges). The ritual use of three is also explicit in such items as: a triangular neckerchief; a Scout badge whose design is the *fleur-de-lis;* the Scout sign, a gesture whose most salient characteristic is three upstretched fingers; the Scout handclasp, accomplished by extending the left hand with the three middle fingers outstretched; and the Scout Oath, which consists of three parts.

Military material culture, so to speak, and military ritual demonstrate the identical pattern. Whether it be ship division into Forward, Amidships, and Aft or the color of anchor chain paint markings (to indicate how much chain is out) into red, white, and blue fifteen-fathom lengths, the trichotomic principle prevails. Military music, that is to say, bugle calls, is based upon three notes, the triad. Noteworthy also is the use of fanfares on ritual or formal occasions. There are either three trumpets playing the tones of the triad in unison or playing three-part harmony. Moreover, it may not be amiss to point out that in terms of bugle-playing technique, the most frequently used method of increasing tonguing speed is known as triple-tonguing. Even more pertinent to the present inquiry is occurrence of triple meter. Ternary time is not common in primitive music, and thus its presence in Western and American music is all the more striking. Besides the glaring example of waltz time, there is the rhythm employed in military ritual drumming. For instance, one pattern is based upon a series of three beats.

This may be contrasted with typical ritual drumming patterns of American Indian culture in which the pattern number is most often four. One such is four beats with the first beat heavily accented. Note well that the concept of the triplet itself is quite a remarkable example of trichotomy. It is in essence the substitution of three notes in place of one. Although ⅜ does not equal ¼, culturally sanctioned and conditioned aesthetics permit, if not encourage, the substitution of three eighth notes in place of one quarter-note beat.

Nonmusical examples of military ritual include the sentry's challenge "Halt, who goes there?" "Advance and be recognized," and "Pass." At Officer's Candidate School (OCS) officer trainees during their three months' sojourn (="ninety-day wonders") learn of the three types of court-martial: summary, special, and general. They may also learn that the final act of military funerals is the firing of three volleys. (One wonders if the act of an assassin in firing three shots at the President is purely fortuitous and one wonders further about the statement of the assassin that he meant to fire three shots instead of one!) The twenty-one gun salute for the President appears to be a combination of two sacred numbers—twenty-one is thrice seven.

The occurrence of three-symbolism in American religion is almost too obvious to require mention. In American culture, three major faiths are distinguished: Catholicism, Protestantism, and Judaism. Judaism can be broken down into three types, Orthodox, Conservative, and Reform. Of course, the Old and the New Testaments provide numerous examples. Noah, who had three sons, sent the dove out of the three-storied ark three times. (See Lehmann 1914:18; and Lease 1919:66 for other Old Testament examples.) Christian examples include the three Magi, Satan's three temptations of Christ, Peter's three denials of Christ, the three crucifixions at Calvary, the three Marys, the three nails, the three days intervening between the burial and the resurrection, and Christ's age of thirty-three. After the resurrection, Christ showed himself three times to his disciples (John 21:14) and asked Peter three times "Lovest thou me?" (John 21:17). Of

course, the ultimate charter for belief in three is the concept of the
Trinity, with its sacred confirmation of the notion of three-in-one.
Christian culture includes the triptych, such mottoes as "faith, hope,
and charity", and a three-movement ritual gesture starting at the
forehead to make the sign of the cross. As for American religions, one
can see that the Mormons' reverence of the three Nephites is just as
patterned as the addition of the concept of Purgatory in Catholicism to
form a third alternative to the previously binary Heaven and Hell.

The nature of culture is such that if one finds a pattern in social
organization and religion, one is likely to find that pattern manifested
in time and language (or vice versa, of course). Whorf, in his celebrated analysis of the relation of thought and behavior to language,
made special mention of the cultural relativity of time concepts. While
his statement "The three-tense system of SAE (Standard Average
European) verbs colors all our thinking about time" (1964:143) does
lean perhaps a little too far in the direction of linguistic determinism,
the keen insight is a valid one. It is of considerable historical interest
that Brinton made the following statement in 1894: "The two universal categories of the understanding (or modes of perception), Space
and Time, invariably present themselves in a threefold aspect: Time
as the Past, the Present, the Future, *as expressed in the grammar of every
language;* Space, as Length, Breadth, and Thickness; or, with reference to position, Above, Beneath, and Here. (1894:169, emphasis
added). Brinton saw the relationship between grammatical categories
and concepts of time. His error lay in assuming the universality of his
own particular native categories. Certainly in American culture, the
continuum of time (and admittedly the concept of continuum is itself
culturally relative) is segmented into past, present, and future. The
day may be divided binarily into night and day, but dawn and
twilight provide middle terms at the two junctures. Day is also divided into morning, noon, and night. Moreover, the twenty-four hour
day is also subject to tripartition. In certain types of work, e.g., in
hospitals, there are commonly three eight-hour work shifts. Noteworthy also is the formal way of referring to a particular day. The reference consists of three parts: month, day, and year, e.g., January 1,
1968, or 1/1/68. The principal time indicators, the watch and the
calendar, refer to three units. The average watch has three hands:
hour, minute, and second. Calendars indicate day, month, and year.
It is of interest that many calendars, in addition to displaying the

current month on any one page, also provide small displays of the month immediately preceding and the month which is to follow. This symbolizes a concern with both past and future while living in the present.

The past, present, and future trichotomy remains constant no matter what the time unit is. Whether one is concerned with day, week, month, or year, there is yesterday, today, and tomorrow. The limiting nature of three is demonstrated by the fact that if one wishes to refer to, let us say, days other than those three, one must do so in reference to the two extremes, e.g., the day before yesterday, the day after tomorrow. There is no independent term available for measures outside of the basic three. In some instances, even dependent terms outside of the limiting three are lacking. Thus one can say last night, tonight, and tomorrow night, but while one can refer easily to the night before last, one cannot with equal idiomatic facility speak of the night after tomorrow night. With weeks, months, or years, one can employ "last, this, and next," and thus weeks falling outside the extremes are the week before last and the week after next. Curiously enough, the same type of structure found in time applies to trinary linear kinship terminology. Ego has parents (=yesterday) and he has children (=tomorrow). Linear relatives beyond these two extremes must be named in reference to one of the two extremes, e.g., grand-*parents* or grand-*children*. Moreover, in either direction, there is something of a trinary terminological limit. Ego has parents, grandparents, and great-grandparents, generational distinctions being signalled by a distinct prefix. Additional distinctions can be made only by successive repetition of the last prefix, e.g., great-great-grandparents. The same holds for ego's children, grandchildren, and great-grandchildren. Note also the incremental repetition of one to three words in parent (1), grandparent (2), and great-grandparent (3). The time-kinship parallel is also obvious in American values. In a scheme like past, present, and future (or man, woman, and child), it is the third and last term which is valued most. Americans are future-oriented and, to the amazement of their enemies, they tend to forget about the past. Similarly, they are child-oriented and they tend to forget about their elders, banishing them to old-age homes or communities.

Still another time trichotomy stems from regarding noon as a midpoint. Time is denoted in reference to noon inasmuch as A.M. and P.M. are before and after noon respectively. In the same fashion, historical

time in American culture is measured with respect to the birth of
Christ. Years are either B.C. or A.D. However, the intial points of reference are separate from the periods of "before" and "after," just as the
present is in theory distinct from the past and the future. Thus noon
is neither A.M. nor P.M. Twelve o'clock is ambiguous and one is required to say twelve midnight or twelve noon. It should be noted that
in Europe generally, an unambiguous *four*-digit time indicator system
is employed. The practical advantages of a four-digit symbol such as
1530 over a three-digit 3:30 are obvious—there are two three-thirties
daily—and this is probably why the American military has adopted
the more efficient four-digit system. Incidentally, a possible
mathematical-logical analogue for the "before" and "after" terms in
reference to an initial point is provided by the usual ways of relating
one term to another. Either a equals b; a is less than b, or a is greater
than b. Distinctions such as a is slightly less than b or a is much less
than b are not culturally defined as relevant or significant. There are
only the three possibilities. Similarly we have three ways of relating
man to nature, man subjugated to nature (less than); man in nature
(equal); and man over nature (greater than); in interpersonal relations,
an individual is inferior (or subordinate), equal, or superior (or
superordinate) to another.

The discussion of time is in part a discussion of the terminology of
time and is thus a discussion of language. In any case, the very nature
of the Sapir-Whorf hypothesis would make one suspect that if
trichotomy were a pattern of American culture, it would also be found
in American English. However, the greater part of Whorf's own consideration of English suggests that English has primarily binary features. Whorf emphasizes that there are basically nouns and verbs
(1964:215), with the nouns of two sorts: individual nouns and mass
nouns (1964:140). Whorf also draws attention to the fundamental
categorical distinction between singular and plural. All this leads him
to see some of the linguistic correlates of the strong tradition of
philosophical dualism in Western civilization and he cites the example
of the dichotomy of form and substance (1964:141). (He might also
have cited active/passive, mind/body, spirit/flesh, and many other
polarities.) While Whorf is undoubtedly correct in his fundamentally
binary analysis there are some trinary features besides the three-tense
system which he might have mentioned. The pronouns are first person, second person, and third person. (The names of these distinctions

are themselves part of the pattern.) In modern English there are no more than three distinct forms of any one pronoun, e.g., he, his, him. Third person nominative singular is divided into he, she, and it, corresponding to the genders masculine, feminine, and neuter. Hoijer's argument (1954:97) that this is strictly a grammatical survival with no semantic correlate is somewhat beside the point, even assuming he is correct. Whether it is actually part of linguistic structure or whether it is simply part of what traditional grammarians say is linguistic structure, the fact remains that in our educational system, the distinction between the three genders is made. What members of a culture think about their language (i.e., folk linguistics) can influence other aspects of culture probably almost as much as the actual linguistic patterning. Linguists with their concern for the latter have tended to ignore folk linguistics, that is, folk analytical categories. Brown (1960:342) has put the matter well in her proposition that "many of the perceptions we derive from language do not arise from anything inherent in the structure of the language itself, but as the result of what we have been *taught* about it". That American grammarians analyze English sentences into actor/action/goal or subject/predicate/object is important culturally, regardless of whether or not this is in fact an accurate delineation of English structure. Grammarians also distinguish simple, compound, and complex sentences. In punctuation rules, one finds three major medial marks: comma, semicolon, and colon, whose orthographic symbolism itself reflects trichotomic structuring (*a*, *ab* and *b*). There are also three principal terminal marks: period, question mark, and exclamation point. The latter marks are allegedly indicators of the three major sentence types: declarative, interrogative, and exclamatory. In another instance of orthographic symbolism, one finds that ellipsis, an indefinite quantity, is signalled by the definite convention of using three periods or asterisks.

Of course, there are actual trinary structural features of English. One of the most important of these is the number of degrees employed with modifiers—specifically, the comparative and superlative. One might even go so far as to conjecture that it is the "good, better, best" paradigm, perhaps more than any other single factor, which has encouraged the concept formation of three classes or three types of merchandise sizes, quality, etc. In a recent study, Deonna has brilliantly pointed out (1954:415) that three is in part a semantic derivative of the superlative degree and cites the roots *ter*, *tri*, and *tre* as evidence. In French, for example, *trés* is a superlative. (In English, one might think of *terr*ific and *tre*mendous. Moreover, etymologies of *triumph*—and *trump* in the game of bridge—might show that three was all-powerful, just as the origins of *terminus*, in the sense of limit and eternity—ternity as an obsolete form of trinity—in the sense of time without limit, or past plus present plus future, or as a synonym for the deity—who is tripartite—may stem from an archaic *ur*-three root.) In any event, Whorf's distinction between nouns and verbs notwithstanding, tripartition in English is an important structural feature. The division of time and history into threes would appear to be influenced by verb action tense (past, present, future), while the division of objects or object qualities into three would seem to be related to the degrees of comparison (correct, more correct, most correct). Whether the relationship of linguistic features to other aspects of culture is causal or only correlative, the fact there are trichotomies of verb tense, modifier degree, pronoun category, and gender tends to support the notion that patterning underlying a culture generally will be evident in language.

That trichotomy is a cognitive category in the sense that individuals tend to perceive in threes is suggested by the results of experiments in gestalt psychology. Continua involving both sight and sound were segmented into groups of three (Köhler 1959:83, 89). However, experiments such as the classic pioneering ones made by Wertheimer (1923) did not take the pattern number three into account. Subjects did tend to see things in threes, but Wertheimer attributed his results to such factors as organization (in terms of proximity) and the grouping of similar forms (such as three dots opposed to three circles). The results might be more a matter of "three" gestalt, an explanation which would no doubt have delighted Wertheimer. Subjects might, for example, see threes even in a continuous line of dots. In any case, it is difficult to isolate such variables as proximity and form similarity when *three* figures are used in the experiment.

This brings us to an important theoretical point and one of the primary purposes of the present paper. Thus far, an attempt has been made to show that the pattern of trichotomy does in fact exist as a native category in Western and, more specifically, American culture. What remains to be seen, however, is how such a native category can unconsciously affect the formation of supposedly objective analytical categories. This is the really insidious part of cultural patterning. No individual can escape his culture and its built-in cultural cognitive categories. Yet many individuals think they have escaped, and they claim to have described the nature of objective reality in culture-free terms. But often what scientists and scholars present as bona fide analytical categories are in fact ethnocentric extensions of their own native categories. While a few analysts specify that their trichotomic models are solely for heuristic purposes (and certainly a tripartite scheme would have both mnemonic and aesthetic value in American culture), many do not do so, and the reader is led to believe that the trichotomic model comes from the data, not from the analyst. Having identified a folk pattern of trichotomy in a variety of aspects of American culture, one is in an excellent position to perceive the arbitrary and culturally determined nature of many of our accepted "objective" analytic schemes.

No doubt there will be those who will be offended by the implication that their analytical categories are but folk or native categories in disguise. They may claim that the analytical categories in question really do correspond to objective reality. (This would also be the argument of those defending the notion of the Trinity.) Others, with a penchant for nit-picking, will be quick to point out that some of the analytical schemes here presented have long been discarded. The point is that all of the following analytical schemes did or do have some standing in American culture. Not just Gaul, but the whole world is divided into three parts. There is animal, vegetable, and mineral. (These and other categories are so deeply embedded in our culture that it may be difficult for some to see their arbitrariness.) Yet is there an absolute difference between plant and animal life or is there a continuum? Similar examples may be taken from almost any discipline. Entomologists define insects as those members of the phylum Arthropoda in which the body is divided into three parts: head, thorax, and abdomen. The question is: are insects truly morphologically tripartite or do we simply see them as tripartite? And what of the trichotomy explicit in the metamorphic continuum of some insects into larva, pupa, and adult? Are the three stages simply a reflection of the same cultural convention which suggests that literature has a beginning, a middle, and an end or that plays commonly be written in three acts?

At least we are consistent, for all the world is conceived and perceived in tripartite terms—*by us*. The continuum of states of matter is

neatly divided into solid, liquid, and gas. The projection of this
scheme to the entire earth results in distinguishing land (solid), sea
(liquid), and air (gas). These in turn are subdivided. The air or atmosphere may be broken down into troposphere, stratosphere, and iono-
sphere, while the earth may be divided into three types of climate
zones: frigid, temperate, and torrid. (Cf. the spatial-geographical divisions such as North, Central (or Middle), and South America or the
East, the Middle West, and the West.) As the world is divided, so is
man. The human ear is divided into the outer, middle, and inner ear;
the brain into cerebrum, cerebellum, and medulla; the small intestine
into the duodenum, the jejunum, and the ileum. Are these divisions
any less arbitrary than the segmentation of human voice range continuum into soprano, mezzo-soprano, and alto (female), and tenor,
baritone, and bass (male)? But the issue is not just taxonomic or
classificatory. When physicians prescribe dosages in threes, e.g., one
pill every three hours or three pills a day, or when infants are given a
three-in-one DPT (diphtheria toxoid, pertussis vaccine, and tetanus
toxoid) shot or a series of three polio shots, the question is whether
this is the most efficacious procedure, medically speaking, or not.
Perhaps the ritual element is in fact an additional beneficial feature.

One can pick up an elementary textbook in any discipline and find
numerous instances of three-determined thinking. It is really astonishing to realize that anthropologists, students of cultural conditioning,
have been so culture-bound in their theoretical formulations. Among
the numerous versions of a three-stages-of-man theory (cf. Comte,
Hegel, and Vico), one thinks of Morgan's savagery, barbarism (which
was subdivided into Opening, Middle and Closing periods), and
civilization, and Frazer's stages of magic, religion, and science. Other
obvious examples of tripartition include Van Gennep's classic analysis
of rites of passage in which he distinguishes rites of separation, transition, and incorporation.

There is just as much three-conditioning evident in the other
branches of anthropology. In physical anthropology, the traditional
conventional number of races is three: Caucasoid, Mongoloid, and
Negroid, although the inadequacy of the classification is well known.
Similarly, European peoples are divided into northern, central, and
southern, that is, Nordic, Alpine, and Mediterranean. In the study of
body measurement and typology, tripartition is also found. (The folk
system of measuring females in terms of bust, waist, and hips is in the

same pattern.) In craniology, for example, the measurements of the various craniometric indices fall invariably into one of three categories (cf. Comas 1960:406–12), Archaeology is even more three-ridden. The three-age system of Stone, Bronze, and Iron is still in vogue (Heizer), but more important are the subdivisions of time periods. Ages are divided into three. Thus the Stone Age is commonly divided into Old, Middle, and New, i.e., Paleolithic, Mesolithic, and Neolithic. The Paleolithic can then be subdivided into Lower, Middle, and Upper Paleolithic. The Upper Paleolithic can then be broken down into Aurignacian, Solutrean, Magdalenian. If this weren't enough evidence to indicate that archaeologists are culture-bound, one should consult V. Gordon Childe's argument that tripartition is a necessary means of establishing chronological sequences in archaeology (1956:66) and that this is true, not because of any Hegelian metaphysics or trinitarian mysticism, but because of the very nature of the material to be seriated. The question is, of course, whether the method of tripartition is really dictated by the nature of the material or is it rather dictated by the nature of the culture of the archaeologist? If human history is a continuum, then the segmentation of a portion of that continuum into ages, stages, or levels is arbitrary.

Anthropology is typical insofar as the three-patterning of its scholarship is concerned. It would be easy to cite hundreds of examples from other disciplines. Yet anthropologists do not seem to have been aware of the pattern. Whorf, one of the pioneers in the study of the cultural conditioning of thought patterns, failed to see the influence of tripartition on his own work. His coinage of the three-word phrase "Standard Average European" is an example. His decision to compare *three* isolates of English—*clean, with, ramrod*—with *three* isolates from Shawnee would be another. (Note also his three-part figure in which he shows how one Hopi word equals three English words and how one English word equals three Eskimo words.) Another indication that anthropologists are not aware of their cultural propensity for tripartition is found in Edward Hall's *The Silent Language*. Hall, in collaboration with George L. Trager, developed an elaborate tripartite scheme which distinguished what were termed formal, informal, and technical levels. However, Hall, an expert on the implicit assumptions of various cultures, claimed that Americans had a bipolar way of analyzing data and that "the ease with which Americans tend to polarize their thoughts about events may make it difficult for them to embrace an approach which employs three categories rather than two" (1959:66).

Having demonstrated that the number three is a folk category in American culture, a folk category which has made inroads into the various analytic categories of academic disciplines, it remains to be seen what the meaning, if any, of the category is. It is one thing to describe a cultural category; it is another to speculate about its origin and meaning. Does the category stem from the family group of father, mother, and child? Is it a reflection of the divine nature of the universe as defined by trinitarian Christian doctrine? A Whorfian would no doubt place language rather than social organization or religion at the source. Thus a Whorfian might claim that the tense system, the first- second- third-person distinctions, and the good-better-best paradigm were the roots of the pattern. A Freudian would argue along different lines (Glenn). Freud suggested that the number three was a masculine symbol, the *phallus cum testiculis*.[1] This is most interesting in the light of Freud's own work: e.g. *Three Contributions to the Theory of Sex*, or the id, ego, superego classification. Incidentally, the standard kinship notation employed by anthropologists would tend to support Freud's view. The triangle represents a male while a circle represents a female. However, the convention of three as a masculine symbol is more probably a manifestation of the traditional symbolism of Western civilization than a cause or origin of trichotomy. Only if one were to argue that male as opposed to female thought was trichotomized and that male thought was a compensatory activity for not being able to give birth to children as females do could one make a case for a most hypothetical origin theory. The only child a man produces is a brainchild. His intellectual project serves as his "baby." His products bear his stamp, the number three, the mark of masculinity. Since the majority of Western constructs and classification schemes have been devised by men rather than women, this could account for the preoccupation with three.[2] This type of explanation would also make clear why aspects of American culture which are exclusively masculine, e.g., the military, the Boy Scouts, baseball, are especially three-ridden. (Note also that the Christian Trinity is all masculine. This would be further evidence that three is male creativity denying or replacing female creativity.) However, like most psychological explanations, this one is highly speculative. One must conclude that it is difficult, if not impossible, to state with any degree of certainty what the ultimate origins of trichotomy might be.

One thing is certain though, and that is that trichotomy is a pattern of American culture. Whether it is related to masculinity or male mental creativity or not, it is, and will probably continue to be, an important cognitive category in American (and Old World) culture. As for how individuals learn about the pattern, there are probably many sources. Three dimensions of space, the three tenses of time, and the good-better-best paradigm all exert some influence. But an American three-year-old has already been exposed to the category in folkloristic form, perhaps before he realizes the space, time, and linguistic features. For are there not three men in a tub? three bags of Baa Baa Black Sheep's wool? three little kittens who lost their mittens? three little pigs? Is not the third item called for by Old King Cole his fiddlers three? Is there an American child who has not heard the story of the three bears? This latter story is a narrative listing of trichotomies in which the mediating third term is invariably "just right." (Note that the third term is associated with the child bear rather than the mother and father bears.) The child is conditioned by his folklore to expect three and his culture does not disappoint him. Language, social organization, religion, and almost all other aspects of American culture confirm the pattern.

Trichotomy exists but it is not part of the nature of nature. It is part of the nature of culture. At this point, if anyone is skeptical about there being a three-pattern in American culture, let him give at least three good reasons why.

The Crowing Hen
and the Easter Bunny

Male Chauvinism in American Folklore

——————————⟫•₿ ₿•⟪——————————

Popular prejudices and stereotypes nourished by
oral tradition have affected the course of history.
—RICHARD M. DORSON
American Folklore and the Historian

I wish you luck
I wish you joy
I wish you first a baby boy.

And when his hair
begins to curl
I wish you then a baby girl.

If a woman comes to see you on the first day of the year before a man,
you will have bad luck.

Jack and Jill
went up the hill
to fetch a pail of water
Jack fell down
and broke his crown
and Jill came tumbling *after*.[1]

The male bias in American culture is not just reflected passively in
American folklore, it is also actively transmitted to each new generation of Americans, often unconsciously or unselfconsciously, through
folkloristic means. Whether it be an autograph book verse, a superstition, or a nursery rhyme, the pattern is unmistakable: male first,
female second.

Even the order of Jack and Jill (as opposed to Jill and Jack) is significant. With the possible exception of "ladies and gentlemen," most of the traditional verbal formulas consistently place males before females, e.g., king and queen (never queen and king); lord and lady; Mr. and Mrs.; his and hers (his or her); boys and girls; man, woman, and child. In American wedding ritual, the couple is pronounced "man and wife" by a male minister, priest, or rabbi. The pronouncement is not "wife and man" or "woman and husband." Furthermore, the term *wife* is by definition a term relative to the man whereas the term used for the groom, *man*, is a term which is independent (as opposed to a relativistic, dependent term such as *husband*).

While on the subject of the term *man*, I might note the psychological implications of the term *woman*. Apart from actual historical and etymological considerations, one might understand *woman* as being an extension or derivative of the basic term *man*. (Centuries ago there were various puns on woman as "man's woe.") In the same way, one could interpret *female* as being derived from *male*—just as *heroine* might be derived from *hero*. On the other hand, one could perfectly well interpret *woman* as a term including *man* just as *female* includes *male*. This would make men a diminished form of women! Possibly the folk interpretation held might be correlated with the sex of the holder of the opinion.

Among the other evidence of male chauvinism in American folk speech, one finds exclamations such as "Oh boy!" "Oh brother!" or "Man!" with no analogues of "Oh girl!" "Oh sister!" or "Woman!" Man-sized is something large and, generally speaking, largeness is associated with males. Compare a "big man" (as in "big man on campus") with the "little woman." The association of smallness with females might be explained on the basis of differences in stature, but such differences cannot account for the striking difference in terms of address: "Man" versus "Baby." Calling a woman "baby" as a term of affection does make her an infant in some sense. Perhaps this is analogous to employing "doll" as a term of address (cf. the phrase "guys and dolls"). "Babydoll" would combine both terms to emphasize the toylike or plaything nature of women as perceived by men. In the same way, the groom's carrying his new bride across the threshold emphasizes the dependent status of women. The strong male must carry the weak female—as though she were a chattel baby. (In symbolic terms, the male must carry her cleanly over the portal all by himself. It is as if to say that he takes all the responsibility for initial sexual entry.)

In investigating male chauvinism in American folklore, I am not considering folkloristic materials which apply equally to males and females. Actually, the vast majority of riddles, superstitions, and other genres probably do not differentiate or discriminate on a sexual basis. One need only examine cures for hiccoughs or warts or peruse the numerous signs of good and bad luck to see that most practices work equally well without regard to the sex of the participant. However, where the sex of the participant or the sex of one of the parties described in the item of folklore is an issue, one is likely to find an instance of preferential male bias. The presence of a woman on board ship or in a mine is alleged to be a cause of bad luck. It is the seventh son, or a "seventh son of a seventh son" who has special qualities more often than a seventh daughter or a "seventh daughter of a seventh daughter." There can, of course, be absolutely no question of the male bias in "It's a man's world" or the male chauvinism of "A woman's place is in the home."

One is tempted to suggest a distinction between sexual differentiation and sexual discrimination. The difficulty here is that what might appear on the surface to be more differentiation turns out upon further reflection to be an example of potential discrimination. For example, there are various traditional means which purport to foretell the sex of an unborn child. If the baby is carried high in some cases, low in others, it will be a boy. But the point is that the majority of these traditional divination techniques specifically refer to boys, not girls. The implication is clearly that boys are desired.

The wish for "first a baby boy" may be related in part to the patronymic custom, surely a classic example of male bias. Women in the same ritual marriage act already mentioned—in which, by the way, they are instructed to "love, honor, and *obey*" while men are asked only to "love, honor, and *cherish*"—have until fairly recently submitted to taking the family names of their husbands as their own. Psychologically, the bride thereafter belongs to her husband, as she previously belonged to her father. In this context, one can see that a bride retaining her "maiden" name is hardly full liberation, if that maiden name is her *father*'s. Full liberation might dictate that a bride keep her mother's name (even if that mother's name was a patronymic survival of a previous generation). In any event, under a strict patronymic system, a family name "dies out" if there is no male issue to carry on the name. It would be an error, I think, to blame the patronymic system per se as a root cause of male chauvinism. It is but one of many indicators of such bias, though it is perhaps a bit more obvious than some of the others I shall discuss.

If prediction of the sex of unborn children is not really neutral, what about the custom of boy babies wearing blue and girl babies wearing pink? Isn't that merely a traditional means of differentiating the sexes at an early age with no particular intent to discriminate? In fairness, one must take the associations of these colors into account. Even the dictionary definition of *pink* as a light tint of crimson, pale reddish purple, shows the bias. Adjectives such as *light* and *pale* coupled with the word *tint*, which implies a color of less than maximum chroma and which hints at something subdued or delicate, carry the message. Blue, in contrast, is a strong color, a primary color, a color associated with "true" (as in "true blue") and perhaps even with sexuality as in the name "Bluebeard!" In other words, the initial color code of the baby's dress signals the conventional sex-assigned behavioral norms. Boys are to be bold and brave, active and aggressive; girls are to be mild and meek, passive and put upon.

Some of the earliest folklore of childhood (e.g., dandling rhymes) serve to instruct both sexes with respect to the differential sex roles:

> This is the way the ladies ride
> Nimble, nimble, nimble, nimble;
>
> This is the way the gentlemen ride,
> A gallop a trop, a gallop a trot.[2]

The easy, gentle pace of the lady's riding style is contrasted with the rough, bouncy one of the gentleman. But perhaps the classic articulation of the prescribed differences between boys and girls is the following:

> What are little boys made of?
> What are little boys made of?
> Snips and snails
> And puppy-dogs' tails,
> That's what little boys are made of.

What are little girls made of?
What are little girls made of?
    Sugar and spice
    And everything nice,
That's what little girls are made of.

Aside from the fact that boys are discussed first, the compositional differences are clear-cut. In the English version, boys are made of frogs and snails.[3] The frog is a standard phallic symbol (as in the Frog Prince fairy tale) [AT 440] which relates how a frog finally succeeds in gaining access to the bed of a princess—and when kissed turns into a handsome prince). In the American versions, we typically find snails and puppy-dogs' tails. The extension of a snail's head and body from its shell might have phallic connotations as well. (The snail's head itself has suggestive horn-like tentacles.) The tail of a puppy dog is also an obvious body extension (much as the tail of a bull or the foot of a rabbit may serve as a phallic substitute).

In contrast, girls are sweet foodstuff—to be eaten. Another rhyme emphasizes the inherent sweetness of girls:

Boys are rotten
made out of cotton.

Girls are handy
made out of candy.

The socially sanctioned saccharine quality of females is confirmed later in life by such terms of endearment as sweetheart, honey bun(ch), sugar, sweetie, sweetie-pie, and the like. It is true that females can and do use these terms to address males, but certainly the early "sugar and spice" image would suggest that these terms were first used by males towards females after which the terms were used reciprocally by both sexes. (On the other hand, it is also possible that the very suggestion that males used the terms first is but another instance of male chauvinism, in this case an instance in folklore scholarship as opposed to the materials of folklore!) In this context, one can appreciate the large number of slang terms for the female or her genitals which draw upon dessert metaphors. Examples include cake, cheesecake, cookie, hair pie, and tart. It is reasonable to assume that such metaphors belong to precisely the same cultural pattern which

begins with little girls being made of sugar and spice. The basic association of females and food may go back to breast-feeding, but the
cultural insistence upon a girl's being a "dish," or the Americanism of
"motherhood and apple pie" or such food for matrimonial thought as
"the way to a man's heart is through his stomach" all tend to restrict
the range of female activity.

The image of domestic servitude as implied by homemaking and
housekeeping is also defined in folklore. It is no doubt an exaggeration
to suggest that a "housewife" is a woman married to a house. But
there are, after all, no "househusbands," though to be sure the initial
portion of the word "husband" means house![4] A representative illustration of the image of a woman as a pretty household drudge is the
following:

> I had a little hen,
>> The prettiest ever seen;
> She washed up the dishes
>> And kept the house clean.
> She went to the mill
>> To fetch some flour,
> And always got home
>> In less than an hour.
> She baked me my bread,
>> She brewed me my ale,
> She sat by the fire
>> And told a fine tale.[5]

One need only compare the image of the dutiful hardworking wife
in the above nursery rhyme with the content of a traditional technique
for obtaining a husband in the first place in order to see the consistency of the pattern. The technique, termed "Dumb Supper," is (or at
any rate was) fairly widespread in the United States. "Two girls
sweep the floor together, set the table, cook a meal, put it on the table,
then open the door and sit and wait. The guest who comes to the table
will be the future intended of one of them. This is called the 'Dumb
Supper.'"[6] The original meaning of "dumb" referred to the require-
ment of remaining silent—as ideal women were supposed to remain
silent. However, in the modern context of women's liberation, the
dumbness might more appropriately refer to the women who would
be foolish enough to accept such a passive, domestic role.

The passivity of the girl in the Dumb Supper who after a certain

point can do little more than wait for a man to arrive is also expressed
in fairy tales. A number of feminists have complained about the image
of women in fairy tales. Typically, heroines get themselves into
trouble and must then be rescued by males. The sleeping heroine, be
she Snow White or Sleeping Beauty, must remain passive until awak-
ened by the kiss of a prince charming.[7]

One of the most serious aspects of any stereotype is the extent to
which it reflects empirical reality. Whether the stereotype causes the
behavior or only mirrors it is not the point. Studies seem to indicate,
for example, that in playing tic-tac-toe, boys and "aggressive" girls
play to win while "conforming" boys and "feminine" girls often play
to draw.[8] In other words, many girls appear to have accepted the
passive, nonaggressive stereotype as a behavioral norm. Consider the
following autograph book verse:

> Here comes love
> Here comes marriage
> Here comes_____(girl's name)_____
> With a baby carriage.

This verse spells out the traditional time-honored *cursus honorum* for
women. No mention is made of a possible career or profession. There
are no alternative options. Women's fulfillment is presumed to come
through romantic love, marriage, and childbearing—in that order.
Note that these rhymes are normally written *by girls for girls!* This
suggests that the inculcation of male chauvinism is so firmly
entrenched that already by the end of elementary school, sex role
norms have been tacitly, passively accepted. Little girls do know
about different professional careers, e.g., rich man, poor man, beg-
garman, thief, doctor, lawyer, Indian chief; but as rich *man*, poor *man*
imply, these are career opportunities for men. A girl, according to the
folklore, does not become a doctor or lawyer; she can only hope for
enough good fortune to marry one! The crucial importance of marriage for women is also signalled by the numerous superstitions predicting permanent spinsterhood, not to mention the popular card
game "Old Maid."[9]

If the female path includes love, marriage, and childbearing, it does
not include sex. Sex is depicted as a male prerogative. Countless jokes

and idioms express the male's attempt to reduce females to sex objects, the hapless victims or prisoners of male sexual aggression: "Find 'em, fuck 'em, and forget 'em" or "Keep them barefoot, pregnant, and in the kitchen." The stereotype includes the well-known double standard whereby girls were supposed to refrain while boys were expected to indulge. Several "rhymes for tickling" reported by W. W. Newell in his *Games and Songs of American Children* show how early this portion of the stereotype is introduced to little girls:

> If you're a little lady, as I take you for to be
> You will neither laugh nor smile when I tickle your knee.

A girl who admits she enjoys sexual stimulation is clearly not a prospective wife. A male may seek a promiscuous female, but he will probably not marry her.

> Old maid, old maid, you'll surely be
> If you laugh or you smile while I tickle your knee.[10]

The double standard can be illustrated by several catches. For example, one asks a girl the question, "Do you know what virgins eat for breakfast?" The victim, thinking the question is a normal joking question or riddle, more than likely answers "No" and thereby implies that she is not a virgin. A more elaborate catch consists of a narrative purporting to explain how to play "Little Red Wolf."

> A boy and a girl are out parked on a lover's lane. The boy asks the girl if she would like to play Little Red Wolf. The girl says she has never heard of the game. The boy says it's easy and offers to teach her. She agrees to try it. First the boy says, "You take off your sweater and throw it in the back seat." The girl does this. "Next you take off your skirt and put it under the front seat." The game continues in this fashion until the girl has only a pair of panties left on. Now the boy says, "You take off your panties and put them in the, in the _____, the _____ [the narrator gestures as though he can't remember the term *glove compartment* — at which point if the tale is told properly, some member of the audience, preferably a girl, will try to assist the apparently faltering narrator by volunteering "glove compartment." The narrator then turns to the dupe and says, "Then *you* have played 'Little Red Wolf.'"]

In both of these catches, the female victim is forced to admit that she has engaged in sexual activity. Indeed, one could go so far as to argue that the very utilization of such catches by boys to girls constitutes a miniature structural model of a seduction attempt.

In contrast, catches designed for male victims stress impotence. Males who are expected to perform are shown to be incapable of such performance. One example consists of someone asking a male if he has heard of the latest scientific studies which have discovered a definite sign of impending impotence. When the victim indicates no, the initial questioner tells him—in an unintelligible whisper or mumble, "It's deafness." The victim then asks "What?" whereupon the victimizer loudly shouts, "IT'S *DEAFNESS!*" The pretense that it was deafness on the part of the victim rather than the whisper/mumble which required the repetition of the answer obviously implies the impending impotence of the victim.

Another catch designed for male victims involves a curious physiological or neurological trait involving the fourth finger of either hand. The prospective male dupe is told to place his thumb on top of the nail of the pinkie of the same hand and to extend the middle three fingers (much as one would do in making the "Scout Sign" in Boy Scout ritual). The extended three fingers are then placed on a flat surface such as a table or desk top so that they lie pressed down hard against the surface. The victim is then told that he will be asked three questions in succession. The questioner will point to one of the fingers after each question. If the answer to the question is yes, the dupe is told that he should wiggle the appropriate finger to so indicate. If the answer is no, the finger should remain still. Starting with the index finger and moving successively to the ring finger, the questioner asks such questions as: Are you male? Do you like sex? and Are you good at it? Since many males are physically unable to move their fourth fingers under these circumstances, the male dupe is usually forced into the embarassing position of admitting sexual inadequacy.

In these catches, we find a reversal of sex norms. Girls are forced to admit that they have had sexual experience; boys are forced to admit that they are incapable of having sexual experience. Such folkloristic forms would appear to be unmistakable socializing carriers of peer group sexual values concerning the double standard, to wit, boys do and girls do not.

The double standard is not limited to adolescents. One need only compare the connotations and nuances of *bachelor* versus *old maid* for an unmarried person. The word *bachelor* in no way implies an absence of sexual activity whereas *old maid* does. Similarly, one might compare "dirty old man" versus "little old lady." Even an aged male is supposed to continue to attempt sexual adventures whereas comparably aged females are supposed to be sexless.

American legends also reflect the double standard, which insists that nice girls don't while nice boys are expected to "sow their wild oats." In a previous analysis of "The Hook,"[11] I tried to suggest that the couple in a parked car in a lover's lane demonstrated both male and female norms. The male hopes to seduce the young woman—it is he who is the hook-armed sex maniac escaped from a mental institution, mentioned by the voice of society or conscience in the radio news bulletin. However, the girl prevails upon her escort to "pull out fast" and take her home. Her honor is preserved and the dangerous hook is caught on the handle of her door or trapped in the closed window on her side of the car. In this legend frequently told by adolescent girls to their peers, the would-be male marauder is symbolically castrated. The double standard is there: boys will try to make out, to "go all the way"; girls should try to return home without having the hook penetrate.

The sexual significance of the car as a mobile bedroom surrogate during adolescence may also be involved in the equally popular legend of the "Vanishing Hitchhiker." Widely reported from all over the United States for the past thirty or forty years,[12] the legend could simply be an articulation of the fear of death. Each year there are hundreds of traffic fatalities and many parents of teenagers rightly worry about the possibility of an automobile accident in which their children might be injured or killed. In the legend, the hitchhiker is nearly always a young woman while the driver of the car is a young man. From this we might infer that it is not dangerous or unacceptable for young men to hitchhike, but that it is for young women. If one accepts the notion that many superstitions and legends are literalizations of metaphors,[13] one might read the vanishing hitchhiker legend as a literal reading of the idea that "a girl who tries to get picked up by a stranger is dead." The ghost's repeated vain attempts to return home further suggest that once a girl has been picked up, she cannot go home again. In the legend of "The Hook," the girl does not yield to temptation and she does return home safely. In the legend of the "Vanishing Hitchhiker," it is the active girl who initiates the encounter in the car with a perfect stranger and she does not return home safely. (In the double standard, only boys can seek out strangers, e.g., in the extreme case, prostitutes; but girls are not supposed to do this.) The punishment is death coupled with the endless repetition of the fruitless effort to return home.

One detail of the legend is also explicable in light of the present interpretation. In most versions, the concerned young man is left with the ghost's material token, a scarf or travelling bag. The reduction of the young woman to a travelling bag or a piece of clothing—such as a scarf which is wrapped around the head—is understandable in terms of the male chauvinistic sexual convention in which women are referred to by men as a single part, usually the vagina, as in "bag," "box," "cunt," "piece of ass." The ghost's leaving a token of herself, a piece of clothing, behind in the car surely suggests that it is something which she has lost and which has been lost permanently. The punishment for the original sin of having been picked up in the first place is ritual reenactment of losing one's token in a car.

Regardless of the validity of the above interpretation of the "Vanishing Hitchhiker," an interpretation which is, admittedly, highly speculative, it should be clear enough that male chauvinism attempts to dictate not only what women should do, but also what women should not do. The statement of the negative is just as important as the statement of the positive. Women should not only act like women (as prescribed and defined by males), but they should not try to act like men. A young girl who forsakes dolls for rough-and-tumble games may risk being called a tomboy. Later in life, after marriage, a woman who exercises decision-making qualities may be accused of "wearing the pants in the family." (The expression is also used by one male to another to indicate that a woman has usurped the traditional role of male dominance in a particular family.) Males assume that females would prefer to be males. "Kiss your elbow and you can turn into a boy."[14] (While it is sometimes reported that a boy can turn into a girl by kissing his elbow, it is evidently more commonly reported as a girl wishing to turn into a boy.)

Perhaps one of the most striking examples of male chauvinism with respect to women attempting to act like men involves a crowing hen. It's bad luck for a hen to crow and a crowing hen is a sign of death.[15] There are many, many versions of the couplet linking whistling maids and crowing hens:

> Whistling maids and crowing hens
> Never come to no good ends.

> A whistling maid and a crowing hen
> Is good to neither God nor man.

Occasionally one finds a version which would seem to reflect a feminist perspective:

> Girls that whistle and hens that crow
> Make their way wherever they go.[16]

But the vast majority of texts are negative. A woman who whistles is acting like a man just as a hen which crows is acting like a rooster. A mid-19th century English version couldn't be more explicit:

> Ill thrives the hapless family that shows
> A cock that's silent and a hen that crows.
> I know not which live more unnatural lives.
> Obeying husbands or commanding wives.[17]

From a male chauvinistic point of view, such a radical departure from the expected passive, docile, sex-stereotyped behavior norm is threatening. One superstition recommends a very specific course of remedial action. If a hen crows and you do not kill her, a member of the family will die within a year.[18] By implication, a woman who acts like a man is unnatural and should be eliminated.

As women who whistle are unnatural and dangerous, so dangerous whistling storms such as hurricanes are assigned female names. However, one of the most impressive folkloristic illustrations of the threatening female who assumes a male position is the witch. In conventional American sexuality, the most common position for sexual intercourse has the man on top and the woman on the bottom, a perfect male chauvinist model of social inequality! In witchcraft this is reversed, for it is frequently the witch who rides a man, for example, by transforming the male victim into a horse (cf. Motif G241.2.1). Even the witch riding on a broomstick indicates her riding on top of and controlling the movements of a symbolic male phallus.

Even more curious than the male insistence that women stay in their place and utterly refrain from acting like males is the fact that males do not place similar restrictions upon their own behavior. In other words, although females may not act like males, males may act like females. Females who act like males are dangerous—crowing hens and broom-riding witches. But males who act like females are not dangerous at all.

This peculiar form of male chauvinism may not be so obvious and, in fact, the suggestion that males may act like females may strike some as a radical hypothesis. Certainly it is true that on the conscious level, American males are desperately afraid of appearing to be feminine in any way. The adjective "effeminate" is highly insulting. A male who is too dependent upon a female—from Mama's boy to henpecked husband—is looked down upon by his male peers and often by females as well. A young boy who plays with dolls and refuses to engage in rough and tumble sports may be labelled "sissy" (from sister?). In the light of this, how can one argue that male chauvinism includes any attempt to act like females?

In his book *Symbolic Wounds,* Bruno Bettelheim noted that in male initiation rites around the world, there was an attempt to imitate female behavior. While on the one hand, the male puberty rites insisted upon the total exclusion of women and proclaimed the independence of men from women, the rites at the same time represented a male borrowing of female activities. The bleeding caused by circumcision or subincision was an attempt to ritually recreate the "natural" menstrual bleeding of females. Similarly, the attempt to have the initiates reborn from males (as opposed to females) also copied much of the form and content of female parturition. Thus ironically, in the very ritual intended to utterly repudiate any dependence upon the female, males acted out female behavior.[19]

While one could argue that such aping of female procreative behavior constitutes convincing evidence of the primary importance of the female vis-à-vis the male, it might also be construed as a male chauvinistic attempt to usurp what is rightfully and naturally female. In this context, man seeks through cultural means to take what woman has through natural means. A patriarchal male-biased society might seek to deny the natural female role by asserting the existence of a pseudo-male activity. Such male assertions frequently occur in folkloristic form.

A male deity's creation of mankind, the creation of woman from out of man's body, God's promise to Abraham that he would father a great nation (with no mention of Sarah), and a male Noah saving all animal connubial pairs by means of an ark-womb which floats for a period roughly corresponding to that of human pregnancy, are all male creation myths from the Old Testament.[20] Whether it is knee babies, a man's reference to his pet project as his "brainchild" or his "baby," or the widespread custom of couvade, we find man's desire to participate in childbirth by himself.[21]

One might object at this point that the folklore cited is Old World folklore, not American folklore. This is true, but male chauvinism didn't start in the United States either. Notions of male superiority are found in Near Eastern and Mediterranean cultures. To a large extent American notions of sex roles and sex stereotypes are derivative. Yet in American folklore, we have retained and even embellished various nonbiblical male creation fantasies which continue the tradition of denying female procreativity while simultaneously asserting male procreativity.

We might first mention Santa Claus. In American tradition, he is an extremely rotund figure with a bulging bag full of goodies. An expectant air fills the days immediately preceding his arrival. He makes his delivery down a chimney, often filling shoes or stockings.[22] Please note that the chimney is the same point of entry for the stork, a second example of a male chauvinistic expression of procreativity. While the sex of the stork is not always specifically mentioned, nearly all of the American informants I have questioned on this point have indicated they had always assumed the stork was male. Certainly the stork's physical characteristic, e.g., long legs and long bill, would tend to support a phallic interpretation. In Europe, there were at one time several trademarks for contraceptives with such titles as "The Stork Ensnared" and "The Stork Imprisoned" in which storks were depicted on labels as being completely tied up or held in a cell behind a barred window.[23] The image of the stork carrying the new babies through the air (just as Santa Claus flies through the air) and dropping them down the chimney is widespread in the United States. It commonly appears, for example, on birth announcements. The stork normally carries the babies in a kind of sling suspended from his bill. It is, thus, the male stork rather than a female figure which *carries* the child. In the same semantic frame, it might be worth noting that just as the stork delivers babies, a doctor (usually male) is said to "deliver" the newborn baby.[24] Perhaps this lexical item is not an example of a male attempt to take credit for a successful birth, but then again it might well be part and parcel of the pattern here delineated.

If anyone doubts that Santa Claus and the stork are male chauvinistic images, what about the Easter bunny? Again as in the case of the stork, the sex of the Easter bunny is not always explicitly stated. Yet informants claim that they have always thought of the Easter bunny as a male. And what does the Easter bunny do? What is his primary mission in life? He brings Easter eggs, female symbols par excellence. Here is another illustration of the would-be male usurpation of the female procreative role.

The crowing hen and the Easter bunny thus show a pseudomythological extension of the double standard. Women are *dis*couraged from doing something while men are *en*couraged to do something. Women should not act like men, but men are free to act like women, albeit in somewhat concealed symbolic form. Both the crowing hen and the Easter bunny would appear to be deep-seated facets of male chauvinism in American culture. They tend to reinforce norms which seek to inhibit the full development of female activities or to falsely claim full male credit for the creation of progeny.

The existence of male chauvinistic folklore is probably far more serious than the custom of patronymic naming or the male insistence upon virginity or marital fidelity so as to better establish biological paternity. It is more serious because it is not so obvious. Generations of American children have been exposed to a wide gamut of folklore ranging from apparently innocuous rhymes such as "I wish you luck, I wish you joy, I wish you first a baby boy," to such traditional creatures of the folk imagination as the stork and the Easter bunny. As folklorists, we know that folklore is a primary vehicle for the communication and continuation of attitudes and values.

The question is: What should be done if the attitudes and values which are being communicated and continued are adjudged faulty? It is my hope that the present investigation will assist those who seek to eliminate the male bias which pervades so much of American society. I do not believe, however, that trying to censor or ban the folklore materials cited above would do much good—even if it were possible to bring censorship to bear upon folklore. It is well to remember that folklore reflects a society. A racist society, for example, is bound to have examples of racist folklore. Merely sweeping the racist folklore under the rug, so to speak, wouldn't eliminate the racist attitudes which produced the folklore in the first place. In the final analysis, it is the society and its attitudes which must be altered, not just the folklore. One must treat the cause of disease, not just the symptoms. On the other hand, to the extent that folklore helps perpetuate racism, prejudice, male chauvinism, stereotypes, etc., we as professional folklorists must point this out at every opportunity. By making the unconscious or unselfconscious conscious, we may raise levels of consciousness. We cannot stop folklore, but we can hold it up to the light of reason and through the unrivaled picture it provides, we may better see what wrongs need righting.

A Psychoanalytic Study
of the Bullroarer

I

"Perhaps the most ancient, widely-spread, and sacred religious symbol in the world," wrote anthropologist Alfred C. Haddon at the conclusion of his extensive essay devoted to the bullroarer (1898:327). "To
study the bull-roarer is to take a lesson in folklore" was Andrew
Lang's comment in a still earlier consideration of the same curious
artifact (1884:31). Robert H. Lowie referred to it as "a subject of apparent triviality but of the utmost ethnographic interest" (1961:311).
We may safely ignore the label of triviality as a mere value judgment,
for as E. B. Tylor wisely observed "In anthropology nothing is in-
significant" (1881:265). By the end of the nineteenth century the bullroarer, hitherto known in Europe only as a children's toy, had become
one of the most controversial and frequently discussed subjects in anthropology, engaging the studious attention of some of the truly distinguished anthropologists of that era (e.g., Frazer, van Gennep,
Haddon, Lang, Marett, Pettazzoni, Schmidt). More recently, Lévi-
Strauss has discussed the bullroarer at some length (1973:411 – 22).

The term *bullroarer* is the English name for a folk toy found in
Britain and in many European countries, e.g., Italy (Pettazzoni 1912b;
Battaglia 1925; Tucci 1954–55). The toy consists of a small thin flat
slat of wood, often in the shape of a long oval or ellipse, with a hole at
one end through which a length of string is tied. The instrument
when swung rapidly with a circular motion makes a whirring hum-
ming sound. Folk names in English for this toy include *roarer*, *bull*,
boomer, *buzzer*, *whizzer*, and *swish* (Marett 1910:400). In German, the
object is known as *Schwirrholz* or *Waldteufel;* in Italian *rombo*.

The folk term *bullroarer* evidently entered the formal anthropological lexicon in 1880 when Fison and Howitt published *Kamilaroi and Kurnai*, a study of the Australian aborigines, though the anthropological acceptance of the term was surely encouraged by Tylor's use and extended mention of it in his review of the book in *The Academy* in April of 1881, and also by Andrew Lang's essay on the subject in 1884. Specifically, the Reverend Lorimer Fison devoted an appendix (E) to the *Tûrndun*, which he described in part as follows:

> When whirled round, or whisked backwards and forwards, it makes a peculiar and slightly humming noise, which also approximates to the sound of the word 'whew'. It much resembles in general character the wooden toy which I remember to have made as a boy, called a 'bull roarer'. The occurrence of such an instrument with us as a toy, and with the Australian savage as an object of mystery used in their ceremonies, suggests that the 'bull roarer' is a survival (Fison & Howitt 1880:267).

The apparent marked contrast between sacred ritual object on the one hand and secular toy on the other was understood as exemplifying unilinear cultural evolution by means of which peoples progressed from savagery to civilization having no visible record of such change other than a few tangible vestigial remains of the earlier period, remains which were dubbed survivals. E. B. Tylor, speaking of the bullroarer, in 1890, commented that "in ancient Greece, modern Australia, North America, and Africa, the instrument is one of sacred purpose. Only in Europe and the United States has it degenerated into a boy's plaything" (1890:163). A more recent comment predicts that "soon the bullroarer will become, among the Ibo, the toy that it is in Europe" (Jeffreys 1949:34).

In his initial report, Fison went on to describe specific examples of bullroarers from different parts of Australia. For instance, among the Chepara on the coast of Southern Queensland, the *bribbun* (bullroarer):

> is kept secret and hidden from light by the head chief, and is considered to possess some mysterious and supernatural power or influence. The women and children are not permitted to see it; if seen by a woman or shown by a man to a woman, the punishment to both is *death*. After the young men have been initiated, each of them receives, to take home with him, a toy or miniature 'bribbun', as a sort of

guarantee of their initiation, and as receiving a small portion of the
virtue which the larger and principal one is supposed to possess
(1880:268).

Since 1880 there has been a considerable body of scholarship devoted to the bullroarer. Some scholars have treated it as a rudimentary
musical instrument (Sachs 1929:10–13; Izikowitz 1935:208–12). Some
have studied the sound made by the bullroarer (Hanika 1952:86–8).
Others have been more concerned with the ritual designs found as
bullroarer decorations (Guiart 1951: Davidson 1953). However, the
majority of studies have been distribution surveys of the occurrence of
the bullroarer in different parts of the world. Surveys include Australia (Mathews 1898; Pettazzoni 1912a) or Australia and New Guinea
(Speiser 1928–29; 156–87; van Baal 1963), Africa (Hirschberg 1940),
and South America (Zerries 1953). Sometimes the surveys are of a
more limited area, e.g., of the Papuan Gulf (Williams 1936a) or India
(Roy 1927) or of the Ibo (Jeffreys 1949) or Dogon (Leiris 1934). More
ambitious scholars attempted worldwide distribution studies (e.g.,
Schmeltz 1896; Frazer 1913:228n.2) of which the most complete is
Zerries's 1942 doctoral dissertation devoted exclusively to the bullroarer. The antiquity of the bullroarer has also been established. It
may have existed in ancient Israel (Budde 1928) and Egypt (Hickmann
1955) and there is some archaeological evidence attesting to its age
(Zerries 1942:161; Heizer 1960) although the authenticity of some of
the alleged artifacts has upon occasion been challenged (cf. Armstrong
1936 and Kitching 1963:23–4, 51). But the demonstration of widespread distribution per se does not explain why the bullroarer should
exist in the first place nor what, if anything, the bullroarer means.

II

Comparative studies do reveal a remarkable uniformity of bullroarer
design and usage. For example, a comparison of Australian and South
American bullroarers shows striking similarities in form and decora-
tion (Bormida 1952:67). But more amazing than the commonality of
bullroarer construction are the parallels in accompanying attitudes and
customs. The bullroarer's specific association with males, often in conjunction with initiation rites, coupled with the corollary characteristic
of being kept secret from females is one of the most consistent attri-

butes of the "bullroarer complex" as Loeb phrased it (1929:283–5). Another important feature is the common linking of the bullroarer with thunder and wind (Zerries 1942:188–93). It would be difficult enough to explain the cross-cultural occurrence of a single artifact, but it is even more of a challenge to explain the entire bullroarer complex. In 1881, Tylor remarked, "It need hardly be said that the extraordinary correspondence in its ceremonial use among races so different as the Kafirs of South Africa and the Australians calls for careful enquiry" (1881:265). Ten years later, Howitt had this to say of the bullroarer: "The universality of its use, and under the same conditions in world-wide localities, is one of the most puzzling questions in this branch of anthropology" (1891a:347 or 1891b:64).

Just as the bullroarer was used as an example of the doctrine of survivals, so its distribution was cited equally by champions of polygenesis and advocates of monogenesis plus diffusion. Andrew Lang believed the bullroarer's distribution to be a manifestation of polygenetic independent invention. The bullroarer shows, he argued, that "similar minds, working with simple means towards similar ends, might evolve the bull-roarer and its mystic uses anywhere. There is no need for a hypothesis of common origin, or of borrowing, to account for this widely diffused sacred object" (1884:31; cf. 42–3). One thing that puzzled Lang particularly, though, was the apparent parallelism between classical Greek and "savage" initiation rites, which included not only the bullroarer but the practice of covering the initiates with filth (e.g., goat dung) or clay. Lang offered no explanation for this. "Both Greeks and savages employ the bull-roarer, both bedaub the initiated with dirt or with white paint or chalk. As to the meaning of the latter very un-Aryan practice, one has no idea" (1884:41).

Robert Lowie, writing in 1920, was also struck by the "occurrence of the same association of ideas in different regions of the globe." But the important issue for Lowie was "not whether the bull-roarer has been invented once or a dozen times," but rather why women should be excluded from seeing or touching the object.

There lies the crux of the matter. Why do Brazilians and Central Australians deem it death for a woman to see the bullroarer? Why this punctilious insistence on keeping her in the dark on this subject in West and East Africa and Oceania? I know of no psychological principle that would urge the Ekoi and the Bororo to bar women from

knowledge about bullroarers and until such a principle is brought to
light I do not hesitate to accept diffusion from a common center as a
more probable assumption (1961:313; cf. Loeb 1929:285).

It is, of course, no surprise that Lowie should be inclined to explain
the distribution of the bullroarer on the basis of monogenesis and subsequent diffusion from a point of origin—just as it was no surprise
that Lang favoured polygenesis as an explanatory principle.

Lowie's interest in diffusion was heavily influenced by German
ethnologists, some of whom saw the wide distribution of the bullroarer as evidence for an extremely old layer of human culture (cf.
Hauer 1923:162: Bormida 1952). Part of the initial great interest in
bullroarers had to do with whether or not they provided an indication
of the existence of so-called high gods among "primitive" peoples (cf.
Schmidt 1909:889–96; Marett 1910). The sound made by the bullroarer was likened to the sound of thunder, which was thought to be
the voice of a deity (cf. Harrison 1912:56–66). This association came
from native testimony. Indeed, it is clear that the sound made an impact even upon unbelieving outsiders. One observer reported:

> There is no doubt whatever about the value of the bull-roarer for
> impressing the uninstructed. Its sound, once heard, remains a vivid
> memory, and even a hardened anthropologist cannot hear that omin-
> ous roar booming through the forest without feeling its power, and
> forgetting for the moment, that it is caused by a bit of wood twirled
> on the end of a string (Blackwood 1935:244).

All in all, it was the use of the bullroarer in initiation ceremonies
which stimulated the most scholarly interest. Frazer's theory of the
bullroarer centered on its initiation function. "Now, what is the meaning of the bull-roarer, that simple, but mysterious, implement which
plays so important a part in the sacred rites of so many savage
peoples? Perhaps the two things which characterise it as a sacred implement most generally are, first, its use at the initiation of lads into
manhood and second, the profound secrecy in which it is kept from
the knowledge and sight of women and children" (1901:318). Frazer
goes on to suggest that the bullroarer serves to impart the power of
propagating the species and that the sound component may signal the
pubertal change from a shrill boyish voice to the deep tones of virile
manhood (1901:319). Frazer cites instances of using bullroarers to

ensure good hunting or a good crop of yams as corroboration of the fertility factor.

Frazer's ingenious theorizing is plausible as far as it goes, but it does not really explain why the bullroarer must be kept from women, the feature of the bullroarer complex that most troubled Lowie. Women are allowed to hear the sound of the bullroarer—indeed, often the bullroarer is used to warn women to keep away. If the bullroarer is phallic—as recent scholarship suggests it almost certainly is (cf. van Baal 1963), why would this need to be kept secret from women? Women are surely aware of the existence and nature of the male phallus. The phallic qualities of male initiates would therefore hardly need to be kept secret. Nor would a purely phallic interpretation of the bullroarer really illuminate the noisemaking characteristic. Why would a phallus be depicted as making a mysterious sound? Neither does Frazer's explanation really account for the use of the bullroarer among many peoples to make wind (Frazer 1913:232; Spier 1928:290: Heizer 1960:7).

III

Various phallic interpretations of the bullroarer have been proposed since Frazer (e.g., Dennett 1968:34, 52–6; Róheim 1926:154, 183, 271; Zerries 1942:197–8: Murphy 1959:94–5; Hiatt 1971:86), but van Baal is easily the most articulate spokesman of this view. In his provocative essay, he states at the outset that his primary concern is to demonstrate "that in Australia and in the southern part of New Guinea the bull-roarer has to be interpreted as a phallic symbol and, consequently, its cult as a phallic cult" (1963:201). However, van Baal completely avoids the issue of why women are banned from the site/ sight of bullroarers. "We will not enter into a discussion of the interesting problem why it is always the community of males which sets out to frighten the community of females by the use of quasi-supernatural means" (1963:202). Yet as the various myth texts cited by van Baal eloquently attest in highly convincing fashion, the exclusively phallic theory of the bullroarer is totally inadequate to explain all the details of the bullroarer complex. Let me cite just one glaring example, which is in fact a most crucial one.

The evidence from a number of myth texts clearly indicates that whatever the bullroarer represents, it was once in the possession of

women, *not* men! Van Baal summarizes a Kiwai myth of the origin of
the bullroarer in which a woman discovers the object. When cutting a
tree, a woman sees a chip of wood fly off with a buzzing sound. She
secured the splinter but that night in a dream she is instructed to give
it to her husband. Van Baal's comment is: "Though by no means uncommon, it certainly is remarkable that the origin of the bull-roarer is
attributed to a woman. We will refrain from speculation upon its
deeper meaning . . ." (1963:205). The original possession or discovery
of the bullroarer by women has been noted but likewise not explained
by other scholars (e.g., Speiser 1928–29: 237; Zerries 1942:225). In an
even more remarkable example, van Baal cites an initiation ceremony
in which two *tjuringa* are bound together to form a ritual object. Van
Baal insists upon calling this object a phallus, despite the fact that the
native language term for the object is *ambilia ekura*, "amnion,"
"womb"! He interprets the data as follows: "The real secret of the
rites is the symbolic inversion of the male genital. The penis is called a
womb . . ." (1963:211). Van Baal fails to answer the question of why a
male should call his penis a womb. Nor does he speculate as to the
significance of the fact that the bullroarer's origin is attributed to a
female.

Another myth text mentioned by van Baal provides an additional
clue. He refers to a myth of the origin of all vegetables. A man kills
his wife. From her dead body, all the vegetables sprouted. However,
the man collects them all and swallows them. Undigested, they pass
through his body into his genital organ. With a new wife, he engages
in sexual intercourse, but he withdraws his organ, allowing all the
vegetables to scatter over the field. This myth would appear to be a
clear-cut example of male envy of female procreativity. The male hero
kills his wife and usurps the female role by literally incorporating the
vegetables which came from her body. His own body and phallus
function as a substitute womb. This symbolic process is paralleled in
many initiation rites where a male spirit or deity is said to swallow
initiates. Later he disgorges them, thereby making the boys into men
(cf. Róheim 1926:141; Zerries 1942:178; Hiatt 1971:83–6).

The semantic connection between bullroarer and female procreativity is found in yet another myth cited by van Baal. In this text:

> the wife of Tiv-r or Kambel, the originator in tribal mythology, is
> pregnant of the bullroarer. Tiv-r hears a soft whining in his wife's

abdomen and is highly intrigued. One bird after another is sent out by
him to extract the mysterious something. At last, while the woman is
stooping down with legs wide apart, brooming the place, a bird man-
ages to get hold of the protruding thing and extract it. It is the first
bull-roarer . . . (van Baal 1963:205–6).

Clearly, in this context, the bullroarer is something which is produced
initially by a woman and is stolen by, and for, men. And this is precisely what I should like to argue is part of the underlying meaning of
the bullroarer complex.

The argument that males are jealous of female parturition and that
this pregnancy envy is reflected in male initiation rites has been made
in detail by Bruno Bettelheim. According to this theory, males seek to
emulate or imitate female procreative powers, even to the extent of
causing bleeding from the male genital area (e.g., through subincision). Actually, it was in 1900 that Mathews remarked how in
Australian aboriginal initiation ritual, the male organ was smeared
with blood "to make the boys believe they had a menstrual flow, like
the women" (1900:635). This insight was thus made long before it was
articulated by Róheim (1949), Ashley-Montagu (1937:302), Bettelheim
(1962), and Hiatt (1971). In the male ritual, boys become men, but
they do so by being reborn. However, this birth or rather rebirth
entails being born *from men*, not women. This stealing, so to speak, of
what was originally a purely female prerogative is paralleled in several
of the bullroarer myths cited above. The bullroarer was discovered
by, or initially belonged to, women. Men, through ritual or other
social sanctions, forced the women to transfer the bullroarer to men.
It is noteworthy that in one New Guinea society, a bullroarer was
named "birth helper" (Neuhauss 1911, III:36). This suggests that the
bullroarer helps men give birth. What is it then that the bullroarer
represents? It represents the male equivalent of female procreativity,
but the question remains of why does it function in symbolic form—
through the making of noise, wind, thunder, etc.?

IV

Lévi-Strauss understands the bullroarer as a figurative phallus
(1973:411), but he also sees an association with what he calls the "rotten world" (and he discusses the bullroarer in a chapter titled in English "Din and Stench" [1973:414]). However, neither Lévi-Strauss

nor, to my knowledge, any other anthropologist has ever referred to the only writer to have discussed in painstaking detail the anal erotic elements of the bullroarer complex. Ernest Jones, in a brilliant essay, "The Madonna's Conception through the Ear," first published in 1914, lucidly articulates the symbolic transformations of the expulsion of intestinal gas (1951:278). Males, he maintains, create by a blowing movement (breath, wind) or by sound. Although Jones does tend to make such categorical statements as the following: "That the idea of thunder is exceedingly apt, in dreams and other products of uncon-scious fantasy, to symbolize flatus, particularly paternal flatus, is well known to all psycho-analysts" (1951:287; cf. Freeman 1968:359–60, 368n.13), he supports his assertions with extensive documentary evi-dence. It is true that there is evidence that flatus has been the subject of ritual worship (Bourke 1891:154–64; cf. Crombie 1884), but flatus is one thing and the crucial question is whether the wind or thunder or the bullroarer stem from this source.

Certainly the notion of wind as a fertilizing principle is extremely widespread as the references for motif T524, Conception from wind, in the *Motif-Index of Folk-Literature*, attest. Jones himself cites Hera's impregnation by the wind to conceive Hephaistos, the East Wind's inpregnation of the virgin Ilmatar in the Kalevala to conceive the wizard Väinämöinen, plus American Indian and other instances. Radcliffe-Brown remarked that in Australia small whirlwinds were thought to make women become pregnant (1912:182). The idea is also to be found in Western cultures, as we can see in a fascinating essay which shows how the wind has been given credit for the impregnation of four types of females: mares, vultures, hens, and women. The author of this essay is not sure just why the wind is involved. "The reason why the wind was chosen as the fecundating agent in all four cases is not at all clear. It will probably have to be sought in some psychological twist of the not quite civilized folk among whom the stories originated" (Zirkle 1936:96). Repeatedly throughout European history, stories of the wind-impregnation of animals were offered as support for the dogma of the virgin birth of Christ. As a matter of fact, the fertilizing principle in the latter case is presumed to be the Holy Ghost. In his essay entitled "A Psycho-analytic Study of the Holy Ghost Concept," Ernest Jones argues that the Holy Ghost is a male substitute for the mother figure (1951:360); and since the concept of ghost is related to spirit, breath, or wind, the Holy Ghost might

also be an example of a fertilizing wind or, to put it somewhat facetiously, "wholly a gust"! (Cf. the discussion of *geist* by Zirkle
1936:126, who also notes that the Latin *spiritus* was a breath as well as
a ghost.)

The semantic or symbolic equivalence of flatus and thunder may
well be universal but unfortunately such types of equations have been
infrequently reported by ethnographers. In Western culture, the
equation is explicit in Aristophanes' *The Clouds*, which dates from 423
B.C. Among the Mundurucú of Brazil, thunder is believed to be the
sound of the spirit Karuparabö's flatus, and rays of lightning are
thought to shoot from his anus (Murphy 1958:21). But the issue is not
really one of seeking exemplifications of the equation so much as demonstrating the relevance of this analytic line of reasoning to the bullroarer. Once again, myths provide critical incontrovertible data.

A Loritja narrative (Strehlow 1908:48, n.9) describes a group of
small men called Maiutu who live in a place called Maiutukunna
which means "the excrement of the Maiutu." Another Loritja narrative which is clearly a cognate tells of a group of small men called
Apuju, a name which means bullroarer (Strehlow 1908:50). Pettazzoni
(1912a:152) realised that Maiutu=Apuju=bullroarer, but he did not
comment on the possible significance of the name of the place where
the Maiutu lived. The sons of the Maiutu were called Inankiri as were
the sons of the Apuju. In an Aranda cognate myth, the sons of the
little men are called *nankara*, which Strehlow informs us is the name
of the large bullroarer (Strehlow 1907:102; cf. Pettazzoni
1912a:153–4). In the light of the present anal erotic hypothesis, it
makes perfect sense for the bullroarer or the father of the bullroarer to
come from a place of excrement.

The Australian aboriginal association of bullroarer with excrement
is strongly suggested by some unusual linguistic evidence. In a mas-
terful survey, E. A. Worms compares roots and stems from a variety
of Australian languages. All of the roots and stems considered are
mythological and religious terms. Again and again, Worms demonstrates that the same roots mean "shadow," "soul," "hidden," and "secret" (1957:734). It is noteworthy that the identical roots frequently
carry the meanings of "ghost" and "bullroarer," a semantic equivalence
which at first glance would seem to confirm the view that the sound of
the bullroarer represents the voice of deceased ancestral spirits (cf.
Hirschberg 1940). But there is yet another association, an association

which evidently disturbed Worms somewhat. In a special supplementary section (1957:764–5), entitled "The problem of *guna* with reference to R. and C. Berndt and to W. Schmidt," Worms questions previous translations of the word *guna* as excrement. He wonders, for example, whether Father Schmidt's translation of *kuanameru*, of the Kurnai of Gippsland (Victoria), as "excreta hawk" might be in error and he quotes Schmidt himself who noted "This compound expresses the disregard of the Kurnai for the important position which the hawk occupies in the religion and mythology of other tribes." Worms bothers to say that "owing to their purely naturalistic conception of natural functions, the use of the word 'excreta' would not necessarily imply a derogatory notion in the minds of the natives as it might in the different European outlook." Nevertheless, since *"gan-, gun-, gin,* the dead, ghost, shadow" is one of the mythological roots considered by Worms, he does go so far as to suggest translating "excreta hawk" as "ancestral hawk" and he offers a similar retranslation of the Berndts' data. I submit that retranslation would be an error, since there is plenty of additional evidence confirming the accuracy of the original translations. In the Loritja narrative collected by Strehlow cited above, the group of small men called Maiutu live in a place called Maiutukunna which Strehlow translates as "excrement of the Maiutu." Similarly, R. H. Mathews in a vocabulary listing from a tribe in Victoria also lists *gunang* as excrement (Mathews 1904:62). Worms unaccountably failed to consult *Eaglehawk and Crow* by Mathew (1899:34, 55, 251), which would have provided conclusive evidence that *kun-/gun-* referred to excrement. In his discussion of the list of cognates and meanings of this single root, Worms includes four which mean bullroarer and two which refer to the decorations on bullroarers (1957:748), more references to bullroarer than are found under any of the other thirty or so roots considered. In the present psychoanalytic framework, it is reasonable for a religious root *gun-/kun* to mean both bullroarer and excrement in addition to "dead, ghost, and shadow." I might add that without such a framework, the excremental meanings of *guna* must remain a "problem," as Worms calls it.

V

There is additional evidence supporting the notion that males attempt to supplant female procreativity through the symbolic creativity of the anus. One finds explicit data linking excrement with initiation ritual—ritual in which bullroarers are employed. (It has been clear almost from the beginning that the psychological rationale underlying bullroarers is closely related to the psychological rationale underlying male initiation rites.) For example, Howitt reports that among the Wiimbaio tribe, a boy goes through several name changes. "A child was spoken of as *Katulya;* a boy of nine or ten years as *Wilyango;* one of ten to fifteen as *Wilyango-kurnundo;* and when fifteen, and before being made a young man, as *Kurno,* that is excrement. When he became a man he would be spoken of as *Thalara*" (1904:739). The reference to *kurno* (cf. *Kurn*undo in the preceding stage) suggests that a boy becomes a man by passing through a fecal ritual. It is as if to say that a man is moulded from feces. Even more striking is an initiation ceremony described by Mathews (1897:321–3) in which the initiates are taken from the main area to a special oval enclosure "called the goonambang (excrement place)." (*Goon* is surely cognate with Worms's *gun-*.) The bullroarers sound and "the guardians say to each other that they suppose Goign is killing all the women and children in the camp. This puts the novices in a great state of anxiety and alarm" (1897:328). Goign is evidently the deity or spirit in charge of the initiation (and his name may well also be a cognate of the root in question). In any case, once assembled in the *goonambang*, the novices watch old men who perform feats of jugglery and exhibit white stones (quartz crystals). "These quartz crystals are believed to be the excrement of Goign" (1897:329; cf. Róheim 1926:435, n.4). In an earlier report of a similar initiation ceremony (Angas 1847, II:224), the initiates at the end are given *mundie*, a term which appears to be cognate with another one of Worms's inventory of mythological roots (1957:753–4). "Mundie is a crystal, believed by the natives to be an excrement issuing from the Deity, and held sacred. It is worn concealed in the hair, tied up in a packet, and is never shown to the women, who are forbidden to look at it under pain of death." The *mundie*, divine excrement, appears to be the functional equivalent of the bullroarer in this instance. Returning to Mathews's account, we learn that on the first night of the arrival of the novices at the excrement place, they are required to eat some human excrement, during which time a bullroarer sounds (1897:331). The term for bullroarer in this society is *goonandhakeea* which Mathews translates as "excrement eater" (1897:324, 331), while the sound of it is said to be the voice of Goign "who would come and

eat them if he got the chance." Finally the boys are shown the bullroarers and they touch their bodies with them. Again it would appear
that boys become men by means of male anal power. Boys are or
become feces as part of the process of being passed through the bodies
of powerful male spirits/monsters. Male birth or rebirth occurs
through the anus.

It might be useful at this point to consider a striking myth of the
origin of the bullroarer as reported by Spencer and Gillen
(1904:498–9, 345). Among the Kaitish, there is a narrative about a
spirit called Atnatu "who derives his name from the fact that he has
no anus." Angry at his children who did not give him Churinga and
perform sacred ceremonies for him, Atnatu dropped them "through a
hole in the sky" along with all the material culture of the Kaitish.
"Atnatu first of all made the Churinga, and swung them up in the sky
when he initiated his offspring, and now he is glad when he hears the
natives on the earth making the bull-roarer sound as they initiate the
boys." In this narrative, we have the equivalence of the sound of the
bullroarer on earth and the sound of thunder in the sky. We also have
the creator of the bullroarer depicted as having no anus although he is
well able to "drop" people and objects through a sky hole.

In another narrative (Spencer & Gillen 1904:420), two men named
Tumana (which means the sound made by the swinging of the bullroarer) heard Atnatu up in the sky making the noise with his
Churinga. The two men wanted to imitate him and they made a bullroarer. Two dogs heard the noise and came to smell the men saying
"Oh they smell very good." The dogs then cut the men's heads off.
Incidentally, the pair of dogs recur in such narratives, sometimes
forming deposits of red ochre "where they voided their excreta"
(1904:279) and sometimes "they lifted their tails over their backs and
yams arose to mark the spot" (1904:435). The lifting of the dogs' tails
to defecate is a detail reminiscent of one of the earliest accounts of
initiation. In a report of an initiation held in January, 1795, the initiators wearing a kind of pseudo-tail, dropped down on all fours "imitating the dogs of the country. Their dress was adapted to this purpose; the wooden sword, stuck in the hinder part of the girdle which
they wore around the waist, did not, when they were crawling on all
fours, look much unlike the tail of a dog curled over his back. Every
time they passed the place where the boys were seated, they threw up
the sand and dust on them with their hands and their feet" (Collins

1798:567). Later the swords [Could the object have been a bullroarer?] are replaced by "long tails made of grass." Then "quickly divesting themselves of their artificial tails, each man caught up a boy, and placing him on his shoulders, carried him off in triumph" to the area where a tooth was removed. The ritual act of throwing sand and dust on the initiates could be construed as symbolic defecation.

It is also of interest that the mythical pair of dogs produce red ochre from feces. If red ochre (with which initiates are often daubed) is a symbol for blood, perhaps menstrual blood (Spencer & Gillen 1898:463; Bettelheim 1962:98; Hiatt 1971:85), then the excretion of red ochre may be parallel to producing "female" bleeding through subincision. Since there is some evidence that the Arunta initiates are called *rukuta* meaning wild dogs (Strehlow 1913:26; Róheim 1926:295), one could argue that the excretion of red ochre is an anal alternative to producing a symbolic surrogate for menstrual blood (as opposed to the genital alternative of subincision). It should be noted that there is a myth which accounts for red ochre as being formed from female sexual organs (Spencer & Gillen 1898:442, 464). (For another instance where the clay used for body adornment is said to be the excrement of a (crocodile) culture hero, see Thomson 1933:523. In this case, the term for clay, *mätän*, looks suspiciously similar to *panmäddaä*, the term for bullroarer.)

The significance of Atnatu's name may have analogues in other cultures. Lévi-Strauss observes that South American Indians "consider the control of excretory functions of paramount importance" and "at least in the myths, that the being most able to resist nature, will *ipso facto* be the most gifted in respect to cultural aptitudes" (1973:427–8). But perhaps the most interesting possible parallel comes from the Chaga of Africa. The central portion of the Chaga initiation ritual concerns the "stopping up of the anus" (Raum 1940:318). The *ngoso*, or plug, is supposed to represent male superiority. "The novices were told that the plug was the sign of manhood and that the guarding of its secret was the foremost duty of all men." The preceptor told the novices, "Don't emit wind in the presence of women and uninitiated youths" (Raum 1940:318). It is worth recalling that one of the most consistent characteristics of the bullroarer is supposedly its ability to make wind. Haddon (1898:306) notes that "at Moa a man would raise the wind by painting himself black all over and whirling a bullroarer." The Paviotso use the bullroarer to raise a wind (Heizer

1960:7; cf. Zerries 1942:129) and the Comanche word for bullroarer, *yuane*, means "warm wind" (Cohen 1973:31). Even in Italy, one folk name for the bullroarer is *far el vento* (Battaglia 1925:201). Just as the bullroarer is not to be seen by women and uninitiated boys, so the Chaga initiates are instructed to keep any "breaking wind" from the same group. Structurally and contextually, the bullroarer on the one hand, and control of such anal acts as defecating and farting on the other, would appear to be functionally equivalent.

The plugging up of the anus by the Chaga has been interpreted as being a male attempt to imitate female pregnancy (Gutmann 1926:364–5; Bettelheim 1962:129). A large number of creation myths, e.g., earthdiver who creates the world from mud, may well reflect the same tendency of men to attempt to rival or surpass women's "natural" procreativity by means of various manipulations of feces (Dundes 1962). But the role of male anal creativity in initiation rites has not apparently been considered by scholars particularly concerned with such rites (cf. e.g., Allen, Hiatt, Loeb, Young). Certainly it is difficult to deny the specific connections between the bullroarer and feces. Sometimes it is a matter of a metaphor as in the case of an Arunta idiom which indicates that the purpose of ritually rubbing the stomach and thighs with a churinga is "to untie their bowels" (Spencer & Gillen 1898:164). But often the evidence is more elaborate. For example, Williams (1936a:29) reports from the Papuan Gulf that when the initiates are finally allowed to see the bullroarer, "a mess of ashes, dirt and stew is plastered on their bodies. When later they return and are asked by their supposedly anxious mothers, 'Did the crocodile bite you?' they answer, 'No, he only dunged on us.'" Williams claims that this narrative is simply a story concocted to fool women about the contents of initiation rituals. However, as van Baal rightly observes (1966:581, 659, 931), such traditional fabrications may well contain elements of symbolic truth. Van Baal himself in an extensive description of myth and ritual in New Guinea reports an even more explicit account (1966:480) involving Sosom, the name of a deity as well as a term for bullroarer. "Finally, Sosom devours all the neophytes and adolescents . . . each time he swallows one, disgorging another through his posterior parts," Here is undeniable male anal birth or rebirth being carried out by a deity whose name means bullroarer!

The anal erotic element of the bullroarer would not only explain its frequent association with wind and thunder, but it would also explain some of the hitherto inexplicable mysterious features of initiation rituals. For example, among the Bororo, there is a combined ritual of death and initiation in which bullroarers represent a large mythical beast. A hunter in disguise serves as the representative of the deceased. Women and children would die at the sight of either him or the bullroarer. Then as part of the initiation, several nude youths plastered with mud represent the mythical animal. Note that since the bullroarers originally represented the animal and the youths plastered with mud represent the same, then in some sense mud-splattered youths are equivalent to the bullroarer. In any case, after caressing the hunter, the youths "frighten the novices with yells and pelt them with mud before allowing them to see the bullroarers" (Lowie 1946:430). If mud is considered to be a substitute for feces, we can see why youths plastered with mud yell (make noise) and throw mud at the initiates. We can also understand the practice which so perplexed Andrew Lang, namely, the cross-cultural occurrence of covering initiates with filth. If men are giving birth to young males through anal means, it follows that there could appropriately be the accompanying signs of anal creation, namely feces and farts. Moreover, we may now see why initiates in some instances are required to drink urine or eat feces (Mathews 1900:637). Whereas parturient women can nurse infants soon after the infants' birth, men cannot; and in male symbolic terms they must offer other body products in lieu of mother's milk, as Róheim suggested some years ago (1942:371).

VI

With respect to the purely phallic interpretation of the bullroarer, it should now be obvious that it cannot account for what appear to be anal components of the bullroarer complex. The phallic interpretation cannot explain the noise of the bullroarer or the myths referring to excrement or to the lack of an anus. Yet the evidence for a phallic aspect of bullroarer is also compelling. Can phallic and anal interpretations be reconciled or are they mutually exclusive?

Once again Ernest Jones has suggested a possible solution, though not with specific mention of the bullroarer. Jones, having demonstrated the anal erotic underpinnings of the Holy Ghost or Holy Spirit, attempts to explain why the Holy Ghost should so often be depicted in the form of a bird (and a dove in particular). He abundantly illustrates the phallic symbolism of birds with special reference to the dove (1951:322–41). He concludes that it is a phallic organ which expels the fertilizing gas, asserting that he has come across the fantasy in individual psychoanalyses in which a person in childhood "considered the male organ to be a continuation of the rectum or its contents" (1951:329). The same reasoning may apply to the bullroarer. This possible double aspect, that is, both phallic and anal, of the bull-roarer might explain why some bullroarers are perceived to have "heads" and "tails" (Williams 1936b:181) and it is noteworthy that they may be swung by the tail. In this connection one may recall that in one account describing the designs inscribed on an Arunta *churinga* (Spencer & Gillen 1898:147), it is the bottom series of circles which are said to represent "the posterior part of the man."

The hypothetical combination of anal and genital elements in the same symbolic behavior may also shed some light on yet another element in the bullroarer complex. A number of scholars have observed that flutes are sometimes substituted for bullroarers (e.g., Speiser 1928–29:187–9; Zerries 1942:225–6; Murphy 1959:94; cf. Murphy's discussion of phallic trumpets in 1960:107–8). In such instances, it is the sacred flute which cannot be shown or played in front of women. The flute in the present context could easily qualify as a "flatulent phallus," that is, as a phallic wind instrument. Thus the Chaga mentor's dictum: "Don't emit wind in the presence of women and uninitiated youths" could apply as well to the playing of flutes as it does to breaking wind or whirling the bullroarer.

The bullroarer's association with thunder reminds us that the thunderbird, a widespread concept in Asia and North America (Hatt 1949:36–40) might be explained in similar fashion. The thunderbird, mentioned *en passant* by Jones (1951:328) would thus appear to be a male phallic bird whose principal powers consist of producing thunder and lightning. The folkloristic associations of thunder might be said to include both phallic and anal features. The sound of thunder would be analogous to the sound of flatus, but the thunderbolts thrown by gods of thunder might be phallic. Freeman points out (1968:363) that thunderbolts are commonly called the "teeth" of thunder spirits, but he failed to relate this metaphorical convention to the custom of knocking out one of the initiate's teeth as part of the initiation ritual (Róheim 1926:354, Bettelheim 1962:94–5). (It is tempting to speculate about the possible similarity in form of the serrated or notched edges of some bullroarers to teeth.)

The ritual removal of one or more of the initiates' teeth was interpreted by Freud as being symbolic castration (1938:924, n.1) and further studies have amply confirmed the phallic symbolism of teeth (cf. Darlington 1929; Kanner 1928). A Greek myth of male procreation (Motif A 1265, Men created from sown dragon's teeth) does suggest that men may use teeth as a means of producing all-male offspring without recourse to women. But if teeth are phallic, as Freud and his followers have suggested; and initiation rites are designed to bring young men to adulthood, why are the teeth removed? How could symbolic castration make a boy into a man?

This raises one of the most difficult and troublesome theoretical questions with respect to initiation rites (and indirectly to the bullroarer). Does initiation make men of boys or does it make women of boys? Previous psychoanalytic interpretations of initiation rites have argued that they were castrative and/or ritual Oedipal dramas. Reik (1962), for example, suggested that adult fathers, jealous of rival sons, insisted upon culturally sanctioned mutilation of the boys' genitals. Bettelheim went further in proposing that it was not that young males had to give up maleness (as in castration) but rather that they were asked to assume femaleness. This is in contrast to most anthropologists who have tended to interpret initiation rituals as rites of passage (Van Gennep 1960) or dramatizations of male identity through solidarity (Young 1965). (For useful summaries of initiation rite theory, see Allen 1967:1–27, Young 1965.) Certainly anthropologists should not ignore evidence of overt feminizing behaviour. For example, among the Nandi, the garb of the boys being circumcised is germane. Before circumcision, the boys are dressed *as girls*. After circumcision, the girls' clothes are exchanged for *women's garments* (Hollis 1909:53–5; cf. Bettelheim 1962:111–13). So there is an apparent paradox and this may be why there is such a split in anthropological and psychoanalytic interpretations. Anthropologists claim that initiation rites make men; psychoanalysts claim that the same rites make men into pseudo-women. One can, however, accept both positions. Initiation rites make boys into men, but they do so by means of feminizing the initiates (cf. Hiatt 1971:88).

Bettelheim has offered an explanation for the feminizing of the initiates, namely, pregnancy envy on the part of males. But if older males can bear young males anew via the anus, why would they need to rely upon subincision and similar ritual acts. Admittedly, Young is too quick to dismiss Bettelheim's theory, arguing (1965:4) that "the recondite character of his interpretation, turning as it does on male envy of the procreative functions of women, is not the sort of thing that a native—or anybody else for that matter—normally brings up in conversation." The ethnographic facts suggest otherwise. There are numerous native statements explicitly equating male subincision with female menstrual bleeding, as Róheim carefully demonstrated in detail (1949; cf. also Bettelheim 1962:105–6, and Allen 1967:17). But there is a legitimate question whether pregnancy envy alone is sufficient to explain circumcision, subincision, etc. If men wish to emulate women in giving birth or rebirth to boys, why would they need to give the symbolic equivalents of female organs to *young* boys? The young boys will not give birth themselves until much later when they are initiators instead of initiates.

VII

I have already suggested that previous analyses of initiation rites have not taken proper cognizance of the possible anal component of initiation rites. I should now like to indicate that there may be another factor which has similarly failed to receive much attention from students of these rites and this factor is the element of homosexuality. If men wish to proclaim themselves entirely independent of women (as the enforced sexual segregation and secrecy would imply), then it is not just menstruation and parturition which are enacted in symbolic terms by men. Rather heterosexual intercourse itself is rejected— temporarily—in favor of homosexual intercourse.

In almost any all-male society or male subsection of society, one finds a distinction between so-called active and passive homosexuality. Typically, the active homosexual has high status and prestige whereas the passive homosexual—who is often considered to be playing the part of a female—has low status and little prestige (cf. Dundes *et al.* 1970). When a young boy leaves the world of women to join the world of men, he finds that the process of becoming a "man" may in fact entail playing the part of a woman. If this is correct, then initiation rites may be seen quite differently from before. A young boy has his masculinity challenged, often through ritual mutilation of his sexual organ, a mutilation which in some societies is specifically labelled as a female genital. He is permitted to join the exclusive society of men where he is informed that males control creativity—commonly in terms of anal, wind-blowing or by means of literal or symbolic manipulations of feces, mud or dust. He may then be asked to serve as the passive sexual object of an aggressive older male. We can now see another possible reason why the creator of the bullroarer in one myth has the name of no-anus. The senior males likewise have no anus in the sense that they are the active rather than passive homosexuals. In no case do they provide anuses, but only phalluses. It is the initiates who must provide anuses—especially as their phalluses have been temporarily put out of commission! This is no idle armchair speculative theory, but is in fact an account closely paralleling empirical ethnographic data.

Only a few anthropologists have remarked upon the possible homosexual elements in male initiation rites. Victor Turner, for example, felt there was such an element in Ndembu initiation, observing that one of the principal initiators, the lodge instructor, had a name which meant "husband of the novices" (1967:223). However, Hiatt (1971:87) specifically rejects this type of interpretation claiming "it would be hard to find empirical grounds for representing these rites as 'guilty homosexual secrets'." Long ago, R. H. Mathews commented, "Among all the aboriginal tribes with which I am acquainted masturbation and sodomy are practised on certain occasions" (1900:636) and he described one such occasion, albeit in rather circumlocutory detail (1896:333–4): "Most of the positions and gestures are very obscene, and some of them disgusting." A much more modern and detailed account is reported by van Baal (1966:479–80). After the young boys have been introduced to Sosom (phallus, bullroarer), they are presented with bullroarers of their clan. Then after having been instructed not to divulge to women anything connected with the ritual, they are led outside to an enclosure where they are "subjected to promiscuous homosexual intercourse." Similarly, Williams in his extended discussion of "initiation and the bull-roarer" (1936b:181–206) among the Keraki notes (194) that following the revelation of the bullroarer to the initiates, the initiates are subjected to sodomy by elders. Van Baal comments (1966:351) that the natives have the distinction between active and passive homosexuals. In Malekula, Deacon reported (1934:261) similar connections of homosexuality with initiation. "Up to the time that a boy assumes the bark-belt, the badge of the adult male, he should not take a boy-lover, but himself plays this role to some older man. It is only after he has donned the bark-belt that he enjoys this privilege."

The rationale offered by natives for homosexual behavior is equally traditional. Van Baal reports that it is to make the young boys grow. Just as reported heterosexual cohabitation is necessary for normal pregnancy to be successful, so growth is dependent upon repeated homosexual intercourse (1966:493). Among the Keraki, Williams notes (1936b:203–4) that sodomy is believed to make the young boys grow. Deacon indicates (1934:262) that the homosexual acts of a young boy's "husband" are thought to cause the boy's male organ to grow strong and large. Van Baal remarks upon the institutionalized homosexual relationship between a boy and an older man (sometimes the boy's mother's brother). The boy may be "mockingly called a girl" (1966:670) and may be subject to the older man's homosexual desires for some years (1966:671, 845; cf. 950–1). It is tempting to speculate whether the distinction between older males and younger "female" boys is analogous to different kinds of bullroarers, e.g., male and female, or large and small bullroarers (Williams 1936a:15; Schmeltz 1896:109). When initiates are presented with small miniature bullroarers, this symbolizes their lesser male status in comparison with older males (who handle the large bullroarers).

The use of the phallic bullroarer in initiation rites may well involve symbolic masturbation. If the bullroarer is phallic and if it is whirled about, then the novices are ritually being taught how to symbolically manipulate their phalluses. Róheim has drawn attention to the onanistic implications of rubbing the bullroarer—often on the male organs of the young boys (1926:231, 257; cf. Mathews 1900:635), citing (1926:443) a custom in which the initiates form a ring and allegedly perform mutual onanism.

VIII

It may now be more clear why the initiation rites must be kept secret from women. Whether it is males attempting to emulate female procreativity by means of anal power, or homosexual intercourse in lieu of heterosexual intercourse, or ritual masturbation, the consistent element is that men seek to live without recourse to women. Williams (1936b:201–2) reports that Keraki initiates are forced to eat lime, which is said to ensure that the young men do not become pregnant as a result of serving as objects of anal intercourse. (This would seemingly be counter evidence to the theory of pregnancy envy!) However, perhaps more significant is the native reasoning that were a corpulent man to succeed in delivering a child, that would reveal that sodomy had taken place, "a revelation which, they say, would cause extreme shame to every man." Engaging in acts normally carried out by women must at all cost be kept from women. The would-be superiority of males would be revealed as a sham if women were allowed to observe. The secrecy permits the males the luxury of thinking they are superior to women or at least of not being dependent upon them or possibly just of enjoying the culturally sanctioned pretense of trying to fool women.

Considering the bullroarer as a flatulent phallus (cf. Saul 1959) makes it possible to account for the overt anal and phallic characteristics found in the bullroarer complex. The hypothesis is in no way incompatible with the idea that the bullroarer is somehow connected with an ancestral (male) spirit, or that it signals male solidarity. Quite the contrary, the specific use of anal and phallic traits make it essential that it be associated with powerful males of the past. The hypothesis does offer an explanation for the common connection of the bullroarer with thunder and windmaking. It is also in accord with accounts of initiation which refer to the initiates in terms of feces, and in similar fashion it makes sense out of the practice which disturbed Lang, namely, that of covering the initiates with filth. It would provide the plausible psychological principle sought by Lowie to explain why the Ekoi and Bororo women must be kept from bullroarers. The male envy factor would also be consonant with myths indicating that originally women had the bullroarer and that men forcibly took it away from the women. It would solve the "problem" raised by Worms as to why *guna* could be an archaic Australian aboriginal term meaning both bullroarer and feces. And finally the present analysis might even explain why the bullroarer has continued on into modern times in Europe.

Euro-American boys have noisemakers which appear to be functional equivalents of the bullroarer. These can be used to annoy, if not frighten, girls. Such toys may also be flatulent phalluses. As the names of the bullroarer proved suggestive in other cultures, so the name *bullroarer* itself may not be without significance. The etymology of *bull*, for instance, does tend to support the flatulent phallus hypothesis. Etymological antecedents of *bull* refer to testicle and penis, but several also refer to swelling and blowing as in a pair of bellows (Klein 1966). A bull is without a doubt a male phallic symbol (as in bullfighting) but there may also be an anal component. To "shoot the bull" at a "bull-session" concerns long*winded* discourse presumably containing some bull*shit*. The roar of a bullroarer would be analogous to a "bronx cheer" or a "raspberry." To razz someone is to direct at him a derogatory flatulent sound (*razz*, from *raspberry tart* which in rhyming slang substitutes for *fart*). One might even go so far as to argue that motor cars and motorcycles express the same double phallic and anal symbolism. A stock car or any car stripped of nonessential items with its engine modified to produce greater speed has been traditionally called a "hot rod" in the United States, a term which strongly suggests phallicism. And the common practice of removing the muffler ensures an extremely loud exhaust noise from the car's rear end. This suggests anal power. The point is that since the bullroarer *is* reported in Europe, even if it is *only* a toy or "boy's plaything," as E. B. Tylor phrased it, whatever cross-cultural explanation is offered to illuminate the functioning of the bullroarer in aboriginal Australia, native North and South America, and Africa, should also be applicable to Europe.

It is my hope that the present hypothetical psychoanalytic consideration of the bullroarer based upon notions of male pregnancy envy, anal eroticism, and ritual homosexuality does satisfactorily explain some of the more puzzling aspects of the bullroarer complex (and initiation rites). Possibly too much emphasis has been given to data from Australia and New Guinea. Still, the worldwide distribution of the bullroarer is undeniable. The ultimate test of the present argument should not be a matter of doctrinaire acceptance or rejection of Freudian-derived theory, but rather how well or how poorly it succeeds in explaining the patterning of ethnographic facts. And that is for the reader to judge.

Into the Endzone for a Touchdown

A Psychoanalytic Consideration
of American Football

I would like to dedicate this essay to Professor David Bidney who taught me that there is no cultural data which cannot be illuminated by a judicious application of theory. I must also thank Nancy Nash and Stuart Blackburn for their helpful comments and suggestions.

In college athletics it is abundantly clear that it is football which counts highest among both enrolled students and alumni. It is almost as though the masculinity of male alumni is at stake in a given game, especially when a hated rival school is the opponent. College fund raisers are well aware that a winning football season may prove to be the key to a successful financial campaign to increase the school's endowment capital. The Rose Bowl and other postseason bowl games for colleges, plus the Super Bowl for professional football teams have come to rank as national festival occasions in the United States. All this makes it reasonable to assume that there is something about football which strikes a most responsive chord in the American psyche. No other American sport consistently draws fans in the numbers which are attracted to football. One need only compare the crowd-attendance statistics for college or professional baseball games with the analogous figures for football to see the enormous appeal of the latter. The question is: what is it about American football that could possibly account for its extraordinary popularity?

In the relatively meager scholarship devoted to football, one finds the usual array of theoretical approaches. The ancestral form of football, a game more like Rugby or soccer, was interpreted as a solar ritual—with a disc-shaped rock or object supposedly representing the sun[1]—and also as a fertility ritual intended to ensure agricultural abundance. It had been noted, for example, that in some parts of England and France, the rival teams consisted of married men playing against bachelors.[2] In one custom, a newly married woman would throw over the church a ball for which married men and bachelors fought. The distinction between the married and the unmarried suggests that the game might be a kind of ritual test or battle with marriage signifying socially sanctioned fertility.[3]

The historical evolution of American football from English Rugby has been well documented,[4] but the historical facts do not in and of themselves account for any psychological rationale leading to the unprecedented enthusiasm for the sport. It is insufficient to state that football offers an appropriate outlet for the expression of aggression. William Arens has rightly observed that it would be an oversimplification "to single out violence as the sole or even primary reason for the game's popularity."[5] Many sports provide a similar outlet (e.g., wrestling, ice hockey, roller derby), but few of these come close to matching football as a spectacle for many Americans. Similarly, pointing to such features as a love of competition, or the admiration of coordinated teamwork, or the development of specialists (e.g., punters, punt returners, field-goal kickers, etc.) is not convincing since such features occur in most if not all sports.

Recently, studies of American football have suggested that the game serves as a male initiation ritual.[6] Arens, for example, remarks that football is "a male preserve that manifests both the physical and cultural values of masculinity,"[7] a description which had previously been applied, aptly it would appear, to British Rugby.[8] Arens points out that the equipment worn "accents the male physique" through the enlarged head and shoulders coupled with a narrowed waist. With the lower torso "poured into skintight pants accented only by a metal codpiece," Arens contends that the result "is not an expression but an exaggeration of maleness." He comments further: "Dressed in this manner, the players can engage in hand holding, hugging, and bottom patting, which would be disapproved of in any other context, but which is accepted on the gridiron without a second thought."[9] Having said this much, Arens fails to draw any inferences about possible ritual homosexual aspects of football. Instead, he goes on to note that American football resembles male rituals in other cultures insofar as contact with females is discouraged if not forbidden. The argument usually given is one of "limited good."[10] A man has only so much energy and if he uses it in sexual activity, he will have that much less to use in hunting, warfare, or in this case, football. I believe Arens and others are correct in calling attention to the ritual and symbolic dimensions of American football, but I think the psychological implications of the underlying symbolism have not been adequately explored.

Football is one of a large number of competitive games which involve the scoring of points by gaining access to a defended area in an opponent's territory. In basketball, one must throw a ball through a hoop (and net) attached to the other team's backboard. In ice hockey, one must hit the puck into the goal at the opponent's end of the rink. In football, the object is to move the ball across the opponent's goal into his endzone. It does not require a great deal of Freudian sophistication to see a possible sexual component in such acts as throwing a ball through a hoop, hitting a puck across a "crease" into an enclosed area bounded by nets or cage, and other structurally similar acts. But what is not so obvious is the connection of such sexual symbolism with an all-male group of participants.

Psychologists and psychoanalysts have not chosen to examine American football to any great extent. Psychologist G. T. W. Patrick, writing in 1903, tried to explain the fascination of the game: "Evidently there is some great force, psychological or sociological, at work here which science has not yet investigated"; but he could offer little detail about what that great force might be.[11] Similarly, psychoanalyst A. A. Brill's superficial consideration of football in 1929 failed to illuminate the psychodynamics of the game.[12] Perhaps the best known Freudian analysis of football is the parody written originally in 1955 in the *Rocky Mountain Herald* by poet Thomas Hornsby Ferril, using the pseudonym Childe Herald, but the essay is more amusing than analytic. Actually his interpretation tends to be more inclined towards ritual than psychoanalytic theory. He suggests "football is a syndrome of religious rites symbolizing the struggle to preserve the egg of life through the rigors of impending winter. The rites begin at the autumn equinox and culminate on the first day of the New Year with great festivals identified with bowls of plenty; the festivals are associated with flowers such as roses, fruits such as oranges, farm crops such as cotton and even sun-worship and the appeasement of great reptiles such as alligators."[13] While he does say that "football obviously arises out of the Oedipus complex," he provides little evidence other than mentioning that college games are usually played for one's alma mater, which he translates as "dear mother." Actually, a more literal translation would be "nourishing mother" (and for that matter, *alumnus* literally means nursling.)

A more conventional psychoanalytic perspective is offered by Adrian Stokes in his survey of ball games with special reference to cricket. Stokes predictably describes football (soccer) in Oedipal terms. Each team defends the goal at their back. "In front is a new land, the new woman, whom they strive to possess in the interest of preserving the mother inviolate, in order, as it were, to progress from infancy to adulthood: at the same time, the defensive role is the father's; he opposes the forward youth of the opposition."[14] Speaking of Rugby football, Stokes proposes the following description: "Ejected out of the mother's body, out of the scrum, after frantic hooking and pushing, there emerges the rich loot of the father's genital." According to Stokes, both teams fight to possess the father's phallus, that is, the ball, in order to "steer it through the archetypal vagina, the goal."[15] Earlier, Stokes had suggested the ball represented semen though he claimed that "more generally the ball is itself the phallus."[16] Folk speech offers some support for the phallic connotation of a ball. One thinks of "balls" for testicles. A man who has "balls" is a man of strength and determination. To "ball" someone is a slang expression for sexual intercourse.[17] On the other hand, while one might agree with the general thesis that there might be a sexual component to both soccer and American football, it is difficult to cite concrete evidence supporting Stokes's contention that the game involves a mother figure or a father surrogate. If psychoanalytic interpretations are valid, then it ought to be possible to adduce specific details of idiom and ritual as documentation for such interpretations. It is not enough for a psychoanalyst to assert ex cathedra what a given event or object supposedly symbolizes.

I believe that a useful way to begin an attempt to understand the psychoanalytic significance of American football is through an examination of football folk speech. For it is precisely in the idioms and metaphors that a clear pattern of personal interaction is revealed. In this regard, it might be helpful first to briefly consider the slang employed in the verbal dueling of the American male. In effect, I am suggesting that American football is analogous to male verbal dueling.

Football entails ritual and dramatic action while verbal dueling is more concerned with words. But structurally speaking, they are similar or at least functionally equivalent. In verbal dueling, it is common to speak about putting one's opponent "down." This could mean simply to topple an opponent figuratively, but it could also imply forcing one's adversary to assume a supine position, that is, the "female" position in typical Western sexual intercourse. It should also be noted that an equally humiliating experience for a male would be to serve as a passive receptacle for a male aggressor's phallic thrust. Numerous idioms attest to the widespread popularity of this pattern of imagery to describe a loser. One speaks of having been screwed by one's boss or of having been given the shaft. Submitting to anal intercourse is also implied in perhaps the most common single American folk gesture, the so-called *digitus impudicus,* better known in folk parlance as *"the finger."* Giving someone the finger is often accompanied by such unambiguous explanatory phrases as "Fuck you!" "Screw you!" "Up yours!" or "Up your ass!."

Now what has all this to do with football? I believe that the same symbolic pattern is at work in verbal dueling and much ritual play. Instead of scoring a putdown, one scores a touchdown. Certainly the terminology used in football is suggestive. One gains yardage, but it is not territory which is kept in the sense of being permanently acquired by the invading team. The territory invaded remains nominally under the proprietorship of the opponent. A sports announcer or fan might say, for example, "This is the deepest *penetration* into (opponent's team name) territory so far" [my emphasis]. Only if one gets into the endzone (or kicks a field goal through the uprights of the goalposts) does one earn points.

The use of the term *end* is not accidental. Evidently there is a kind of structural isomorphism between the line (as opposed to the backfield) and the layout of the field of play. Each line has two ends (left end and right end) with a "center" in the middle. Similarly, each playing field has two ends (endzones) with a midfield line (the fifty-yard line). Ferril remarked on the parallel between the oval shape of the football and the oval shape of most football stadiums,[18] but I submit it might be just as plausible to see the football shape as an elongated version of the earlier round soccer or Rugby ball, a shape which tends to produce two accentuated ends of the ball. Surely the distinctive difference between the shape of a football and the shape of the balls used in most other ball games (e.g., baseball, basketball, soccer) is that it is not perfectly spherical. The notion that a football has two "ends" is found in the standard idiom used to describe a kick or punt in which the ball turns over and over from front to back during flight (as opposed to moving in a more direct, linear, spiraling pattern) as an "end over end" kick.

The object of the game, simply stated, is to get into the opponent's endzone while preventing the opponent from getting into one's own endzone. Structurally speaking, this is precisely what is involved in male verbal dueling. One wishes to put one's opponent down; to "screw" him while avoiding being screwed by him. We can now better understand the appropriateness of the "bottom patting" so often observed among football players. A good offensive or defensive play deserves a pat on the rear end. The recipient has held up his end and has thereby helped protect the collective "end" of the entire team. One pats one's teammates' ends, but one seeks to violate the endzone of one's opponents!

The trust one has for one's own teammates is perhaps signalled by the common postural stance of football players. The so-called three-point stance involves bending over in a distinct stooped position with one's rear end exposed. It is an unusual position (in terms of normal life activities) and it does make one especially vulnerable to attack from behind, that is, vulnerable to a homosexual attack. In some ways, the posture might be likened to what is termed *presenting* among nonhuman primates. *Presenting* refers to a subordinate animal's turning its rump towards a higher ranking or dominant one. The center thus presents to the quarterback—just as linemen do to the backs in general. George Plimpton has described how the quarterback's "hand, the top of it, rests up against the center's backside as he bends over the ball—medically, against the perineum, the pelvic floor."[19] We know that some dominant nonhuman primates will sometimes reach out to touch a presenting subordinate in similar fashion. In football, however, it is safe to present to one's teammates. Since one can trust one's teammates, one knows that one will be patted, not raped. The traditional joking admonitions of the locker room warning against bending over in the shower or picking up the soap (thus presumably offering an inviting target for homosexual attack) do not apply since one is among friends. "Grabass" among friends is understood as being harmless joking behavior.

The importance of the "ends" is signalled by the fact that they alone among linemen are eligible to receive a forward pass. In that sense, ends are equivalent to the "backs." In symbolic terms, I am arguing that the end is a kind of backside and that the endzone is a kind of erogenous zone. The relatively recently coined terms *tight end* and *split end* further demonstrate the special emphasis upon this "position" on the team. The terms refer to whether the end stays close to his neighboring tackle, e.g., to block, or whether he moves well away from the normally adjacent tackle, e.g., to go out for a pass. However, both *tight end* and *split end* (cf. also *wide receiver*) could easily be understood as possessing an erotic nuance.

I must stress that the evidence for the present interpretation of American football does not depend upon just a single word. Rather, there are many terms which appear to be relevant. The semantics of the word *down* are of interest. A down is a unit of play insofar as a team has four downs in which to either advance ten yards or score. A touchdown, which earns six points, refers to the act of an offensive player's possessing the ball in the opponent's endzone. (Note it is not sufficient for the player to be in the endzone; it is the ball which must be in the zone.) In a running play, the ball often physically touches the endzone and could therefore be said to "touch down" in that area. However, if an offensive player catches a pass in the endzone, the ball does not actually touch the ground. The recent practice of "spiking" the ball, in which the successful offensive player hurls the ball at the ground as hard as he can, might be construed as an attempt to have the football physically touch down in the endzone. In any case, the use of the word *touch* in connection with scoring in football does conform to a general sexually symbolic use of that term. The sexual nuances of *touch* can even be found in the Bible. For example, in I Corinthians 7:1–2, we find "It is good for a man not to touch a woman. Nevertheless to avoid fornication, let every man have his own wife" (cf. Genesis 20:6; Proverbs 6:29). Touching can be construed as an aggressive act. Thus to be touched by an opponent means that one has been the victim of aggression. The game of "touch football" (as opposed to "tackle" football) supports the notion that a mere art of touching is sufficient to fulfill the structural (and psychological) requirements of the basic rules. No team wants to give up a touchdown to an opponent. Often a team on defense may put up a determined goal-line stand to avoid being penetrated by the opponent's offense.

The special spatial nature of the endzone is perhaps indicated by the fact that it is not measured in the one hundred yard distance between the goal lines. Yet it is measured. It is only ten yards deep; a pass caught by an offensive player whose feet are beyond the end line of the endzone would be ruled incomplete.

Additional football folk speech could be cited. The object of the game is to "score," a term which in standard slang means to engage in sexual intercourse with a member of the opposite sex. One "scores" by going "all the way." The latter phrase refers specifically to making a touchdown.[20] In sexual slang, it alludes to indulging in intercourse as opposed to petting or necking. The offensive team may try to mount a "drive" in order to "penetrate" the other team's territory. A ball carrier might go "up the middle" or he might "go through a hole" (made by his linemen in the opposing defensive line). A particularly skillful runner might be able to make his own hole. The defense is equally determined to "close the hole." Linemen may encourage one another "to stick it to 'em," meaning to place their helmeted heads (with phallic-symbolic overtones) against the chests of their opposite numbers to drive them back or put them out of the play.

A player who scores a touchdown may elect to "spike" the ball by hurling it down towards the ground full force. This spiking movement confirms to all assembled that the enemy's endzone has been penetrated. The team scored upon is thus shamed and humiliated in front of an audience. In this regard, football is similar to verbal dueling inasmuch as dueling invariably takes place before one or more third parties. The term *spike* may also be germane. As a noun, it could refer to a sharp-pointed long slender part or projection. As a verb, it could mean either "to mark or cut with a spike" (the football would presumably be the phallic spike) or "to thwart or sabotage an enemy." In any event, the ritual act of spiking serves to prolong and accentuate the all-too-short moment of triumph, the successful entry into the enemy's endzone.

The sexual connotations of football folk speech apply equally to players on defense. One goal of the defensive line is to penetrate the offensive line to get to the quarterback. Getting to the offensive quarterback and bringing him down to the ground is termed "sacking the quarterback." The verb *sack* connotes plunder, ravage, and perhaps even rape. David Kopay, one of the few homosexuals in professional football willing to admit a preference for members of the same sex, commented on the nature of typical exhortations made by coaches and others:

> The whole language of football is involved in sexual allusions. We were told to go out and "fuck those guys"; to take that ball and "stick it up their asses" or "down their throats." The coaches would yell, "knock their dicks off," or more often than that, "knock their jocks off." They'd say, "Go out there and give it all you've got, a hundred and ten per cent, shoot your wad." You controlled their line and "knocked" 'em into submission. Over the years I've seen many a coach get emotionally aroused while he was diagramming a particular play into an imaginary hole on the blackboard. His face red, his voice rising, he would show the ball carrier how he wanted him to "stick it in the hole."[21]

The term *rape* is not inappropriate and in fact it has been used to describe what happens when an experienced player humiliates a younger player: "That poor kid, he was raped, keelhauled, he was just *destroyed*. . . ."[22] Kopay's reference to *jock* as phallus is of interest since *jock* is a term (short for *jockstrap*, the article of underapparel worn to protect the male genitals) typically used to refer generally to athletes. Calling an athlete a *jock* or a *strap* thus tends to reduce him to a phallus. A *jocker* is used in hobo slang and in prison slang to refer to an aggressive male homosexual.[23] (The meaning of *jock* may well be related to the term *jockey* insofar as the latter refers to the act of mounting and riding a horse.)

Some of the football folk speech is less obvious and the interpretation admittedly a bit more speculative. For example, a lineman may be urged to "pop" an opposing player, meaning to tackle or block him well. Executing a perfect tackle or block may entail placing one's helmet as close as possible to the middle of the opponent's chest. The use of the verb *pop* strongly suggests defloration, as in the idiom "to pop the cherry" referring to the notion of rupturing the maidenhead in the process of having intercourse with a virgin.[24] In Afro-American folk speech, "pop" can refer to sexual penetration.[25] To "pop" an opponent thus implies reducing him to female-victim status. Much of the sexual slang makes it very clear that the winners are men while the losers are women or passive homosexuals. David Kopay articulates this when he says, "From grade school on, the curse words on the football field are about behaving like a girl. If you don't run fast enough to block or tackle hard enough you're a pussy, a cunt, a sissy."[26] By implication, if a player succeeds, he is male. Thus in the beginning of the football game, we have two sets or teams of males. By the end of the game, one of the teams is "on top," namely the one which has "scored" most by getting into the other team's "end zone." The losing team, if the scoring differential is great, may be said to have been "creamed."

It is tempting to make something of the fact that originally the inner portion of the football was an inflated animal bladder. Thus touching the enemy's endzone with a bladder would be appropriate ritual behavior in the context of a male homosexual attack. However, it could be argued that the bladder was used simply because it was a convenient inflatable object available to serve as a ball.

If the team on offense is perceived in phallic terms, then it is the quarterback who could be said to be nominally in charge of directing the attack. In this context, it may be noteworthy that a quarterback intending to pass often tries to stay inside of the "pocket," a deployment of offensive players behind the line of scrimmage designed to provide an area of maximum protection.[27] A pants pocket, of course, could be construed as an area where males can covertly touch or manipulate their genitals without being observed. "Pocket pool," for example, is a slang idiom for fondling the genitals,[28] an idiom which incidentally may suggest something about the symbolic nature of billiards. The quarterback, if given adequate protection by his "pocket," may be able to "thread the needle," that is, throw the ball accurately, past the hands of the defensive players, into the hands of his receiver. The metaphor of threading the needle is an apt one since getting the thread through the eye of the needle is only preparatory for the act of "sewing." (Note also that "to make a pass" at someone is a conventional idiom for an act of flirtation.) Once the ball is in his possession, the receiver is transformed from a passive to an active role as he tries to move the ball as far forward as possible.

While it is possible to disagree with several of the interpretations offered of individual items of folk speech cited thus far, it would seem difficult to deny the overall sexual nature of much of football (and other sports) slang. The word *sport* itself has this connotation and has had it for centuries. Consider one of Gloucester's early lines in *King Lear* when he refers to his bastard son Edmund by saying "There was good sport at his making" (I,i,23) or in such modern usages as "sporting house" for brothel[29] or "sporting life" referring to pimps and prostitutes.[30] In the early 1950s, kissing was commonly referred to by adolescents as a "favorite indoor sport," presumably in contrast to outdoor sports such as football. It should also be noted that *game* can carry the same sexual connotation as *sport*.[31]

I have no doubt that a good many football players and fans will be skeptical (to say the least) of the analysis proposed here. Even academics with presumably less personal investment in football will probably find implausible, if not downright repugnant, the idea that American football could be a ritual combat between groups of males attempting to assert their masculinity by penetrating the endzones of their rivals. David Kopay, despite suggesting that for a long time football provided a kind of replacement for sex in his life and admitting that football is "a real outlet for repressed sexual energy,"[32] refuses to believe that "being able to hold hands in the huddle and to pat each other on the ass if we felt like it" is necessarily an overt show of homosexuality.[33] Yet I think it is highly likely that the ritual aspect of football, providing as it does a socially sanctioned framework for male body contact—football, after all, is a so-called body contact sport—is a form of homosexual behavior. The unequivocal sexual symbolism of the game, as plainly evidenced in folk speech, coupled with the fact that all of the participants are male, make it difficult to draw any other conclusion. Sexual acts carried out in thinly disguised symbolic form by, and directed towards, males and males only, would seem to constitute ritual homosexuality.

Evidence from other cultures indicates that male homosexual ritual combats are fairly common. Answering the question of who penetrates whom is a pretty standard means of testing masculinity cross-culturally. Interestingly enough, the word *masculine* itself seems to derive from Latin *mas* (male) and *culus* (anus). The implication might be that for a male to prove his masculinity with his peers, he would need to control or guard his buttocks area while at the same time threatening the posterior of another (weaker) male. A good many men's jokes in Mediterranean cultures (e.g., in Italy and in Spain) center on the *culo*.

That a mass spectacle could be based upon a ritual masculinity contest should not surprise anyone familiar with the bullfight. Without intending to reduce the complexity of the bullfight to a single factor, one could nonetheless observe that it is in part a battle between males attempting to penetrate one another. The one who is penetrated loses.

If it is the bull, he may be further feminized or emasculated by having various extremities cut off to reward the successful matador. In this context, we can see American football as a male activity (along with the Boy Scouts, fraternities, and other exclusively male social organizations in American culture) as belonging to the general range of male rituals around the world in which masculinity is defined and affirmed. In American culture, women are permitted to be present as spectators or even cheerleaders, but they are not participants. Women resenting men's preoccupation with such male sports are commonly referred to as football widows (analogous to golf widows). This too suggests that the sport activity is in some sense a substitute for normal heterosexual relations. The men are "dead" as far as relationships with females are concerned. In sport and in ritual, men play both male *and* female parts. Whether it is the verbal dueling tradition of the circum-Mediterranean[34] in which young men threaten to put opponents into a passive homosexual position, or the initiation rites in aboriginal Australia and New Guinea (and elsewhere) in which younger men are subjected to actual homosexual anal intercourse by older members of the male group,[35] the underlying psychological rationale appears to be similar. Professional football's financial incentives may extend the playing years of individuals beyond late adolescence, but in its essence American football is an adolescent masculinity initiation ritual in which the winner gets into the loser's endzone more times than the loser gets into his!

"To Love My Father All"
A Psychoanalytic Study
of the Folktale Source of King Lear

The study of folklore in literature entails at least two distinct methodological steps: identification and interpretation.[1] The first step is to identify accurately and fully a possible folkloristic element or form occurring in a given literary (con)text. This is an empirical, objective process which can be verified by any literary scholar sufficiently conversant with the normal critical apparatus employed by folklorists. Once the identification has been successfully completed, the more difficult task of interpretation may be attempted. Interpretation, unlike identification, is often subjective and is not necessarily empirically demonstrable. Frequently, interpretations are like beauty insofar as they lie primarily in the eyes of the beholders rather than in the literary text analyzed. This is why interpretations, especially psychoanalytic ones, are commonly criticized as being "read into" rather than being "read out of" the text.

One problem with the twofold methodology of identification and interpretation is that both steps are all too rarely achieved. Folklorists for their part are too often wont to stop after making identifications. Accordingly one finds scholarly contributions consisting of little more than long lists of "proverbs" in the works of so and so. Such lists of proverbs, nursery rhymes, or allusions to children's games typically fail to include any attempt to explain why a particular proverb, rhyme, or children's game was used by a particular poet in a particular literary context.

Literary scholars unfamiliar with folkloristics are guilty of a different error. Such scholars are not averse to plunging headlong into interpretation without benefit of proper identification of folkloristic source material. The vast majority of literary source studies assume literary, not folklore, precursors and the inevitable search is invariably for a missing manuscript rather than an oral tale. Literate scholars falsely believe that the authors they study must have read rather than heard an earlier version of the story line. This is despite the fact that the literate scholars themselves have heard folktales, legends, and jokes all their lives. Without considering folkloristic sources for literature would-be critics are deprived of an absolutely essential means of seeing how poets transform the common clay of folk imagination into a literary masterpiece.

It is not undue defensiveness or disciplinary chauvinism on the part of folklorists when they decry their literary colleagues' failure to utilize conventional folkloristic identification tools. The sad fact is that far too many professional students of literature are totally ignorant of such aids. Thus it is perfectly possible to write entire books on Homer's use of folktale and have such books published by reputable academic presses without revealing any knowledge whatsoever of the tale type index—an indispensable vade mecum which has been available since 1910. Neither Rhys Carpenter, *Folk Tale, Fiction and Saga in the Homeric Epics*, published by the University of California Press in 1946, nor Denys Page, *Folktales in Homer's Odyssey*, published by Harvard University Press in 1973, refers to the tale type index, or, for example, to the fact that tale type 1137, The Ogre Blinded (Polyphemus) is an identifiable, independent folktale which certainly must have been incorporated by Homer into the *Odyssey*. Similarly, there are surely Chaucerian scholars who are not aware of all of the dozen and a half tale types cognate with various *Canterbury Tales*.[2]

In Shakespearean criticism, one does find some awareness of the relationship of several of his plots to folktales, but typically these relationships are described in the vague, imprecise language of critics apparently ignorant of folklore scholarship. It is clear, for instance, that *Cymbeline* is related to tale type 882, The Wager on the Wife's Chastity; *The Taming of the Shrew* to tale type 901, Taming of the Shrew; and *Merchant of Venice* to a combination of motif L211, Modest choice; three caskets type, and tale 890, A Pound of Flesh.[3] Not only do most conventional Shakespearean scholars merely allude in passing to possible "old stories rooted in the popular faith" to borrow (and alter slightly) Coleridge's well-turned phrase, but they rarely, if ever, stop to consider the psychological implications of the folktale plot lying at the base of a given work of literature. In short, they do not always properly identify possible folktale sources; and without such identification, they are in no position to make a judicious psychological or, for that matter, any other type of interpretation of literature derived from folklore.

So the study of folklore in literature cannot be expected to advance so long as folklorists identify without interpreting and literary critics interpret without identifying folklore sources. It serves little purpose for folklorists to point accusing fingers at literary critics when they themselves undertake only the first of the two steps. Identifying a folktale source for a Shakespearean play does not per se automatically yield aesthetic and psychological insights into the meaning of either the tale or the play. Identification is simply no substitute for interpretation.

In the case of *King Lear*, it has long been recognized that the plot was borrowed in part from folklore. Specifically, the often discussed love-test of the opening scene has been recognized as tale type 923, Love Like Salt. In 1886, Hartland even labelled the first of what he considered to be five distinct types of "The Outcast Child" as the "King Lear type"; and not long thereafter, in 1892, Marian Roalfe Cox in her *Cinderella*, one of the first major full-length comparative studies of a folktale, elected to call the initial elements in Cap o' Rushes (tale type 510B) "King Lear judgment—Loving like salt."[4] Many of the standard studies of the sources of the play acknowledge the folkloristic origins of the love-test. Perrett devotes considerable notice in his 1904 monograph while Bullough in 1973 briefly mentions the appearance of the love-test in a Grimm tale.[5] (Here incidentally is another illustration of my contention that literary scholars are unaware of folklore scholarship. Perrett writing in 1904 did not have a tale type index to consult, but there is no excuse for any scholar writing after 1910 not to know of the tale type index.) On the other hand, Muir in his otherwise useful 1957 survey of the principal sources of *King Lear* makes no mention whatever of the folktale, Love Like Salt.[6] I hope to show that not only is the folktale in question a crucial source for *King Lear*, but that it is not possible to understand much of the inherent dramatic power of the play without knowledge of the underlying folktale and its essential psychological dimensions.

The folktale contains the basic plot consisting of an initial love test in which a king asks his three daughters to declare their love for him.

The third, his favorite, answers that her love is like salt and she is forthwith banished by the outraged king. The folktale typically ends with the marriage of the third princess—as most *Märchen* end with marriage, a fact confirmed by Propp's *Morphology of the Folktale*.[7] Normally, the king and his favorite daughter are reconciled at the end of the tale. Different versions of the folktale manifest interesting details. For example, in one version, the father becomes insane and the heroine's care restores him to his senses. In another, the father falls dead upon recognizing the heroine.[8]

One very important point is that in the folktale the central figure is the daughter-heroine. In fairy tales, the protagonists are almost always sons or daughters, not parents. This means that in the underlying source of *King Lear*, the central figure is the analogue to Cordelia. It follows that Shakespeare's emphasis upon Lear—one must keep in mind that Cordelia is technically absent for the bulk of the action of the play—is a critical literary change from the folklore source.

We have not yet finished with the task of identification. Not only is the daughter the central figure in the folktale, but the general tale involved is closely related to, and perhaps a subtype of, Cinderella, one of the most popular tales in the world. This is a feature of the identification of the folktale which has not been sufficiently appreciated by students of the play. Cox in her pioneering study of Cinderella called the story subtype C, Cap o' Rushes, but in a more recent comprehensive investigation of Cinderella by Swedish folklorist Anna Birgitta Rooth, the tale is considered to belong with Catskin under the same general plot rubric. In Rooth's 1951 study of the Cinderella cycle, this grouping of Cap o' Rushes and Catskin is labelled Type B1 and it corresponds to Aarne-Thompson tale type 510B, The Dress of Gold, of Silver, and of Stars.[9] Tale type 510B is somewhat distinct from tale type 510A, Cinderella, which is probably the best known version of the Cinderella plot. (Nevertheless, Stith Thompson's grouping of 510A, Cinderella, and 510B, The Dress of Gold, of Silver, and of Stars, under the same basic tale type number, reflects the probable cognation of the subtypes.)

The similarity of Catskin, which Cox called type B, and Cap o' Rushes (Cox's type C) was recognized by Cox herself. In fact, the only differentiating incidents were the occurrence of the "King Lear judgement" and the "Outcast Heroine" in Cap o' Rushes. These incidents were not found in Catskin. However, in Catskin were the functionally equivalent incidents of "Unnatural father" and "Heroine flight".[10] This is of enormous significance in seeking to understand *King Lear*. The summary of tale type 510B, The Dress of Gold, of Silver, and of Stars, which includes both Catskin and Cap o' Rushes, begins: "Present of the father who wants to marry his own daughter." The principal constituent motifs in the tale type include M 255, Deathbed promise concerning the second wife; T 511.1, Lecherous father; S 322.1.2, Father casts daughter forth when she will not marry him; T 311.1, Flight of maiden to escape marriage. Usually the queen on her deathbed makes the king promise to marry only someone who can wear her ring.[11] After the queen's death, the king tries in vain to find someone only to discover that the ring fits his own daughter. In another folktale motif, the king decides to marry the woman who most resembles his recently deceased wife and that person turns out to be his daughter. The gist of all this is that the "love like salt" plot appears to be a weakened form of the folktale plot in which a "mad" father tries to marry his own daughter. In making this assertion, it is not just a matter of identifying "love like salt" as a folklore motif, but rather of identifying its typical context as part of tale type 510B, The Dress of Gold, of Silver, and of Stars.

The theme of incest is a powerful one and it would be no surprise to learn that it provides one of the most important undercurrents of *King Lear*. It should be recognized that the theme occurs in somewhat muted form in the play. It is not as overt as in the folktale where the king demands his daughter's hand in marriage. This is how it is expressed in tale type 510B and in tale type 706, The Maiden Without Hands. In *King Lear*, the love test is rather a matter of a daughter's declaring her total love of her father "To love my father all" (I, i, 104).

A number of psychoanalytically oriented critics have remarked on the possible incest theme in the play. Bransom in 1934 ever so timidly and hesitatingly suggested at the very end of his book *The Tragedy of King Lear* that a factor which might have influenced Lear's conduct was "an old, repressed, incestuous passion for one of his daughters." Bransom was careful to warn readers in his introduction that they might prefer to omit his final chapter if they found the subject distasteful. Freud in a letter written to Bransom about his book agreed that "the secret meaning of the tragedy" had to do with Lear's "repressed incestuous claims on the daughter's love."[12] Earlier, in 1913, Freud had himself written about *King Lear* in his essay "The Theme of the Three Caskets" in which, interestingly enough, he compared Cordelia with Cinderella, but he made no reference to incest. Rather he suggested that Cordelia symbolized death, an interpretation which has not received much enthusiasm from critics sympathetic to psychoanalysis.[13] More recent psychoanalytic treatments of *King Lear* have also drawn attention to the incest theme. Pauncz went so far as to speak of a "Lear Complex," as a kind of a reverse Oedipus complex, referring to a father's being sexually attracted to his daughter.[14]

None of the critics who see an incest theme in *King Lear* appear to be aware of the existence of the same theme in folktale sources from which the play is definitely derived, but there is sufficient textual evidence in the play itself for them to cite in support of their interpretation. Lear during the storm scene specifically refers to incest (III, ii, 55). Later he maintains that he "will die bravely like a smug bridegroom" (Iv, vi, 194) and in the final meeting with Cordelia, Lear depicts himself and Cordelia as lovebirds "Come, let's away to prison. We two alone will sing like birds i' th' cage" (V. iii, 8.9). The incestuous nature of the love-test is also hinted at by France's astonishment upon hearing Lear's surprising denunciation of Cordelia. "This is most strange! That she . . . should . . . Commit a thing so monstrous to dismantle So many folds of favor. Sure, her offence Must be of such unnatural degree . . ." (I, i, 216–223). It may or may not be germane that the adjective "monstrous" was in fact used on another occasion by Shakespeare to refer to father-daughter incest. The final lines of *Pericles* begin: "In Antiochus and his daughter you have heard/Of monstrous lust the due and just reward." (V, iii, 85–86; cf. the father-daughter incest riddle in *Pericles*, I.i, 64–71.)

All the psychoanalytic readings of the play treating the incest theme, and that includes Freud's later one, agree that it is a matter of father-daughter incest. This stems in part from their looking at the drama from Lear's point of view rather than Cordelia's. This may be appropriate in view of the centrality of Lear in the play, but insofar as the basic plot structure comes from a daughter-centered fairy-tale, it is *in*appropriate. In brief, the fairy tale evidence would suggest that it is "daughter-father" incest rather than "father-daughter" incest! Furness once remarked "that of all departments of Shakespearian study none seems . . . more profitless than this search for the sources whence Shakespeare gathered his dramas."[15] The error of this incredible statement is just as serious for psychoanalytic literary criticism as it is for literary criticism in general. I submit that psychoanalysts and several literary critics may have erred in reading *King Lear* as a literal expression of incestuous desires on the part of a father figure. What the folktale behind the play and very likely the play itself does entail is *a projection of incestuous desires on the part of the daughter*. In this sense, the plot revolves around Cordelia, not Lear; and as we shall see, a great many details which have puzzled critics for some time may be explained.

First, a word about projection might be in order. Projection is a defense mechanism which translates unacceptable or taboo inner thoughts to an external outer object with the thoughts in question then neatly attributed to the external object. In Freud's terms, "I hate him" becomes "He hates me."[16] Projection obviates any feelings of guilt inasmuch as the original crime is displaced onto the object of the initial guilt-producing wish. The subject (original wisher) has become the object (victim) while the original intended victim has become the doer of the guilty deed. Projection in myth and folktale is common enough. Otto Rank in *The Myth of the Birth of the Hero* showed convincingly how the son's Oedipal wish to remove the father (so as to have sole access to the mother) is a taboo one. So in the resultant folkloristic projection, it is not the son-hero who wishes to get rid of his father but father, the wicked father figure, who tries to get rid of the son figure. The son is thereby able to slay the villainous father figure without guilt.[17]

In comparable daughter-centered fairy tales, the girl would like to eliminate her mother and marry her father. Many folktales begin with the queen or original mother already dead—perfect wish fulfillment! So in *King Lear*, there is no Queen Lear—leaving the father available as a sexual object for his daughters. But just as the son's wish to marry his mother is taboo, so the daughter's wish to marry her father is equally so. Consequently, in the fairy tale projection, it is always the father who insists upon marrying his own daughter. The specific details of how the dying queen insists that the new wife must be just like her would appear to reflect the common fantasy of a girl wishing to literally replace her mother—with respect to being her father's mate. The daughter either looks just like her mother or she is the only one who fits into her mother's wedding ring. (Cf. Kent's use of a ring to summon Cordelia, III, i, 47.)

If the present interpretation is correct, then it is perfectly true that

King Lear and its folktale source concerns a girl's inability to express her (sexual) love for her father. The interpretation explains not only why there is no Queen Lear, but also why Cordelia's husband appears so little in the play. The play is about a daughter-father relationship, not a wife-husband relationship. This is why, dramatically speaking, Cordelia's husband, "France," cannot appear in the final act. Cordelia's line "O dear father. It is thy business that I go about" (IV, iv, 23–24) is perhaps more than an obvious Christian echo of Jesus explaining, after having been found in the temple, "wist ye not that I must be about my Father's business?" (Luke, 2:49). It affirms that Cordelia is primarily concerned with her father, not her husband. Possibly there may even be a double meaning in "It is thy business that I go about" meaning both that it is her father's fault that she is wandering around, and that she is engaged in looking after his interests. In any case, it is the emotional reunion of daughter and father which provides the only logical and psychological denouement for such a plot.

The present interpretation also illuminates the punishment of Cordelia. Many critics have been bothered by Cordelia's death. In many of the literary versions of the story, Cordelia takes her own life. Perrett, for example, observes how common this ending is, but he is troubled by such a "meaningless" suicide since "it is not connected in any way with the events of the story proper."[18] From the psychoanalytic perspective, the story is a daughter's incestuous projection, not a father's. For this reason, Lear is quite right when he claims that he is "a man more sinn'd against than sinning." The original sin is Cordelia's. Once again, the available evidence from folklore is helpful. In tale type 706, The Maiden Without Hands, we have another extremely popular fairy tale which begins with a father's incestuous wish to marry his daughter. The daughter's response is to cut off her hands—perhaps signalling in a rather macabre punning way that she refuses to give her "hand" in marriage to her father. In any case, the point is that the girl punishes herself as a response to a "crime" purportedly about to be committed by her father. (In terms of female masturbatory behavior, it would be appropriate for a girl to cut off her "sinning" hands as a suitable punishment for indulging in incestuous thoughts about her father.) Thus if Cordelia is a sinner, then it is poetic justice to have her guilt lead her to suicide. Of course, Shakespeare elected to depart from the literary sources of his plot and Cordelia does not take her own life. The suicide is shifted to Goneril.

In the present context, it is noteworthy that the apparent motivation for Goneril's decision is unrequited lust (for Edmund).[19]

The fairy tale projection also helps explain Cordelia's relationship to her two sisters, who are obviously the wicked older sisters (often stepsisters) in Cinderella and other *märchen*. Among sisters, there is commonly sibling rivalry for the affection of the father. Each daughter wants to be her father's very favorite. In theory Cordelia ought to be pleased, for Lear admits publicly that he "lov'd her most" (I, i, 124). But in the fairy tale, overt sexuality on the part of the girl is denied. The adamant denial of sexuality and unadulterated purity of Cordelia is contrasted throughout the play with the unabashed animality and sexuality of both Goneril and Regan.[20]

The marked contrast between Cordelia and her sisters is also indicated by the sexual symbolism of speech. Speech is sexual; dumbness, not speaking, is asexual. Cordelia is unable or unwilling to speak. Her name, which may derive etymologically from heart (*cor*), may be related to Lear's request for her heart (I, i, 106), but she cannot heave her heart into her mouth (I, i, 94). Freud interpreted Cordelia's dumbness as a representation of death, an interpretation not incompatible with the asexuality suggested here. If dumbness is death, then speaking is life. Among other examples of the sexuality of speech, there is Albany's attempt to communicate that his wife is sexually unavailable to Edmund: "My lady is bespoke" (V, iii, 90). Regan refers to Goneril's "most speaking looks" before admitting that Edmund and she "have talk'd" (IV, v, 30) which means presumably that they have come to some sexual understanding.[21]

Understanding *King Lear* as a transformation of a folktale fantasy concerned with a daughter's disguised incestuous love of her father also affords insight into the particular verbiage used by Goneril and Regan in the love-test itself. Goneril declares "A love that makes breath poor and speech unable" (I, i, 61). Whether there is gasping or panting in the delivery of the lines is irrelevant,[22] for the words themselves hint of passion. Regan's response to the love-test includes mention of the "very deed of love" as well as reference to her "most precious square of sense" (I, i, 72, 75).[23] Regan, one may recall, is later to speak bluntly of the "forefended place," referring again to the female genital area (V, i, 10). Such teasing seductive allusions are in accord with a daughter's sexual fantasies revolving around her father.

The final reunion of Cordelia with Lear provides her triumph over her sibling rivals. In the very first scene of the play, Cordelia has to suffer her father's asking for the love of her two older sisters before he gets around to asking her for her love. In the final scene, however, Cordelia has her father all to herself. She even asks, "Shall we not see these daughters and sisters?" (V, iii, 7), but Lear emphatically says no and speaks of himself and Cordelia as "two alone" in the lovebird metaphor. Without either rival mother or rival sisters, Cordelia enjoys the culmination of her Electra complex fantasy for but a brief instant before being led away with her father to prison and death.

One could interpret the struggle between Goneril and Regan for the sexual attentions of Edmund as another reflection of sibling rivalry. Moreover, since a father is a married man, a daughter must commit adultery in order to gain his sexual favors, and this might explain the single curious reference to Lear's wife. Here the sexual rivalry is not between siblings, but between daughter and mother. In Lear's meeting with Regan, he tells her that if she weren't glad to see him, he would divorce himself from her mother's tomb because it would hold an adulteress (II, iv, 131). This implies that if Regan weren't glad to see him, she couldn't be his true daughter. But it also evokes a daughter's various fantasies concerning her rivalry with her mother for her father. From the daughter's point of view, if the daughter possesses the father, then the mother is the outsider, the adulteress.

In terms of the initial argument of this essay, we have provided both identification and interpretation. The objective identification was made of the love-test as more than simply "Love like salt." Rather, it belongs to a major form of the Cinderella cycle, a folktale whose normal form includes an overt paternal demand for an incestuous relationship with a daughter. If nothing else, this more complete identification of the ultimate source for *King Lear* would tend to support those many critics, including Freud himself, who have claimed that there is an underlying theme of father-daughter incest in the play. The more subjective and speculative interpretive portion of the essay, however, suggests that the fairy tale in question is a remarkable example of projection. Through projection, the basic daughter-father incest wish is transformed into an attempted father-daughter incest act. This does not mean that there are not fathers who are sexually attracted to their own daughters. There most surely are. But the existence of such paternal desires in no way precludes the existence of an Electra complex. To argue that it does would be tantamount to claiming that seductive behavior on the part of mothers towards sons rules out the possibility of the existence of the Oedipus complex. Clearly such parental fantasies add fuel to the fire of children's fantasies. (The confusion of generations is suggested in *King Lear* when Cordelia seems to be both daughter and mother to Lear.) The point is that incestuous desires may be mutual on the part of both daughter and father.

Some may doubt the wisdom of applying a modern concept such as projection to the artistic materials of past centuries. Yet in *King Lear* we find striking evidence for the plausibility of projection as a psychological device or defense mechanism. Lear himself (IV, vi, 156–158) demonstrates considerable insight into the nature of projection: "Thou rascal beadle, hold thy bloody hand! Why does thou lash that whore? Strip they own back. Thou hotly lusts to use her in that kind For which thou whipp'st her." In the same way, fathers should not punish daughters for indulging in sexual fantasies which fathers themselves hold and consciously or unconsciously encourage. We can see other examples of projection in the play. The daughter's anger because her father doesn't love her best is transformed in the fairy tale into the king's anger because his daughter doesn't love him best (to the exclusion of husbands present or future). Similarly, the daughter's wish to turn her home into a brothel (where she can more easily seduce her father) is transformed into her accusation that it is the father and his retinue which is making the house into a brothel " . . . our court . . . more like a tavern or a brothel Than a grac'd palace" (I, iv, 250).

In his book *Psychoanalysis and Shakespeare*, Norman Holland mentions that although Freud planned to attempt a synthesis of folkloristic and psychoanalytic approaches to *King Lear*, he never did so.[24] The present essay is intended to be a first step towards that synthesis. If valid, then the delineation of the projection pattern of the fairy tale underlying *King Lear* may provide a new perspective for students of the play. To be sure, one must be careful to separate the fairy tale source and the Shakespeare play. Even if the psychoanalytic argument broached here were adjudged applicable to the fairy tale, it does not necessarily follow that it must be equally so to the play. The play represents a literary reworking of folk material and more importantly it reflects an older male's reworking of a female-centered fairy tale. Whether Shakespeare's choice of subject matter and treatment stems from autobiographical factors is a moot question. Sharpe suggests that there might be a connection between the writing of *King Lear* in 1606 and Shakespeare's relationship with his own daughters—e.g., Susannah was married in 1607.[25] In this connection, one is tempted to venture the view that one possible reason for Shakespeare's giving vent to such vitriol with respect to the sexuality of women in *King Lear* as opposed to his witty and positive treatment in other plays[26] might be his normal father's repugnance at the thought of his "innocent" daughter becoming a sexual object for men (himself included).[27]

Regardless of any possible "play-as-biography" significance of the present interpretation of the play, it is at any rate safe to say that Shakespeare's utilization of a folktale plot involves much more than changing the fairy tale happy ending into a poignant, powerful tragedy.[28] Crucial is the emphasis upon the father-figure in a standard daughter-father fantasy. In other words, *King Lear* is a girl's fairy tale told from the father's point of view. Upon the fairy tale frame have been woven intricate philosophical and religious patterns which reveal the marvellous complexity of man.[29] Yet despite the sophistication of the overlay, the strongly articulated attitudes towards sexuality, the unmistakable expression of sibling rivalry, and the playing out of the Electra complex in *King Lear* provide abundant evidence for the view that the fairy tale frame is never really absent. That a "kissing cousin" of Cinderella, one of the world's most beloved and celebrated fairy tales, could have been metamorphosed into one of the great literary dramatic masterpieces of the stage is an eternal tribute to the unequalled creative genius of Shakespeare.

The Hero Pattern
and the Life of Jesus

The New Testament in general and the life of Jesus in particular have not received much critical attention from folklorists. This is in marked contrast to the considerable body of folklore scholarship devoted to the Old Testament. Frazer could pen a three-volume work entitled *Folklore in the Old Testament*, but he said relatively little about folklore in the New Testament. Similarly, Frazer devoted a considerable portion of his monumental *Golden Bough* to "Dying and Reviving Gods," most of them Near Eastern, but he said next to nothing about their possible relationship to the life of Jesus. Lord Raglan in his fascinating delineation of the hero pattern was perfectly willing to take three examples from the Old Testament—Joseph, Moses, and Elijah—but he does not so much as mention Jesus, despite the fact that the life of Jesus is demonstrably as similar to Raglan's twenty-two incident hero pattern as the lives of the three Old Testament heroes he does cite.

Perhaps one reason for the neglect of the New Testament by folklorists is a combination of prejudice and self-interest. Folklorists as well as folk feel ambivalence towards folklore. On the one hand, there is pride in folklore insofar as it represents a traditional expression of one's heritage. On the other hand, to the extent that folklore is considered to be synonymous with error and fallacy (and to the extent that the folk are considered to be the *vulgus in populo*), one tends to be ashamed of one's folklore and may even repudiate it. Raglan, for example, was anxious to show that the lives of traditional heroes were "folklore" rather than history. Thus it was perfectly all right to argue that Old Testament or Jewish heroes were folkloristic rather than historical. But heaven forbid that a proper member of the British House

of Lords should apply this line of reasoning to the life of Jesus! Moses
might be folklore but Jesus was history or, to put it another way,
Moses was "false" while Jesus was "true." Raglan even went so far as
to remark that "the compilers of the 'historical' books of the Old Testament were not historians writing for students, but theologians writing for the faithful" (Raglan 1956:112), an observation, which, of
course, could be equally well applied to the New Testament!

This may be a somewhat exaggerated statement of Lord Raglan's
position; but since he does not discuss Jesus, it would appear reasonable to assume that he felt Christ was fact while Moses was fiction. (In
1958 Lord Raglan told Professor Albert B. Friedman that of course he
had thought of Jesus in connection with the hero pattern, but that he
had no wish to risk upsetting anyone and therefore he elected to avoid
even so much as mentioning the issue—personal communication from
Professor Friedman, April, 1977.) To be sure, Raglan does not
categorically deny the historicity of any of the heroes he considers. It
is rather their common biographies which he labels as nonhistorical.
Moses and the others may have lived, but inevitably the folk reportings of their lives tend to conform to the hero pattern. The common
biographical pattern, Raglan claimed, derived from a common ritual
pattern, namely, ritual regicide. In this articulation of myth-ritual
theory, Raglan offers no suggestion of why ritual regicide should have
arisen. Actually, myth-ritual theory rarely, if ever, accounts for ultimate origins. To say myth comes from ritual is not to say where the
alleged ritual came from.

Inasmuch as Raglan and others insist upon referring to the accounts
of heroes as myths, it might be appropriate to indicate that if one
defines myth in the folkloristic sense of a sacred narrative explaining
how the world and man came to be in their present form, then it is
abundantly clear that Raglan's hero narratives are *not* myths. The narrative which originally inspired Raglan to undertake his hero pattern
study was Oedipus, which folklorists recognize as a folktale, namely
Aarne-Thompson tale type 931 (Thompson 1961). The story of
Oedipus is not a myth. Similarly, the story of Perseus, also analyzed
by Raglan, is generally considered by folklorists to be a version of
Aarne-Thompson tale type 300, The Dragon-Slayer. Many of the
narratives treated by Raglan, e.g., Arthur, Robin Hood, are legends
rather than myths. What this means is that the hero pattern articulated by Raglan (and a number of other scholars) is part of folktale and

legend, not myth. I would argue that the lives of Joseph, Moses, Elijah, and Jesus would, from the folklorists' point of view, be considered legends (cf. Bascom 1965).

If folklorists have neglected the life of Jesus, it cannot be said that theologians concerned with reconstructing the biography of Christ have not been concerned with folklore (though they usually insist upon referring to folklore under the misleading rubric of "myth"). The various "quests for the historical Jesus" invariably set as their goal the disentangling of fact from fiction, history from folklore. It would be a gross understatement to say that there exists a proliferation of books and monographs devoted to the life of Jesus. It would take more than one lifetime to read them all, assuming one had the requisite polyglot linguistic competence to do so. However, it is possible to note the consistent concern with attempting to separate out the folkloristic elements from the New Testament so as to come as close as humanly possible to unalloyed "gospel" truth.

The utilization of comparative folklore materials to illuminate the historicity of portions of the New Testament is by no means anything new. Celsus (circa 178), writing an anti-Christian tract in the second century, compared the virgin birth of Jesus with Greek myths about Danae, Melanippe, Auge, and Antiope. Furthermore, in speaking of the resurrection, he asked why, if other stories are myths, should the Christian account be regarded as "noble and convincing" (Grant 1961:73, 75)? There is other evidence attesting to the early recognition of possible analogues or parallels to the story of Jesus. For example, Justin Martyr, also writing in the second century, used a form of the comparative method in two distinct ways. On the one hand, he implies that the existence of analogues weakens the credibility of the Jesus narrative. Into the mouth of Trypho the Jew in his "Dialogue with Trypho," Justin put the following argument: "Besides, in Greek mythology there is a story of how Perseus was born of Danae, while she was a virgin, when the one whom they call Zeus descended upon her in the form of a golden shower. You Christians should be ashamed of yourselves, therefore, to repeat the same kind of stories as these men, and you should, on the contrary, acknowledge this Jesus to be a man of mere human origin" (Justin Martyr 1948:254). On the other hand, Justin in "The First Apology" actually used the existence of comparable stories as an argument for believing in the story of Jesus. "When, indeed, we assert that the Word, our Teacher Jesus Christ, who is the first-begotten of God the Father, was not born as the result of sexual relations, and that He was crucified, died, arose from the dead, and ascended into Heaven, we propose nothing new or different from that which you say about the so-called sons of Jupiter. You know exactly the number of sons ascribed to Jupiter by your respected writers: Mercury, who was the interpretative word and teacher of all; Aesculapius, who, though himself a healer of diseases, was struck by a thunderbolt and ascended into heaven; Bacchus, who was torn to pieces; Hercules, who rushed into the flames of the funeral pyre to escape his sufferings; the Dioscuri, the sons of Leda; Perseus, the son of Danae; and Bellerophon, who, though of human origin, rose to heaven on his horse Pegasus" (Justin Martyr 1948:56–57). Justin goes on to claim that such Greek myths had been invented by demons to counterfeit and thereby demean the true and miraculous events in the life of Jesus. "And, Trypho (I said), when I hear it asserted that Perseus was born of a virgin, I know that this is another forgery of that treacherous serpent" (Justin Martyr 1948:262, 57, 92, 259).

The problem of how to treat apparent or actual parallels to biblical materials has yet to be solved. If the same narrative exists in a variety of cultures, why is one version of the story singled out as being true or valid while all others are dismissed as being false or untrue? This fundamental question, which invariably arises from any honest application of the comparative method, continues to bedevil conscientious students of theology. Gunkel put the matter thus: " . . . it should not be forgotten that many of the legends of the Old Testament are not only similar to those of other nations, but are actually related to them by origin and nature. Now we cannot regard the story of the Deluge in Genesis as history and that of the Babylonians as legend" (Gunkel 1964:10). A number of alternatives exist. One can stubbornly cling to the notion that one's own version of the narrative is God's truth and simply not worry about the probable or possible cognate versions of the narrative in other cultures. A second possibility is to accept all versions of the narrative as God's truth. A third possibility is to accept the comparative data as bona fide evidence for the multiple existence of a narrative (thereby confirming the narrative as folklore) and to remove it from the sacred canon. This is, generally speaking, the course which has been followed by scholarly theologians. The folklore elements are to be identified and then culled out of the Bible. Through this process of "demythologizing," unadulterated sacred truth will remain.

I do not propose to survey all of the various attempts to de-mythologize the Old and New Testaments, for truly there is a massive amount of scholarship devoted to the subject (cf. Doane, Saintyves, Henderson, Childs, and Ohler). However, it might be useful to cite several of the earlier illustrations of the trend. One of the most influential treatises was the *Leben Jesu* of David Friedrich Strauss, first published in 1835. Using a modified form of the comparative method, Strauss viewed the four gospels as variants and he tried to isolate con-tradictory elements. One of his principles was: "An account which shall be regarded as historically valid, must neither be inconsistent with itself, nor in contradiction with other accounts" (Strauss 1892:88). His honest detailing of the contradictory elements as part of his elaborate effort to apply "the notion of the mythus to the entire history of the life of Jesus" (1892:65) led to a veritable ground swell of vituperative criticism from both his peers and the general public. The book cost Strauss his teaching position and his academic career (Schweitzer 1968:71; McCown 1940:6). Twentieth-century folklorists can nevertheless appreciate his accurate awareness of the difference between the narrative genres of myth and legend (Strauss 1892:62) even though he stubbornly chose to use the term *mythus* to refer to the folkloristic patterns underlying Christ's biography. Folklorists can cer-tainly empathize with such statements as "The knowledge of the fact, that the Jews were fond of representing their great men as the children of parents who had long been childless, cannot but make us doubtful of the historical truth of the statement that this was the case with John the Baptist; knowing also that the Jews saw predictions everywhere in their writings of their prophets and poets, and discovered types of the Messiah in all the lives of holy men recorded in their Scriptures; when we find details in the life of Jesus evidently sketched after the pattern of these prophecies and prototypes, we cannot but suspect that they are rather mythical than historical" (Strauss 1892:89). The field of comparative folklore was scarcely sufficiently developed at the time Strauss wrote for him to have been able to cite parallels from non-Judeo-Christian traditions.

By the end of the nineteenth century, various advocates of a 'myth' approach to the life of Jesus were much more sophisticated in terms of knowledge of other narrative traditions, but at the same time they were much less convincing in their arguments because of rigid adher-ence to one or another particular theory of interpretation: e.g., solar mythology. So another German critic, Arthur Drews, in his book *The*

Christ Myth, which appeared initially in 1909, sought to "prove that more or less all the features of the picture of the historical Jesus, at any rate all those of any important religious significance, bear a purely mythical character, and no opening exists for seeking an historical figure behind the Christ myth" (Drews 1911:19). Drews, called by one scholar "perhaps the outstanding representative of the denial of the historicity of Jesus in the twentieth century" (McCown 1940:71), attempted through tortuous reasoning to show that the sun god who dies in winter to rise again in the spring is related to a fire god, specifically the Indic Agni. A brief example of Drews' specious use of comparative folklore should suffice: "At dawn, as soon as the brightening morning star in the east announced that the sun was rising, the priest called his assistants together and kindled the fire upon a mound of earth by rubbing together two sticks in which the God was supposed to be hidden. As soon as the spark shone in the 'maternal bosom,' the soft underpart of the wood, it was treated as an 'infant child.'" He concludes, "There is no doubt that we have before us in the Vedic Agni cult the original source of all the stories of the birth of the Fire-Gods and Sun-Gods" (Drews 1911:99–100), adding later "Accordingly we have before us in the story of the transfiguration in the Gospels only another view of the story of the Light-God or Fire-God, such as lies at the root of the story of the baptism of the Christian Saviour" (1911:127). One must keep in mind that the reigning folklore theories of the day included both Indic origins and solar mythology. In any case, the flawed reasoning and faulty scholarship of Drews and other would-be folklore Bible critics of the period were fairly easy to attack. (Conybeare's *The Historical Christ* published in 1914, for example, did so with a good deal of acerbic glee!)

The excesses of solar mythologists may be partly responsible for the failure of later students of the history of religion and folklorists to have made any concerted effort to systematically consider the life of Jesus Christ as a variant of a standard European (or perhaps Indo-European) hero pattern. (The hero pattern in question actually includes Semitic as well as Indo-European exemplars.) Biblical scholars have shown a willingness to draw upon developments in folklore and mythology research. Bultmann, for example applies Olrik's celebrated "epic laws of folk narrative" to biblical materials (1963:188–189). But neither Bultmann, Dibelius, nor Boman makes mention of the extensive research devoted to the hero pattern. Even with the recent tendency to consider and even to embrace structural folklore studies, e.g., Propp (Ricoeur 1975:39–51) or Lévi-Strauss (Patte 1976, cf. Leach 1975), I am not aware of any application of Raglan's hero pattern, published in the mid-1930s, to the life of Jesus.

The hero pattern has been the subject of frequent discussion for over a century, but few of the discussions have even so much as mentioned the possible relevance of the pattern to Christ. E.B. Tylor in an essay written in 1863 noted the widespread stories of children being brought up by animals and he referred specifically to Romulus and Remus, Moses, and Cyrus. But it was not until the posthumous publication of J.G. von Hahn's "Arische Aussetzungs-und-Rückkehr-Formel" (The Aryan Expulsion and Return Formula) in 1876 that modern hero pattern research may be said to have been properly launched. Von Hahn used the biographies of fourteen heroes to arrive at a sixteen-incident biographical paradigm. Von Hahn's pioneering effort passed virtually unnoticed by folklorists with perhaps the single exception of Alfred Nutt, who applied the pattern to Celtic materials in 1881. The heroes analyzed by von Hahn included Perseus, Hercules, Oedipus, Romulus and Remus, Siegfried, Cyrus, Karna, and Krishna.

Some of the subsequent hero studies centered on Cyrus. In 1882, Adolf Bauer published a comprehensive monograph. In the first part of "Die Kyros-Sage und Verwandtes," Bauer concentrated upon different versions of the Cyrus story, but in the second part he discussed such possible cognates as Romulus and Remus, Siegfried, Karna, and Sargon. Bauer also noted that the expulsion of children, miraculous rescue from water, the nursing by an animal, and the foster parenthood undertaken by a shepherd, fisherman, or some other poor individual were widely found in *märchen* as well (Bauer 1882: 566–570). Other studies of Cyrus appeared including Heinrich Lessmann's *Die Kyrossage in Europa* in 1906. Lessmann gave a summary of the hero pattern (1906:49–50), but it was far less detailed than von Hahn's of 1876.

In 1908 French folklorist Emmanuel Cosquin published a fascinating essay entitled "Le Lait de la Mére et Le Coffre Flottant." Taking a Javanese Moslem legend as a point of departure, Cosquin proceeded to show the parallelism of the biographies of Sargon, Romulus and Remus, Perseus, Karna, Cyrus, Judas, and Moses. He also documented the existence of the same or similar pattern in folktales. Cosquin's essay stimulated further discussion (Hertel), including a study of the pattern in Jewish tradition apart from the Old Testament (Lévi). In 1909 Otto Rank published his brilliant monograph *The Myth of the Birth of the Hero* in which he used fifteen biographies as the basis of his formulation of the hero pattern. (The heroes analyzed by Rank were: Sargon, Moses, Karna, Oedipus, Paris, Telephus, Perseus, Gilgamesh, Cyrus, Tristan, Romulus, Hercules, Jesus, Siegfried, and Lohengrin.) Rank is unique among early students of the hero pattern in that he included the life of Jesus as one of his representative biographies. Rank chose to give a composite narrative synopsis of the hero pattern rather than giving a detailed listing of individual incidents.

Additional studies of the hero appeared. In 1911 came Karl Schmeing's dissertation, *Flucht- und Werbungssagen in Legende*, which was largely concerned with Christian saint's legends. In 1916, Paull Franklin Baum published a lengthy discussion of the medieval legend of Judas, remarking that "practically the whole of Judas' story can be related by means of the 'formulas' to which Hahn has reduced a large mass of myth and Heldensage" (1916:594, n. 39). Baum was attempting to determine whether the Judas story was a direct derivative of the Oedipus plot or whether it could have developed independently. Baum argued that the existence of a standard, distinct hero pattern involving a mother's dream of a son predestined to a wicked career, the exposure of the newborn child on the sea, his rescue and murder of his father, and the unconscious incest with his mother tended to suggest that the Judas story was not necessarily a conscious borrowing from Oedipus (Baum 1916:590, 603). In 1925, Eugene S. McCartney surveyed some forty classical versions of animal-nurtured children including Romulus and Remus, Cyrus, Paris, Aesculapius, Gilgamesh, and a host of lesser-known figures. In 1928 Vladimir Propp's *Morphology of the Folktale* was published. This important study might be said to outline the typical biography of a hero or heroine as it is found in fairy tales (Aarne-Thompson tale types 300–749). Since the story of Perseus is similar to tale type 300, The Dragon-Slayer, and since Oedipus is tale type 931 (though strictly speaking this tale type doesn't fall in the Aarne-Thompson tales of magic category analyzed by Propp [1968:19]), one might well expect Propp's analysis to apply to the hero pattern. However, Propp is concerned solely with the fairy tale genre. His pattern ends with the marriage of the hero. In other words, Propp's scheme does not provide the full life of a hero ending with the hero's death. This is not a criticism of Propp but rather an acknowledgment that the fairy tale genre ends with marriage, not death. Most hero narratives are, or were told as, true stories; they are legends rather than fairy tales. For this reason, Propp's pioneering morphology of the fairy tale has only limited applicability to the totality of the legendary hero pattern.

In 1933 Alexander Haggerty Krappe wrote a brief essay in which he pointed out the similarity of the stories of Moses, Cyrus, Zeus, and Perseus. In 1934 Lord Raglan published his paper "The Hero of Tradition," which shortly thereafter (1936) formed the basis of his book *The Hero*. Raglan's hero pattern is one of the most ambitious inasmuch as he used the biographies of twenty-one heroes to illustrate a proposed scheme consisting of twenty-two incidents. Raglan wrote in complete ignorance of earlier scholarship devoted to the hero, and he was therefore unaware of the previous studies of von Hahn and Rank, for example. Raglan was parochial in other ways too. For one thing, the vast majority of his heroes came exclusively from classical (mostly Greek) sources. The first twelve heroes he treats are: Oedipus, Theseus, Romulus, Heracles, Perseus, Jason, Bellerophon, Pelops, Asclepios, Dionysos, Apollo, and Zeus. Raglan could have strengthened his case had he used some of the same heroes used by von Hahn and Rank and other scholars, e.g., such heroes as Sargon and Cyrus. On the other hand, one overall advantage of the fact that von Hahn, Rank, and Raglan made independent investigations of essentially the same textual material is the support it provides for the reliability of their hypothesized accounts of the hero pattern. In other words, since all three were able to inductively extrapolate hero biographical incident sequences from a more or less common body of data, sequences which reveal a fairly high degree of uniformity, it is more reasonable to defend the proposition that an empirically demonstrable hero biography pattern for (Indo-)European (and Semitic) heroes exists.

Before considering the pattern as described by von Hahn, Rank, and Raglan, it should be mentioned that the steady stream of hero pattern studies has continued. Joseph Campbell in his 1956 work *The Hero with a Thousand Faces* tries to delineate a "monomyth" which might apply to heroes from all cultures. However, Campbell's pattern is a synthetic, artificial composite which he fails to apply in toto to any one single hero. Campbell's hero pattern, unlike the ones formulated by von Hahn, Rank, and Raglan, is not empirically verifiable, e.g., by means of inductively extrapolating incidents from any one given hero's biography. In 1964 Gerhard Binder considered stories of exposed children citing no less than one hundred twenty-one examples from a variety of European and Asian cultures. For the present purposes, however, it is doubtful whether an overly ambitious attempt to define a universal hero pattern allegedly applicable to all human societies or an intensive study of one specific incident, e.g., the exposure of infant heroes, is as useful as an empirical study of the entire life stories of individual heroes. Let us therefore briefly consider the patterns of von Hahn, Rank, and Raglan.

Von Hahn (1876)	*Rank (1909)*	*Raglan (1934)*
1. hero of illegitimate birth	child of distinguished parents	mother is royal virgin
2. mother is a princess	father is a king	father is a king
3. father is a god	difficulty in conception	father related to mother
4. prophecy of ascendance	prophecy warning against birth (e.g., parricide)	unusual conception
5. hero abandoned	hero surrendered to the water in a box	hero reputed to be son of god
6. suckled by animals	saved by animals or lowly people	attempt (usually by father) to kill hero
7. hero raised by childless shepherd couple	suckled by female animal or humble woman	hero spirited away
8. hero is high-spirited	———	reared by foster parents in a far country
9. he seeks service abroad	hero grows up	no details of childhood
10. triumphant homecoming	hero finds distinguished parents	goes to future kingdom

11. slays original persecutors and sets mother free	hero takes revenge on his father	is victor over king, giant dragon or wild beast
12. founds cities	acknowledged by people	marries a princess (often daughter of predecessor)
13. extraordinary death	achieves rank and honors	becomes king
14. reviled because of incest and dies young	———	for a time he reigns uneventfully
15. hero dies as an act of revenge by an insulted servant	———	he prescribes laws
16. he murders his younger brother	———	later, he loses favor with gods or his subjects
17. ———	———	driven from throne and city
18. ———	———	meets with mysterious death
19. ———	———	often at the top of a hill
20. ———	———	his children, if any, do not succeed him
21. ———	———	his body is not buried, but nevertheless
22. ———	———	he has one or more holy sepulchers

It is difficult to compare the three patterns. Von Hahn had sixteen incidents, Rank did not divide his pattern into incidents as such, and

Raglan had twenty-two incidents. Raglan himself admitted that his choice of twenty-two incidents (as opposed to some other number of incidents) was arbitrary (Raglan 1956:186). So one could hardly expect complete agreement among the three pattern studies in terms of the number of incidents. Rank, because of his particular psychoanalytic bias, tended to emphasize the birth of the hero and for this reason he seems to have slighted the death of the hero. It is not my purpose in any case to try to reconcile the differences between von Hahn, Rank and Raglan. Nor am I interested in comparing the relative importance of individual incidents or traits in any of the schemes. Cook's statistical analysis of Raglan's pattern revealed two things. One was that the pattern was *not* truly cross-cultural. It did not apply, generally speaking, to selected American Indian, African, or Oceanic heroes. Moreover, even among the European heroes selected by Raglan, not all the traits occurred with the same frequency. Only one of the twenty-two traits occurred in the biographies of all twenty-one heroes: trait 11, the victory over the king *et al.* Five of the traits (3, 4, 15, 16, 19) occurred in only eleven or twelve biographies (Cook 1965:149). The point is that there is some arbitrariness in Raglan's selection of traits. Raglan remarks that he used the story of Oedipus as his starting point although he gives no particular justification for doing so. But this may be why Oedipus earns an almost perfect score of twenty-one points (out of twenty-two), the highest score of any hero Raglan considered. (Theseus and Moses both score twenty.)

There have been relatively few follow-up studies utilizing the Raglan scheme. Just as Nutt had applied von Hahn's pattern to Celtic material, so Rees (1936) applied Raglan's pattern successfully to a number of Celtic saints—including Saint Patrick. More recently, Utley applied the pattern somewhat tongue-in-cheek to the biography of Abraham Lincoln and found that Lincoln scores no less than the full twenty-two points (Utley 1965:4, 28). The significance of Utley's essay is that it underscores the distinction between the individual and his biography with respect to historicity. The fact that a hero's biography conforms to the Indo-European hero pattern does not necessarily mean that the hero never existed. It suggests rather that the folk repeatedly insist upon making their versions of the lives of heroes follow the lines of a specific series of incidents. Accordingly, if the life of Jesus conforms in any way with the standard hero pattern, this proves nothing one way or the other with respect to the historicity of Jesus.

To determine to what extent, if any, the life of Jesus might be related to the standard Indo-European hero pattern, one might ask which version of the life of Jesus is the one to choose. Biblical scholars are wont to distinguish sharply between the different versions told in each of the four gospels. A distinction is also made between the synoptic gospels (Matthew, Mark, and Luke) and the gospel of John. Moreover, the materials in the four gospels are often considered separately, as being more authoritative, from details contained in the so-called apocryphal gospels. As a folklorist, I find it difficult to give a priori preference or precedence to one or more versions of a legend as opposed to other versions. As a genre, legend rarely exists in any one single version in any community in the world. Rather, a cluster of legends surrounds an important political or religious figure. It may be that no one individual in a community can relate the entire legendary life history of a particular figure. For this reason, a folklorist normally collects as many versions of a legend as possible before trying to reconstruct a composite notion of a legendary figure's life story. In the present instance, I have chosen to regard all four gospels as primary sources for the life of Jesus although I will on occasion cite what I consider to be relevant data from the apocrypha. I do not intend to treat Jesus as miracle worker or healer or religious teacher. Rather, my purpose is to examine his life in the light of the hero pattern as this pattern has been described by folklorists.

If one wished to apply Raglan's twenty-two incident pattern to the life of Jesus, one might include (1) virgin mother, (4) unusual conception, (5) hero reputed to be son of god, (6) attempt to kill hero, (7) hero spirited away [flight into Egypt], (8) reared by foster parents [Joseph], (9) no details of childhood, (10) goes to future kingdom, (13) becomes "king" [cf. the mock title of king of the Jews: INRI], (14) "reigns" uneventfully for a time, (15) prescribes laws, (16) loses favor with some of his "subjects" (e.g., Judas), (17) driven from throne and city, (18) meets with mysterious death, (19) at the top of a hill, (21) body is not buried, and (22) he has a holy sepulcher. While one may well quibble about the applicability of one or two of Raglan's twenty-two points, it would appear that Jesus would rate a score of seventeen (which would rank him closer to Raglan's ideal hero paradigm than Jason, Bellerophon, Pelops, Asclepios, Apollo, Zeus, Joseph, Elijah, and Siegfried). If one accepts the validity of the general outlines of the European hero pattern as delineated by Raglan (and others), then it would appear reasonable to consider that the biography of Jesus does in fact conform fairly well to this pattern.

Raglan's pattern provides a new vantage point for those who seek to understand the life of Jesus as it is reported in the gospels. For example, Bible scholars have bemoaned the lack of information about the youth and growing up of Jesus. Luke and John tell us almost nothing of the period between birth and adulthood. The point is that this is precisely the case with nearly all heroes of tradition. That is why Raglan included his trait 9 "We are told nothing of his childhood" (1956:174).

The versions of the pattern delineated by von Hahn and Rank are also helpful. For example, both include the animal nurse detail. It is tempting to see an echo of this incident in Jesus being born in a manger (Luke 2:12). The word "manger" (cognate with French *manger*, to eat) does refer to a box or trough from which animals feed. The image of the manger is thus consonant with the animal nurse incident in the hero pattern. It is true that no animal participates in the actual nursing of Jesus, but the later iconographic tradition of having an ox and ass watching over the infant Jesus (cf. Ziegler) might possibly be related to this part of the hero pattern (cf. Rank 1956:52, n. 7). There is no scriptural authority for the iconographic tradition though there is a passage in Isaiah (1:3) "The ox knoweth his owner, and the ass his master's crib." A striking piece of evidence confirming the present analysis of the manger detail as part of the hero pattern comes from one of the New Testament apocrypha, namely, the Protevangelion of James the Lesser. In this account, the manger as a box or trough clearly functions as the floating chest in which the imperiled infant male is esconced. Moreover, the placement of Jesus in the manger immediately follows Herod's massacre of the innocents, a sequence following the hero pattern to the letter: "Then Herod perceiving that he was mocked by the wise men, and being very angry, commanded certain men to go and to kill all the children that were in Bethlehem, being two years old and under. But Mary hearing that the children were to be killed, being under much fear, took the child, and wrapped him up in swaddling clothes, and laid him in an ox-manger" (Protevangelion 16:1–2). Then follows a sudden shift to John the Baptist and his mother Elizabeth who take flight from Herod's decree. In other words, the hero pattern continues to be followed but with different personages filling the traditional slots.

Another detail possibly illuminated by the hero pattern consists of presence of the shepherds at the nativity scene. Dibelius (1932:75) discusses at some length the traditionality of having a shepherd present at the birth of a hero or god. While only two of the thirty-two versions of "the literary motif of the exposed child" surveyed by Redford have shepherd rescuers, there are commonly comparable figures such as three herdsmen, a fisherman, a farmer, etc. (Redford 1967:225). Von Hahn did have as his seventh incident "Hero raised by childless shepherd couple." The inference to be drawn is that in Luke's account, the shepherds' role is diminished—they come to observe rather than to save the newborn infant (Luke 2:8–20). Nevertheless, it could be argued that the shepherds do constitute another reflection of the influence of the overall hero pattern.

There is a methodological issue which it might be well to mention and that is that the above observations were facilitated by the perspective provided by a knowledge of the general Indo-European hero pattern. Previous scholarship, in my opinion, has been greatly handicapped by its self-imposed parochial nature. The comparative approach may have been employed, but the comparisons were typically restricted or partial. A comparison of the birth of Jesus with just the birth of Moses (e.g., Bourke, Winter) or with just a possible Egyptian (Brunner-Traut) or Indic (Kennedy) precursor failed to yield the same insights. The comparative method requires more than a limited comparison with only one or two presumed parallels. I submit that biblical scholars have failed to utilize the relevant comparative tools available from folkloristics. The error of making too limited a comparison, e.g., Jesus with Moses, has another dimension. By comparing only a single element of the hero pattern, e.g., just the virgin birth, scholars deprive themselves and their readers of perceiving the entire pattern. Thus Dibelius treats the virgin birth and the manger-child as two separate legends (1932:80) whereas I am arguing that both elements are part of single legendary hero sequence. Bultmann (1963:3) makes clear that his aim is to reconstruct the history of the "individual units of the tradition", a praiseworthy and useful goal to be sure, but the atomistic study of small units can unfortunately result in seeing trees instead of the forest.

Having established, albeit tentatively, that the life of Jesus is a variant of the standard biography of the hero of tradition, we have tried to note similarities in the life of Jesus and in the hero pattern. But of equal importance are the differences between the life of Jesus and the typical hero. From our folkloristic vantage point, we can observe just how Jesus departs from the pattern. Recalling Raglan's trait sequence, we can easily see that what is "missing" from the life of Jesus are traits 11 and 12: a victory over a king, giant, dragon or wild beast; and a marriage with a princess. (One might go so far as to argue that to the extent that Jesus resisted the temptations of Satan (Matthew 4:1–11; Luke 4:1–13) he could be said to have vanquished a villainous antagonist. And in this same connection, it is of interest that in one of the apocryphal accounts of Christ's infancy, namely, the Gospel of Pseudo-Matthew (chapter 23), Jesus descends from his mother's lap to tame threatening dragons. But there can be no question that Jesus does not marry a princess.) In theory, that is, according to the folkloristic hero pattern, Jesus should have taken revenge upon Herod (or some other authority figure) and married his daughter.

The absence of marriage with a princess provides a significant clue to the particular worldview which produced the various versions of the life of Jesus. It was a male-oriented worldview which denied power to females—the one female power acknowledged was that of procreation. Women from Eve to Delilah to Salome were not to be trusted. If one wished to consider the life of John the Baptist in the light of the hero pattern, one can see that instead of the hero marrying the king's daughter, he is beheaded at her request (Mark 6:17–41). Propp's thirty-one function analysis of Russian fairy tale structure ends with the hero's or heroine's wedding which further supports the notion that traditional narratives included a marriage. It is thus the denial of women generally and the failure of Jesus to marry which sets him apart from other Indo-European heroes.

The significance of the lack of marriage in some versions of the Christian ideal (cf. the continuing argument over the necessity of celibacy for the truly devout) is even more crucial when one considers the possible psychological implications of the European hero pattern. Up to this point, we have considered only formal features of comparison with respect to the life of Jesus and the hero pattern. But pattern description is not an end in itself. Describing a pattern is but one step towards the end of studying meaning. What, if anything, does the European hero pattern mean? and how does its meaning bear on our understanding of the life of Jesus? To attempt to answer such questions, we must venture into the treacherous areas of interpretation and speculation. It is one thing to point out empirically verifiable parallels between one narrative and another; it is quite another to offer an interpretation of the possible meaning(s) of such narratives.

For an understanding of the psychological significance of the hero pattern, we must turn first to the insightful analysis offered by Otto Rank in 1909. Rank made a number of extremely astute observations about the hero pattern. First, he suggested there were three actors: the hero and his parents. Second, he explained that the pattern exemplified the psychological principle of projection inasmuch as the son who would like to get rid of his father is transformed into a father who tries to get rid of his son. Through this projection, the son is freed from any guilt caused by hating his father since the father is depicted as a wicked villainous figure. Third, the son's Oedipal wish to repudiate his father (so as to have his mother all to himself) finds its ultimate expression in the virgin birth (Rank 1959:81). There have been numerous folkloristic studies of the virgin birth (Charencey, Hartland, Van Gennep, Saintyves) though not nearly so many as theological studies of the same phenomenon (cf. the bibliography in Boslooper), but none have offered a more fascinating (and persuasive) interpretation of this puzzling detail. A son who is born of a virgin can deny that his father ever had sexual access to his mother.

Despite his brilliant insights, Rank went astray on one point and unfortunately it was a major point in his analysis. Rank interpreted the placing of the infant hero in a box floating in water as the "symbolic expression of birth." Rank's extended emphasis upon the importance of the alleged "birth" symbolism (as opposed to his application of Freud's Oedipal rationale to the lives of heroes) perhaps anticipated his later book *The Trauma of Birth* in which he argued that it was the act of being born which was primarily responsible for adult neuroses. Rank, in fact, attempted to offer his birth trauma theory as a rival theory to Freud's Oedipus complex. In any event, there are some serious theoretical difficulties in this aspect of Rank's analysis of the hero pattern which one must remember Rank called "the myth of the *birth* of the hero."

For one thing, the hero is *not* surrendered to the water in a box in all versions of the hero biography. Von Hahn is more accurate when he refers to the abandonment of the hero. The child is just as often abandoned on land as at sea. Redford's study of thirty-two versions of the "literary motif of the exposed child" shows that only twelve have a watery place of abandonment. Thus Moses is abandoned in water but Oedipus is abandoned in the wilds. Slightly more than half of the specific heroes selected by Rank himself for his analysis have the water abandonment. What this means is that the hero pattern is *not* dependent upon the particular motif of S 331, Exposure of child in boat (floating chest). The critical motif is rather M 371, Exposure of infant to avoid fulfillment of prophecy. Since the hero's biography can conform to the overall pattern without reference to exposure to water, Rank's analysis of the hero pattern in terms of birth trauma would seem to be in error.

There are other problems with Rank's birth analysis. Consider the fact that the hero is already born when he is abandoned. Why would he need to be born again? Consider also that in several versions of the hero story involving water, the protagonist is abandoned *with* his mother, as Rank (1959:79) himself observed, and they are *both* placed in the box or floating chest, e.g., the case of Perseus. Since the mother is placed in the chest, is she also being born or reborn? Holley in his study of "the floating chest" suggests, not very convincingly, that "the presence of the mother in the chest, a mythological doubling of the function of the chest itself" is related to a supposed ritual involving a mother-goddess and a young child-god who must be reborn to ensure the earth's annual vegetative fertility (1949:45).

I should stress that the weakness of Rank's interpretation of the birth symbolism of the hero pattern in no way affects the aptness of his more or less Oedipal reading of the pattern. After the father has gotten rid of his son (which in terms of inverse projection means "after the son has gotten rid of his father"), he is invariably nursed by a kindly animal or peasant woman. It was Cosquin in 1908 who specifically pointed out the repeated connection between the act of exposing the hero and his being suckled. In some of the legends discussed by Cosquin, the act of nursing is initiated to prevent sexual relations. For example, in the Javanese Moslem legend which inspired Cosquin's research, an ascetic cures a king's daughter after the king had promised to embrace Islam. The king has the ascetic sheik marry the princess but the ascetic returns to his home without her. The princess gave birth to a handsome son but at the same time an epidemic breaks out. The king's astrologers claim the baby is the cause of the calamity. The king builds a watertight chest and placing the infant in it, he throws the chest into the sea. A passing ship notices a strange light and picks up the chest. The infant is turned over to the ship's owner, a woman. The woman raises the child and after some time conceives a grand passion for him. The boy then says to her that if she will uncover her breasts, he will remedy the situation. She does so and the boy nurses. By this means, the woman becomes the proper mother of the boy. (For references to additional mythological parallels to symbolic nursing as a means of ritual adoption, see Deonna's excellent essay "La légende de Pero et de Micon et l'allaitement symbolique" (1955:5–50) and Renard 1964:616 n. 1.) Presumably the act of nursing cures the woman of her passion for the boy. (In terms of projection, the boy's passion for the mother (surrogate) is transformed into her passion for him and so the alleged curative act for *her* problem provides an opportunity for him to fulfill *his* desire.) In some versions of the story, it is stated that the miracle consists of the fact that the woman was able to produce milk even though she had never given birth to a child. In still other Indic and Javanese legends, the abandoned boys return to their original homeland to attack the king. The king's wife, their mother, squirts milk into their mouths, thereby proving to the boys her relationship to them. Cosquin suggests that these legends may be cognate with the stories of Sargon, Romulus and Remus, Moses, Judas, etc.

I submit that the act of nursing is a confirmation of the mother-child constellation vis-à-vis the father. In many societies, a father must abstain from sexual intercourse so long as his wife is nursing a baby. Thus the longer an infant nurses, the more he succeeds in keeping his father away. In terms of the hero pattern, one finds a variety of means for the hero to keep his father away from his mother. The unusual means of conception, the virgin birth, and the emphasis upon abandonment plus nursing are all techniques for denying the father. (For numerous creation myths from East Indonesia which tell of the mother-son bond to the exclusion of a visible father image, see Muensterberger 1939.) Since breast-feeding in biblical times might have lasted as long as three or four years, according to Patai (1959:194–197), this would have solidified the mother-child relationship. It is worth noting also that Jesus was the firstborn—assuming that he did have brothers and sisters. His frequent depiction in iconography and art in the act of nursing from his mother suggests that he succeeds as no other firstborn ever has insofar as he is never displaced by younger sibling rivals. Von Hahn's delineation of the hero pattern ends with the hero murdering his younger brother. It is not certain just how common this is (though it does occur), but it would seem to reflect a sibling rivalry component of the hero pattern. (For the notion that Jesus and Judas might represent "brothers," see Tarachow 1960:546.)

The importance of the mother-infant nursing configuration in the hero pattern is suggested by one of the numerous ancient etymologies for the names "Romulus" and "Remus," which derives them from *"ruma"* or *"rumis,"* allegedly old Latin words for "breast" (McCarthy 1935:32, citing Plutarch and Pliny). Regardless of the linguistic validity of what might be a folk etymology, the fact that it was proposed at all supports the notion that the heroes are closely associated with the act of suckling. If the etymology were accurate, it would seemingly apply to the current name Rome and thus support Rank's general notion of the city as a mother symbol (cf. the modern word 'metropolis' derived from the Greek for mother and city) and his particular observation that "the seven hills of Rome correspond to the teats of the she-wolf" (1952:18, n. 2).

Other philological data is less suspect. For example, in Latin and in derivative languages, the words for mother and breast are similar if not identical. Even in English, "mamma" can refer affectionately to one's mother or to the breast. The semantic connection between mother and breast-feeding makes both logical and psychological sense (and may have been a factor in the decision of Linnaeus to coin the term "mammalia" to refer to the class of animals whose young are brought forth alive and then nourished with milk from the mother's breasts). Also relevant is the likelihood that the Latin word for son, *filius*, appears to have meant originally "suckling" from the Latin root *felare*, "suck"—cf. fellatio—(Buck 1949:105). The English word *daughter* is also of interest in this connection. Buck (1949:106) claims the root connection is obscure. It agrees in form with Sanskrit *duh* "milk" and with a Greek root meaning fashion or make, but Buck remarks that "in neither case is there a convincing semantic explanation." One wonders if a daughter isn't perceived as a milk-maker (as opposed to a son who sucks). Females give; males take (cf. Thass-Thienemann 1957:30).

It is tempting to argue from linguistic data that being thrown into or onto a body of water does not so much symbolize birth, as Rank contended, as it symbolizes being thrown onto a mother. The word for sea in Latin is *mare* which could conceivably be related to *mater*. (In French, the words *mer* and *mere* are homophonic.) I am not arguing that the words for sea and mother are related in all languages or even in all Indo-European languages. But the phonetic if not etymological similarity of the words for sea and mother in even one language is surely of interest. One wonders if the name "Mary" isn't derived from either sea or mother. The origins of the name are obscure but Mary may be related to the name Miriam which could be construed as containing the Hebrew *yam* meaning sea. (Ernest Jones in his extended discussion of the "MR" root (1951b:326–339) suggests that "milk" is related to it.) It is certainly curious that in Latin the word for lake is *lacus* and the word for milk is *lac*. The floating "chest" might be literally just that, a floating female bosom. (cf. in French *boite* and *poitrine*). This would explain Cosquin's observation that there was a close connection between the floating chest and the giving of maternal milk. Please note that the association exists *regardless* of the validity of the above admittedly highly speculative philological musings.

The importance and antiquity of the mother-child nursing configuration is well attested in mythology and art. Besides such traditions as Juno suckling Hercules (Deonna 1955:31–38; Renard 1964), there is considerable evidence from the ancient Near East. Statues show Ishtar nursing a child or the cow-headed Egyptian goddess Hathor suckling Osiris (Jeremias 1911, I:118). Sometimes the image takes the form of cow nursing a calf with the characteristic motif of the maternal cow twisting its head around so as to see or lick the young calf (Matthiae 1962). The configuration was found in Egypt, Syria, and Mesopotamia. This bovine imagery is present in both the Old and New Testament. Samson refers to his bride as a heifer in his suggestive metaphor rebuking her kinsmen who with her help were able to answer his neck riddle: "If ye had not plowed with my heifer, ye had not found out my riddle" (Judges 14:18). The ashes of a ritually slain heifer were used to purify the unclean. The requirements were: a red heifer without spot, wherein is no blemish, and upon which never came yoke. In any case, a heifer is, so to speak, a virgin cow. In terms of such an imagery pattern, one is reminded of the centrality in Mithraism of killing the bull (a father figure?) coupled with the worship of the golden calf (a son figure?) (Exodus 32:1–8). The mythological association of a heifer or cow with a mother figure is

also attested in the Greek story of Zeus' affair with Io (plus the formulaic epithet "cow-eyed," used to describe Hera). One could cite
numerous examples of gods mating with cows in Sumerian and
Canaanite myths (Astor 1965:80–92). There is even Neolithic evidence of this metaphorical pattern which includes the head of a bull
on a wall, right next to which are two protruding human breasts (Mellaart 1963:72).

Although the cow was perhaps one of the most logical forms of the
animal nurse motif, other animals apparently served equally well.
Wolves, goats, and dogs on occasion provided the necessary source of
milk. One of the most curious nurturant agents consisted of bees, e.g.,
in the case of Zeus. It might be worth mentioning that the combination of milk and honey associated with the idyllic "paradise" of earliest
infancy could well account for the presence of the same nutrient
combination in the promised land or afterlife paradise. One thinks of
"and the hills shall flow with milk" (Joel 3:18) and the image of the
ideal of "honey and milk" under the tongue (Song of Solomon 4:11).
The idiom of "a land flowing with milk and honey" as a metaphor for
abundance occurs no fewer than twenty-one times in the Bible (Beck
and Smedley 1971:167). One might logically assume that infants were
in fact fed milk and honey (Usener 1902, Roheim 1940:182). Guidi
1903:241) argued that the biblical phrase should be translated as milk
with honey rather than milk and honey. In any event, the parallelism
of earliest infancy with the concept of afterlife suggests an infantile
origin for the equation of *Urzeit* and *Endzeit*, as Gunkel and others
refer to the beginning and end of human time on earth. Some scholars
have suggested an infantile origin for paradise, but they tend to think
that the model is the prenatal state (Rank 1952:116, 162, n.1, Rubenstein 1972:147, 165). I think it is more reasonable to argue that
postnatal breast-feeding is a more likely infantile model, especially in
view of such phrases as "the hills shall flow with milk." In this regard,
a passage from the Coptic Gospel of Thomas (Plate 85, lines 20–22) is
germane: "Jesus saw children being suckled. He said to his disciples,
'These children who are being suckled are like those who enter the
Kingdom'" (cf. Isaiah 66:10–13).

The semantic connection between honey and milk is also suggested
by the curious coincidence that the initial portion of the English word
milk is phonetically similar to the Latin root for honey *mel*. Thus
combining the Latin words for honey and milk would be *mel lac*,

which is close to Gothic *miluks* (cf. Danish *melk*,, Old English *meolc*, Polish *mleko*, Russian *moloko*, etc. Buck 1949:385). Another association between honey and milk comes from an equation of bees and breasts (Bradley 1973) supported by such mythological data as the many-breasted Artemis of Ephesus, a mother goddess of western Anatolia, having her cult administered by a group of sixty priestesses called bees "melissai" (Mellaart 1963:80). The notion of Zeus, father of the gods, as an infant being nurtured by bees is also suggestive in philological terms. *Abba* is Aramaic for father (Mark 14:36))cf. *babbo* in Italian). Bee in Latin is *apis*. French *abbé*, the head of an abbey, is at least homonymically similar to French *abeille*, bee. If one were specula-tively inclined, one might be tempted to see a parallel between the social organization (and nurturant qualities) of bees and abbeys. With respect to man-made objects, Bradley (1973:304) remarks that until relatively recently, men tended to build beehives in the shape of the human breast. Even if one rejects some of the questionable etymologi-cal speculation crossing unrelated languages (Aramaic and French), there remain to be explained such facts as Zeus' being nursed by bees or the many-breasted Artemis' having helpers called *"melissai"* (bees).

What is at issue here is not the symbolism of bees and honey, or the difficulties of a dubious etymological equation so much as trying to understand one of the principal elements in the Indo-European (and Semitic) hero pattern. The abandonment and exposure of the infant and his being rescued by an animal that suckles him could very well represent the deep-seated anxiety produced by weaning. But whether he is displaced by a younger sibling or engaged in a struggle with the father for exclusive possession of the mother, the hero of the hero pattern finds an ideal solution. He succeeds in separating his parents and in being lavishly and lovingly nursed. It should be noted that the basic plot of a son who desires to separate his father from his mother is also to be found in myth.

The hero pattern, as I have noted, is rather a matter of the genres of legend and folktale. But in the widespread creation myth of the world parents (motif A 625, World parents: sky-father and earth-mother as parents of the universe), we find that the sky-father has descended upon the earth-mother to beget the world. Often the culture hero pushes the sky away (motif A 625.2, Raising of the sky), leaving him alone with his earth-mother. (In Egypt, it is the sky which is female and the earth which is male, but the crucial point is that they are torn asunder.) It has been suggested that in those myths in which father sky leaves mother earth in the morning, we find a parallel to the custom of visit marriage. "When morning comes, the man, like Uranos, must leave the woman. Therefore the myths have merely transferred what happens every morning to the first morning of the beginning of the universe" (Numazawa 1953:34). I might add that the withdrawal of the father either for a day or for a longer period of time (e.g., if there were multiple households as is not uncommon in societies with polygamous marriage) might through a projection of the infantile experience account for the idea of *deus otiosus*, in which a creator departs after having completed the initial act of (pro) creation.

Once armed with the hypothetical possibility that the stories of gods are child's projections of parents, one can more easily understand what previous generations have considered trivial or absurd narratives. For example, Hooke in *Middle Eastern Mythology* (1963:131) describes the Babylonian flood myth as follows: "In the Babylonian myth of the Flood the gods decided to destroy mankind for the rather absurd reason that they had become so noisy that they prevented the gods from sleeping at nights." If one reads "parents" for "gods" and "infants" for "mankind," one can see that the absurdity is not absurd at all. Rather, we have another version of the child's wish to disturb or separate the parents in bed.

In the separation of parents in folk narrative, the son ideally seeks to possess the mother while the daughter seeks to have the father for herself. The projection of Oedipal or Electral complexes in the Bible is a subject which deserves separate study. For the Electra complex, for example, one might profitably examine the story of Lot. His wife is turned to salt—the elimination of the mother is a common bit of wishful thinking in girl-centered fairy tales. This removes the principal rival for the father's affections. In the case of Lot, his daughters succeed in seducing him (Genesis 19:30–36).

This world parent creation myth is extremely widespread (Fischer, Numazawa, Staudacher) and it was common in classical Greek tradition (Maròt). It is of interest that in perhaps the best-known Greek version, Kronos castrates Uranos as he approaches his consort Gaia. The castration of the father by the son would, like the virgin birth, be an ultimate expression of the son's repudiation or rejection of his father.

The relationship of castration to the hero pattern, however, is not always attached to the son's success. Castration is sometimes applied to the son. For example, the story of Attis, though not treated by von Hahn, Rank, or Raglan, appears to be related to the hero pattern. (Attis is mentioned by Redford as an example of the literary motif of the exposed child and by McCartney as an example of an animal-nursed infant (Redford 1967:212, McCartney 1925:22).) Attis, the son of Nana, was conceived by contact with a pomegranate (from a tree growing from the severed phallus of a previous son of a mother-goddess). Disgraced by this miraculous conception, Nana's father Sangarius exposes the baby, who is rescued and suckled by a goat. Attis grows up to become the beloved of the mother-goddess Cybele. Eventually, Attis castrates himself. In one version, Zeus responds to the plea to bring Attis back to life by granting only that his body should not decay, that his hair should continue to grow, and that his little finger should remain alive and move (Weigert-Vowinkel 1938:356).

In the story of Attis and comparable heroes, we find that the mother-goddess figure becomes absolutely infatuated with a son figure. It is the mother who passionately pursues the son. This seems to be another instance of projection in the hero pattern (Weigert-Vowinkel 1938:371). Just as the father's attempt to eliminate the son is a projection of the son's wish to eliminate the father, so the son's wish to love his own mother, love in a sexual sense, that is, is projected onto the mother figure. (Cf. the Javanese Moslem legend cited by Cosquin in which it is the mother-rescuer who suddenly conceives a grand passion for the grown youth.) In the case of Jesus, he is pursued by women; he does not pursue them. It is women who seek him out and who come to the sepulcher. Even Frazer after his exhaustive consideration of the various major mother-son constellations in the ancient Near East does "surmise that the Easter celebration of the dead and risen Christ was grafted upon a similar celebration of the dead and arisen "Adonis" and, further, that "the type, created by Greek artists, of the sorrowful goddess with the dying lover in her arms, resembles and may have been the model of the *Pietà* of Christian art, the Virgin with the dead body of her divine Son in her lap" (Frazer 1964:356). Frazer, to be sure, draws no inferences whatsoever of the possible further implications of seeing a parallel between the relationship of various sets of mother-son lovers and the relationship of Mary and Jesus. (For a truly remarkable examination of the erotic symbolism of the *Pietà* tradition, see Steinberg 1970.)

The possible parallelism between Mary and Jesus and the widespread mother-son mythological pattern has frequently been noted. Ishida, in several ambitious studies of mother-son relationships in folk narrative, documents the antiquity and distribution of the pattern. In east Asian tradition, he finds a three-element pattern consisting of (1) a divine boy from the water world, (2) the boy's miraculous birth, or no mention of his father, and (3) his mother or a motherlike female is worshipped with him (Ishida 1956:411) Sometimes the male is very small in size (1964:31). In some tales, a small snake is put in a cup but it "grew so quickly during the course of each night that soon no container was big enough to hold it" (1964:33). Ishida concludes that the east Asian tradition is part of a larger pattern and that the pattern of a mother-goddess coupled with a small male deity was widespread in "the entire pre-Aryan and probably pre-Semitic cultural zone of the ancient Orient from Southwest Asia to the Eastern Mediterranean" (1964:49). In this pattern, "the Mother, a goddess of fertility, was often accompanied by a young male deity who was both her son and her consort: Isis with Horus, Astaroth with Tammuz, Kybele with Attis, Rhea with the young Zeus. Everywhere she bore her son by parthenogenesis; then, in union with him, she bore all living things" (1964:49–50). Ishida continues, "Even after the Christian conquest of paganism, the Mother maintained her prominence as an object of pious worship, holding in her arms the baby Jesus, the divine child" (1964:51). He also comments upon the frequency of an incestuous marriage between mother and son (1964:45–48). Earlier, both Freud and Jones had commented upon the similarity of the relationship between Mary and Jesus to the mother-son pattern common in the Near East (Freud 1913:152–53; Jones 1951a:370–71.) Jones argued that the maternal component of the sacred nuclear family of father, mother, and son was replaced in early Christianity by the Holy Ghost, thereby making an all-masculine Trinity (Jones 1951a:210; cf. Rank 1952:121–29). He felt that the suppression of a mother goddess followed the example of the highly partriarchal Hebrew tradition. Accordingly, he insisted that Mary represented a weakened version of the mother-goddess figure. The psychoanalytic position has been summarized as follows: "It has been recognized, for example, that Mary represents a sort of younger sister of the great goddesses of love of antiquity; and that her relationship with Jesus was an incestuous one, in the tradition of such mother-goddesses and their son-husbands, for instance, Ishtar and Tammuz, Astarte and Adonis, Isis and Osiris, Cybele and Attis. Within this tradition, then, Jesus' crime was an incestuous one, part of which was an attempt to equal or to displace his father, and for this reason he has to die" (Reider 1964:523).

The delineation of the mother-son pattern reveals both that the life of Jesus belongs to it *and* that it departs from it in several respects. Jesus does not have an incestuous relationship with Mary nor in fact does he have a sexual relationship with any woman. It is true, however, that there is far more mention of Mary in the Gospels than of Joseph. The extremely low profile of Joseph, a father figure, would tend to support the idea that the life story of Jesus does concern a mother-son relationship. Occasional father-son rivalry does occur in some of the apocryphal gospels. The Infancy Gospel of Thomas contains several examples. In one instance (chapter 5), an angry Joseph violently pulls the ear of the boy Jesus. In another (chapter 13), Jesus helps Joseph solve a carpentry problem. Joseph, in the process of constructing a couch, ineptly makes one piece of wood shorter than another and he doesn't know what to do. Jesus instructs him to lay the two pieces down alongside each other. Jesus then grasps the shorter beam and stretches it, making it equal with the longer piece. The possible phallic significance of this deed is obvious enough. Yet the overall lack of sexuality in Jesus and his failure, as noted earlier in this discussion, to marry a princess, as dictated by the norms of the hero pattern, suggest a departure from the mother-son bond.

One way of appreciating the departure of Jesus from the Near Eastern mother-son pattern is to consider how the relationship of Jesus to Mary changed over the centuries. A most compelling piece of data bearing on the relationship of Mary and Jesus to the general mother-son pattern is the rise of Mariolatry. The folk, in effect, have over the course of centuries succeeded in redressing the imbalance caused by the particular male-centered worldview which created the Gospel accounts of the life of Jesus. It is as though the paradigm of the mother-son pattern re-asserted itself. Over the years, the worship of Mary restored the mother goddess to the place she would have held if the Jesus biography had conformed more closely to the original hero pattern. I shall not attempt here to recapitulate the complex history of hyperdulia, but suffice it to say that in the centuries since the first articulations of the life of Jesus, there have been as many or more sightings of the Virgin Mary on the surface of the earth than sightings of Jesus. It is the Virgin Mary who has continued to intervene in the affairs of men and whose appearances have inspired the construction of numerous sacred shrines, e.g., Lourdes, Fatima, etc. By the end of medieval times, the Virgin Mary had assumed many of the attributes of the mother figure in the hero pattern. An eminent art historian remarked on what to him seemed the curious depiction of the Virgin Mary as the bride of Christ. "However anomalous such a union may appear to us, the conception of Mary as the bride of Christ (in addition to being his mother and daughter) was current in the Late Middle Ages" (Meiss 1951:109, cf. Steinberg 1970:237–238). From the perspective afforded by a knowledge of the hero pattern, we can see that the notion of Mary as mother and bride is but a reaffirmation of the very same details noted by Ishida: "the Mother, a goddess of fertility, was often accompanied by a young male deity who was both her son and her consort."

If Jesus is a cognate of the son figure in the mother-son pattern then we may wish to consider the manner of his death in this light. It is curious to see how St. Augustine (though in a passage which may not have been written by him) viewed the crucifixion: "Like a bridegroom Christ went forth from his chamber; he went out with a presage of his nuptials into the field of the world. . . . He came to the marriage-bed of the cross, and there, in mounting it, he consummated his marriage. And when he perceived the sighs of the creature, he lovingly gave himself up to the torment in place of his bride, and he joined himself to the woman for ever" (Jung 1967:269). Numerous symbolic interpretations of the crucifixion exist, e.g., it has been analyzed as a scapegoat ritual (Runeberg), but it is not clear how many scholars would concur with St. Augustine's sexual reading of the event. Yet the sexual component of the crucifixion is also signalled by its being subsumed under the term *Passion*, which connotes both suffering and also strong amorous feeling. Later folk narratives can be adduced to support a sexual interpretation of the cross. In the legend of St. Elizabeth of Hungary, a suspicious husband rushes into the saint's bedroom and whisks off the blankets to discover the crucified Jesus in his wife's bed (Thurston and Attwater 1956:387). There is also a folktale (Aarne-Thompson tale type 1359C, Husband prepares to castrate the crucifix) in which a discovered paramour assumes the pose of the crucified Jesus until the husband prepares to take action against him.

St. Augustine, or the author of the passage attributed to St. Augustine, may have been intuitively correct in stating that the crucifixion contained a metaphorical meaning of marriage or sexual intercourse, but it is also true that the crucifixion implies punishment and a denial of intercourse. Again from the perspective of the hero pattern, we can observe that it is not uncommon for the hero's masculinity to be threatened. Samson, betrayed by Delilah, is shaved by his enemies. The loss of hair, perhaps a form of symbolic castration, results in a loss of strength. Samson is also blinded, and blindness often serves as an expression of symbolic castration. Oedipus, after killing his father and marrying his mother, self-inflicts blindness—just as Attis self-inflicts literal castration. The symbolism of the cross is surely multifaceted, but it is conceivable that it has, as a symbol of life, a phallic dimension. For those who doubt the possibility of a phallic component in the Bible, it might be well to recall that if one swears by all that is holy, it may be significant that one swears by the phallus. "And the servant put his hand under the thigh of Abraham his master, and sware to him concerning that matter" (Genesis 24:2, 9 cf. Genesis 47:29, Jeremias 1911, II:77, n. 1). From this custom, we get our idiom of giving *testi*mony and for that matter ultimately the names of Old and New Testament. (The phallic nature of the cross might also illuminate the practice of nuns wearing one around the neck—to protect their maiden heads? and especially the custom of monks wearing one exposed and hanging down from the waist.)

If the cross has a phallic component, then it is of interest that according to John (19:17), Jesus carried his own cross. (Matthew 27:32 and Mark 15:21 say that one Simon bore the cross while Luke 23:26 implies that Simon merely helped Jesus carry it.) In any event, Jesus, having denied the father (by being born of a virgin), yields to the father by being nailed to a symbolic phallus. (Earlier nineteenth-century interpretations of the cross as phallic failed to see it in the context of the entire hero pattern.) If the number three is a masculine or phallic symbol (Dundes 1968), then the image of Christ being one of three crucified might be relevant. As the figure in the middle, he would be the phallus—with the two thieves being testicles. (Cf. Allegro's controversial assertion (1970:35) that the name Jesus stems from a Sumerian word which means "semen.")

The idea of castration being an extreme form of the denial of sexuality is found in the New Testament. According to Matthew (19:12),

Jesus himself refers specifically to men making themselves into eunuchs for the kingdom of heaven's sake. "For there are some eunuchs, which were so born from their mother's womb; and there are some eunuchs, which were made eunuchs of men: and there be eunuchs, which have made themselves eunuchs for the kingdom of heaven's sake" (cf. Nock 1925, and Phipps 1973:144).

The humiliation of the son in terms of masculinity is exacerbated in the crucifixion insofar as Jesus is physically penetrated—both by the nails and by the spear which is later thrust into his side. In circum-Mediterranean male verbal dueling, there is honor for the active penetra*tor*, for the male who puts his opponent down just as for the matador who sinks his sword into the bull; there is only shame for the passive victim who is penetra*ted*. The distinction also applies to active and passive homosexuals—as is clear from accounts of pederasty in classical Greece and modern Turkey (cf. Vanggaard 1972; Dundes, Leach, and Özkök 1970). In this case, Jesus is curiously hoist on his own petard by being nailed to a symbolic phallus which entails his being penetrated by male representatives of an authority figure.

The paradoxical irony of being put to *death* on a symbol of *life*, the cross, is reminiscent of the Garden of Eden story. The crucifixion is the continuation of the Eden story (with Eve and Mary, Adam and Jesus explicitly equated). In Eden, discovery of the tree of *life* resulted in *death* thereafter for mankind. (Several references in the New Testament specifically refer to the cross as a tree, e.g., Acts 5:30; 1 Peter 2:24.) More importantly we find a continuity of theme. Twentieth-century ethnography confirms that in Mediterranean cultures, "Sex, sin and death [are] related; similarly virginity, continence, and life" (Campbell 1964:280). The original sin was sexual in nature (Levy, Róheim) and the result was the origin of death (Cohon, Morgenstern, Krappe 1928). Similarly, the crucifixion involves sexuality, sin, and death. In Eden, disobedience led to forfeiting the tree of life; in the case of Jesus, obedience led to being nailed to it.

Yet if the crucifixion is a form of symbolic castration, analogous to a similar incident in the lives of other heroes, it is not the end. A hero can evidently overcome even an obstacle of this magnitude. Recall that the hair of Samson's head began to grow again after he was shaven, and he regained enough strength to pull down the pillars and the temple of his enemies (Judges 16:22–30). Similarly, in the previously cited version of Attis, Zeus granted that his hair should continue to grow and that his little finger should remain alive and move, indications that the castration is rescinded or transcended (Weigert-Vowinkel 1938:372). So in the life story of Jesus, the hero is able to rise from the dead, a phallic triumph of the highest order. D.H. Lawrence in his fictionalized life of Jesus, originally entitled "The Escaped Cock," depicts Jesus as being rescued by a young virgin devotee of Isis: ". . . He crouched to her, and he felt the blaze of his manhood and his power rise up in his loins, magnificent. 'I am risen!'. . . ." (Lawrence 1952:444, 386–393, cf. Garth 1950:40, n. 52). At least the irrepressible Lawrence refrained in his literary 'exejesus' from punning on Jesus having a "cross" to "bare"! (In English, a punster might well have been tempted by the potential double entendre of a "second coming" meaning both a second advent and a second orgasm.) The association of the "erection" of a phallus with the notion of resurrection has been suggested by scholars not at all influenced by psychoanalytic thought. For example, Jeremias in his respected treatise, *The Old Testament in the Light of the Ancient East*, remarks that "the phallus planted by Bacchus at the gate of Hades is a symbol of the Resurrection" (1911 I:122, n. 2). Metaphorically, it certainly makes sense for an erect phallus to represent the overcoming of death; and this is surely involved in the shape and form of memorial monuments (consider the appropriateness of the Washington Monument erected by grateful Americans for the *father* of their country).

In the light of the present interpretation of the 'crucifiction,' it may not be amiss to remember the individual to whom the risen Christ first appeared. If the resurrection is a form of re-erection, then it would be reasonable for the observer of this marvel to be a woman. Matthew (28:1) indicates that Mary Magdalene and the other Mary came to the sepulcher where an angel told them Jesus wasn't there and asked them to tell the disciples. Mark (16:9) says that Jesus appeared first to Mary Magdalene, while John (20:14–18) reports that Jesus revealed himself first to Mary Magdalene in the famous scene where Jesus orders her not to touch him.

Phipps has astutely pointed out (1973:67) that the word *touch* might possibly carry a nuance of sexual intercourse, especially since it does so elsewhere in the Bible. In 1 Corinthians 7:1–2, we find "It is good for a man not to touch a woman. Nevertheless to avoid fornication, let every man have his own wife. . . . " In Genesis 20:6, Abraham told Abimelech that Sarah was his sister, not his wife, which led

Abimelech to believe that Sarah was available to him as a partner. God prevented Abimelech from taking advantage of the misunderstanding by appearing to him in a dream to explain the situation: "for I also withheld thee from sinning against me: therefore suffered I thee not to touch her." Similarly in Proverbs 6:29, "So he that goes in to his neighbour's wife; whosoever toucheth her shall not be innocent." Whether touching refers simply to a physical caress or serves as a euphemism for intercourse, there would seem to be a definite sexual connotation. So when Jesus tells Mary Magdalene, the very first person to see him "arisen" not to "touch" him, it is at least within the realm of logical possibility that Jesus is fending off a sexual advance.

Mary Magdalene had been healed of evil spirits—seven devils had been cast out of her life (Luke 8:2, Mark 16:9). She is generally identified as the repentant sinner whom Jesus forgave (Luke 7:37–50). The implication is that she was a prostitute (cf. Phipps 1970:64–67, 1973:69, Garth 1950:21) and she is so regarded in popular Christian iconography. The critical question is why should Jesus appear first to a reformed prostitute whose name just coincidentally happens to be the same as that of his own mother? From the point of view of the mother-son pattern, Jesus should be a son-consort. This would require a Mary mother and a Mary bride (cf. Leach 1975). There is some evidence of a tradition which declared that Mary Magdalene was the wife of Jesus (Phipps 1970:64, 137–38), a tradition recorded in the Gospel of Philip (Wilson 1962:35). For example, a passage from this source reads "And the consort of [Christ is] Mary Magdalene. [The Lord loved Mary] more than [all] the disciples, and kissed her on her [mouth] often" (Wilson 1962:39). This tradition of Mary Magdalene being the wife of Jesus is perhaps as old as the second century and it continued for centuries, e.g., at least up until the sixteenth century (Garth 1950:73).

The double tradition of a Virgin Mary and a harlot Mary is a long-standing one. The initial situation of an unmarried virgin's becoming pregnant has always suggested adultery and whoring. In Redford's survey of thirty-two examples of "the literary motif of the exposed child," he found three motivations for the exposure. The first was exposure because of shame at the circumstances of the child's birth. The second was the prophecy of parricide or some similar misfortune for those in power. The third was a general massacre, i.e., motif M375, Slaughter of innocents to avoid fulfillment of prophecy.

(The third motivation appears to be a special adaptation of the second.) Shame, then, is the crucial factor in fourteen instances (of thirty-two examples) and the shame commonly involves illegitimate birth or perhaps using the birth as prima facie evidence of the prior occurrence of sexual promiscuity. So in Matthew (1:18–19), it is told "Now the birth of Jesus Christ was on this wise: When as his mother Mary was espoused to Joseph, before they came together, she was found with child of the Holy Ghost. Then Joseph her husband, being a just man, and not willing to make her a public example, was minded to put her away privily." An angel convinces him to do otherwise and Joseph knew (sexually) his wife "not till she had brought forth her firstborn son" (Matthew 1:25). But even if Mary is not a reformed harlot (cf. Phipps 1973:106), Mary Magdalene certainly seems to be one.

Freud has explained the psychological origin of the 'harlot' component of the mother figure in terms of the shock of a young boy's discovery that his very own mother must have indulged in sexual activities with his father. In Freud's words, "he says to himself with cynical logic that the difference between his mother and a whore is not after all so very great since basically they both do the same thing" (Freud 1910:171). Thus Jesus born of a virgin Mary reveals his resurrection first to a harlot Mary. It is tempting to see a parallel to Jesus' possible relationship with a harlot in the story of Samson. There can be no question about Samson's consorting with a harlot (Judges 16:1). Interestingly enough, after Samson meets the harlot, he takes the doors of the gate of the city and carries them away. Jesus rolled the stone away from the door of his sepulcher right before he revealed himself to Mary Magdalene. However, Jesus, in contrast with Samson, rejects the woman's overtures.

What is the significance, if any, of the fact that the life of Jesus seems to be related to the European or Indo-European hero pattern? What sense can we make of his attitudes towards women? We have seen that one important omission in terms of the standard hero pattern is the failure of Jesus to marry a princess. How can one explain the resurgence of the Virgin Mary in so many circum-Mediterranean cultures? Ernest Jones suggested that the Protestant Reformation was in part a reactionary attempt to oppose Mariolatry and to restore the original Christian version of the hero pattern (Jones 1951a:372). I would add that in the circum-Mediterranean area where the original mother-son pattern was so strongly entrenched, such Protestantism reform has not had much impact. The cult of the Virgin in Greece, Italy, France, Spain, and Ireland continues. The question is why should the mother-son paradigm be so strong in this geographical-cultural area. It is one thing to describe a pattern; it is quite another to explain its origin or psychological significance. Surely there are critical factors which might account for the phenomenal success and continued appeal of this religious pattern.

To the extent that religious or sacred family structure mirrors ordinary human family structure, one might reasonably look at Mediterranean family organization. The isomorphism between family structure among the gods and among men is signalled in Roman mythology by the very name of the head of the gods, Jupiter, the latter portion of which is cognate with Sanskrit *pitar-* (cf. Latin *pater*) which means father. The equation of divine and human family is explicit in Christianity inasmuch as God is termed the father, Jesus is the son, and Mary the mother of God. (Even the name 'pope' etymologically comes from father. Priests continue to be addressed as father while various religious orders insist upon using family kinship terms such as brothers and sisters.)

Circum-Mediterranean social organization traits include rigid sexual segregation. Men associate with one another, leaving women largely to themselves. Men tended to marry late and often in serial succession according to birth order (cf. Genesis 29:26). In modern Greece, for example, sons, or sometimes just the youngest son, are supposed to wait to marry until all the daughters of the house are married (Westermarck 1922 I:373, Campbell 1964:178, Slater 1968:24). A man might marry a woman much younger than himself. According to Joachim Jeremias, the usual age for a Jewish girl to be betrothed at the time of Jesus was between twelve and twelve-and-a-half (1969:365). Slater reminds us of a tradition that Helen was abducted when she was only twelve (1968:392). If a man took a second wife, the chances were that the second wife would be much younger than the man. In the contemporary Near East, one of the rationales given for selecting a young wife is that a young bride will be strong enough to take care of the man when he has grown old (Granqvist 1931:42–43). In ancient Greece, the age at which males married was estimated to be around thirty (Slater 1968:26). Certainly the traditional view is that Joseph was much, much older than Mary—just as Laius was much older than Jocasta, and for that matter, just as Freud's father was twenty years older than his mother! (Wellisch 1955:32, 38).

The age differential coupled with the enforced sexual segregation meant that affection-starved wives often poured their unrequited love upon their sons. The sons thereby became husband-substitutes for their own mothers. I believe this may be why there are so many son consorts for so many mother goddesses in the Near East. However, the husband-hating and resenting females tended to smother (the verb choice is intentional) their sons, making it difficult for the boys to break away from the world of women to join the sexually segregated domain of men. Sons in their later struggles with distant or strict fathers would often ask their mothers to intervene on their behalf. The communication chain would involve a son asking his mother to ask his father for some boon rather than the son's asking the father directly. (So adult males found it comfortable to ask favors from the Virgin Mary or to request her to act as intermediary to God the father.)

Sons raised in such an atmosphere might well develop excessive feelings of attachment towards their mothers to the point where they wished to possess the mothers and to do away with their fathers completely. The Oedipal situation was reinforced by the social realities and it is understandable how a warm, proximate, succoring mother could be worshipped in favor of a distant, sometimes uncaring father.

Women in Mediterranean societies were invariably divided into two categories: good and bad. The good, the virgins, were mothers and wives and they were not to be thought of in sexual terms; sisters and daughters were to be guarded against sexual attacks by outsiders. The evil women were harlots and they were perceived in sexual terms. Since all women, according to this worldview, had inherent predispositions to become evil, the good women had to be protected from such temptations or rather from tempting other men by being guarded behind walls, veils, and the general overall protection of male members of the immediate family. Good women were expected to be virgins and to produce a son. Thus a virgin mother-wife who produces a son is truly an ideal model of Mediterranean male chauvinistic values. Since "good" women were not supposed to enjoy sexuality, men often sought mistresses in addition to wives. This attitude also encouraged neglected mothers to lavish undue affection upon their sons, the affection they might have offered their husbands. According to Slater, who has brilliantly analyzed this pattern, Greek boys learned to fear mature women, a factor which also led them to prefer much younger wives (who would not smother or dominate them). Again, these younger wives, not being able to manage their older husbands, would give their affection to their sons and so the cycle would continue ad infinitum (Slater 1968:45, 52, 132, 307). With a distant or absent father, a son raised in a mother-dominated household (often sleeping with the mother until replaced by a younger sibling) might take on cross-sex identificational characteristics which could be construed as effeminacy (Slater 1968:224, 227).

I do not pretend to have given an exhaustive description of Mediterranean family dynamics, but if the holy family represents a projection of human family roles, then perhaps what Nelson has described for Mexico (1971:74) may apply to Mediterranean cultures generally. She suggests that the Virgin Mary provides a female ideal (mother, wife) but there is no clear counterpart for the male. Joseph is regarded as a cuckold, God is too remote to be perceived as a role model, and Jesus for all his compassion—or because of it—is effeminate. (On the other hand, the cultural relativity of the projective aspects of Christ must also be taken into account. It has been suggested [Richardson, Pardo, and Bode 1971:247], for example, that in Catholic Latin America Christ provides a model of how to suffer [e.g., on the cross] whereas in Protestant North America, the emphasis is on the resurrection or the conquering of death, a distinction which, if valid, might well be correlated with critical differences in general worldview.)

In Mediterranean family structure, one of the crucial problems for boys remains breaking the strong bond existing between them and their mothers so as to join the world of mature men. I suggest that the hero pattern in general and the life of Jesus in particular are an expression of this problem. In this sense, the hero pattern is analogous to male puberty rites. In male initiation rites, young boys are separated from their mothers to join a males-only group. The male initiates are born again, but this time from exclusively male progenitors. The rebirth ceremony often involves a ritual mutilation of the phallus, e.g. circumcision or subincision. These mutilations explicitly entail a feminization of the initiates. (The incised urethra may be referred to as a vulva and the bleeding is likened to menstrual bleeding, etc.) The young boys are deemed inferior to the older males and they must play the parts of women (sometimes in homosexual activities) to demonstrate this (Dundes, 1976). Yet the ceremony permits the boys to join the world of adult men, to become one with their fathers.

Jesus must leave the world of women to join a males-only group (his disciples). Then he undergoes symbolic castration to join (be at one with his) father. As the symbolic castration is no more devastating than ritual circumcision/subincision, Jesus, like male initiates everywhere, is reborn, resurrected. Evidence supporting the notion that the life of Jesus involves a rejection of the mother in favor of the father includes Jesus' response to the woman who praised Mary: "Blessed is the womb that bare thee, and the paps which thou has sucked". Jesus replied, "Yea, rather, blessed are they that hear the word of God and keep it" (Luke 11:27–28). In other words, father's word is more important than mother's womb and breasts. There is also Jesus' direct rebuff of Mary, "Woman, what have I to do with thee?" (John 2:4). In initiation ritual, a boy is required to reject his mother so as to be accepted by his father. While Jesus refuses to allow Mary Magdalene to touch him (John 2:17), he specifically invited doubting Thomas to do so (John 20:27). Jesus rejects women and accepts men.

From the perspective of an individual male trying to choose between remaining on earth with his mother or joining his father in heaven, we see the crucifixion as a critical state in which the child is suspended between his parents (cf. Edelheit 1974:195). After resurrection, Jesus shakes off Mary Magdalene's attempt to "touch" him and he leaves the world of women to join his heavenly father. Joining one's father in afterlife is a continuation of a conventional metaphor in the Old Testament. Heidel thoroughly documents (1963:144–146) the use of the idiom "to lie down with one's fathers" or "to sleep with one's fathers" as a formula signifying death. In a partriarchally determined worldview, just as one would ideally deny the role of woman in childbirth—Eve is created from Adam's body (rather than vice versa), so similarly in death, one would not be laid to rest in mother earth. Rather one would be said to lie or sleep with one's father or to be "carried by the angels into Abraham's bosom" (Luke 12:22). So it is a father's bosom rather than a mother's which serves a euphemism for the land of the dead. And so it is that Jesus is described as the "only begotten Son, which is in the bosom of the Father" (John 1:18).

I have tried to show that the life of Jesus must be understood as a version, a very special version, of the standard Indo-European hero pattern. The life of Jesus is related to the lives of Cyrus, Romulus and Remus, Oedipus, Moses, and many, many other heroes. But his life must also be understood in relation to the norms of Near Eastern and circum-Mediterranean family structure. Freud was essentially correct in observing that whereas Judaism is a religion of the father, Christianity was a religion of the son (Freud 1939:88, 136; 1913:154. Cf. Tarachow 1960:550, who argues that the Judaic pattern renounced the Oedipal object, that is, the mother figure; whereas the Christian pattern retained the Oedipal object.) But Freud did not spell out the full implications of the Holy Family being in some sense a projection of ideal or typical earthly families. If we add a psychoanalytic perspective to both the hero pattern and Mediterranean family structure, we might summarize the life of Jesus as follows: A young virgin is impregnated by her heavenly father, a plot element which contains the appeal of the Electra complex for females. The pregnant virgin is then married to a man much older than she, perhaps old enough to be her father. The infant Jesus is imperiled by a threat on his life by Herod. In one version (Protevangelion), Mary wraps him in swaddling clothes and places him in a manger for protection. In psychoanalytic terms, the son's wish to get rid of the father is translated into the father's attempt to eliminate the son. (We know that Mediterranean fathers specifically wanted sons—as proof of masculinity and to continue the patronymic line.) The son succeeds in keeping his mother to himself (eventually represented in Christian art in the form of the Madonna del Latte). However, unlike the majority of heroes in the hero pattern who kill their father figures and who marry their mothers or a mother surrogate, Jesus yields to (paternal) authority and is crucified. He renounces the world of women to join the world of men and to become one with his father. A mother watching her son agonize in a suspended state over leaving the protective world of women to join the men's world (leaving the mother for the father, leaving the earth for heaven) is common enough in Mediterranean family dynamics. The resurrection suggests a triumph over symbolic castration. He reveals himself to Mary Magdalene, a harlot counterpart of his mother Mary, but he refuses to allow her to "touch" him. By becoming one with his father, Jesus achieves the Oedipal ideal of being his own begetter (thus assuming his father's sexual role with his mother). So Jesus has it both ways: he is the dutiful son obeying a distant, powerful father, but he becomes one with that father—just as boys growing up in circum-Mediterranean households have to learn to progress from a close and prolonged association with protective mothers to a world of men dominated by elders to a time finally when they themselves become distant fathers to their own children as they seek virgin wives and attempt not to become cuckolded (like Joseph).

The life of Jesus cannot be understood in isolation from the cultural context from which it arose. Nor can it be understood apart from comparable hero patterns in cognate cultures. Nor finally can it be understood without reference to the social and psychological factors inherent in the circum-Mediterranean and Near Eastern form of the family.

References

Who Are the Folk?

Bauman, Richard 1971. Differential Identity and the Social Base of Folklore. *Journal of American Folklore* 84:31–41.

Boggs, Ralph Steele 1948. Lo 'primitivo' y Lo Material en el Folklore. *Revista del Instituto Nacional de la Tradición* 1:30–35.

Burne, Charlotte Sophia 1914. *The Handbook of Folklore*. London: Sidgwick & Jackson.

Dundes, Alan 1965. *The Study of Folklore*. Englewood Cliffs, N.J.: Prentice-Hall.

———. 1966. The American Concept of Folklore. *Journal of the Folklore Institute* 3:226–49.

Foster, George M. 1953. What is Folk Culture? *American Anthropologist* 55:159–73.

Hultkrantz, Åke 1960. *General Ethnological Concepts*. Copenhagen: Rosenkilde and Bagger.

Jacovella, Bruno 1948. Nota de la Redacción. *Revista del Instituto Nacional de la Tradición* 1:35–38.

Lang, Andrew 1884. The Method of Folklore. In *Custom and Myth*, pp. 10–28. London: Longmans, Green, and Co.

Legros, Élisée 1962. *Sur les noms et les tendances du folklore*. Liège: Éditions du Musée Wallon.

Paredes, Americo 1969. Concepts about Folklore in Latin America and the United States. *Journal of the Folklore Institute* 6:20–38.

Redfield, Robert 1947. The Folk Society. *American Journal of Sociology* 52:293–308.

Simpson, Georgiana R. 1921. *Herder's Conception of 'Das Volk'*. Chicago: University of Chicago Libraries.

The Curious Case of the Wide-mouth Frog

Dahl, R. 1964. *Charlie and the Chocolate Factory*. New York: Alfred A. Knopf.

George, K. 1958. The Civilízed West Looks At Primitive Africa: 1400–1800, A Study in Ethnocentrism. *Isis* 49:62–72.

Kurath, H., and McDavid, R. 1961. *The Pronunciation of English in the Atlantic States*. Ann Arbor, Michigan: University of Michigan Press.

McDavid, R. 1951. Dialect Differences and Inter-group Tensions. *Studies in Linguistics*. 9:27–33.

———. 1953. Some Social Differences in Pronunciation. *Language Learning* 4:102–16.

Reed, C. 1967. *Dialects of American English*. Cleveland and New York: The World Publishing Company.

Toll, R. 1974. *Blacking Up: The Minstrel Show in Nineteenth-century America*. New York: Oxford University Press.

Thinking Ahead: *A Folkloristic Reflection of the Future Orientation in American Worldview*

Abrahams, Roger D., and Hickerson, Joseph C. 1964. Cross-fertilization Riddles. *Western Folklore* 23:253–57.

Adams, Don 1960. The Monkey and the Fish: Cultural Pitfalls of an Educational Adviser. *International Development Review* 2:22–24. Reprinted in Dundes 1968:504–10.

Brunvand, Jan Harold 1963. A Classification for Shaggy Dog Stories. *Journal of American Folklore* 76:42–68.

Dundes, Alan 1965. *The Study of Folklore*. Englewood Cliffs, N.J.: Prentice-Hall.

———. 1968. *Every Man His Way: Readings in Cultural Anthropology*. Englewood Cliffs, N.J.: Prentice-Hall.

Erdész, Sándor 1961. The World Conception of Lajos Ami, Storyteller. *Acta Ethnographica* 10:327–44.

Forde, Daryll 1954. *African Worlds: Studies in the Cosmological Ideas and Social Values of African Peoples*. London: Oxford University Press.

Foster, George M. 1966. World View in Tzintzuntzan: Re-examination of a Concept. In *Summa Anthropologica, en homenaje a Roberto J. Weitlaner*. Mexico, D.F.: Instituto Nacional de Antropología e Historia.

Geertz, Clifford 1957. Ethos, World-view and the Analysis of Sacred Symbols. *Antioch Review* 17:421–37. Reprinted in Dundes 1968:301–15.

Heilbroner, Robert L. 1959. *The Future As History*. New York: Harper & Row.

Jacobs, Melville 1959. *The Content and Style of an Oral Literature*. Chicago: University of Chicago Press.

Kluckhohn, Clyde 1949. The Philosophy of the Navaho Indians. In *Ideological Differences and World Order*, edited by F. S. C. Northrup. New Haven: Yale University Press.

Kluckhohn, Florence Rockwood 1953. Dominant and Variant Value Orientations. In *Personality in Nature, Society and Culture*, edited by Clyde Kluckhohn, Henry A. Murray, and David M. Schneider. 2d ed. New York: Alfred A. Knopf.

Lee, Dorothy 1950. Codifications of Reality: Lineal and Nonlineal. *Psychosomatic Medicine* 12:89–97. Reprinted in Dundes 1968:329–43.

Malinowski, Bronislaw 1922. *Argonauts of the Western Pacific*. New York: E. P. Dutton.

Raymond, Joseph 1954. Attitudes and Cultural Patterns in Spanish Proverbs. *The Americas* 11:57–77.

Redfield, Robert 1952. The Primitive World View. *Proceedings of the American Philosophical Society* 96:30–36.

––––––. 1953. Primitive World View and Civilization. In *The Primitive World and Its Transformations*. Ithaca: Cornell University Press.

––––––. 1959. Anthropological Understanding of Man. *Anthropological Quarterly* 32:3–21.

Shimkin, D. B., and Sanjuan, Pedro 1953. Culture and World View: A Method of Analysis Applied to Rural Russia. *American Anthropologist* 55:329–48.

Tillich, Paul 1966. The Decline and the Validity of the Idea of Progress. In *The Future of Religions*, edited by Jerald C. Brauer. New York: Harper & Row.

Vogt, Evon Z. 1955. *Modern Homesteaders: The Life of a Twentieth-century Frontier Community*. Cambridge, Mass.: Harvard University Press.

Williams, Robin M., Jr. 1952. *American Society: A Sociological Interpretation*. New York: Alfred A. Knopf.

Wet and Dry, the Evil Eye: *An Essay in Indo-European and Semitic Worldview*

Abraham, Karl 1913. *Dreams and Myths: A Study in Race Psychology*. New York: Journal of Nervous and Mental Disease Publishing Company.

Andree, Richard 1878. *Ethnographische Parallelen and Vergleiche*. Stuttgart: Verlag von Julius Maier. [evil eye, pp. 35–45]

Anon. 1902. Chez les Wallons de Belgique. *Kryptadia* 8:1–148.

Anon. 1887. The Evil Eye. *The Celtic Magazine* 12:415–18.

Arditi, Michele 1825. *Il fascino, e l'amuleto contro del fascino presso gli antichi*. Naples.

Ball, R.A. 1967. The Evil Eye in *Christabel*. *Journal of the Ohio Folklore Society* 2:47–71.

Basil, Saint 1950. *Ascetical Works*. Translated by Sister M. Monica Wagner. New York: Fathers of the Church, Inc.

Bel, Alfred 1903. La Djâzya, Chanson Arabe. *Journal Asiatique*, Dixieme Série, 1:311–66. [evil eye, pp. 359–65]

Bellucci, Giuseppe 1909. Sul Bisogno di Dissetarsi Attribuito All'Anima dei Morti. *Archivio per l'Antropologia e le Etnologia* 39:211–29.

Bergen, Fanny D. 1890. Some Saliva Charms. *Journal of American Folklore* 3:51–59.

Berry, Veronica 1968. Neapolitan Charms Against the Evil Eye. *Folk-Lore* 79:250–56.

Bienkowski, P. 1893. Malocchio. In *Eranos Vindobonensis*, pp. 285–303. Vienna: Alfred Holder.

Blackman, Aylward M. 1912. The Significance of Incense and Libations in Funerary Temple Ritual. *Zeitschrift für Ägyptische Sprache und Altertumskunde* 50:69–75.

Blum, Richard, and Blum, Eva 1965. *Health and Healing in Rural Greece*. Stanford: Stanford University Press.

————. 1970. *The Dangerous Hour: The Lore of Crisis and Mystery in Rural Greece*. London: Chatto & Windus.

Bonner, Campbell 1950. *Studies in Magical Amulets Chiefly Graeco-Egyptian*. Ann Arbor: University of Michigan Press.

Borneman, Ernest 1971. *Sex in Volksmund*. Hamburg: Rowohlt.

Brav, Aaron 1908. The Evil Eye among the Hebrews. *Ophthalmology* 5:427–35.

Browne, Peter 1716. *A Discourse of Drinking Healths*. London: Henry Clements.

Budge, E. A. Wallis 1909. *The Liturgy of Funerary Offerings*. London: Kegan Paul.

————. 1930. *Amulets and Superstitions*. London: Humphrey Milford. [evil eye, pp. 354–65]

Cadbury, Henry J. 1954. The Single Eye. *Harvard Theological Review* 47:69–74.

Cadoux, C. J. 1941–42. The Evil Eye. *The Expository Times* 53:354–55.

Callisen, S.A. 1937. The Evil Eye in Italian Art. *Art Bulletin* 19:450–62.

Camera Cascudo, Luis da 1949. Gorgoneion. In *Homenaje a Don Luis de Hoyos Sainz*, Vol. 1, pp. 67–77. Madrid: Gráficas Valera.

Campbell, Åke 1933. Det onda ögat och besläktade föreställningar i svensk folk-tradition. *Folkminnen och folktankar* 20:121–46.

Canaan, T. 1914. *Aberglaube und Volksmedizin in Lande der Bibel*. Abhandlungen des Hamburgischen Kolonialinstituts, Band XX. Hamburg: L. Friederichsen. [evil eye, pp. 28–32]

————. 1929. Water and 'The Water of Life' in Palestinian Superstition. *Journal of the Palestinian Oriental Society* 9:57–69.

Caquot, André, and du Mesnil du Buisson, R. 1971. La seconde tablette ou 'Petite amulette' d'Arslan-Tash. *Syria* 48:391–406.

Casalis, Matthieu 1976. The Dry and the Wet: A Semiological Analysis of Creation and Flood Myths. *Semiotica* 17:35–67.

Charles, R. H. 1908. *The Testaments of the Twelve Patriarchs*. London: Adam and Charles Black.

Comhaire, Jean L. 1958. Oriental Versions of Polyphem's Myth. *Anthropological Quarterly* 31:21–28.

Conybeare, F. C. 1899. The Testament of Solomon. *The Jewish Quarterly Review* 11:1–45.

Coote-Lake, E. F. 1933. Some Notes on the Evil Eye Round the Mediterranean Basin. *Folklore* 44:93–98.

Corso, Rose 1959. The Evil Eye. *Polish Folklore* 4:6.

Coss, Richard 1974. Reflections on the Evil Eye. *Human Behavior* 3:16–22.

Crawford, O. G. S. 1957. *The Eye Goddess*. London: Phoenix House Ltd.

Crombie, J. E. 1892. The Saliva Superstition. In *The International Folk-Lore Congress 1891, Papers and Transactions*, edited by Joseph and Alfred Nutt, pp. 249–58. London: David Nutt.

Crooke, W. 1968. *The Popular Religion and Folklore of Northern India*. 2 vols. Delhi: Munshiram Manoharlal.

Cross, Frank Moore 1974. Leaves from an Epigraphist's Notebook. *Catholic Biblical Quarterly* 36:486–94.

Cutileiro, José 1971. *A Portuguese Rural Society*. Oxford: Clarendon. [evil eye, pp. 273–78]

Dawkins, R.M. 1937. Alexander and the Water of Life. *Medium Aevum* 7:173–92.

De Cunha, John 1886–89a. On the Evil Eye among the Bunnias. *Journal of the Anthropological Society of Bombay* 1:128–32.

———. 1886–89b. On the Belief in the Evil Eye among the Modern Persians. *Journal of the Anthropological Society of Bombay* 1:149–53.

Del Rio, Martinus Antonius 1599–1600. *Disquisitionum magicarum* libri sex. Lovanii.

Dennys, N. B. 1876. *The Folk-Lore of China*. London: Trübner.

Deonna, Waldemar 1939. Croyances Funéraires: La soif des morts; Le mort musicien. *Revue de l'Histoire des Religions* 119:53–81.

———. 1955. *De Télesphore au "moine bourre": Dieux, génies et démons encapuchonnés*. Berchem-Bruxelles: Latomus.

———. 1965. *Le Symbolisme de l'Oeil*. Paris: Éditions E. de Broccard.

Diego Cuscoy, Luis 1969. Mal de Ojo, Amuletos, Ensalmos y Santiguadores en la Isla de Teneriffe. In *Etnologia y Tradiciones Populares*, pp. 499–520. Zaragoza: Institución "Fernando El Católico."

Dionisopoulos-Mass, Regina 1976. The Evil Eye and Bewitchment in a Peasant Village. In *The Evil Eye*, edited by Clarence Mahoney, pp. 42–62. New York: Columbia University Press.

Djordjevíc, Tihomir R. 1934. Zle oĉi verovanju muslimana u Ohridu. *Glasnick Etnografski Muzej* 9:1–30.

———. 1938. Zle oĉi verovanju južnih Slovena. *Srpski etnografski zbornik* 53:1–347.

Dodwell, Edward 1819. *A Classical and Topographical Tour Through Greece, During the Years 1801, 1805, and 1806*. 2 vols. London: Rodwell and Martin.

Donaldson, Bess Allen 1938. *The Wild Rue: A Study of Muhammadan Magic and Folklore in Iran*. London: Luzac & Co. [evil eye, pp. 13–23]

Doutté, Edmond 1909. *Magie et Religion dans L'Afrique du Nord*. Alger: Typographie Adolfe Jourdan. [evil eye, pp. 317–27]

Dundes, Alan 1962. From Etic to Emic Units in the Structural Study of Folktales. *Journal of American Folklore* 75:95–105.

———. 1968. The Number Three in American Culture. In *Every Man His Way*, pp. 401–24. Englewood Cliffs, N.J.: Prentice-Hall.

———. 1971. Folk Ideas as Units of Worldview. *Journal of American Folklore* 84:93–103.

Ebeling, Erich 1949. Beschwörungen gegen den Fiend und den bösen Blick aus dem Zweistromlande. *Archive Orientálni* 17:172–211.

Edwardes, Charles 1889. *Sardinia and the Sardes*. London: Richard Bentley and Son.

Edwards, Dennis 1971. The 'Evil Eye' and Middle Eastern Culture. *Folklore Annual* (Austin, Texas) 3:33–40.

Eisen, M. J. 1927. Kuri silm. *Eesti Kirjandus* 21:34–43, 153–60.

Eiszler, Lydia 1889. Das böse Auge. *Zeitschrift des Deutschen Palestina-Vereins* 12:200–222.

Elworthy, Frederick Thomas 1958. *The Evil Eye: The Origins and Practices of Superstition*. 1895. Reprint. New York: Julian Press.

Erikson, Erik H. 1977. *Toys and Reasons: Stages in the Ritualization of Experience*. New York: Norton.

Evans, H. C. 1925. The Evil Eye. *Psyche* 6(1):101–6.

Feilberg, H.F. 1901. Der böse Blick in nordischer überlieferung. *Zeitschrift für Volkskunde* 11:304–30, 420–30.

Ferenczi, Sandor 1956. On Eye Symbolism. In *Sex and Psycho-Analysis*, pp. 228–33. New York: Dover.

Foster, George M. 1965. Peasant Society and the Image of Limited Good. *American Anthropologist* 67:293–315.

———. 1972. The Anatomy of Envy: A Study in Symbolic Behavior. *Current Anthropology* 13:165–202.

———. 1978. Hippocrates' Latin American Legacy: "Hot" and "Cold" in Contemporary Folk Medicine. In *Colloquio in Anthropology*, Vol 2, edited by R. K. Wetherington, pp. 3–19. Dallas: Southern Methodist University, The Fort Burgwin Research Center.

Foulks, Edward; Freeman, Daniel M.A.; Kaslow, Florence; and Madow, Leo 1977. The Italian Evil Eye: Mal Occhio. *Journal of Operational Psychiatry* 8(2):28–34.

Frachtenberg, Leo J. 1918. Allusions to Witchcraft and Other Primitive Beliefs in the Zoroastrian Literature. In *The Dastur Hoshang Memorial Volume*, pp. 399–453. Bombay: Fort Printing Press. [evil eye, pp. 419–24]

Freud, Sigmund 1959. The 'Uncanny'. *Collected Papers*, Vol. 4, pp. 368–401. New York: Basic Books.

Frey, Dagobert 1953. *Dämonie des Blickes*. Akademie der Wissenschaften und der Literatur, Abhandlungen der Geistes- und Sozialwissenschaftlichen Klasse. Jahrgang 1953, no. 6. Mainz: Verlag der Akademie der Wissenschaften und der Literatur in Mainz.

Friedenwald, Harry 1939. The Evil Eye (Ayin Hara-ah). *Medical Leaves* 44–48.

Fries, Karl 1891. The Ethiopic Legend of Socinius and Ursula. *Actes de Huitième Congrès International des Orientalistes*, Vol. 2, Section Semitique, pp. 55–70. Leiden: E. J. Brill.

Frommann, Joannes Christianus 1675. *Tractatus de Fascinatione*. Norimbergae.

Gaidoz, Henri 1912. Jules Tuchmann. *Mélusine* 11:148–51.

Gallini, Clara 1973. *Dono e Malocchio*. Palermo: S. F. Flaccovio.

Gardiner, Alan H. 1916. A *Shawabti*-Figure with Interesting Names, The Evil Eye in Egypt. *Proceedings of the Society of Biblical Archaeology* 38:129–30.

Gaster, M. 1900. Two Thousand Years of a Charm Against the Child-Stealing Witch. *Folk-Lore* 11:129–62.

Gaster, Theodor H. 1973. A Hang-up for Hang-ups. The Second Amuletic Plaque from Arslan Tash. *Bulletin of the American Schools of Oriental Research* 209:18–26.

Gennep, Arnold van 1932. *Le Folklore du Dauphiné*. 2 vols. Paris: G.P. Maisonneuve.

———. 1967. *The Semi-Scholars*. London: Routledge & Kegan Paul.

Georges, Robert A. 1962. Matiasma: Living Folk Belief. *Midwest Folklore* 12:69–74.

Giancristofaro, Emiliano 1970. Viaggio nel Mondo Magico Abruzzese: Il malocchio. *Rivista Abruzzese* 23:180–93.

Gifford, Edward S. 1957. The Evil Eye in Medical History. *American Journal of Ophthalmology* 44:237–43.

————. 1958. *The Evil Eye: Studies in the Folklore of Vision.* New York: Macmillan.

————. 1971. The Evil Eye in Philadelphia. *Pennsylvania Folklife* 20:58–59.

Glenn, Justin 1978. The Polyphemus Myth: Its Origin and Interpretation. *Greece & Rome* 25:141–55.

Gollancz, Hermann 1912. *The Book of Protection: Being a Collection of Charms.* London: Oxford University Press.

González Palencia, Angel 1932. La Doncella Que Se Sacó Los Ojos. *Revista de la Biblioteca, Archivo Y Museo* 9:180–200, 272–94.

Gordon, Benjamin L. 1937. Oculus Fascinus (Fascination, Evil Eye). *Archives of Ophthalmology* 17:290–319.

Gouldner, Alvin W. 1965. *Enter Plato.* New York: Basic Books.

Grebe, Mariá Ester, Rajs, Dana, and Segura, José 1971. Enfermedades populares chilenas. Estudio antropológico de cuatro casos. *Cuadernos de la Realidad Nacional* 9:207–38. [evil eye, pp. 227–30]

Greenacre, Phyllis 1925–26. The Eye Motif in Delusion and Fantasy. *American Journal of Psychiatry* 82:553–79.

Gregory, Lady 1920. *Visions and Beliefs in the West of Ireland,* First Series, Vol. 1. New York: G. P. Putnam. [evil eye, pp. 127–52]

Grierson, George A. 1900. The Water of Life. *Folk-Lore* 11:433–34.

Grossi, Vincenzo 1886. *Il Fascino e La Jettatura nell' Antico Oriente.* Milano-Torino: Fratelli Dumolard Editori.

Grünbaum, M. 1877. Beiträge zur vergleichenden Mythologie aus der Hagada. *Zeitschrift der Morgenländischen Gesellschaft* 31:183–359. [evil eye, pp. 258–66]

Gubbins, J. K. 1946. Some Observations on the Evil Eye in Modern Greece. *Folk-Lore* 57:195–97.

Günther, R. T. 1905. The Cimaruta: Its Structure and Development. *Folk-Lore* 16:132–61.

Gutierrez, Joannes Lazarus 1653. *Opusculum de Fascino . . .* Lugduni.

Hanauer, J. E. 1935. *Folk-Lore of the Holy Land.* London: The Sheldon Press.

Haimowitz, Morris L., and Haimowitz, Natalie Reader 1966. The Evil Eye: Fear of Success. In *Human Development: Selected Readings,* edited by Morris L. Haimowitz and Natalie Reader Haimowitz, 2d ed., pp. 677–85. New York: Thomas Y. Crowell.

Hampden, Doreen 1955. The Evil Eye. *The Countryman* 51:272–74.

Hand, Wayland D. 1976. The Evil Eye in its Folk Medical Aspects: A Survey of North America. *Actas del XLI Congreso Internacional de Americanistas,* Mexico, 2 al 7 de Septiembre de 1974. Vol. 3, pp. 183–89. Mexico City.

Hardie, Margaret M. [Mrs. F. W. Hasluck] 1923. The Evil Eye in Some Greek Villages of the Upper Haliakmon Valley in West Macedonia. *Journal of the Royal Anthropological Institute* 53:160–72.

Harfouche, Jamel Karem 1965. *Infant Health in Lebanon:* Customs and Taboos. Beirut: Khayats. [evil eye, pp. 81–106]

Hauschild, Thomas 1979. *Der böse Blick—Ideengeschichtliche und sozialpsychologische Unterschungen.* Beiträge zur Ethnomedizin, Ethnobotanik und Ethnozoologie. Band 7. Hamburg.

Hazard, Willis Hatfield 1890–91. A Syriac Charm. *Journal of the American Oriental Society* 15:284–96.

Hemmer, Ragnar 1914. *Det onda ögat i skandinavisk folktro.* Helsinki.

Henderson, George 1911. *Survivals in Belief Among the Celts*. Glasgow: James Maclehose and Sons.

Herber, J. 1927. La Main de Fathma. *Hespéris* 7:209–19.

H[errmann], A[ntal] 1888. Rumänische Besprechungsformel gegen den bösen Blick. *Ethnologische Mitteilungen aus Ungarn* 1:175–76.

Hildburgh, W. L. 1908. Notes on Some Contemporary Portuguese Amulets. *Folk-Lore* 19:213–24.

———. 1944. Indeterminability and Confusion as Apotropaic Elements in Italy and Spain. *Folk-Lore* 55:133–49.

———. 1946. Apotropaism in Greek Vase Paintings. *Folk-Lore* 57:154–78, 58:208–25.

———. 1951a. Psychology Underlying the Employment of Amulets in Europe. *Folk-Lore* 62:231–51.

———. 1951b. Some Spanish Amulets Connected with Lactation. *Folk-Lore* 62:430–48.

Hirsch, Emil G. 1892. The Evil Eye. *The Folk-Lorist* 1:69–74.

Hocart, A. M. 1938. The Mechanism of the Evil Eye. *Folk-Lore* 49:156–57.

Honea, Kenneth 1956. Buda in Ethiopia. *Wiener Völkerkundliche Mitteilungen* 4:20–24.

Hopkins, E. Washburn 1905. The Fountain of Youth. *Journal of the American Oriental Society* 26:1–67, 411–15.

Hornell, James 1923. Survivals of the Use of Oculi in Modern Boats. *Journal of the Royal Anthropological Institute* 53:289–321.

———. 1924. The Evil Eye and Related Beliefs in Trinidad. *Folk-Lore* 35:270–75.

———. 1938. Boat Oculi Survivals: Additional Records. *Journal of the Royal Anthropological Institute*. 68:339–48.

Ibn Khaldûn 1967. *The Muqaddimah: An Introduction to History*. Vol. 3. 2d ed. Translated by Franz Rosenthal. Princeton: Princeton University Press.

Jahn, Otto 1855. Über den Aberglauben des bösen Blicks bei den Alten. *Berichte über Verhandlungen der königlich sächsischen Gesellschaft der Wissenschaften zu Leipzig*, Philologisch-Historische Classe 7:28–110.

Johnson, Clarence Richard 1924–25. The Evil Eye and Other Superstitions in Turkey. *Journal of Applied Sociology* 9:259–68.

Jones, Ernest 1910. The Action of Suggestion in Psychotherapy. *Journal of Abnormal Psychology* 5:217–54.

———. 1951a. *Essays in Applied Psycho-Analysis*. Vol 2, Essays in Folklore, Anthropology and Religion. London: Hogarth Press.

———. 1951b. *On the Nightmare*. New York: Liveright Publishing Corporation.

Jones, Louis C. 1951. The Evil Eye among European-Americans. *Western Folklore* 10:11–25.

Jorio, Andrea de 1832. *La Mimica degli Antichi*. Naples: Dala stamperia e cartiera del Fibreno.

Joshi, Purushottam Balkrishma 1886–89. On the Evil Eye in the Konkan. *Journal of the Anthropological Society of Bombay* 1:120–28.

Kinsey, Alfred C., Pomeroy, Wardell B., and Martin, Clyde E. 1948. *Sexual Behavior in the Human Male*. Philadelphia: W. B. Saunders.

Kirshenblatt-Gimblett, Barbara, and Lenowitz, Harris 1973. The Evil Eye (The Good Eye) Einehore. *Alcheringa* 5:71–77.

Klein, Melanie 1957. *Envy and Gratitude: A Study of Unconscious Sources.* New York: Basic Books.

Koenig, Otto 1975. *Urmotiv Auge.* Munich: R. Piper & Co.

Krappe, Alexander Hagerty 1927. *Balor with the Evil Eye.* New York: Columbia University Institut des Études Françaises.

Kuriks, O. 1930. Kuri silm ja tema pilgu maagiline mõju. *Eesti Arst* 9:265–75.

La Barre, Weston 1962. *They Shall Take Up Serpents: Psychology of the Southern Snake-Handling Cult.* Minneapolis: University of Minnesota Press.

Landtman, Gunnar 1939. Tron på det onda ögat i svenska Finland. *Bodkavlen* 18:34–42.

Lane, Edward William 1895. *An Account of the Manners and Customs of the Modern Egyptians.* London: Alexander Gardner.

Lawson, John Cuthbert 1910. *Modern Greek Folklore and Ancient Greek Religion.* Cambridge: Cambridge University Press. [evil eye, pp. 8–15]

Legman, G. 1968. *Rationale of the Dirty Joke: An Analysis of Sexual Humor.* New York: Grove Press.

———. 1975. *No Laughing Matter: Rationale of the Dirty Joke: 2nd Series.* New York: Breaking Point.

Leite de Vasconcellos, J. 1925. *A Figa: Estudio de Etnografia Comparativa.* Porto: Araujo & Sobrinho.

Lévi-Strauss, Claude 1969. *The Elementary Structures of Kinship.* Boston· Beacon Press.

Lilienthal, Regina 1924. Eyin ho-re. *Yidishe filologye* 1:245–71.

Lindquist, Edna W. 1936. Rue and the Evil Eye in Persia. *The Moslim World* 26:170–75.

Lloyd G. E. R. 1964. The Hot and the Cold, the Dry and the Wet in Greek Philosophy. *Journal of Hellenic Studies* 84:92–106.

Löwinger, Adolf 1926. Der Böse Blick nach judischen Quellen. *Menorah* 4:551–69.

Lopasic, Alexander 1978. Animal Lore and the Evil-eye in Shepherd Sardinia. In *Animals in Folklore,* edited by J. R. Porter and W.M.S. Russell, pp. 59–69. Totawa, New Jersey: Rowman and Littlefield.

McCartney, Eugene S. 1943. Praise and Dispraise in Folklore. *Papers of the Michigan Academy of Science, Arts and Letters* 28:567–93.

McCown, Chester Charlton 1922. *The Testament of Solomon.* Leipzig: J.C. Hinrichssche Buchhandlung.

McDaniel, Walter Brooks 1918. The *Pupula Duplex* and Other Tokens of an "Evil Eye" in the Light of Ophthalmology. *Classical Philology* 13:335–46.

MacHovec, Frank J. 1976. The Evil Eye: Superstition or Hypnotic Phenomenon. *American Journal of Clinical Hypnosis* 19:74–79.

McKenzie, Dan 1927. *The Infancy of Medicine: An Enquiry into the Influence of Folk-Lore upon the Evolution of Scientific Medicine.* London: Macmillan. [evil eye, pp. 225–62]

Mackenzie, William 1895. *Gaelic Incantations, Charms and Blessings of the Hebrides.* Inverness: Northern Counties Newspaper and Printing and Publishing Company.

Maclagan, R. C. 1902. *Evil Eye in the Western Highlands.* London: David Nutt.

Magaldi, Emilio 1932. Di un particuloare ignorato e strano del culto della dea Fortuna. *Il Folklore Italiano* 7:97–110.

Mallowan, M. E. L. 1947. Excavations at Brak and Chagar Bazar. *Iraq* 9:1–266.

Maloney, Clarence, ed. 1976. *The Evil Eye.* New York: Columbia University Press.

Marugj, Giovanni Leonardo 1815. *Capricci sulla jettatura.* Naples: Dalla tipographia de L. Nobile.

Mather, Frank Jewett 1910. The Evil Eye. *Century Magazine* 80:42–47.

Meerloo, Joost A. M. 1971. *Intuition and the Evil Eye: The Natural History of a Superstition.* Wassenaar: Servire.

Meisen, Karl 1950. Der böse Blick und anderer Schadenzauber in Glaube und Branch der alten Völker und in frühchristlicher Zeit. *Rheinisches Jahrbuch Für Volkskunde* 1:144–77.

———. 1952. Der böse Blick, das böse Wort und der Schadenzauber durch Berührung im Mittelalter und in der neuren Zeit. *Rheinishces Jahrbuch für Volkskunde* 3:169–225.

Meltzl de Lomnitz, Hugo 1884. Le mauvais oeil chez les Arabes. *Archivio per lo Studio delle Tradizioni Popolari* 3:133–34.

Michaelis, A. 1885. Sarapis Standing on a Xanthian Marble in the British Museum. *Journal of Hellenic Studies* 6:287–318.

Millingen, James 1821. Some Observations on an Antique Bas-relief, on which the Evil Eye, or Fascinum, is represented. *Archaeologia* 19:70–74.

Minturn, Leigh, and Hitchcock, John T. 1966. *The Rajputs of Khalapur, India.* New York: John Wiley.

Modi, Jivanji Jamshedji 1924. A Few Notes From and On Recent Anthropological Literature. *Journal of the Anthropological Society of Bombay* 13:113–31. [evil eye, pp. 123–28]

Monger, G. P. 1975. Further Notes on Wedding Customs in Industry. *Folk-Lore* 86:50–61.

Montgomery, James A. 1910–11. Some Early Amulets from Palestine. *Journal of the American Oriental Society* 31:272–81.

———. 1913. *Aramaic Incantation Texts from Nippur.* University of Pennsylvania, The Museum, Publications of the Babylonian Section, Vol. 3. Philadelphia: University Museum.

Moret, Alexandre 1902. *De Charactère Religieux de la Royauté Pharaonique.* Annales de Musee Guimet 15. Paris: Ernest Leroux.

Moretti, Pietrina 1955. Contro il Malocchio del Bestiame in Sardegna. *La Lapa* 3:105.

Mundt, Theodor 1870. Der Blick ist der Mensch. *Europa* 10:298–306.

Murgoci, A. 1923. The Evil Eye in Roumania, and its Antidotes. *Folk-Lore* 34:357–62.

Naff, Alixa 1965. Belief in the Evil Eye among the Christian Syrian-Lebanese in America. *Journal of American Folklore* 78:46–51.

Napier, James 1879. *Folk-Lore or Superstitious Beliefs in the West of Scotland within this Century.* Paisley: Alex. Gardner.

Nefzawi, Shaykh 1963. *The Perfumed Garden of the Shaykh Nefzawi.* Translated by Richard F. Burton. Edited by Alan Hull Walton. London: Neville Spearman.

Nicholson, Frank W. 1897. The Saliva Superstition in Classical Literature. *Harvard Studies in Classical Philology* 8:23–40.

Odelstierna, Ingrid 1949. *Invidia, Invidiosus, and Invidiam facere: A Semantic Investigation.* Uppsala Universitets Årsskrift 1949:10. Uppsala: A.-B. Lundequistska.

O'Flaherty, Wendy Doniger 1969. The Symbolism of the Third Eye of Śiva in the Purānas. *Purāna* 11:273–84.

————. 1975. *Hindu Myths*. Baltimore: Penguin.

O'Neil, Bernard 1908. The Evil Eye. *The Occult Review* 8:5–18.

Onians, Richard Broxton 1951. *The Origins of European Thought About the Body, the Mind, the Soul, the World, Time, and Fate*. Cambridge: Cambridge University Press.

Oyler, D. S. 1919. The Shilluk's Belief in the Evil Eye. *Sudan Notes and Records* 2:122–28.

Park, Roswell 1912. The Evil Eye. In *The Evil Eye, Thanatology and Other Essays*, pp. 9–31. Boston: Gorham Press.

Parry, Albert 1933. *Tattoo: Secrets of a Strange Art as Practised among the Natives of the United States*. New York: Simon and Schuster.

Percy, J. Duncan 1942–43. An Evil Eye. *The Expository Times* 54:26–27.

Perdrizet, Paul 1900. Mélanges Epigraphiques. *Bulletin de Correspondace Hellénque* 24:285–323. [evil eye, pp. 291–99]

————. 1922. *Negotium Perambulans in Tenebris:* Études de démonologie Gréco-Orientale. Strasbourg: Libraire Istra.

Pitrè, Guiseppe 1889. La Jettatura ed il Malocchio. *Biblioteca delle Tradizioni Popolari Siciliane*, Vol. 17, pp. 235–49. Palermo: Libreria L. Pedone Lauriel.

————. 1913. Jettatura e Malocchio. Scongiuri, Antidoti ed Amuleti. *Biblioteca delle Tradizioni Popolari Siciliane*, Vol. 25, pp. 193–211. Palermo: Libreria Internazionale A. Reber.

Plutarch 1969. *Plutarch's Moralia*. Vol. 7. Translated by Paul A. Clement and Herbert B. Hoffleit. London: William Heinemann.

Potts, William John 1890. The Evil Eye. *Journal of American Folklore* 3:70.

Probst-Biraben, J.H. 1933. La Main de Fatma et Ses Antécédents Symboliques. *Revue Anthropologique* 43:370–75.

————. 1936. Les Talismans contre le Mauvais Oeil. *Revue Anthropologique* 46:171–80.

Quatremère, Étienne Marc 1838. Proverbes Arabes de Meidani. *Journal Asiatique*, III Série, 5:209–58. [evil eye, pp. 233–43]

R., E. 1879. The Evil Eye. *Cornhill Magazine* 39:184–98.

Reitler, Rudolf 1913. Zur Augensymbolic. *Internationale Zeitschrift für Ärztliche Psychoanalyse* 1:159–61.

Reminick, Ronald A. 1974. The Evil Eye Belief Among the Amhara of Ethiopia. *Ethnology* 13:279–91

Riemschneider, Margarete 1953. *Augengott und heilige Hochzeit*. Leipzig: Koehler und Amelang.

Roback, A. A. 1938. *Psychological Aspects of Jewish Protective Phrases*. Bulletin of the Jewish Academy of Arts and Sciences, no. 4. New York: Jewish Academic of Arts and Sciences.

Roberts, John M. 1976. Belief in the Evil Eye in World Perspective. In *The Evil Eye*, edited by Clarence Maloney, pp. 223–78. New York: Columbia University Press.

Róheim, Géza 1952. The Evil Eye. *American Imago* 9:351–63.

————. 1955. *Magic and Schizophrenia*. New York: International Universities Press.

————. 1972. *The Panic of the Gods and Other Essays*. New York: Harper Torchbooks.

Rolfe, Eustace Neville, and Ingleby, Holcombe 1888. *Naples in 1888*. London: Trübner. [evil eye, pp. 106–26]

Rolleston, J. D. 1942. Ophthalmic Folk-Lore. *The British Journal of Ophthalmology* 26:481–502.

Rousseau, Pierrette Bertrand 1976. Contribution à l'étude de mauvais oeil en Corse. *Ethnopsychologie: revue de psychologie des peuples* 31:5–18.

Rypka, Jan 1965. Der böse Blick bei Niẓámí. *Ural-Altaische Jahrbücher* 36:397–401.

Salillas, Raphael 1905. *La Fascinación en España*. Madrid: Eduardo Arias.

Salomone-Marino, Salvatore 1882. Rimedj e Formole contro le Jettatura. *Archivio per lo Studio delle Tradizione Popolari* 1:132–34.

Sastriar, E. N. Mahadeva 1899. The Evil Eye and the Scaring of Ghosts. *Journal of the Asiatic Society of Bengal* 68(3):56–60.

Schmidt, Bernhard 1913. Der böse Blick und Ähnlicher Zauber im Neugriechischen Volksglauben. *Neue Jahrbucher für das Klassische Altertum Geschichte und Deutsche Literatur* 31:574–613.

Schnippel, Emil 1929. Dill als Mittel gegen den bösen Blick. *Zeitschrift für Volkskunde* 39:194–95.

Schoeck, Helmut 1955. The Evil Eye: Forms and Dynamics of a Universal Superstition. *Emory University Quarterly* 11:153–61.

Schwartz, W. 1877. Der (rothe) Sonnenphallos der Urzeit. Eine mythologisch-antropologische Untersuchung. *Zeitschrift für Ethnologie* 6:167–88, 409–10.

Seligmann, S. 1910. *Der Böse Blick und Verwandtes: Ein Beitrage zur Geschichte des Aberglaubens aller Zeiten und Völker*. 2 vols. Berlin: Hermann Barsdorf Verlag.

———. 1913. Antike Malocchio-Darstellungen. *Archiv für Geschichte der Medizin* 6:94–119.

———. 1922. *Die Zauberkraft des Auges und das Berufen: Ein Kapitel aus der Geschichte des Aberglaubens*. Hamburg: L. Friederichsen & Co.

Servadio, Emillio 1936. Die Angst vor dem bösen Blick. *Imago* 22:396–408.

Shrut, Samuel D. 1960. Coping with the 'Evil Eye' or Early Rabbinical Attempts at Psychotherapy. *American Imago* 17:201–13.

Simeon, George 1973. The Evil Eye in a Guatemalan Village. *Ethnomedizin* 2:437–41.

Simon, Maurice 1948. *Berakoth (The Babylonian Talmud)*. London: Soncino Press.

Smith, C. Ryder 1941–42. An Evil Eye (Mark vii. 22). *The Expository Times* 53:181–82.

———. 1942–43. The Evil Eye. *The Expository Times* 54:26.

Smith, Kirby Flower 1902. Pupula Duplex. In *Studies in Honor of Basil L. Gildersleeve*, pp. 287–300. Baltimore: Johns Hopkins Press.

Spiegelberg, Wilhelm 1967. Der böse Blick in altägyptischen Glauben. *Zeitschrift für Ägyptische Sprache und Altertumskunde* 59:149–54.

Spooner, Brian 1976. Anthropology and the Evil Eye. In *The Evil Eye*, edited by Clarence Maloney, pp. 279–85. New York: Columbia University Press.

Stein, Howard F. 1974. Envy and the Evil Eye Among Slovak-Americans: An Essay in the Psychological Ontogeny of Belief and Ritual. *Ethos* 2(1):15–46.

Stillman, Yedida 1970. The Evil Eye in Morocco. In *Folklore Research Center Studies*, Vol. 1, edited by Dov Noy and Issachar Ben Ami, pp. 81–94. Jerusalem: Magnes Press.

Stocchetti, Sara 1941. Interpretazione Storico-criticadi una Diffusa Superstitione Popolare. *Lares* 12:6–22.

Story, William W. 1860. Roba di Roma: The Evil Eye and Other Superstitions. *Atlantic Monthly* 5:694–704.

———. 1877. *Castle St. Angelo and the Evil Eye*. London: Chapman and Hall.

Sumner, William Graham 1960. *Folkways*. 1906. Reprint. New York: Mentor.

Taylor, Archer 1951. *English Riddles from Oral Tradition*. Berkeley and Los Angeles: University of California Press.

Thompson, Arthur 1907. The Secret of the Verge Watch: A Study in Symbolism and Design. In *Anthropological Essays Presented to Edward Burnett Taylor*, pp. 355–59. Oxford: Clarendon Press.

Thompson, R. Campbell 1904. *The Devils and Evil Spirits of Babylonia*. Vol. 2. London: Luzac and Co.

———. 1908. *Semitic Magic: Its Origins and Development*. London: Luzac & Co.

Thompson, Stith 1955–58. *Motif-Index of Folk-Literature*. 6 vols. Bloomington: Indiana University Press.

Thurston, Edgar 1907. *Ethnographic Notes on Southern India*. Madras: Government Press. [evil eye, pp. 253–58]

———. 1912. *Omens and Superstitions of Southern India*. London: T. Fisher Unwin. [evil eye, pp. 109–20]

Tourney, Garfield, and Dean J. Plazak 1954. Evil Eye in Myth and Schizophrenia. *Psychiatric Quarterly* 28:478–95.

Tuchmann, Jules 1884–1901. La Fascination. *Mélusine* 2–10 passim.

Tylor, E. B. 1890. Notes on the Modern Survival of Ancient Amulets Against the Evil Eye. *Journal of the Royal Anthropological Institute* 19:54–56.

———. 1892. Exhibition of Charms and Amulets. In *Papers and Transactions of the International Folklore Congress 1891*, pp. 387–393. London: David Nutt.

Vairus, Leonardus 1589. *De Fascino Libre tres . . .* Venetiis.

Valla, Filippo 1894. La Jettatura (*Ocru malu*) in Sardegna (Barbagia). *Archivio per lo Studio delle Tradizioni Popolari* 13:419–32.

Valletta, Nicola 1787. *Cicalata sul Fascino Volgarmente detto Jettatura*. Naples.

Van Buren, E. Douglas 1955. New Evidence Concerning an Eye-Divinity. *Iraq* 17:164–75.

Vega, Juan José Hurtado 1968. 'El Ojo': Creencias y Prácticas Médicas Populares en Guatemala. *Tradiciones de Guatemala* 1:13–25.

Vereecken, J. L. Th. M. 1968. A Propos du mauvais oeil. *L'hygiène mentale* 57(1):25–38.

Vijaya-Tunga, J. 1935. The Evil Eye. *The Spectator* 154:1011–12.

Villena, Enrique de 1917. Tres Tratados. 1422. Reprint. *Revue Hispanique* 41:110–214.

Vuorela, Toivo 1967. *Der Böse Blick im Lichte der Finnischen Überlieferung*. Folklore Fellows Communication 201. Helsinki: Academia Scientiarum Fennica.

Wace, Alan J. B. 1903–1904. Grotesques and the Evil Eye. *The Annual of the British School at Athens*, no. 10. (Session 1903–1904), pp. 103–14.

Wagner, Max Leopaldo 1913. Il Malocchio e credenze affini in Sardegna. *Lares* 2:129–50.

Weakland, John H. 1956. Orality in Chinese Conceptions of Male Genital Sexuality. *Psychiatry* 19:237–47.

Weinreich, Otto 1909. Helios, Augen heiland. *Hessische Blätter für Volkskunde* 8:168–73.

West, John O. 1974. Mal Ojo. In *The Folklore of Texas Cultures*, Publications of the Texas Folklore Society 38, edited by Francis Edward Abernethy, pp. 82–84. Austin: The Encino Press.

Westermarck, Edward 1904. The Magic Origin of Moorish Designs. *Journal of the Royal Anthropological Institute* 34:211–22.

———. 1926. *Ritual and Belief in Morocco*. Vol. 1. London: Macmillan. [evil eye, pp. 414–78]

Weston, Stephen 1821. Further Observations on the Bas-relief, supposed to represent the Evil Eye. *Archaeologia* 19:99–101.

Williamson, Marjorie 1932. Les Yeux Arrachés, *Philological Quarterly* 11:149–62.

Wolters, Paul 1909. Ein Apotropaion aus Baden im Aargau. *Bonner Jahrbücher* 118:257–74.

Woodburne, A. Stewart 1935. The Evil Eye in South Indian Folklore. *International Review of Missions* 24:237–47.

Zammit-Maempel, G. 1968. The evil eye and protective cattle horns in Malta. *Folk-Lore* 79:1–16.

The Number Three in American Culture

Abbot, A.E. 1962. *The Number Three: Its Occult Significance in Human Life.* London: Emerson Press.

Ben Cheneb, Mohammed 1926. Du nombre Trois chez les Arabes. *Revue Africaine* 67:105–78.

Brinton, Daniel G. 1894. The origin of sacred numbers. *American Anthropologist* 7:168–73.

Brough, J. 1959. The tripartite ideology of the Indo-Europeans: an experiment in method. *Bulletin of the School of Oriental and African Studies* 22:69–95.

Brown, Dora Worrall 1960. Does language structure influence thought? *ETC: A Review of General Semantics* 17:339–45.

Buckland, A.W. 1895. Four, as a sacred number. *Journal of the Anthropological Institute* 25:96–102.

Childe, V. Gordon 1956. *Piecing Together the Past.* New York: Frederick A. Praeger.

Comas, Juan 1960. *Manual of Physical Anthropology.* Springfield: Charles C. Thomas.

Crawley, E.S. 1897. The origin and development of number symbolism. *Popular Science Monthly* 51:524–34.

Deonna, W. 1944. Trois, superlatif absolu. *L'Antiquité Classique* 23:403–28.

Dumézil, Georges 1958. *L'idéologie tripartite des Indo-Européens.* Brussels: Collection Latomus 31.

Erben, Karel Jaromir 1857. O dvojici a o trojici v bàjeslovi slovanskèm ("About the number two and the number three in Slavic mythology"). *Casopis Musea Kralovsti Ceskeho* 31:268–86; 390–415.

Freud, Sigmund 1953. *A General Introduction to Psychoanalysis.* Garden City: Permabooks.

Geil, William Edgar 1926. *The Sacred 5 of China.* Boston and New York: Houghton and Mifflin.

Glenn, Jules 1965. Sensory determinants of the symbol three. *Journal of the American Psychoanalytic Association* 13:422–34.

Göbel, Fritz 1935. *Formen und Formeln der epischen Dreiheit in der griechischen Dichtung.* Stuttgart: W. Kohlhammer.

Goudy, Henry 1910. *Trichotomy in Roman Law.* Oxford: Clarendon Press.

Gunther, R.F. 1912. Worauf beruht die Vorherrschaft der Drei in Menschen? *Nord und Sud* 142:313–25.

Hall, Edward T. 1959. *The Silent Language.* New York: Fawcett Publications.

Heizer, Robert F. 1962. The background of Thomsen's three-age system. *Technology and Culture* 3:259–66.

Hoijer, Harry 1954. *Language in Culture.* Chicago: University of Chicago Press.

Jacobs, Melville 1959. *The Content and Style of an Oral Literature.* Chicago: University of Chicago Press.

Kirfel, Willibald 1948. *Die dreikopfige Gottheit.* Bonn: Ferd, Dummlers Verlag.

Kohler, Wolfgang 1959. *Gestalt Psychology.* New York: Mentor Books.

La Sorsa, Saverio 1963. Il numero 3 nella terapia popolare. *Annali di Medicina Navale* 68:171–74.

Lease, Emory B. 1919. The number three, mysterious, mystic, magic. *Classical Philology* 14:56–73.

Lehmann, Alfred 1914. *Dreiheit and dreifache Wiederholung im deutschen Volksmarchen.* Leipzig: Buchdruckerei Robert Noske.

Littleton, C. Scott 1967. Toward a genetic model for the analysis of ideology: the Indo-European case. *Western Folklore* 26:37–47.

Lowie, Robert H. 1925. Five as a mystic number. *American Anthropologist* 27:578.

May, Earl Chapin 1932. *The Circus from Rome to Ringling.* New York: Duffield and Green.

Morgan, Lewis H. 1876. Ethnical periods. *Proceedings of the American Association for the Advancement of Science* 24:206–74.

Muller, Raimund 1903. Die zahl 3 in sage, dichtung und kunst. In *XXX Jahresbericht der K.K. Stauts-Oberrealschule in Teschen am Schlusse des Schuljahres* 1902–1903, pp. 1–23. Teschen: K. und K. Hofbuchdruckerei Karl Prochaska.

Olrik, Axel 1909. Epische Gesetze der Volksdichtung. *Zeitschrift für Deutsches Al tertum* 51:1–12. Reprinted in translation in Alan Dundes, ed., *The Study of Folklore,* pp. 129–41. Englewood Cliffs, N.J.: Prentice-Hall, 1965.

Paine, Levi Leonard 1901. *The Ethnic Trinities and Their Relations to the Christian Trinity.* Boston and New York: Houghton, Mifflin and Company.

Parsons, Elsie Clews 1916. The favorite number of the Zuni. *Scientific Monthly* 3:596–600.

Post, Emily 1960. *Etiquette.* 10th ed. New York: Funk and Wagnalls.

Seifert, Josef Leo 1954. *Sinndeutung des Mythos: Die Trinitat in den Mythen der Urvolker.* Wien, Munchen: Verlag Herold.

Simmel, Georg 1902. The number of members as determining the sociological form of the group. *American Journal of Sociology* 8:1–46, 158–96.

Strand, T.A. 1958. *Tri-Ism: The Theory of the Trinity in Nature, Man and His Works.* New York: Exposition Press.

Tavenner, Eugene 1916. Three as a magic number in Latin literature. *Transactions of the American Philological Association* 47:117–43.

Usener, H. 1903. Dreiheit. *Rheinisches Museum für Philologie* 58:1–47, 161–208, 321–62.

Wertheimer, Max 1923. Untersuchungen zur lehre von der gestalt. *Psychologische Forschung* 4:301–50.

Whorf, Benjamin L. 1964. *Language, Thought and Reality.* Cambridge Mass.: The MIT Press.

A Psychoanalytic Study of the Bullroarer

Allen, M. R. 1967. *Male Cults and Secret Initiations in Melanesia.* Melbourne: Melbourne University Press.

Angas, George French 1847. *Savage Life and Scenes in Australia and New Zealand.* 2d ed. 2 vols. London: Smith, Elder, and Co.

Armstrong, A. Leslie 1936. A Bull-roarer of Le Moustier Age from Pin Hole Cave, Creswell Crags, Derbyshire. *The Antiquaries Journal* 16:322–23.

Ashley-Montagu, M. F. 1937. *Coming Into Being Among the Australian Aborigines.* London: George Routledge.

Baal, J. Van 1963. The Cult of the Bull-roarer in Australia and Southern New Guinea. *Bijdragen Tot de Taal-, Land- en Volkenkunde* 119:201–14.

———. 1966. *Dema: Description and Analysis of Marind-Anim Culture (South New Guinea).* The Hague: Martinus Nijhoff.

Battaglia, Raffaello 1925. Sopravvivenze del rombo nelle provincie venete. *Studi e Materiali Storia delle Religioni* 1:190–217.

Bettelheim, Bruno 1962. *Symbolic Wounds: Puberty Rites and the Envious Male.* New York: Collier Books.

Blackwood, Beatrice 1935. *Both Sides of Buka Passage.* Oxford: Clarendon Press.

Bourke, John G. 1891. *Scatalogic Rites of All Nations.* Washington, D.C.: W. H. Lowdermilk.

Bromida, Marcelo 1952. Pampidos y Australoides; Coherências Ergológicas y Míticas. *Archivos Ethnos* 1 (2):51–82.

Brown, A. R. 1912. Beliefs Concerning Childbirth in Some Australian Tribes. *Man* 12:180–82.

Budde, Karl 1928. Das Schwirrholz Werkzeug der alttestamentlichen Totenbeschwörung? *Zeitschrift für die alttestamentliche Wissenschaft* 46:75–76.

Cohen, Saul 1973. The Bullroarer, *El Palacio* 78 (4):29–33.

Collins, David 1798. *An Account of the English Colony in New South Wales.* Vol. 1. London: T. Cadell and W. Davies.

Crombie, J. W. 1884. A Curious Superstition. *Folklore Journal* 2:172–73.

Darlington, H. S. 1929. Tooth Evulsion and Circumcision. *Psychoanalytic Review* 16:272–90.

Davidson, Daniel Sutherland 1953. The Possible Source and Antiquity of the Slate Churingas of Western Australia. *Proceedings of the American Philosophical Society* 97:194–213.

Deacon, A. B. 1925. The Kakihan Society of Ceram and New Guinea Initiation Cults. *Folk-Lore* 36:332–61.

————. 1934. *Malekula: A Vanishing People in the New Hebrides.* London: George Routledge.

Dennett, R. E. 1968. *Nigerian Studies.* London: Frank Cass & Co.

Dundes, Alan 1962. Earth-Diver: Creation of the Mythopoeic Male. *American Anthropologist* 64:1032–51.

Dundes, Alan; Leach, Jerry W.; and Özkök, Bora 1970. The Strategy of Turkish Boys' Verbal Dueling Rhymes. *Journal of American Folklore* 83:325–49.

Figura, Franz 1896. Das Schwirrholz in Galizien. *Globus* 70:226.

Fison, Lorimer, and Howitt, A. W. 1880. *Kamilaroi and Kurnai.* Melbourne: George Robertson.

Frazer, J. G. 1901. On Some Ceremonies of the Central Australian Tribes. *Report of the Australasian Association for the Advancement of Science* 8:312–21.

————. 1913. *The Golden Bough* Vol. 9, Baldur the Beautiful. London: Macmillan.

Freeman, Derek 1968. Thunder, Blood, and the Nicknaming of God's Creatures. *Psychoanalytic Quarterly* 37:353–99.

Freud, Sigmund 1938. *The Basic Writings of Sigmund Freud.* New York: Modern Library.

Gennep, Arnold Van 1906. Les deux doctrines religieuses et le rhombe sacré. In *Mythes et Légendes d'Australie*, pp. lxviii-lxxxi. Paris: E. Guilmoto.

————. 1960. *The Rites of Passage.* London: Routledge & Kegan Paul.

Guiart, Jean 1951. Rhombes et Tjurungas Australiens: Etudes des motifs decoratifs et de leur symbolique. *Etudes Melanesiennes.* n.s.3(5):45–57.

Gutmann, Bruno 1926. *Das Recht der Dschagga.* Arbeiten zur Entwicklungspsychologie 7. Munich: C. H. Beck'she Verlagsbuchhandlung.

Haddon, Alfred C. 1898. The Bull-Roarer. In *The Study of Man*, pp. 277–327. London: John Murray.

Hanika, Josef 1952. Der r-Laut in Fruchtbarkeitsriten und das Schwirrholz. *Bayerisches Jahrbuch für Volkskunde* 1952:79–90.

Harrison, Jane Ellen 1912. *Themis: A Study of the Social Origins of Greek Religion.* Cambridge: Cambridge University Press.

Hatt, Gudmund 1949. *Asiatic Influences in American Folklore.* Copenhagen: Ejnar Munksgaard.

Hauer, J. W. 1923. Das Schwirrholz und das magische corpus delicti. In *Die Religionen: Ihr Werden, Ihr Sinn, Ihre Wahrheit*, pp. 154–62. Berlin: W. Kohlhammer.

Heizer, Robert F. 1960. Some Prehistoric Bullroarers from California Caves. Reports of the University of California Archaeological Survey no. 50, Papers on California Archaeology 78:5–9.

Hiatt, L. R. 1971. Secret Pseudo-Procreation Rites Among the Australian Aborigines. In *Anthropology in Oceania*, edited by L. R. Hiatt and C. Jayawardena, pp. 77–88. Sydney: Angus and Robertson.

Hickmann, Hans 1955. Unbekannte aegyptische Klangwerkzeuge (Aerophone), I. Schwirrholz und Schwirrscheibe. *Die Musikforschung* 8:151–57.

Hirschberg, Walter 1940. Der Ahnencharakter des afrikanischen Schwirrholzes. *Ethnos* 5:112–121.

Hollis, A.C. 1909. *The Nandi: Their Language and Folk-Lore.* Oxford: Clarendon Press.

Howitt, A. W. 1891a. Address by the President (Anthropology). *Report of the Australasian Association for the Advancement of Science* 3:342–53.
———. 1891b. The "Bull Roarer" of Some Australian Tribes. *New Zealand Journal of Science* n.s. 1:94.
———. 1904. The Native Tribes of South-East Australia. London: Macmillan.
Izikowitz, Karl Gustav 1935. *Musical and Other Sound Instruments of the South American Indians.* Göteborg: Elanders Boktryckeri Aktiebolag.
Jeffreys, M.D.W. 1949. The Bull-Roarer among the Ibo. *African Studies* 8:23–34.
Jones, Ernest 1951. *Essays in Applied Psycho-Analysis* Vol. 2, Essays in Folklore, Anthropology and Religion. London: The Hogarth Press.
Kanner, Leo 1928. The Tooth as a Folkloristic Symbol. *Psychoanalytic Review* 15:37–52.
Kitching, James W. 1963. *Bone, Tooth and Horn: Tools of Palaeolithic Man.* Manchester: Manchester University Press.
Klein, Ernest 1966. *A Comprehensive Etymological Dictionary of the English Language.* 2 vols. Amsterdam: Elsevier Publishing Company.
Lang, Andrew 1884. The Bull-Roarer: A Study of the Mysteries. In *Custom and Myth*, pp. 29–44. London: Longmans, Green, and Co.
———. 1910. Savage Supreme Beings and the Bull-Roarer. *Hibbert Journal* 8:665–67.
Leiris, Michel 1934. Rhombes Dogon et Dogon Pignari. *Bulletin du Musée d'Ethnographie du Trocadero* 7:3–10.
Lévi-Strauss, Claude 1973. *From Honey to Ashes.* New York: Harper and Row.
Loeb, Edwin M. 1929. Tribal Initiations and Secret Societies. *University of California Publications in American Archaeology and Ethnology* 25:249–88.
Lowie, Robert H. 1946. The Bororo. Handbook of South American Indians, Vol. I., pp. 419–34. Bureau of American Ethnology 43. Washington: Government Printing Office.
———. 1961. *Primitive Society.* New York: Harper Torchbooks.
Marett, R. R. 1910. Savage Supreme Beings and the Bull-roarer. *Hibbert Journal* 8:394–410.
Mathew, John 1899. *Eaglehawk and Crow: A Study of the Australian Aborigines.* London: David Nutt.
Mathews, R. H. 1896. The Boro, or Initiation Ceremonies of the Kamilaroi Tribe, Part II. *Journal of the Anthropological Institute of Great Britain and Ireland* 25:318–39.
———. 1897. The Keeparra Ceremony of Initiation. *Journal of the Anthropological Institute of Great Britain and Ireland* 26:320–340.
———. 1898. Bullroarers used by the Australian Aborigines. *Journal of the Anthropological Institute of Great Britain and Ireland* 27:52–60.
———. 1900. Phallic Rites and Initiation Ceremonies of the South Australian Aborigines. *Proceedings of the American Philosophical Society* 39:622–38.
———. 1904. The Native Tribes of Victoria: Their Languages and Customs. *Proceedings of the American Philosophical Society* 43:54–70.
Murdoch, John 1890. The 'Whizzing-Stick' or 'Bull-Roarer' on the West Coast of Africa. *American Anthropologist* 3:258.
Murphy, Robert, F. 1958. *Mundurucú Religion.* University of California Publications in American Archaeology and Ethnology, Vol. 49, no. 1. Berkeley and Los Angeles: University of California Press.

————. 1959. Social Structure and Sex Antagonism. *Southwestern Journal of Anthropology* 15:89–98.

————. 1960. *Headhunter's Heritage.* Berkeley and Los Angeles: University of California Press.

Neuhauss, R. 1911. *Deutsch Neu-Guinea.* 3 vols. Berlin: Verlag Dietrich Reimer.

Pettazzoni, Raffaele 1911. Un rombo australiano. *Archivio per l'Antropologia e la Etnologia* 41:257–70.

————. 1912a. Mythologie Australienne du Rhombe. *Revue de l'Histoire des Religions* 65:149–70.

————. 1912b. Sopravvivenze del rombo in Italia. *Lares* 1:63–72.

————. 1924. Il rombo. In *I Misteri: Saggio di una teoria storico-religiosa,* pp. 1–40. Bologna: Nicola Zanichelli.

Raum, O.F. 1940. *Chaga Childhood.* London: Oxford University Press.

Reik, Theodor 1962. The Puberty Rites of Savages. In *Ritual: Four Psychoanalytic Studies,* pp. 91–166. New York: Grove Press.

Róheim, Géza 1926. *Social Anthropology: A Psychoanalytic Study in Anthropology and A History of Australian Totemism.* New York: Boni and Liveright.

————. 1942. Transition Rites. *Psychoanalytic Quarterly* 11:336–74.

————. 1949. The Symbolism of Subincision. *American Imago* 6:321–28.

Roy, Rai Bahadur Sarat Chandra 1927. The Bull-Roarer in India. *Journal of the Bihar and Orissa Research Society* 13:54–61.

Sachs, Curt 1921. *Geist und Werden der Musikinstrumente.* Berlin: Verlag von Dietrich Reimer.

Saul, Leon J. 1959. Flatulent Phallus. *Psychoanalytic Quarterly* 28:382.

Schmeltz, J.D.E. 1896. Das Schwirrholz. *Verhandlungen des Vereins für Naturwissenschaftliche Heimatforschung Unterhaltung zu Hamburg* 9:92–127.

Schmidt, P.G. 1908. Die Stellung der Aranda unter den australischen Stämmen. *Zeitschrift für Ethnologie* 40:866–901.

————. 1912. Sur la mythologie australienne des rhombes (bull-roarer). *Anthropos* 7:1059–60.

Schwartz, F.L.W. 1879. *Wolken und Wind, Blitz und Donner: Ein Beitrag zur mythologie und culturgeschichte der urzeit.* Berlin: Verlag von Wilhelm Hertz.

Seidel, H. 1896a. Das Schwirrholz in Hinterpommern und Rügen. *Globus* 70:340.

————. 1896b. Das Schwirrholz in Westpreussen. *Globus* 70:67–68.

Speiser, Felix 1928–29. Uber Initiationen in Australien und Neu-Guinea. *Verhandlungen der Naturforschended Gesellschaft in Basel* 40(2):53–258.

Spencer, Baldwin, and Gillen, F.J. 1898. *The Native Tribes of Central Australia.* London: Macmillan.

————. 1904. *The Northern Tribes of Central Australia.* London: Macmillan.

Spier, Leslie 1928. Havasupai Ethnography. *Anthropological Papers of the American Museum of Natural History* 29:81–392.

Strehlow, Carl 1907. *Die Aranda- und Loritja-Stämme in Zentral-Australien.* I. Teil. Mythen, Sagen und Märchen des Aranda-Stammes in Zentral-Australien. Frankfurt: Joseph Baer & Co.

————. 1908. *Die Aranda- und Loritja-Stamme in Zentral-Australien.* II. Teil. Mythen, Sagen und Märchen des Loritja-Stammes. Frankfurt: Joseph Baer & Co.

————. 1913. *Die Aranda- und Loritja-Stämme in Zentral-Australien.* IV. Teil, I.

Abteilung. Das Soziale Leben der Aranda-und Loritja-Stämme. Frankfurt: Joseph Baer & Co.

Thompson, Stith 1955–58. *Motif-Index of Folk-Literature*. 6 vols. Bloomington: Indiana University Press.

Thomson, Donald F. 1933. The Hero Cult, Initiation and Totemism on Cape York. *Journal of the Royal Anthropological Institute* 63:453–537.

Tucci, Giovanni 1954–55. Contributo allo studio del rombo. *Rivista di Etnografia* 8–9:1–16.

Turner, Victor 1967. *The Forest of Symbols*. Ithaca: Cornell University Press.

Tylor, E.B. 1881. Review of Kamilaroi and Kurnai. *The Academy* 19:264–66.

———. 1890. Discussion. *Journal of the Anthropological Institute of Great Britain and Ireland* 19:163.

Williams, F.E. 1936a *Bull-Roarers in the Papuan Gulf*. Territory of Papua. Anthropology, Report no. 17. Port Moresby: Walter Alfred Bock.

———. 1936b *Papuans of the Trans-Fly*. Oxford: Clarendon Press.

Worms, E.A. 1957. Australian Mythological Terms: Their Etymology and Dispersion. *Anthropos* 52:732–68.

Young, Frank W. 1965. *Initiation Ceremonies: A Cross-Cultural Study of Status Dramatization*. Indianapolis: Bobbs-Merrill.

Zerries, Otto 1942. *Das Schwirrholz*. Stuttgart:Strecker and Schröder.

———. 1953. The Bull-Roarer among South American Indians. *Revista do Museu Paulista* 7:275–309.

Zirkle, Conway 1936. Animals impregnated by the wind. *Isis* 25:95–130.

The Hero Pattern and the Life of Jesus

Allegro, John M. 1970. *The Sacred Mushroom and the Cross*. New York: Bantam.

Astour, Michael C. 1965. *Hellenosemitica: An Ethnic and Cultural Study in West Semitic Impact on Mycenaean Greece*. Leiden: E.J. Brill.

Bascom, William 1965. The Forms of Folklore: Prose Narratives. *Journal of American Folklore* 78:3–20.

Bauer, Adolf 1882. Die Kyros-Sage und Verwandtes. *Sitzungsberichte der Philosophisch-Historischen Classe der Kaiserlichen Akademie der Wissenschaften* 100:495–578.

Baum, Paull Franklin 1916. The Mediaeval Legend of Judas Iscariot. *Publications of the Language Association* 31:431–632.

Beck, Bodog F., and Smedley, Dorée 1971. *Honey and Your Health:* A Nutrimental, Medicinal and Historical Commentary. New York: Bantam.

Binder, Gerhard 1964. *Die Aussetzung des Konigskindes Kyros und Romulus*. Beiträge zur Klassischen Philologie 10. Meisenheim am Glan: Verlag Anton Hain.

Boman, Thorleif 1967. *Die Jesus-Uberlieferung im Lichte der neueren Volkskunde*. Göttingen: Vandenhoeck and Ruprecht.

Boslooper, Thomas 1962. *The Virgin Birth*. Philadelphia: The Westminster Press.

Bourke, Myles M. 1960. The Literary Genius of Matthew 1–2. *Catholic Biblical Quarterly* 22:160–75.

Bradley, Noel 1973. Notes on Theory-Making, on Scotoma of the Nipples and on the Bee as Nipple. *International Journal of Psycho-Analysis* 54:301–14.

Brunner-Traut, Emma 1960. Die Geburtsgeschichte der Evangelien im Lichte ägyptologischer Forschungen. *Zeitschrift für Religions-und Geistesgeschichte* 12:97–111.

Buck, Carl Darling 1949. *A Dictionary of Selected Synonyms in the Principal Indo-European Languages.* Chicago: University of Chicago Press.

Bultmann, Rudolf 1958. *Jesus Christ and Mythology.* New York: Charles Scribner's Sons.

———. 1963. *The History of the Synoptic Tradition.* Oxford: Basil Blackwell.

Campbell, J.K. 1964. *Honour, Family, and Patronage.* New York: Oxford University Press.

Campbell, Joseph 1956. *The Hero with a Thousand Faces.* New York: Meridian.

Charencey, Hyacinthe de 1879. *Le Fils de la Vierge.* Havre: Imprimerie Lepelletier.

Childs, Brevard S. 1960. *Myth and Reality in the Old Testament.* Studies in Biblical Theology no. 27 London: SCM Press.

Cohon, Samuel S. 1919. The Origin of Death. *Journal of Jewish Lore and Philosophy* 1:371–96.

Conybeare, Fred. C. 1914. *The Historical Christ.* London: Watts & Co.

Cook, Victor 1965. Lord Raglan's Hero—A Cross Cultural Critique. *Florida Anthropologist* 18:147–54.

Cosquin, Emmanuel 1908. Le Lait de la Mère et le Coffre Flottant. *Revue des Questions Historiques* 83:353–425.

Deonna, W. 1955. *Deux études de symbolisme religieux.* Collection Latomus 18. Berchem-Bruxelles: Latomus.

Dibelius, Martin 1932. *Jungfrauensohn und Krippenkind.* Sitzungsberichte der Heidelberger Akademie der Wissenschaften, Philosophisch-historische Klasse 22, 4. Abhandlung.

Dibelius, Martin 1935. *From Tradition to Gospel.* New York: Charles Scribner's Sons.

Doane, T.W. 1882. *Bible Myths and Their Parallels in Other Religions.* New York: The Commonwealth Company.

Drews, Arthur 1911. *The Christ Myth.* Chicago: Open Court Publishing Company.

Dundes, Alan 1968. The Number Three in American Culture. In *Every Man His Way.* Englewood Cliffs, N.J.: Prentice-Hall. Pp. 401–24.

———. 1976. A Psychoanalytic Study of the Bullroarer. *Man* 11:220–38.

Dundes, Alan, and Jerry W. Leach and Bora Özkök 1970. The Strategy of Turkish Boys' Verbal Dueling Rhymes. *Journal of American Folklore* 83:325–49.

Edelheit, Henry 1974. Crucifixion Fantasies and Their Relation to the Primal Scene. *International Journal of Psycho-Analysis* 55:193–99.

Fischer, Henri Théodore 1929. *Het Heilig Huwelik van Hemel en Aarde.* Utrecht: Drukkerij J. van Boekhoven.

Frazer, James 1918. *Folklore in the Old Testament.* 3 vols. London: Macmillan.

———. 1964. *The New Golden Bough.* New York: Mentor.

Freud, Sigmund 1910. A Special Type of Choice of Object Made by Men. *Standard Edition* 1957, 11:162–75. London: The Hogarth Press.

———. 1913. *Totem and Taboo. Standard Edition* 1955, 13:1–161. London: The Hogarth Press.

———. 1939. *Moses and Monotheism. Standard Edition* 1964, 23:7–137. London: The Hogarth Press.

284 REFERENCES

Garth, Helen Meredith 1950. *Saint Mary Magdalene in Mediaeval Literature.* The Johns Hopkins University Studies in Historical and Political Science 67 (3). Baltimore: John Hopkins University Press.

Gennep, Arnold van 1904. Lucina sine concubitu (III), notes ethnographiques. *La Revue des Idees* 1:554–58.

Granqvist, Hilma 1931. *Marriage Conditions in a Palestinian Village*, Vol. I. Helsinki: Societas Scientiarum Fennica.

Grant, R.M. 1961. *The Earliest Lives of Jesus.* London: S.P.C.K.

Guidi, I. 1903. Une Terre Coulant du Lait avec du Miel. *Revue Biblique* 12:241–44.

Gunkel, Hermann 1964. *The Legends of Genesis.* New York: Schocken.

Hartland, Edwin Sidney 1894–96. *The Legend of Perseus.* 3 vols. London: David Nutt.

Hahn, Johann Georg von 1876. *Sagwissenschaftliche Studien.* Jena: F. Mauke.

Heidel, Alexander 1963. *The Gilgamesh Epic and Old Testament Parallels.* Chicago: University of Chicago Press.

Henderson, Ian 1952. *Myth in the New Testament.* Studies in Biblical Theology no. 7. London: SCM Press.

Hertel, Johannes 1909. Zu den Erzählungen von der Muttermilch und der schwimmenden Lade. *Zeitschrift für Volkskunde* 19:83–91.

Holley, N.M. 1949. The Floating Chest. *Journal of Hellenic Studies* 69:39–47.

Hooke, S.H. 1963. *Middle Eastern Mythology.* Baltimore: Penguin.

Ishida, Eiichirô 1956. The Mother-Son Complex in East Asiatic Religion and Folklore. In *Die Wiener Schule der Volkerkunde.* Vienna. pp. 411–19.

Ishida, Eiichirô 1964. Mother-Son Deities. *History of Religions* 4:30–52.

Jeremias, Alfred 1911. *The Old Testament in the Light of the Ancient East.* 2 vols. New York: G.P. Putnam's Sons.

Jeremias, Joachim 1969. *Jerusalem in the Time of Jesus.* London: SCM Press.

Jones, Ernest 1951a. *Essays in Applied Psychoanalysis*, Vol. II, Essays in Folklore, Anthropology and Religion. London: The Hogarth Press.

Jones, Ernest 1951b. *On the Nightmare.* New York: Liveright.

Jung, C.G. 1967. *Symbols of Transformation.* 2nd ed. Princeton: Princeton University Press.

Justin Martyr, Saint 1948. *Writings of Saint Justin Martyr.* New York: Christian Heritage.

Kennedy, J. 1917. The Gospels of the Infancy, The Lalita Vistara, and the Vishnu Purana: Or the Transmission of Religious Legends Between India and the West. *Journals of the Royal Asiatic Society of Great Britain and Ireland* 209–43; 469–540.

Krappe, Alexander Haggerty 1928. The Story of the Fall of Man. *Nieuw Theologisch Tijdschrift* 17:242–49.

Krappe, Alexander Haggerty 1933. La naissance de Moise. *Revue de l' Histoire des Religions* 107:126–133.

Lawrence, D.H. 1952. *The Later D.H. Lawrence.* New York: Alfred A. Knopf.

Leach, Edmund 1976. Jesus, John and Mary Magdalene. *New Society* 34:686–88.

Lederer, Wolfgang 1967. Historical Consequences of Father-Son Hostility. *Psychoanalytic Review* 54:248–76.

Lessmann, Heinrich 1906. *Die Kyrossage in Europa.* Wissenschaftliche Beilage zum Jahresbericht Uber die Städtische Realschule zu Charlottenburg. Ostern.

Lévi, Israel 1910. Le Lait de la Mére & Le Coffre Flottant. *Revue des Etudes Juives* 59:1–13.

Levin, A.J. 1957. Oedipus and Samson: The Rejected Hero-child. *International Journal of Psycho-Analysis* 38:105–16.

Levy, Ludwig 1917. Sexualsymbolik in der biblischen Paradiesgeschichte. *Imago* 5:16–30.

McCartney, Eugene S. 1925. Greek and Roman Lore of Animal-Nursed Infants. *Papers of the Michigan Academy of Science, Arts and Letters* 4:15–42.

McCown, Chester Charlton 1940. *The Search for the Real Jesus:* A Century of Historical Study. New York: Charles Scribner's Sons.

Maròt, Károly 1951. Die Trennung von Himmel und Erde. *Acta Antiqua* 1:35–66.

Matthiae, Paolo 1962. Il motivo della vacca che allatta nell'iconografia del vicino oriente antico. *Revista degli Studi Orientali* 37:1–31.

Meiss, Millard 1951. *Painting in Florence and Siena After the Black Death.* Princeton: Princeton University Press.

Mellaart, James 1963. Excavations at Catal Hüyük, 1962. *Anatolian Studies* 13:43–100.

Morganstern, Julian 1919. The Sources of the Paradise Story. *Journal of Jewish Lore and Philosophy* 1:105–23; 225–40.

Münsterberger, Warner 1939. *Ethnologische Studien an Indonesischen Schopfungsmythen* Ein Beitrag zur Kultur-Analyse Südostasiens. The Hague: Martinus Nijhoff.

Nelson, Cynthia 1971. *The Waiting Village:* Social Change in Rural Mexico. Boston: Little, Brown.

Nock, Arthur Darby 1925. Eunuchs in Ancient Religion. *Archiv fur Religionswissenschaft* 23:25–33.

Numazawa, Frank Kiichi 1946. *Die Weltanfänge in der Japanischen Mythologie.* Paris: Librairie du Recueil Sirey.

Numazawa, Frank Kiichi 1953. Background of Myths on the Separation of Sky and Earth from the Point of View of Cultural History. *Scientia* 88:28–35.

Nutt, Alfred 1881. The Aryan Expulsion-and-Return Formula in the Folk and Hero Tales of the Celts. *The Folklore Record* 4:1–44.

Ohler, Annemarie 1969. *Mythologische Elemente im Alten Testament.* Düsseldorf: Patmos-Verlag.

Patai, Raphael 1959. *Sex and Family in the Bible and the Middle East.* Garden City: Doubleday.

Patte, Daniel 1976. *What is Structural Exegesis?* Philadelphia: Fortress Press.

Phipps, William E. 1970. *Was Jesus Married?* New York: Harper & Row.

Phipps, William E. 1973. *The Sexuality of Jesus.* New York: Harper & Row.

Propp, Vladimir 1968. *The Morphology of the Folktale.* Austin: University of Texas Press.

Raglan, Lord 1934. The Hero of Tradition. *Folklore* 45:212–31.

Raglan, Lord 1956. *The Hero:* A Study in Tradition, Myth, and Drama. New York: Vintage.

Rank, Otto 1952. *The Trauma of Birth.* New York: Robert Brunner.

Rank, Otto. 1959. *The Myth of the Birth of the Hero.* New York: Vintage.

Redford, Donald B. 1967. The Literary Motif of the Exposed Child. *Numen* 14:209–28.

Rees, Alwyn D. 1936. The Divine Hero in Celtic Hagiology. *Folklore* 47:30–41.

Reider, Norman 1960. Medieval Oedipal Legends about Judas. *Psychoanalytic Quarterly* 29:515-27.

Renard, Marcel 1964. Hercule allaité par Junon. In Marcel Renard and Robert Schilling, eds., *Hommages a Jean Bayet*. Collection Latomus 70. Bruxelles-Berchem: Latomus. Pp. 611–18.

Richardson, Miles, and Marta Eugenia Pardo and Barbara Bode 1971. The Image of Christ in Spanish America as a Model for Suffering. *Journal of Inter-American Studies and World Affairs* 13:246–57.

Ricoeur, Paul 1975. Biblical Hermeneutics. *Semeia* 4:29–148.

Róheim, Géza 1940. The Garden of Eden. *Psychoanalytic Review* 27:1–26; 177–99.

Rubenstein, Richard L. 1972. *My Brother Paul*. New York: Harper and Row.

Runeberg, Arne 1952. *Jesu Korsfiästelse*. Stockholm: Natur och Kultur.

Saintyves, Pierre [Nourry, Emile Dominique] 1906. *Les Vierges Méres et les naissances miraculeuses*. Paris: E. Nourry.

———. 1923. *Essais de Folklore Biblique*. Paris: E. Nourry.

Saliba, John A. 1975. The Virgin-Birth Debate in Anthropological Literature: A Critical Assessment. *Theological Studies* 36:428–54.

Schmeing, Karl 1911. *Flucht- und Werbungssagen in der Legende*. Münster: Aschendorffsche Buchdruckerei.

Schweitzer, Albert 1968. *The Quest of the Historical Jesus*. New York: Macmillan.

Slater, Philip E. 1968. *The Glory of Hera:* Greek Mythology and the Greek Family. Boston: Beacon Press.

Staudacher, Willibald 1968. *Die Trennung von Himmel und Erde*. 2d ed. Darmstadt: Wissenschaftliche Buchgesellschaft.

Steinberg, Leo 1970. The Metaphors of Love and Birth in Michelangelo's *Pietàs*. In Theodore Bowie and Cornelia V. Christenson, eds., *Studies in Erotic Art*. New York: Basic Books, Pp. 231–335.

Strauss, David Friedrich 1892. *The Life of Jesus*. 2nd ed. London: Swan Sonnenschein.

Tarachow, Sidney 1960. Judas the Beloved Executioner. *Psychoanalytic Quarterly* 23:528–54.

Taylor, Archer 1964. The Biographical Pattern in Traditional Narrative. *Journal of the Folklore Institute* 1:114–129.

Thass-Thienemann, Theodore 1957. Oedipus and Sphinx: The Linguistic Approach to Unconscious Fantasies. *Psychoanalytic Review* 44:10–33.

Thompson, Stith 1955–58. *Motif-Index of Folk-Literature*. 6 vols. Bloomington: Indiana University Press.

Thompson, Stith 1961. *The Types of the Folktale*. Helsinki: Academia Scientiarum Fennica.

Thurston, Herbert, and Donald Attwater, eds. 1956. *Butler's Lives of the Saints*. Vol. IV. New York: P.J. Kennedy & Sons.

Tylor, E. Burnet 1863. Wild Men and Beast-Children. *Anthropological Review* 1:21–32.

Usener, Hermann 1902. Milch and Honig. *Rheinisches Museum für Philologie* 57:177–95.

Utley. Francis Lee 1965. *Lincoln Wasn't There or Lord Raglan's Hero*. CEA Chap

Book. Supplement to CEA Critic 22, no. 9. Washington, D.C.: College English Association.

Vanggaard, Thorkil 1972. *Phallos:* A Symbol and Its History in the Male World. New York: International Universities Press.

Weigert-Vowinkel, Edith 1938. The Cult and Mythology of the Magna Mater from the Standpoint of Psychoanalysis. *Psychiatry* 1:347–78.

Wellisch, E. 1955. *Isaac and Oedipus.* New York: Humanities Press.

Westermarck, Edward 1922. *The History of Human Marriage.* 3 vols. New York: Allerton Book Company.

Wilson, R. McL. 1962. *The Gospel of Philip.* New York: Harper & Row.

Winter, Paul 1954–55. Jewish Folklore in the Matthaean Birth Story. *Hibbert Journal* 55:34–42.

Ziegler, Joseph 1952. Ochs und Esel an der Krippe. *Munchener Theologische Zeitschrift* 3:385–402.

Notes

———————⟫⟩ ⟨⟨———————

Who Are the Folk?

1. This text was collected in December 1975 in Martinez, California, by two of my students, Johnny Green and Pamela Yazman, from Laura Kingston, a bank vice president. Jokes not specifically credited come from the author's own repertoire.

2. The text was collected in March 1974 by Andrea Magnani, who had heard the joke told by Charles Fulkerson, conductor of the orchestra at Humboldt State in California. It should be noted that from the audience's point of view, the violins are on the left and the violas on the right.

3. The text was collected by Philip Lyons from Ed Prentice in July 1974 in San Francisco.

4. The text was collected by Michael McKenna from Carl N. Cole in June 1964 in Berkeley. Mr. Cole reported hearing the story at the Passionist Seminary in St. Louis, circa 1950.

5. This text also was collected by Michael McKenna, from Father Adrian McKenna, a secular Catholic priest, in July 1964 in Oakland.

6. This text was collected by Marcia Skolnick from her father, Dr. Alex Skolnick, a psychiatrist, in December 1964 in San Mateo, California. Dr. Skolnick, who described reform Judaism as "a hemorrhage without the blood," said he first heard the joke in San Francisco in 1958.

7. This text was collected by Michael Ziegler in November 1976 from himself. He first heard the joke from Rabbi Harold Schulweis, a Conservative rabbi, at Temple Sinai in Oakland in 1974.

8. This joke was collected by an engineering student who heard it told by Professor Lester C. Dubins, Department of Statistics, University of California, Berkeley, in an upper-division statistics course in the fall of 1969.

9. This text was collected by John Morthland from himself in March 1969. He first heard it in Berkeley in 1967.

10. This text was collected by Lia Jackson from Carolina Clare in January 1965 in Berkeley.

11. This text was collected by Joyce Paviso from Crandall Bay in April 1964 in Berkeley.

12. This is just as I heard the joke except that in the original version it was a labor organizers' meeting in Denver. Denver was actually the city mentioned in the version of the joke I heard sometime in the 1960s.

Texture, Text, and Context

1. For a more extended discussion of the unavoidable pitfalls facing the folklorist who would define superstitions in terms of belief or genesis, see Alan Dundes, "Brown County Superstitions," *Midwest Folklore* 11 (1961):26–28.

2. According to Richard M. Dorson, folklore, to be considered folklore, must "live in people's mouths for at least several generations." *Bloodstoppers and Bearwalkers* (Cambridge, 1952), p. 7. While Dorson does suggest that the term "tradition" is more important than "oral," he essentially defines folklore as oral traditional texts. See *American Folklore* (Chicago, 1959), p. 2, and *Buying the Wind* (Chicago, 1964), p. 1. See also Francis Lee Utley, "Folk Literature: An Operational Definition," *Journal of American Folklore* 74 (1961):194.

3. William Bascom put the matter thus: "All folklore is orally transmitted, but not all that is orally transmitted is folklore." See "Folklore and Anthropology," *JAF* 66 (1953):285. (The question remains whether or not 'all folklore is orally transmitted.')

4. Francis Lee Utley, "Folk Literature: An Operational Definition," *JAF* 74 (1961):197, 204.

5. Elli-Kaija Köngäs Maranda, "The Concept of Folklore," *Midwest Folklore* 13 (1963):85.

6. The need for definition also extends to the most basic terms in folklore scholarship. What is the difference, it any, between "version" and "variant"? According to Stith Thompson, "It is customary to call each example of an item of folklore a variant." But "if the idea of variation is not foremost in the mind of the speaker, he is more likely to use the term *version*." Says Thompson, "There is otherwise no difference in the use of these two terms." But is the distinction simply a matter of a folklorist's subjective state of mind? If one examines ten texts of a proverb or folktale, one could distinguish between versions and variants. Contrary to what Thompson says, any iteration of a text is a version. Thus if one had ten texts of a particular proverb, one would have ten versions of that proverb. Versions which depart to a lesser or greater degree from the more typical forms can be labelled variants. Thus all variants must by definition be versions, but not all versions are necessarily variants. The obvious difficulties are first the determination of 'typical forms,' and second the question of how different does a version have to be before it can be termed a variant? For Thompson's views, see "variant," in Maria Leach, ed., *The Standard Dictionary of Folklore, Mythology and Legend*, Vol. II (New York, 1950), pp. 1154–55.

7. Archer Taylor, *The Proverb* (Hatboro, 1962), p. 3. This kind of thinking is not far removed from the mysticism advocated by Richard Chase when he explains that one does not have to be "an authority" (Professional folklorist) to tell whether folklore is genuine or not. "You know by the feel, by a tingling in your scalp, by an indefinable something inside you when you hear the song sung, or the tale told, or the tune played." *American Folk Tales and Songs* (New

York, 1956), p. 19. One wonders whether future generations of folklorists will continue to be satisfied with this approach to the science of folklore.

8. Stith Thompson, *Narrative Motif-Analysis as a Folklore Method*, Folklore Fellows Communications No. 161 (Helsinki, 1955), p. 7; "Folktale," in Maria Leach, ed., *The Standard Dictionary of Folklore, Mythology and Legend*, Vol. I (New York, 1949), p. 408.

9. Three is not only the ritual number of the folk, but of folklorists as well. In Euro-American culture, many of the standard classification schemes in folklore scholarship as in most disciplines are patently tripartite. Folklorists familiar with the subdivisions of folk narrative: myth, legend, and folktale; of folktale: animal tales, ordinary folktales, and jokes/anecdotes; and of motifs: actor, item, and incident; will probably not be bothered by the present triadic scheme.

10. For a discussion of texture, see Alan Dundes, "Trends in Content Analysis: A Review Article," *Midwest Folklore* 12 (1962):36. For specific considerations of texture in particular genres, see Thomas A. Sebeok, "The texture of a Cheremis incantation," *Mémoires de la Société Finno-Ougrienne* 125 (1962):523–37; Maung Than Sein and Alan Dundes, "Twenty-Three Riddles from Central Burma," *JAF* 77 (1964):72–73.

11. C. W. v. Sydow, *Selected Papers on Folklore* (Copenhagen, 1948), pp. 12–13.

12. One of the most elaborate attempts is Charles T. Scott's "A Linguistic Study of Persian and Arabic Riddles: A Language-Centered Approach to Genre Definition," an unpublished University of Texas doctoral dissertation (1963).

13. For further discussion of the distinction between folkloristic and linguistic structure, see Robert A. Georges and Alan Dundes, "Toward A Structural Definition of the Riddle," *JAF* 76 (1963):117, nn. 15, 18.

14. Even such excellent studies as Thomas Rhys Williams, "The Form and Function of Rambunan Dusun Riddles," *JAF* 76 (1963):95–110; and John Blacking, "The Social Value of Venda Riddles," *African Studies* 20 (1961):1–32, fail to provide this kind of concrete context data.

15. Robert A. Georges and Alan Dundes, "Toward A Structural Definition of the Riddle," *JAF* 76 (1963):111–118.

16. These typical remarks are from Maung Wun, "Burmese Riddles," *Journal of the Burma Research Society* 40 (1957):2, and Y. M. Sokolov, *Russian Folklore*, trans. Catherine Ruth Smith (New York, 1950), p. 283, respectively.

17. See Martha Wolfenstein, *Children's Humor* (Glencoe, 1954), pp. 114–15.

18. The tale is Motif N13, Husbands wager that they will be able to do what wives tell them to do. For an English version, see E. M. Wilson, "Some Humorous English Folk-Tales, Part Two," *Folk-Lore* 49 (1948):282–83. A version which appeared originally in an upstate New York newspaper in 1840 was recently reprinted by Julia Hull Winner in her article, "Wit and Humor A Century Ago," *New York Folklore Quarterly* 19 (1963):56–61. The present texts were collected in Lawrence, Kansas, in May 1963 by Mrs. Betty Ann Henderson.

19. In a version I heard in Bloomington, Indiana, in 1962, the incidents were slightly different. The first husband is driving home and he accidentally runs over a bit of the lawn as he turns into his driveway. The wife says, "That's right, run all over the flower bed." The second husband dozes in his

easy chair and accidentally burns a tiny hole when his cigarette comes into contact with the chair. The wife says, "That's right, burn up all the funiture." The third incident is the same as in the present text except that the punch line is accompanied by a gesture in which the raconteur cups his two hands together as if concealing the detached object in question. Note, incidentally, how well this and the preceding joke exemplify the pattern number of three in American jokelore.

20. *Russian Folklore*, p. 285.

21. T. S. Eliot, *Selected Essays*, New Edition (New York, 1950), pp. 124–25.

22. Alan Dundes, "From Etic to Emic Units in the Structural Study of Folktales," *JAF* 75 (1962):102.

23. Alan Dundes, "Trends in Content Analysis: A Review Article," *Midwest Folklore* 12 (1962):37.

Projection in Folklore: *A Plea for Psychoanalytic Semiotics*

1. Ruth Benedict, "Folklore," *Encyclopaedia of the Social Sciences*. VI (New York, 1931), pp. 288–93.

2. Stith Thompson, *Motif-Index of Folk-Literature*. 6 vols. (Bloomington, 1955–58). For a discussion of some of the more widespread narrative elements in the world, see Clyde Kluckhohn, "Recurrent Themes in Myths and Mythmaking," *Daedalus* 88 (1959):266–79, reprinted in Alan Dundes, ed., *The Study of Folklore* (Englewood Cliffs, N.J.: 1965), pp. 158–68. For a balanced account of the Jungian view, see Wilson M. Hudson, "Jung on Myth and the Mythic," in *The Sunny Slopes of Long Ago*, Publications of the Texas Folklore Society XXXIII (Dallas, 1966), pp. 181–97. For a more partisan treatment, see Marie Louise von Franz, *An Introduction to the Interpretation of Fairy Tales* (New York, 1970).

3. For details of the menehune, see Katharine Luomala, *The Menehune of Polynesia and Other Mythical Little People of Oceania*, Bernice P. Bishop Museum Bulletin 203 (Honolulu, 1951).

4. Vladimir Propp, *Morphology of the Folktale* (Austin, 1968). For my adaptation of Propp's function, see "From Etic to Emic Units in the Structural Study of Folktales," *Journal of American Folklore* 75 (1962):95–105, reprinted in Alan Dundes, *Analytic Essays in Folklore* (The Hague, 1975), pp. 61–72. For an indication of trends in the semiotic study of folk narrative, see Claude Bremond, *Logique du récit* (Paris, 1973) and William O. Hendricks, *Essays on Semiolinguistics and Verbal Art*, Approaches to Semiotics 37 (The Hague, 1973). For a useful survey of structuralism, see Robert Scholes, *Structuralism in Literature: An Introduction* (New Haven, 1974).

5. For a representative collection of office-copier folklore, see Alan Dundes and Carl R. Pagter, *Urban Folklore from the Paperwork Empire* (Austin, 1975).

6. P. Bogatyrev and R. Jakobson, "Die Folklore als besondere Form des Schaffens," in *Verzameling van Opstellen Door Oud-Leerlingen en Bevriende Vakgenooten Opgedragen Aan Mrg. Prof. Jos. Schrijnen* (Donum Natalicium Schrijnen) (Nijmegen-Utrecht, 1929), pp. 900–913.

7. My sources for the definition of projection include: Leopold Bellak, "The Concept of Projection: An Experimental Investigation and Study of the

Concept," *Psychiatry* 7 (1944):354; Gardner Lindzey, *Projective Techniques and Cross-Cultural Research* (New York, 1961), pp. 25–31; and Ludwig Eidelberg, ed., *Encyclopedia of Psychoanalysis* (New York, 1968), p. 331.

8. Justus Buchler, ed., *Philosophical Writings of Peirce* (New York, 1955), p. 88.

9. Sigmund Freud, *The Basic Writings of Sigmund Freud* (New York, 1938), p. 164. One distinct advantage of Freud's approach as opposed to Jung's is the possibility of reconciling it with cultural relativism. It was Kardiner, among others, who demonstrated how specific projective systems might be derived from particular cultural contexts. See Abram Kardiner, *The Individual and his Society* (New York, 1939) and *The Psychological Frontiers of Society* (New York, 1945). Jung's projections in theory cannot easily be reconciled with cultural relativism inasmuch as they are presumed to be genetic, innate, a priori, inherited, *pre*-cultural archetypes. Jung is quite clear on this point. "One encounters projections, one does not make them." "The primitive mentality does not invent *myths*, it experiences them. Myths are original revelations of the pre-conscious psyche, involuntary statements about unconscious psychic happenings." "For the archetype, of course, exists a priori." "Archetypes are . . . autonomous elements of the unconscious psyche which were there before any invention was thought of." "We must therefore assume that they correspond to certain collective (and not personal) structural elements of the human psyche in general, and, like the morphological elements of the human body, are *inherited*." "The archetype—let us never forget this—is a psychic organ present in all of us." See *Psyche & Symbol: A Selection from the Writings of C. G. Jung*, Violet S. de Laszlo, ed. (Garden City, 1958), pp. 8, 117, 15, 108, 123.

10. Gardner Lindzey, *Projective Techniques and Cross-Cultural Research* (New York, 1961). There have been relatively few attempts to study folklore as projection. See Bert Kaplan, "Psychological Themes in Zuni Mythology and Zuni TAT's," *The Psychoanalytic Study of Society* 2 (1962):255–63; George R. Horner, "Folklore as a Psychological Projective System," *The Conch* III, no. 1 (March, 1971):3–13. See also J. L. Fischer, "The Sociopsychological Analysis of Folktales," *Current Anthropology* 4 (1963):235–95, and the section entitled "The Analysis of Folklore" in Victor Barnouw, *Culture and Personality* (Homewood, Ill., 1963), pp. 301–24. One of the best studies of the projective aspect of folklore is Melville Jacobs, *The Content and Style of an Oral Literature* (Chicago, 1959).

11. This is a standard jump rope rhyme. See Roger D. Abrahams, *Jump Rope Rhymes: A Dictionary* (Austin, 1969), p. 51, #148, for references to several dozen versions of "Fudge, fudge." For another jump rope rhyme with obvious sibling rivalry, see Abrahams, pp. 79–80, #224, "I had a little brother," with the very tense of the verb in the first line revealing wishful thinking.

12. One of the first studies of this important characteristic of folklore is Franz Ricklin, *Wishfulfillment and Symbolism in Fairy Tales* (New York, 1915).

13. Sigmund Freud, *A General Introduction to Psycho-Analysis* (New York, 1953), p. 170.

14. Tale type numbers refer to Stith Thompson, *The Types of the Folktale*, FFC 184 (Helsinki, 1961). Jack and the Beanstalk is tale type 328. The Boy Steals the Giant's Treasure.

15. For further psychoanalytic commentary on this tale, see Alan Dundes, ed., *The Study of Folklore* (Englewood Cliffs, 1965), pp. 107–13.

16. The motif number is from Stith Thompson, *Motif-Index of Folk-*

Literature, 6 vols. (Bloomington, 1955–58). The separation of the parents is included under motif A625.2, Raising of the sky.

17. Henry Nash Smith, *Virgin Land: The American West as Symbol and Myth* (New York, 1957).

18. For a slightly more detailed consideration of the George Washington legend, see Alan Dundes, "On the Psychology of Legend," in Wayland Hand, ed., *American Folk Legend: A Symposium* (Berkeley and Los Angeles, 1971), pp. 26–29.

19. I must here express my thanks to Dr. Donald H. Stanford for having first called my attention to the possible psychological significance of the lunar landing. Dr. Stanford, a psychiatrist, had two patients, both latent homosexuals, who were seriously affected by the lunar landing. Both required hospitalization immediately following their television viewing of the landing. Dr. Stanford contacted me initially to inquire about mythological or folkloristic associations surrounding the moon. Subsequent discussions with Dr. Stanford convinced me that the folkloristic features of the lunar mission did have psychological significance not just for his patients but for Americans generally. For other interpretations of the lunar mission, see Joseph Campbell, "The Moon Walk–The Outward Journey," in *Myths to Live By* (New York, 1972), pp. 233–49; and Ian I. Mitroff, *The Subjective Side of Science: A Philosophical Inquiry into the Psychology of the Apollo Moon Scientists* (New York, 1974).

20. For Cox's study, see Marian Roalfe Cox, *Cinderella*, Publications of the Folk-Lore Society XXXI (London, 1892). For the statistics on the number of versions containing the glass slipper, as well as a discussion of *vair*, see Cox, p. 506. For an earlier discussion of *vair*, see W. R. S. Ralston, "Cinderella," *Nineteenth Century*, 6 (1879):832–53.

21. This rhyme is #108 in the standard collection, Iona and Peter Opie, *The Oxford Dictionary of Nursery Rhymes* (Oxford, 1959), pp. 128–29. "The old woman who lived in a shoe" is #546 in the same collection, pp. 434–35. Even the conservative Opies seem aware of the symbolism inasmuch as they note that "the shoe has long been symbolic of what is personal to a woman until marriage." Similarly, Swedish folklorist Anna Birgitta Rooth in her comprehensive modern study of Cinderella has a brief discussion of "The shoe as a sexual symbol." See Rooth, *The Cinderella Cycle* (Lund, 1951), pp. 104–05. For other folkloristic data concerning shoes, see Paul Sartori, "Der Schuh im Volksglauben," *Zeitschrift des Vereins für Volkskunde* 4 (1894):41–54; 148–80; 282–305; 414–27; and James F. Crombie, "Shoe-Throwing at Weddings," *Folklore* 6 (1895):258–81. For early studies of the erotic symbolism of shoes, see the entries under "Shoe, Symbolism of," in Roger Goodland, *A Bibliography of Sexual Rites and Customs* (London, 1931), p. 739.

22. For further discussion of the medical school cadaver legend and the preceding grandmother legend, see Dundes, "On the Psychology of Legend," in Wayland Hand, ed., *American Folk Legend*, pp. 31–36.

23. For a general discussion of this point, see Eldridge Cleaver, "As Crinkly as Yours," in Alan Dundes, ed., *Mother Wit from the Laughing Barrel: Readings in the Interpretation of Afro-American Folklore* (Englewood Cliffs, 1972), pp. 9–21.

24. Roald Dahl, *Charlie and the Chocolate Factory* (New York, 1964), pp. 72–76.

25. I am indebted to Professor Arthur Asa Berger of San Francisco State

University for the suggestion that Star Trek might be viewed as a projection of American values. For details of Star Trek, see David Gerrold, *The World of Star Trek* (New York, 1973). It might be argued that Star Trek's crew represents the entire world rather than just the United States, but the world appears to be ethnocentrically defined much as it is in the "World Series" baseball championships in which the "world" boils down to just American (plus one Canadian) entries.

26. Otto Rank, *The Myth of the Birth of the Hero* (New York, 1959), p. 81.

27. Sigmund Freud, *Collected Papers*, III (New York, 1959), p. 449. I have no desire to become embroiled in any controversy over terminology. My impression is that psychologists may not have sufficiently differentiated various subtypes of projection. Bellak has proposed the term "inverted projection" to refer to instances where reaction formation takes place prior to outward projection. Thus "I love him" becomes "I hate him" through reaction formation and then "I hate him" becomes "He hates me" through projection. See Gardner Lindzey, *Projective Techniques and Cross-Cultural Research*, pp. 29–30.

28. *The Myth of the Birth of the Hero*, p. 80.

29. Carl Darling Buck, *A Dictionary of Selected Synonyms in the Principal Indo-European Languages* (Chicago, 1949), p. 103.

30. For a more complete analysis of the elephant joke cycle, see Roger D. Abrahams and Alan Dundes, "On Elephantasy and Elephanticide," *Psychoanalytic Review* 56 (1960):225–41, reprinted in Dundes, *Analytic Essays in Folklore*, pp. 192–205. Incidentally, the play on "color" might be another example of the literalization of metaphor occurring in folkloristic projections.

31. Paul Bouissac, "Poetics in the Lion's Den: The Circus Act as a Text," *Modern Language Notes* 86 (1971):845–57. For other essays by Bouissac, see "Pour une sémiotique du cirque," *Semiotica* 3 (1970):93–120; "On Jugglers and Magicians: Some Aspects of the Semantics of Circus Performances," *Journal of Symbolic Anthropology* 1 (1973):127–45.

32. Ujamlal Kothari in his brief essay, "The Animals and Their Symbolic Meanings," *American Imago* 19 (1962):157–62, tends to be a bit simplistic and overly doctrinaire. In the American rodeo, he sees the cowboy as ego with the wild animals (horse, bull) as id. In the circus animal show, he similarly labels the trainer as ego and the animals as id. Nevertheless, his attempt to view rodeo and circus acts as projections of individual psychology helped stimulate my analysis of Bouissac's data.

33. John M. Ingham, "The Bullfighter: A Study in Sexual Dialectic," *American Imago* 21 (1964):95–102.

34. For relevant scholarship, see Archer Taylor, *The Shanghai Gesture*, FFC 166 (Helsinki, 1956), reprinted in Taylor, *Comparative Studies in Folklore: Asia-Europe-America* (Taipei, 1972), pp. 293–366.

35. Edward Sagarin, *The Anatomy of Dirty Words* (New York, 1962), p. 143. Some of the scholarship on the word includes Allen Walker Reed's essay, "An Obscenity Symbol," *American Speech* 9 (1934):264–78, and Leo Stone, "On the Principal Obscene Word of the English Language," *International Journal of Psycho-Analysis* 35 (1954):30–56. If I were as speculatively venturesome as Stone, I might propose that the *cul* in the word "mas*cul*ine" were related to the Latin root *culus* for buttocks, implying that a man as opposed to a boy exercised complete control over his anal area, that is, he kept it safe from homosexual phallic attack. For a Turkish example of this widespread Mediter-

ranean ritual means of proving one's masculinity, see Alan Dundes, Jerry W. Leach, and Bora Özkök, "The Strategy of Turkish Boys' Verbal Dueling Rhymes," *Journal of American Folklore* 83 (1970):325–49.

36. Clifford Geertz, "Deep Play: Notes on the Balinese Cockfight," *Daedalus* 101 (1972):1–37, reprinted in Geertz, *The Interpretation of Cultures* (New York, 1973), pp. 412–53.

37. If *gin* were understood as a snare or net, then a virgin would be literally a 'man trap'! In any case, words like *Virgin* and *virago* indicate that women are described using men as a basic frame of reference.

The Curious Case of the Wide-mouth Frog

1. This text was collected from Lisa Payne, a student at Thornton Junior High School in Fremont, California, in June 1976.

2. This version was collected from Holly C. Dorst who first heard it in Rock Island, Illinois, in 1971. (I am indebted to folklorist John Dorst for collecting the joke from his wife.)

3. This text was collected from Beckie Olson, a student at Thornton Junior High School in Fremont, California, in May 1976. I must also express my thanks to folklorist Steve Kassovic for reminding me of an older joke which utilizes the same range of punch lines as the wide-mouth frog joke. In the older joke, the punch line is uttered by a woman after she is told by a man that just as the size of a man's nose indicates the size of his phallus so the size of a woman's mouth indicates the size of her vagina.

4. This would seem to be parallel to the case of the elephant in the elephant joke cycle. The superphallic elephant made a number of attempts to conceal himself by changing color. "Why do elephants wear green tennis shoes? To hide in the tall grass." "Why do elephants paint their toenails red? To hide in cherry trees." Part of the white stereotype of the black man includes the idea that the black would like to change his color to white. Whites' label of blacks as "colored" supports the interpretation. In any case, the absurdity of an elephant's trying to disguise his nature by wearing green tennis shoes or painting his toenails red is analogous to the wide-mouth frog's altering its speech pattern. The elephant remains an elephant just as the frog remains a frog. For an extended consideration of the elephant joke cycle, see Alan Dundes and Roger D. Abrahams, "On Elephantasy and Elephanticide," *The Psychoanalytic Review* 56 (1969):225–41 (reprinted in Alan Dundes, *Analytic Essays in Folklore* (The Hague: Mouton, 1975), pp. 192–205).

5. I am greatly indebted to Dell Hymes for assistance in spelling out the important features of the phonological symbolism of 'wide-mouth frog' and for other invaluable editorial suggestions.

6. In support of the present interpretation (linking frogs and blacks symbolically) I might note a song sung by one of the principal "Muppet" (puppet) characters in the popular educational television series for children, "Sesame Street." Kermit, who is a frog, sings "It's not so easy being green," which is understood by most viewers to refer to the difficulties of being 'colored,' i.e., black, in a white society. The didactic television song is, of course, a conscious attempt to fight racism. In contrast, the wide-mouth frog joke is an unconscious attempt to indulge in racism. Consider, for example, the implications of the view that a wide-mouth frog parent is so ignorant as not to

know what to feed its babies. Doesn't part of the white stereotype include the belief that many (lower-class) black parents provide inadequate care for their small children?

The Number Three in American Culture

1. Freud was by no means the first to suggest that the number three might be related to phallic symbolism. See, for example, Thomas Inman, *Ancient Faiths Embodied in Ancient Names*, I (London 1868), 76, n. 1, 89. As a matter of fact, the folk had also interpreted the number three in phallic terms long before Freud. For an example from modern Greek folklore, see Curt Wachsmuth, *Das alte Griechenland im neuen* (Bonn, 1864), p. 80, n. 24. Since anthropologists frequently "discover" data which is already known (to the people in the culture under study), they can understand how a modern student of symbols could "discover" an interpretation which was in some sense already known to the people who use these symbols.

2. One small bit of personal biographical data does support this thesis. The author first began to jot down examples of "threes" while awaiting the arrival of his third child. However, it was not until some time after the child's birth that it occurred to the author that his mentally straining to produce examples of threes might be a curious idiosyncratic form of intellectual couvade!

The Crowing Hen and the Easter Bunny

1. Emphasis added. Most of the folklore cited in this essay honoring Professor Richard M. Dorson is in such common usage as not to require documentation. However, a version of "I wish you luck" may be found in Iona and Peter Opie, *The Lore and Language of Schoolchildren* (Oxford: Clarendon Press, 1969), p. 299; for the superstition, see Wayland D. Hand, ed., *Popular Beliefs and Superstitions from North Carolina, The Frank C. Brown Collection of North Carolina Folklore*, vols. 6 and 7 (Durham: Duke University Press, 1961), #3890; for "Jack and Jill," see Iona and Peter Opie, *The Oxford Dictionary of Nursery Rhymes* (Oxford: Clarendon Press, 1951), p. 224.

2. Iona and Peter Opie, *Nursery Rhymes*, p. 257.

3. Ibid, p. 100.

4. If one could ignore etymological evidence, it would be tempting to speculate about a possible cognation of the words *wife* and *with*. *With* connotes proximity, close relationship, and association. A housewife would thus be a female belonging with a house and presumably the house (*hus*) belongs to the man, the *hus*band. The word *woman* could similarly derive from "with man." Actually, *woman* does apparently come from "wife-man" (cf. Old English *wifmon*). In this event, *woman* or *wife* would in verbal terms be defined as an adjunct to the male rather than having a separate linguistic identity. (A married woman whose husband died would then be "without" or a "*widow*.") Unfortunately, any plausibility of the above semantic reasoning notwithstanding, standard dictionaries (such as the *Oxford English Dictionary*) do not indicate any historical connection whatsoever between the words *wife*, *with*, and *widow*.

5. Opie, *Nursery Rhymes*, p. 202.

6. Hand, *Popular Beliefs and Superstitions from North Carolina*, #4322-4327.

7. For a typical popular account of the implications of the passive role of women in fairy tales, see Rollo May and Robert J. Levin, "Sleeping Beauty: The Problem of the Unawakened Woman," *Redbook* 127, no. 5 (September 1966):63, 145-47, 153, 160-61. Less lucid but of some relevance is Marie-Louise von Franz, *Problems of the Feminine in Fairy Tales* (Zurich: Spring Publications, 1972). There is, of course, extensive research devoted to stereotypic differentiation of male and female roles. For a useful survey, see Arlie Russell Hochschild, "A Review of Sex Role Research," *American Journal of Sociology* 78 (1973):1011-29.

8. See Brian Sutton-Smith and John M. Roberts, "Studies of an Elementary Game of Strategy," *Genetic Psychology Monographs* 75 (1967):3-42; or Brian Sutton-Smith, "Achievement and Strategic Competence," in Elliott M. Avedon and Brian Sutton-Smith, *The Study of Games* (New York: John Wiley, 1971), pp. 488-97. One could argue that it is not so much that "feminine" girls play to draw rather than play to win as it is a matter of male investigations labeling girls who play to draw as being "feminine." This in turn raises the question of whether it is possible for a male to study male chauvinism objectively! Yet there is folkloristic evidence which suggests that it is easier for males to break away from original family ties than for females: "A son is a son until he takes a wife; a daughter's a daughter all of her life." (One could, however, interpret this as a male simply shifting his dependence to a wife instead of a mother. At issue would be the difficult relationship between mother-in-law and daughter-in-law.) The point is that "aggressive," "active" behavior may not always be so simple to identify.

9. For typical texts of superstitions warning of impending spinsterhood, see Hand, *Popular Beliefs and Superstitions from North Carolina*, #4661-4705.

10. William Wells Newell, *Games and Songs of American Children* (New York: Dover, 1963), p. 174.

11. Alan Dundes, "On the Psychology of Legend," in Wayland D. Hand, ed., *American Folk Legend: A Symposium* (Berkeley and Los Angeles: University of California Press, 1971), pp. 29-31. For a feminist critique of my interpretation of "The Hook," see Rosan Jordan de Caro, "A Note on Sexocentrism in Folklore Studies," *Folklore Feminists Communication* 1 (Fall 1973):5-6.

12. This is motif E332.3.3.1, The Vanishing Hitchhiker. For an indication of its distribution, see Ernest W. Baughman, *Type and Motif Index of the Folktales of England and North America*, Indiana University Folklore Series no. 20 (The Hague: Mouton, 1966), p. 148; or see Richard K. Beardsley and Rosalie Hankey, "The Vanishing Hitchhiker," *California Folklore Quarterly* 1 (1942):303-35; "A History of the Vanishing Hitchhiker," *California Folklore Quarterly* 2 (1943):13-25; and Louis C. Jones, "Hitchhiking Ghosts in New York," *California Folklore Quarterly* 3 (1944):284-92.

13. This is an important theoretical point which deserves separate treatment. One of the critical differences between proverbs and superstitions concerns the distinction between "literal" and "metaphorical." Proverbs are mainly metaphorical while superstitions are literal. Thus "Lightning never strikes twice" is a superstition if it is literally believed (so that an individual might seek sanctuary in a thunderstorm by standing near a tree previously hit by lightning). "Lightning never strikes twice" functions as a proverb if used

metaphorically to refer to the unlikelihood of some unpleasant event (such as an illness or accident) recurring. But although superstitions (and legends based upon superstition) may be literally understood and believed, they may still involve a metaphor. For example, "A baby should be carried upstairs before downstairs so that it will rise in life." (*Popular Beliefs and Superstitions from North Carolina,* #210.) This practice, if carried out, would entail a literal enactment of the metaphorical notion of "rising" to success in life. (All homeopathic magic is essentially a literalization of metaphor.) Another example of a literalization of a metaphor, namely, "to fight like cats and dogs," is found in the following: "To break up a couple, a conjurer took some of the tracks of each while the ground was wet, rolled this up in brown paper, and put some whiskers of a cat and those of a dog in with it. She ties this up in a sack and leaves until the earth is dry. When it has dried she throws it all into the fire, and the two will henceforth fight like cats and dogs." See Ruth Bass, "Mojo," in Alan Dundes, ed., *Mother Wit from the Laughing Barrel* (Englewood Cliffs, N.J.: Prentice-Hall, 1973), p. 384.

14. Hand, *Popular Beliefs and Superstitions from North Carolina,* #152.

15. Ibid., #5248–57, 7192–94. See also Thomas Rogers Forbes, *The Midwife and the Witch* (New Haven: Yale University Press, 1966), pp. 1–3.

16. Hand, *Popular Beliefs and Superstitions from North Carolina,* #8492. For the more common versions, see #8493–95.

17. William Henderson, *Notes on the Folk-Lore of the Northern Counties of England and the Borders,* 2d ed. Publications of the Folk-Lore Society 2 (London: W. Satchell, Peyton, & Co., 1879), p. 43.

18. Hand, *Popular Beliefs and Superstitions from North Carolina,* #5250, 5257. Forbes translates a German version: "When the hen crows before the cock/ And the woman speaks before the man/Then the hen should be roasted/And the woman beaten with a cudgel." See Forbes, *The Midwife and the Witch,* p. 2.

19. It is not possible to summarize the enormous amount of data Bettelheim presents in support of his novel hypothesis. I recommend that the interested reader consult Bruno Bettelheim, *Symbolic Wounds: Puberty Rites and the Envious Male* (London: Thames and Hudson, 1955).

20. Such male creation myths have been discussed previously. See, for example, Erich Fromm, *The Forgotten Language* (New York: Grove Press, 1951), p. 234; Bettelheim, *Symbolic Wounds,* pp. 109–10, and Alan Dundes, "Earth-Diver: Creation of the Mythopoeic Male," *American Anthropologist* 64 (1962):1032–51.

21. For a consideration of the "knee baby" phenomenon, see Noel Bradley, "The Knees as Fantasied Genitals," *Psychoanalytic Review* 57 (1970):65–94. For couvade behavior in the modern United States, see Wayland D. Hand, "American Analogues of the Couvade," in W. Edson Richmond, ed., *Studies in Folklore* (Bloomington: Indiana University Press, 1957), pp. 213–29.

22. For more detailed discussion of Santa Claus as a remarkable male childbearing figure, see Richard Sterba, "On Christmas," *Psychoanalytic Quarterly* 13 (1944):79–83; Adriaan D. De Groot, *Saint Nicholas: A Psychoanalytic Study of his History and Myth* (The Hague: Mouton, 1965), p. 130–31.

23. Robert Meadows, *A Private Anthropological Cabinet* (New York: Falstaff Press, 1934), illustrations 481 and 482.

24. An interesting piece of protest folklore, popular in the early 1970s, is based upon the bias in make-up of the medical profession. "A man and his son

are in a serious automobile accident. The man is killed, but the boy is rushed to the emergency room of the hospital. When he is brought into the operating room, the surgeon says, 'I cannot operate on this boy because he is my son.' How can this be?" Answer: the surgeon is a woman, the boy's mother.

Into the Endzone for a Touchdown: *A Psychoanalytic Consideration of American Football*

1. W. Branch Johnson, "Football, A Survival of Magic?" *The Contemporary Review* 135 (1929):228.
2. Johnson, 230–31; Francis Peabody Magoun, Jr., "Shrove Tuesday Football," *Harvard Studies and Notes in Philology and Literature* 13 (1931):24, 36, 44.
3. Johnson, 230.
4. David Riesman and Reuel Denney, "Football in America: A Study in Cultural Diffusion," *American Quarterly* 3 (1951):309–25.
5. William Arens, "The Great American Football Ritual," *Natural History* 84 (1975):72–80. Reprinted in W. Arens and Susan P. Montague, ed., *The American Dimension: Cultural Myths and Social Realities* (Port Washington, 1975), 3–14.
6. Arnold R. Beisser, *The Madness in Sports* (New York, 1967); Shirley Fiske, "Pigskin Review: An American Initiation," in *Sport in the Socio-Cultural Process*, M. Marie Hart ed. (Dubuque, 1972), 241–258; and Arens, 72–80.
7. Arens, 77.
8. K. G. Sheard and E. G. Dunning, "The Rugby Football Club as a Type of 'Male Preserve': Some Sociological Notes," *International Review of Sport Sociology* 3–4 (1973):5–24.
9. Arens, 79.
10. George M. Foster, "Peasant Society and the Image of Limited Good," *American Anthropologist* 67 (1965):293–315.
11. G. T. W. Patrick, "The Psychology of Football," *American Journal of Psychology* 14 (1903):370.
12. A. A. Brill, "The Why of the Fan," *North American Review* 228 (1929):429–34.
13. Childe Herald [Thomas Hornsby Ferril], "Freud and Football," in *Reader in Comparative Religion*, eds. William A. Lessa and Evon Z. Vogt (New York, 2d ed., 1965), 250–52.
14. Adrian Stokes, "Psycho-Analytic Reflections on the Development of Ball Games, Particularly Cricket," *International Journal of Psycho-Analysis* 37 (1956):185–92.
15. Stokes, 190.
16. Stokes, 187.
17. Bruce Rodgers, *The Queens' Vernacular: A Gay Lexicon* (San Francisco, 1972), 27; Dennis Wepman, Ronald B. Newman, and Murray B. Binderman, *The Life: The Lore and Folk Poetry of the Black Hustler* (Philadelphia, 1976), 178.
18. Herald, 250.
19. George Plimpton, *Paper Lion* (New York, 1965), 59.
20. Kyle Rote and Jack Winter, *The Language of Pro Football* (New York, 1966), 102.

21. David Kopay and Perry Deane Young, *The David Kopay Story* (New York, 1977), 53–54.
22. Plimpton, 195, 339.
23. Harold Wentworth and Stuart Berg Flexner, *Dictionary of American Slang* (New York, 1967), 294; Rodgers, 155.
24. Vance Randolph, *Pissing in the Snow & Other Ozark Folktales* (Urbana, 1976), 9.
25. Wepman, Newman and Binderman, 186.
26. Kopay and Young, 50–51.
27. Rote and Winter, 130.
28. Rodgers, 152.
29. Wentworth and Flexner, 511.
30. Wepman, Newman and Binderman, *The Life.*
31. Rodgers, 92; Wepman, Newman and Binderman, 182.
32. Kopay and Young, 11, 53.
33. Kopay and Young, 57.
34. Cf. Alan Dundes, Jerry W. Leach, and Bora Özkök, "The Strategy of Turkish Boys' Verbal Dueling Rhymes," *Journal of American Folklore* 83 (1970):325–49.
35. Cf. Alan Dundes, "A Psychoanalytic Study of the Bullroarer," *Man* 11 (1976): 220–38.

"To Love My Father All": *A Psychoanalytic Study of the Folktale Source of* King Lear

1. Alan Dundes, "The Study of Folklore in Literature and Culture: Identification and Interpretation," *Journal of American Folklore* 78(1965):136–42; reprinted in Dundes, *Analytic Essays in Folklore* (The Hague, 1975), pp. 28–34.
2. Unfortunately, the best and the most comprehensive survey of possible and probable relationships between Chaucer's *Canterbury Tales* and traditional tale types is located in a fairly obscure publication, namely, a report of an international congress, which appeared as a volume (XXII) of the Greek folktale journal *Laographia*. See Francis Lee Utley, "Some Implications of Chaucer's Folktales," in *IV International Congress for Folk Narrative Research in Athens*, Georgios A. Megas, ed., (Athens, 1965), pp. 588–99.
3. The standard reference for tale types is Stith Thompson's second revision of Antti Aarne's *The Types of the Folktale*, FF Communications 184 (Helsinki, 1961). Motif numbers refer to Stith Thompson, *Motif-Index of Folk-Literature*, 6 vols., (Bloomington, 1955–58). For a sample of how folklorists approach folktales in Shakespeare, see Max Lüthi, "Shakespeare und das Märchen," *Zeitschrift für Volkskunde* 53 (1956–57):141–49; reprinted in Lüthi, *Volksmärchen und Volkssage: Zwei Grundformen Erzrahlender Dichtung* (Bern, 1961), pp. 109–117; Katherine M. Briggs, "The Folds of Folklore," *Shakespeare Survey* 17 (1964):167–79; and Jan Harold Brunvand, "The Folktale Origin of The Taming of the Shrew," *Shakespeare Quarterly* 17 (1966):345–59. For *King Lear* in particular, see Giuseppe Cocchiara, *La Leggenda di Re Lear* (Torino, 1932), which is briefly summarized in F.D. Hoeniger, "The Artist Exploring the Primitive: King Lear," in Rosalie L. Colie and F. T. Flahiff eds., *Some Facets of King Lear: Essays in Prismatic Criticism* (Toronto, 1974), pp. 98–100. (I am indebted to my colleague Norman Rabkin for the latter reference.)

4. E. Sidney Hartland, "The Outcast Child," *Folk-Lore Journal* 4 (1886):308–49; Marian Roalfe Cox, *Cinderella*, Publications of the Folk-Lore Society 31 (London, 1892), pp. xxv, 80–86.

5. Wilfrid Perrett, *The Story of King Lear from Geoffrey of Monmouth to Shakespeare* Palaestra XXXV (Berlin, 1904), pp. 9–15, 27, 283; Geoffrey Bullough, *Narrative and Dramatic Sources of Shakespeare*, Vol. VII (London, 1973), p. 271.

6. Kenneth Muir, *Shakespeare's Sources*, I, Comedies and Tragedies (London, 1961), pp. 141–66.

7. Vladimir Propp, *Morphology of the Folktale* (Austin 1968). The final function of Propp's series of thirty-one which he claims comprises the basic structure of Russian fairy tales is "The Hero is Married and Ascends the Throne." Since the first function is "One of the Members of a Family Absents Himself from Home," Propp's morphology would appear to suggest that fairy tales depict in the form of fantasy the movement of a young man or woman away from the initial family situation towards the formation of a new family unit through marriage.

8. Cox, *Cinderella*, pp. 85, 81.

9. Anna Birgitta Rooth, *The Cinderella Cycle* (Lund, 1951), pp. 14–15, 19–20.

10. Cox, *Cinderella*, p. xxv.

11. Rooth, p. 10. Even though Stith Thompson does treat "Love Like Salt" as a distinct tale type (923), he does, in the discussion of its plot, refer explicitly and exclusively to the analysis of tale type 510, Cinderella and Cap o' Rushes, for its content. This implies that the "Love Like Salt" story can be considered as an abridged form of the basic tale type 510.

12. J.S.H. Bransom, *The Tragedy of King Lear* (Oxford, 1934), pp. 221, 9. For a useful discussion of Freud's interpretations of *King Lear*, see Norman N. Holland, *Psychoanalysis and Shakespeare* (New York, 1964), pp. 64–66.

13. Sigmund Freud, "The Theme of the Three Caskets," in *Collected Papers*, Vol. IV (New York, 1959), pp. 244–56, reprinted in M.D. Faber, *The Design Within: Psychoanalytic Approaches to Shakespeare* (New York, 1970), pp. 195–206. For an account of the reaction to Freud's early interpretation of *King Lear*, see Kenneth Muir, "Some Freudian Interpretations of Shakespeare," *Proceedings of the Leeds Philosophical and Literary Society* 7 (1952):47. Judging from other surveys of psychoanalytic criticism of *King Lear*, Freud's first interpretation has had little impact. See Holland, *Psychoanalysis and Shakespeare*, pp. 214–19, and M.D. Faber, *The Design Within*, pp. 207–31.

14. Arpad Pauncz, "Psychopathology of Shakespeare's "King Lear," *American Imago* 9 (1952):57–78. Other discussions of the father-daughter incest theme in the play include: John Donnelly, "Incest, Ingratitude and Insanity: Aspects of the Psychopathology of King Lear," *Psychoanalytic Review* 40 (1953):149–53; F.L. Lucas, *Literature and Psychology* (Ann Arbor, 1957), pp. 62–71; Mark Kanzer, "Imagery in King Lear," *American Imago* 22 (1965):3–13; Paul A. Jorgensen, *Lear's Self-Discovery* (Berkeley and Los Angeles, 1967), pp. 128–29; S.C.V. Stetner and Oscar B. Goodman, "Lear's Darker Purpose," *Literature and Psychology* 18 (1968):82–90; William H. Chaplin, "Form and Psychology in *King Lear*," *Literature and Psychology* 19(3, 4; 1969):31–45; Simon O. Lesser, "Act One, Scene One, of Lear." *College English* 32 (1970–71):155–71; and Leslie Fiedler, *The Stranger in Shakespeare* (New York, 1972), pp. 209–20. Sometimes critics sense the nature of the father-daughter rela-

tionship without actually mentioning the word incest. See, for example, Stanley Cavell, "The Avoidance of Love: A Reading of *King Lear*," in *Must We Mean What We Say?* (New York, 1969), pp. 267–353.

15. Horace Howard Furness, ed. *A New Variorum Edition of Shakespeare: King Lear* (Philadelphia, 1880), p. 383.

16. Freud articulated this particular transformation in a 1911 paper. See "Psycho-Analytic Notes Upon an Autobiographical Account of a Case of Paranoia (Dementia Paranoides)," *Collected Papers*, Vol. III (New York, 1959), p. 499. In the present fairy tale context, the relevant transformation would be "I love him" becoming "He loves me."

17. Otto Rank, *The Myth of the Birth of the Hero* (New York, 1959), p. 72.

18. Perrett, p. 241. Chambers was also troubled by Cordelia's suicide in the majority of literary versions of the plot. See R. W. Chambers, *King Lear* (Glasgow, 1940).

19. M.D. Faber, "Some Remarks on the Suicide of King Lear's Eldest Daughter," *University Review* 33 (1967):313–317. With respect to the assessment of guilt, it is tempting to see a shift from Lear's saying "I did her wrong" (I, v, 25) about Cordelia to his saying "You do me wrong . . ." (IV, vii, 44) to Cordelia.

20. Robert Bechtold Heilman, *This Great Stage: Image and Structure in King Lear* (Baton Rouge, 1948), pp. 93, 104.

21. Bransom, p. 160, n. 1.

22. S. C. V. Stetner and Oscar B. Goodman, "Lear's Darker Purpose," *Literature and Psychology* 18 (1968):86.

23. Paul A. Jorgensen, *Lear's Self-Discovery* (Berkeley and Los Angeles, 1967), p. 128; Stetner and Goodman, p. 86; Marvin Rosenberg, *The Masks of King Lear* (Berkeley, 1972), pp. 53, 134. In considering the content of the answers of the daughters to their father's request for a declaration of love, one is reminded of the third daughter's response in the folktale: "love like salt." The sexual symbolism of salt (as in *salacious*) has been extensively investigated by Ernest Jones who even mentions the folktale in question. See "The Symbolic Significance of Salt in Folklore and Superstition," in *Essays in Applied Psychoanalysis*, Vol. II, Essays in Folklore, Anthropology and Religion (London, 1951), pp. 22–109. Shakespeare did not use the "love like salt" phrase so common in the folktale source, but it is interesting that he does have Lear refer to himself as "a man of salt" (IV, vi, 191). Presumably the reference is simply to crying (salty tears). Still the line does come after a mention of his "most dear daughter" and immediately before his stated intention to "die bravely like a smug bridegroom."

24. Holland, pp. 66, 215.

25. Ella Freeman Sharpe, "From *King Lear* to *The Tempest*," in *Collected Papers on Psycho-Analysis* (London, 1950), p. 216. See also William H. Chaplin, "Form and Psychology in *King Lear*," *Literature and Psychology* 19(3, 4; 1969):45, n. 7. In this connection, Holland, p. 65, reminds us that Freud confessed to Ferenczi that his interest in the play was very probably conditioned by his own close relationship to his daughter Anna.

26. Eric Partridge, *Shakespeare's Bawdy* (New York, 1960).

27. Cf. Robert H. West, "Sex and Pessimism in *King Lear*," *Shakespeare Quarterly* 11 (1960):58.

28. Katherine M. Briggs, "The Folds of Folklore," *Shakespeare Survey* 17

(1964):172. Of course, the very use of fairy tale as signalled by the love-test scene at the outset probably serves to suggest to the audience that there is likely to be a happy ending. This makes the final outcome of the play even more tragic than it would have been without the explicit fairy tale frame.

29. It cannot be stressed too strongly that a psychoanalytic reading of *King Lear* is but one interpretation of a play which has inspired dozens. Too often psychoanalytic critics give the impression that they believe their reading is *the*, rather than *a*, meaning of a literary text. The folkloristic and psychoanalytic perspectives utilized in this essay do not pretend to explicate all facets of the play.